T0294371

BOMBER BOY

Night, 9/10 June 1940. Somewhere over occupied Europe.

The primary target for the Hampden bombers of No.50 Squadron were the marshalling yards at Eindhoven. Dereck French and his crew were flying in appalling visibility. Flares were dropped at intervals in the hope of finding a landmark. The bomber lost height gradually after each flare drop. Suddenly, all hell broke loose!

'Anti-aircraft guns hosed streams of projectiles of all colours of tracer at us, coming from all directions, including head on. Finally a shell hit us, to the rear of the pilot's seat. It blew a hole in the side of the plane, destroying the hydraulic gear; shell fragments went past me into the instrument panel, some lodged in my right arm but most of them hit the armour plate behind the pilot's seat. This armour plate was an innovation that had been fitted only a few days earlier. Thank heavens for it, or I should have been cut in half.'

Frantically, Dereck dived to ground level and pulled out just above a wide river. As they hurtled along, almost skimming the surface of the water, the enemy gunners could not bring the speeding Hampden into their sights. Multi-storied warehouse buildings flashed by on each side. At last, they were in the clear. He turned for home. Although the narrow confines of the bomber's fuselage made it difficult, the crew managed to wrap a tourniquet around his injured arm. But something else was wrong. He became aware of warm wetness flowing into his flying boots. Blood? Was he bleeding so much that his boots were filling with blood?

He reached down to touch the mess in his boots...

BOMBER BOY
MY LIFE AS A BOMBER PILOT

DERECK FRENCH DFC & BAR
EDITED BY DENNIS NEWTON

AMBERLEY

To Barbara, Sue, Rooney, Pam, and Chris.
And to Dereck and all those who served.

First published 2020

Amberley Publishing
The Hill, Stroud
Gloucestershire, GL5 4EP

www.amberley-books.com

British Library Cataloguing in Publication Data.
A catalogue record for this book is available from the British Library.

ISBN 978 1 4456 8465 9 (hardback)
ISBN 978 1 4456 8466 6 (ebook)

Typesetting by Aura Technology and Software Services,
India. Printed in the UK.

Contents

Acknowledgements

When Dereck French first contacted me, it was not long after I'd had my first book on Australians in the Battle of Britain published by the Australian War Memorial. He issued me with a challenge.

'Okay, you've written about the fighter boys, what about the bomber boys?'

This presented a rare opportunity, the chance to meet someone who had actually been there and done that. After corresponding back-and-forth, my wife Helen and I visited Barbara and Dereck French at Nagambie, Victoria, in 1993. We met a remarkable couple and began a lasting friendship. There were many common interests, in particular for Barbara and Helen gardening, especially Australian native plants; and for Dereck and me, Australian history, especially Australians in the Royal Air Force in the early years of the Second World War.

Dereck's memorabilia was amazing. On his wartime experiences it included his diary, letters he had written home to his family in Australia during the war, official records, his Flying Log Book and a journal he had written about the war during his early farming years. There was so much and he was so helpful. Many books published after the end of WW2 have presented versions of events which too often consisted of half-truths because of wartime censorship and the inaccessibility of official records. Most who had taken part in those times had either been killed or had passed away since then. More recently, with wartime censorship lifted and official records in most cases readily accessible, accurate telling of the history has improved, but at the same time the personal touch has declined because so many more have passed away. With Dereck's help there was a much better chance to present the whole story of those tumultuous times.

After Dereck passed away, Barbara and Rooney asked me to put together his story. Dereck was one of the finest of the 'bomber boys', and I thank them for the rare privilege. My great regret is that I was unable to finish the work earlier.

The depth of Dereck's records was unique. Ever the perfectionist, he had noted down everything in his life, incident by incident, combining and refining the stories over and over, to form candid documented accounts. They were a collection of histories for his family. There was much to examine. Most was detailed but some parts were sketchy outlines. What should be included in this book? What should remain private and omitted? What should be amalgamated with outside material that has come to light? It was important that the work should faithfully portray Dereck's own personal experiences within the overall drama of the war.

This is not the biography of his very full life. What follows is largely Dereck's memoir that tries to capture the dramatic time when Britain's very survival was at stake, particularly during the desperate days of 1940. Much of it is written using Dereck's own words in the way I believe he would feel comfortable with. It is meant to be a tribute to a man I greatly respect, a man of courage, a 'bomber boy' whose achievements and service should not be forgotten.

My first thanks therefore go to Barbara French, Sue Buckingham, Rooney Fields, Pam Mathieson, and Chris Coster for allowing me access to the French files and for unreservedly supporting the project.

This work could not have reached completion without the generous help and support of many other people and organisations. These people include Alex Gould, Grant Lindeman, Jack Lawson, Bryan Philpott, Reg Moore, Tom Scott, Beryl Olive, Greg Graham, Robert Kirby, Michael Veitch, Roy Chappell, Tom Roberts, Jack Cannon, Bob Jaggers, Richard Osborne and Mike Taylor.

The organisations included the RAAF Museum Point Cook, with special thanks to David Gardiner, Australian War Memorial (AWM), Military Aircraft Photographs (MAP), and the Imperial War Museum (IWM). Of course, members of the staff of Amberley Publishing deserve special mention.

Above all, I acknowledge the unstinting help and patience of my wife, Helen, and son, Scott, and thank them for their great support.

Many thanks to all involved. If any have been overlooked, I apologise for the unintended omission.

Dennis Newton

Abbreviations

AASF	Advanced Air Striking Force
ABDA	American-British-Dutch-Australian Command
AC	Aircraftman
AFC	Air Force Cross, Australian Flying Corps
AHQ	Air Headquarters
AI	Aircraft Interception (airborne radar equipment)
AIF	Australian Imperial Force
A/Cmdr	Air Commodore
AM	Air Marshal
AOC	Air Officer Commanding
AOC-in-C	Air Officer Commanding-in-Chief
ARP	Air Raid Precautions
ASR	Air-Sea Rescue
AVM	Air Vice Marshal
BAFF	British Air Forces in France
BEF	British Expeditionary Force
Brig	Brigadier
BV	Blohme and Voss
Capt	Captain
Cdr	Commander
C-in-C	Commander-in-Chief
CIB	Criminal Investigation Branch
CMF	Citizens' Military Forces
CO	Commanding Officer
Col	Colonel
Cpl	Corporal
DFC	Distinguished Flying Cross
DFM	Distinguished Flying Medal

DH	de Havilland
Do	Dornier
DSO	Distinguished Service Order
E/A	Enemy Aircraft
EATS	Empire Air Training Scheme
EFTS	Elementary Flying Training School
FAA	Fleet Air Arm
F/Lt	Flight Lieutenant
F/O	Flying Officer
F/Sgt	Flight Sergeant
FW	Focke-Wulf
GAF	German Air Force
Gen	General
GOC	General Officer Commanding
Gp/Capt	Group Captain
He	Heinkel
HMS	His Majesty's Ship
HQ	Headquarters
IFF	Identification Friend-or-Foe airborne radar identification device
Ju	Junkers
Lt	Lieutenant
Lt/Col	Lieutenant-Colonel
Lt/Gen	Lieutenant-General
Maj	Major
Maj/Gen	Major-General
Me	Messerschmitt. See Note 2, Chapter 7.
NCO	Non-commissioned Officer
NZ	New Zealand
O	Observer
Ops	Operations
ORB	Operations Record Book
OTU	Operational Training Unit
P/O	Pilot Officer
POW	Prisoner of War
RAAF	Royal Australian Air Force
RAF	Royal Air Force
RAN	Royal Australian Navy
RCAF	Royal Canadian Air Force
RDF	Radio Direction Finding (Radar)
RFC	Royal Flying Corps
RN	Royal Navy

RNAS	Royal Naval Air Service
RNZAF	Royal New Zealand Air Force
RSL	Returned Services League (of Australia)
R/T	Radio Transmitter
SAAF	South African Air Force
SASO	Senior Air Staff Officer
Sgt	Sergeant
Sqn	Squadron
USAAF	United States Army Air Force
USN	United States Navy
VC	Victoria Cross
WAG	Wireless Air Gunner
W/Cdr	Wing Commander
W/Ldr	Wing Leader
W/O	Warrant Officer
W/T	Wireless Telegraphy

Foreword

Some Australians who were in the British Isles when war broke out in September 1939 – working, at university or just visiting – volunteered on the spot to serve in Britain's armed forces. When they did they found that many other Australians were already there before them. In fact, there were more Australian pilots in the Royal Air Force (RAF) than there were in the Royal Australian Air Force (RAAF) back home!

In the days after the First World War it had been regarded as desirable to organize the emerging new air forces of the British Empire nations as much as possible along common lines. When Australian government representatives attended the Imperial Conference of 1923 in London, RAF representatives proposed a system of building up reserves through the attendance of RAAF officers at training courses in England, and by offering short service commissions in the RAF to a number of the pilots trained each year at RAAF Point Cook in Victoria, Australia. From that year on, when S/Ldr Adrian Cole was approved to be the first to go, RAAF officers could attend the RAF Staff College at Andover and up to thirty RAAF officers passed through the college before the Second World War. Other exchange schemes were implemented as well.

Meanwhile, towards the end of 1926, the first seven Point Cook graduates chosen for RAF short service commissions sailed for England. By the time the RAAF closed this opportunity for Point Cook graduates in July 1938 (the RAAF wanted to retain the pilots it trained for its own expansion programme), a total of 149 had transferred to England under the scheme.

That was not the end of it. Applications for short service commissions in the RAF continued to be advertised in the Australian press until at least the middle of 1939 but those who were accepted at this later stage did not have the benefit of initial flying training at Point Cook. Others still came nevertheless, some travelling to England at their own expense.

Many who were already there at the outbreak of war achieved high distinction. They included such men as Hughie Edwards, the first Australian pilot awarded the Victoria Cross; Donald Bennett of Pathfinder fame; Leslie Clisby,[1] the war's first Australian ace; Pat Hughes,[2] the highest-scoring Australian ace of the Battle of Britain; Gordon Olive,[3] the first commander of the only RAAF night fighter squadron; and Robert Bungey,[4] the first Australian to command the first Australian Spitfire squadron in RAF Fighter Command.

But the very first of these young Australian pilots to win battle honours in the Second World War was Dereck Jack French.

This is his story...

1

Dereck

All the world's a stage,
And all the men and women merely players:
They have their exits and their entrances;
And one man in his time plays many parts...

William Shakespeare[1]

And so it was with Dereck French:

'He was a picturesque and turbulent character.'

Jack Lawson, Adjutant of 455 (RAAF) Squadron[2]

'He lived and travelled in Britain, Egypt, and India, flew on daily bombing raids over Germany, experienced the death of friends and comrades on a daily basis, met many of the leading figures in RAF Fighter and Bomber Command, and was privy to the huge social changes in British life.'

Sue Buckingham, daughter[3]

'I thought of him as an intellectual snob. He was critical of anyone who could not hold an educated conversation.'

Chris Coster, daughter[4]

'I soon discovered him to be a highly engaging, well-read and sensitive person of great wit and intelligence.'

Michael Veitch, writer and television host[5]

'Dar had a wonderful range of friends and gave freely of his time and knowledge to them all – but only if he liked them.'

Rooney (Ann) Fields, daughter[6]

He could be strong willed:

'At a welcome home party interest was taken in a female guest, who was also on the lookout for a new relationship, there was definitely chemistry at work. Soon a marriage proposal, with conditions, leave home and become a farmer, otherwise no marriage.'

Barbara Mary French, née Rigg[7]

He could be intensely loyal:

'In spite of his experience in the UK he remained aggressively Australian.'

Jack Lawson[8]

He could be quick to judge others:

'Dar would challenge people on meeting them for the first time, testing their knowledge or attitudes toward various issues and would categorise each person.'

Pam Mathieson, daughter[9]

'He was ... outraged to be "carpeted" next morning by an insensitive Station Commander who abused him for "throwing away bombs to the value of his annual salary". French could hardly believe his ears. Incredulously he tried to explain that in terrible weather, jettisoning the bombs had possibly made the difference between saving and losing the aircraft. He rapidly recognised that reason and common sense was not one of that officer's strong points.'

Robert Kirby, author and historian[10]

He was a fighter:

'Dereck fascinated me primarily because he was the only pilot I met who had operated during the early, primitive stages of the European air campaign.'

Michael Veitch[11]

'He was the first Australian decorated in the War.'

Jack Lawson[12]

'French's air force career must have been one of the most turbulent and colourful experienced by any Australian.'

Jack Cannon, journalist[13]

'He had no time for those who feigned "disability" or "essential services" to avoid joining the services. In fact, he considered many of these "shirkers" had prospered during the war years.'

Sue Buckingham[14]

'His keenness for all things which he considered to be getting on with the war was unequalled, but he always remained his own judge of what things amounted to getting on with the war. His freely expressed exercise of his judgment did not always make for popularity with station administration officers and their kind.'

Jack Lawson[15]

He was adventurous:

'During the winter years he explored extensive inland areas and over time travelled by "tinnie" along the full length of the Murray River. Many of these trips were done on his own – he was very happy with his own company and probably no one else would have put up with his travelling ways.'

Pam Mathieson[16]

He was a researcher:

'Dar was always reading and researching the history and culture of the Australian Aborigines and developed a comprehensive library on the topic. He searched for aboriginal artefacts on his trips up inland during the winter.'

Pam Mathieson[17]

'He made wonderful records of the habitats and nesting habits of the mallee fowl in the area just north of Swan Hill and we regularly spent hours silently walking – stalking these magnificent birds to find their unusual mound nests.'

Rooney Fields[18]

He was a leader:

'He became one of the RAF's most daring officers and passed on his knowledge to several famous flyers, including Australian "Dam Buster" Mickey Martin...'

Jack Cannon[19]

'He was a god to "A" Flight and remains to all who knew him, a legendary and stormy figure.'

Jack Lawson[20]

He was an environmentalist:

'He had always been passionate about the environment, but it seemed those war years made this pursuit more precious.'

Sue Buckingham[21]

He could be eccentric:

'The main motto Dar used throughout life was "Is it a want, or a need?" He never wore socks on his feet and even while dairy farming only used scraps of rag around his feet in his gum-boots. He felt that since we could only wear one pair of shoes at a time, we only needed one pair of shoes.'

Pam Mathieson[22]

'His battered old suit case with the label D. J. French RAF was taken on all his trips away from home tied up with a leather belt and sporting a bullet hole which he claimed was put there by Tammy Fraser's uncle.'

Pam Mathieson[23]

He could stir up anger:

'As children we were only allowed to watch the ABC news and to this day I delight in turning this off at 7pm to watch some idiotic soap opera – just in defiance.'

Rooney Fields[24]

He could hold a grudge:

'His early experience of attending an RSL meeting when his identity and rank was questioned influenced his lifelong antipathy to this organisation.'

Sue Buckingham[25]

He had an in-built sense of fun:

'I remember as a child and teenager he would stride into our bedroom very early in the morning before he headed off to the dairy chanting prose attributed to Omar Khayyam, "Awake for Morning in the bowl of night" … and always adapted the ending by finishing off with, "Wake up you lazy bastards."'

Pam Mathieson[26]

He noticed the smallest details:

'His meeting at a dinner with Churchill resulted in us being allowed to eat peas by 'scooping' them. This was Churchillian table etiquette, and so it was for us.'

Sue Buckingham[27]

He could be difficult:

'Dar was a reluctant attendant at family get-togethers and it was usually easier if he did not come as he usually had his words of criticism offered to us or his grandchildren.'

Rooney Fields[28]

'I can remember at least two times on Christmas day, when Mum had gone to considerable effort to prepare an amazing Christmas lunch, he would announce at the last minute he was going fishing for the day and he did just that.'

Pam Mathieson[29]

And the greatest difficulty was within himself – difficulty in revealing his real feelings to those closest to him:

'As a child I do not recall Dar showing any affection such as a cuddle or a kiss to either Mum or any of his daughters.'

Pam Mathieson[30]

'I suffered major depression … I felt I had to be strong and never give up. I was hospitalized. This was the first time I ever saw Dar show any affection towards me. He actually cried when he met me in hospital and hugged me. It was unbelievably amazing.'

Chris Coster[31]

This was Dereck. And so to his story...

2

Early Days

Dereck French was born on 16 December 1915 in Melbourne:

I was born in my parents' first home at 334 Glenlyon Road, Brunswick, but have no memory of life there. However, I heard later that while at Brunswick I became very ill, so much so that it was assumed that I would die. I was suffering from gastroenteritis. During this period, I went with my mother to stay with her sister, May McNeil, in Sydney, and while there, May, in desperation to find a cure for my condition, suggested that I be given a glass of brandy. This did the trick and cured me, which was good, although the cure proved to be habit-forming.

While still of pre-school age we went to live in Mont Clair Avenue, Brighton, of which I have vague memories, mainly of forming a friendship with a boy of my own age, the son of a neighbour called Solomon. Our next move was to give support to my widowed grandmother, Annie Hanham, née Bryson, who lived alone at 948 Lygon Street, North Carlton. From this stage of my life my memories are very clear. I remember starting my school life at Princes Hill State School in Arnold Street, North Carlton. My mother had attended there as a child and my brother Neil was a pupil when I first went there.

We learned some discipline, the headmaster being Mr Milrae, a man with an earlier military background. He had us attend the Brunswick Baths in Dawson Street, Brunswick, where most of us learned to swim. A school activity which I liked, and which was to be of great use to me in later life, was what was known as 'sloyd' (woodworking). We learned to handle woodworking tools and to make simple articles such as potato mashers or, if one was capable, a letter box.

It was from the school playground that I saw my first aeroplane. It was I think an Italian aviator flying over Melbourne University, giving a flying display.

This was most likely Marquis Francesco di Pinedo, with his engineer Ernesto Campanelli, who in Savoia S.16*ter* flying boat No. 5247-25340 *Gennariello* reached Melbourne on 9 June 1925. The aircraft was completely overhauled and serviced at RAAF Point Cook before its return flight to Italy. It eventually departed from Sydney for Tokyo on 6 August 1925 and arrived in Rome on 7 November. Over the six months and three weeks of their round trip the Italian pair covered approximately 33,500 miles in 360 hours of flying. This same flying boat, still wearing RAAF badges on its fuselage, was discovered by RAAF personnel during the Allied advance through Italy in 1945.

The North Carlton district at that time was not very prosperous; most families seemed to struggle along with little, while my family appeared to be well-off. We had a very good home to live in, a car (Ford T Model) when cars were few, a telephone and a weekend retreat, my father having bought about 11 acres (4.45 ha) of bush at Beaconsfield, on which we built a shack and later a house.

In the 1920s, Beaconsfield was a small farming township 29 miles south-east of Melbourne, outside the Victorian capital's metropolitan area. It is now regarded as a rural suburb, but is still sparsely populated.

The Lygon Street house, 'Summerhill', occupied an imposing site in the street. It had been built by Dr Kirkland in 1875, when it had been known as Killarney Cottage. After various alterations and changes of occupants it was sold in 1885 to my grandfather, George Hanham, and remained in Hanham hands, eventually being inherited by my mother Nellie French, née Hanham, who sold it in 1930 for £1,850 ($3,700). In 1993 it was again sold, this time for $350,000!

At the rear of the house were stables with a loft and a large shed, and in our time, a detached bungalow which Neil and I used as our bedroom. It was a wonderful place in which to grow up. The stables were served by a laneway, which was the regular access route of the regular tradespeople: Chinese greengrocer; the 'rabbito' selling rabbits still in their skins; and the 'fisho', who hawked fish around the town.

Across the lane was a church facing Drummond Street which we at times attended with our grandmother, Annie Hanham, a very religious Scottish lady. Each week she gave Neil and me threepence each and once suggested that if we attended any form of church service during the week our threepence would be increased to sixpence – we became instant Christians. Another church which played a part in our lives was St Michael's in Macpherson Street where we attended Sunday school (Neil was buried there). One day when returning home from there at the corner of Lygon and Richardson Streets, I saw, for the first time, a man killed. He came out of the Rising Sun Hotel and began lifting the feet of a horse tethered at the horse trough outside. The horse lashed out with its hooves and hit the man in the head, killing him instantly.

My mother was the youngest of the Hanham children and was, in my opinion, 'spoiled rotten'. The spoiling was continued by my father, the effect of which she carried with her until her death. When I was about four or five years of age I took an instant dislike to her. This was due to the fact that she had been unable to catch me to punish me for a misdemeanour I had committed and had promised that should I surrender quietly I would receive no punishment. I accepted the promise and was rewarded by having a cane swagger stick broken over my backside. I am afraid that I never forgave her for this break of trust.

Half of our house in Lygon Street was occupied by our family; the other half was the home of my grandmother who lived independently. She had a distrust of new-fangled things such as electricity and used it to a minimum. It was her custom each night to retire early and to read her Bible by the light of a bedside candle.

At about 10.00 p.m. one night, we were awakened by noise and great activity in Lygon Street. We found that grandmother's bedroom was on fire. It appears that she had fallen asleep while reading and the candle had set fire to her bed. The local fire-brigade and hordes of onlookers were in Lygon Street. Neil and I witnessed the activity from the top of a tall pear tree beside our bungalow. My father attempted to rescue grandmother and received smoke damage to his lungs. Eventually the fire was extinguished and grandmother was taken to the hospital, where she developed pneumonia and died. The house reeked of smoke for weeks, the worst of which came from a half-burnt horsehair mattress.

Although I considered grandmother Hanham to be remote when I was a child, I realised later that she had been a very capable person. Born in Scotland, she was taken by her family to Prince Edward Island, Nova Scotia, Canada, and later to Australia, picking up talents as she went. She would have been a great asset to my grandfather, doing most of his bookkeeping and writing and after his death in 1908 continuing to manage his eleven properties until her death in 1924.

My mother inherited 948 Lygon Street and we continued to live there for another six years when we moved to 27 Milroy Street, Brighton, a house my father had bought in 1923. After the death of grandmother Hanham, the half of the house at Lygon Street was let to a very interesting family, the Besters. Old Mrs Bester had earlier been left with three children and had supported them by making chocolate in her kitchen and hawking it from door to door. Her product must have been a great success, for when they were with us the kitchen industry had grown to be housed in a large factory in Drummond Street, Carlton, where they traded under the name of Besters Sweets. During this period, which was the beginning of the Great Depression, many people walked off their farms. One such chap left his farm in Queensland and walked south looking for work and help. He came to 948 for food and was given a job by George Bester cutting bracken fern on the Kinglake block.

I suffered from a bad stutter. I don't know its origin. It could have been a genetic fault as several Brysons had similar afflictions, although I tended to blame my mother for causing it with her impatience and belittling of my endeavours. It stayed with me for years and was an embarrassing disability, especially during my teenage years, when I was reluctant to speak or ask questions in class, which became a barrier to learning. With maturity it became less of a problem and finally none at all.

At the end of 1927, I had received my Merit Certificate which in those days meant one could go out into the world and earn a living, or go on to Secondary School. I followed Neil and went on to University High School (UHS), which was in those days an élite school where admission was by scholarship only. Neil had won a scholarship to attend the school although I don't remember being awarded one; perhaps I was admitted due to my father's influence.

UHS was in those days housed in a fine old building in Lygon Street immediately south of the Melbourne General Cemetery. Our home was in the first block to its north, an easy walk either along Lygon Street or through the cemetery. The cemetery route had great appeal and I used it often, getting to know the whereabouts of points of interest: the Hanham graves; the graves of the early pioneers; and the Chinese burial section where the mourners left food and incense sticks as offerings.

After several years at UHS in Lygon Street, the school moved to its new building in Storey Street, Parkville, on a site which had been part of the Melbourne Hay Market in the early days. By this time my family had sold 948 Lygon Street and we had gone to live at our house in Kilroy Street, North Brighton.

UHS was different from other secondary schools. Apart from its selective entry conditions, it was based on a British system of form names (Remove, Lower VA, VA, Pass 6, etc.), while it was almost experimental in the gender basis of the classes, some forms being entirely girls or all boys while others were mixed. I was fortunate to pass through a series of mixed sex classes, which made me realise that females were scholastically as good, if not better than, males.

My time at UHS I think of as the 'fallow' period of my education when I had no particular aim and did not make much effort. This attitude changed abruptly at the end of my third year. I failed to gain my Intermediate Certificate and had to repeat the year. This hurt my pride and changed my attitude to study. I gained my Intermediate Certificate at the next attempt and went on to Form Pass 6.

I was well into this year of study when it was suggested that I should take a job that was on offer at a firm of jute merchants, Calcutta Company Pty Ltd at 475 Collins Street, Melbourne. I commenced work there as office boy – a general dogsbody, licking stamps, buying lunches for the ladies in the office, etc. – and soon knew the layout of the business section of the city very well. Calcutta Co. Pty Ltd was a worldwide organisation dealing mainly as traders of jute, although it also dealt as exporters of Australian butter and apples from Tasmania, and as an importer of rock salt. My pay was £1 ($2) per week, which was the norm for that type of job, but which barely paid for my fares and living expenses. I paid four shillings (40c) a week board and most weeks borrowed it back during the week. This was Depression time and any job was better than no job.

After about a year with the firm the manager, Mr H. G. Hawken, called me to his office and told me that I should look for another position. (Twelve years later he contacted me and asked that I attend a dinner given in my honour by the firm. I attended this at the Mitre Tavern and was given a cheque for £50 in appreciation of my war services – a nice gesture.)

Being unemployed should have been a blow to me, but it was not. Many of my contemporaries were in the same state, or had taken jobs they did not like. As my father was a public servant we had some money coming in to the house, although at that time he was not on full pay. In 1930 he had been certified as suffering from TB, in those times a killer disease, and had been put on sick leave on reduced pay. He was eventually declared to be cured of the disease and returned to full-time work. Apart from this, my mother had inherited and sold the Hanham home in Lygon Street, the proceeds of which helped us to keep afloat. During this time we did not appear to want for anything. Quite a few of my local friends were also out of work so we got together and used our time looking for jobs, playing tennis or swimming at the North Road beach.

I remember searching for work with Jack Gunn (unemployed ex-Caulfield Grammar) when we went to Melbourne. He would approach every shop and office on one side of Collins Street and ask for work, while I would try the other side of the street, usually without success. I remember once getting as far as to an interview with the manager of a firm who asked my name, and then told me that he knew my father. While I was in his office, he phoned my Dad and told him to give me £5, to send me to Sydney and let me sink or swim. I did not get the £5.

A group of us attended the Congregational Church in Gardenvale Road most Sunday evenings, not for religious inspiration but for the social contacts involved. After church most nights we went to my home for a sing-song around our pianola. Several of this group were already members of the militia (Citizens Military Force or CMF) so I also joined. Our unit was a horse-drawn field artillery unit centred at Chapel Street, Windsor, and carried out its exercises from there on open paddocks around Mulgrave, and once a year a large camp at Seymour where we actually fired our 18 lb guns – all good fun for a teenager. My main purpose in joining this unit was to be taught to ride a horse military fashion. The other reason was that we were paid four shillings per day for parades, etc.

On joining I found that I was too young to ride and looked forward to the day I could do so. This came on a day that the unit was transported to the Remount Depot in Sturt Street, South Melbourne, where we were to pick up our horses and ride them to Chapel Street; so far, so good. Until then I had received little or no training in military horse handling and had little idea of what might happen. I had, however, ridden a few farm animals and a few at riding schools near Mentone. On this occasion I was wearing the usual Artillery uniform complete with a bandolier and vicious spurs. We were allotted our mounts, mounted and proceeded to leave the depot when I, without thinking, pressed the spurs into my horse and it was off at a gallop. I clung on grimly and managed to steer it around the first street corner, but we were beaten to the next corner by a Model T Ford which the horse decided to pass by going under it and taking me with it. The crash made a mess of the horse, the car, me and my uniform, yet we were still mobile. The horse was bleeding from its knees and I was bleeding from mine, so I climbed aboard again and rode back to the depot. No one there seemed surprised or worried. The NCO in charge brought out a large enamel basin of carbolic acid and water and gave my damaged parts a good dabbing. He then went to the horse and gave it the same treatment. My trip to Chapel Street was abandoned and I spent the balance of the day searching for a doctor who could give me an anti-tetanus injection. It was not a good start to a riding career with the Australian Army.

A near neighbour of ours in Milroy Street was Mr G. Chittleborough, who was the head of the Kernot Engineering School of the Melbourne Technical College (MTC, now the RMIT). He suggested to my father that I take a three-year course of study at the MTC for the Diploma of Electrical and Mechanical Engineering. I started the course at the beginning of 1934 and enjoyed every minute of it. During the course we did an amount of practice engineering work and made many visits to engineering projects in Victoria, Tasmania and NSW. The last of these was a tour of Tasmania looking at some of the larger engineering enterprises there including Queenstown, various hydro-electric works, Cadbury's Chocolate Factory and the Electrolytic Zinc works.

During term holidays I took part in some very interesting bush walks in the mountains, which usually meant carrying our gear and food for about a week in our rucksacks, or I worked as an engineering apprentice at the Commonwealth Munitions Works at Maribyrnong gaining good workshop experience.

While on the engineering tour of Tasmania, we – Hughie Gunther, a fellow student, and I – noticed an advertisement in a paper inviting applications for cadetships with the RAAF. The positions entailed a year of study and flying training at Point Cook, after which one could expect to graduate as officer pilots in the RAAF with the chance of transferring to the RAF. We both applied rather half-heartedly, especially on my part as I had almost completed my course of study, having only a few supplementary exams to do. I had already been accepted to join the Electrical Department of the Melbourne City Council in early 1937 as their assistant-assistant engineer on the princely salary of £250 ($500) per annum.

A few weeks later I learned that my application for cadetship had been accepted while Hughie Gunther's had been rejected, because, as he said, 'I'm a bloody Catholic.' Hughie remained in the engineering profession, became a major in the 9th Division, Royal Engineers, 2nd AIF, during WW2, and was decorated, but died shortly after the war.

Admission to the RAAF involved a series of interviews and medical examinations at Melbourne's Victoria Barracks. I must have passed satisfactorily as I joined the remainder of No. 21 Course for induction into the service on 18 January 1937 at Point Cook.

3

Point Cook

During the First World War, Britain and Australia were the only Commonwealth countries to have their own flying corps. At its height, the Australian Flying Corps (AFC) had four operational units, No. 1 Squadron in the Middle East and Nos 2, 3 and 4 Squadrons in France on the Western Front. Four more AFC squadrons were set up for training in England. Numerous Australians who were already overseas, mostly in the AIF, joined the AFC or Britain's RFC or Royal Naval Air Service (RNAS). The exploits of these men built up an enviable reputation for skill, courage and audacity. The RNAS amalgamated with the RFC to form the Royal Air Force (RAF) on 1 April 1918.

After the war to end all wars, the AFC was replaced by the Australian Air Corps (AAC) and its squadrons were disbanded. The AAC manned Point Cook airfield south-west of Melbourne more or less as a caretaker and the government constituted a new Air Board on 9 November 1920. It recommended the forming of an 'Australian Air Force'. Lt/Col Richard Williams, the very first Australian to win his 'wings' in 1914, was the First Air Member of the AAC Air Board, and on the 31st, as Wing Commander Williams, he became the first air member and Director of Intelligence and Organisation of the Air Board for the Australian Air Force. The king approved using the prefix 'Royal' the following June and, effective from 31 August 1921, the Royal Australian Air Force (RAAF) came into being. Personnel strength on its formation consisted of 21 officers and 130 enlisted men. The new service also had 151 aircraft. This total included 128 war surplus aircraft (less one that was lost in 1920) with supporting equipment presented by the British Government in appreciation of Australia's part in the Great War.

Like the aviation industry in general, the period between the two world wars for the new service was difficult, particularly at first. It was a time of survival, gradual development, fighting for funding and trying to acquire up-to-date equipment. Expansion was far from rapid, particularly during the years of the worldwide Great Depression in the early 1930s.

Meanwhile, it was seen as desirable and practical to develop the air forces of the British Empire along common lines as far as possible. At the Imperial Conference in London in 1923, Britain's representatives proposed a system of reserve training for RAAF officers at courses in England through a system of short service commissions in the RAF. These commissions would be made available to a proportion of the pilots trained annually at Point Cook. Graduating cadets could nominate themselves for five-year short service commissions in the RAF, with their year at Point Cook counting as their first year.

As an incentive to agree to this uniform scheme, Britain's Air Ministry offered to credit £1,500 Sterling per head to a special fund in London from which Australia could draw to pay for goods and services to be provided to the RAAF. Australia's fledgling air force was only two years old at the time and it stood to benefit enormously. There were advantages all around. By adopting this method, it was reasoned that a reserve of trained aircrew would be built up which could be drawn on to reinforce RAF squadrons in an emergency, and Australia would benefit when the men returned home after four years of practical operational training at British expense.

The first cadets were selected from the Point Cook course that completed training at the end of October 1926. Seven graduates – not ten as originally stipulated – sailed for England the following month to begin their RAF service. The RAF soon showed interest in retaining some of the men for a longer period of time, perhaps even permanently. Subject to a satisfactory financial adjustment, the Commonwealth was agreeable. When Britain announced measures to build up her air strength in 1935 because of growing tensions in Europe, the Air Ministry suggested extending the short service commission scheme from five to six years. Again, Australia's Air Board had no objection.

Next, the RAF's Chief of Air Staff, Air Chief Marshal Sir Edward Ellington, said that his service was looking for as many as fifty Australian pilots in 1936 and it got them, twenty-five each from the year's January and July classes. Another large course began at the start of 1937 and Dereck French was among the new recruits.

We were issued with uniforms and service equipment and allotted our quarters. Most of the cadets were accommodated in rooms in the existing barrack blocks but some of us were each allotted a well-fitted tent, a row of which were behind the barracks. Our rate of pay was £3/10/- ($7) per week, uniforms supplied.

My immediate neighbours were Jack Galvin and A. F. P. James, both of whom became good friends. Jack Galvin remained with the RAAF and during the war rose to the rank of wing commander and then suddenly resigned his commission – an act which for a permanent air force officer was almost impossible in wartime. I met him again years later at the 50th anniversary of our graduation which had been held at Point Cook in December 1937. He seemed to be uncomfortable when the termination of his service appointment was mentioned. In 1993 he wrote a letter to me explaining the circumstance leading up to his resignation, which I felt was written by him to clear his name before he passed on. The letter certainly explained the highly politically oriented event. It appears that as a wing commander he was ordered to preside at the court martial of a politician, then an officer in the RAAF who was charged with an offense which had resulted in the loss of a Catalina flying boat. This should have been a normal court martial but before it sat he was presented with the findings he was to establish! All of the characters involved in the case are named in the letter, which possibly gives a true picture of the RAAF in Australia in wartime as just another political tool.

A. F. P. James (Francis James, as he was later known) left an even more controversial story. He arrived at Point Cook with a large old domed cabin trunk which he said contained his typewriter and part of his library. When asked how many books were in his library and whether he had read them all, he answered that he had been reading three books a day since birth, an impossibility which indicated to us that he would tell any story if he thought he had a chance of being believed. He did not adjust to service schedules and discipline and eventually was placed more or less under house arrest in his tent while his case was investigated. His meals were served in his tent and were supposed to come from the Cadet's Mess, but by an unusual form of persuasion he possessed his came to him from the Officer's Mess.

Although confined to camp, he frequently absented himself to attend a series of classical music concerts held in Melbourne, again using his remarkable powers of persuasion to induce the guard personnel at the main gate to allow him to leave and re-enter the aerodrome. He was sent for mental assessment in Melbourne. I remember being told of his interview with a psychiatrist who asked him only two questions: 'Do you enjoy a good cigar?' and 'Do you enjoy a good joke?'

He eventually became too much for the RAAF authorities and my diary entry records, 'A. F. P. James kicked out 19/5/37'. I believe that the official reason given for his discharge was, 'Not amenable to service discipline'. He later made his way to England and joined the RAF. I met him once early in the war in Lincoln dressed as a RAF sergeant pilot.

During 1941, I was visiting a friend at Rauceby RAF Hospital when I met him again. He was then a patient under psychological investigation, as he had been wearing several strange ribbons below his flying wings. I have a photograph of him in this garb that includes RAAF wings, which to my knowledge he was not entitled to wear, and the strange ribbons. One group he claimed he earned in the Chinese-Japanese war, the other group in the Spanish Civil war.

On returning to my home aerodrome I received a phone call from the group captain in charge of the hospital. He had learned that I had known James in Australia and asked for my opinion of his mental state at that time. I told him that I considered James to be sane but eccentric. A.F.P.J. was released and returned to his fighter squadron. The next I heard from him was a roneoed letter he sent from a German hospital where he was being held as a POW. He apparently used his strange powers of persuasion again and was returned to England as one of a prisoner exchange scheme before the end of the war.

Post-war, A.F.P.J. again contacted me by sending a supply of his religious paper, *The Anglican*, and subsequently a bill for same. We kept in touch intermittently over the years until his death in 1990. He was an unusual character, a compulsive stirrer who could be described as regards his service life in the way Air Chief Marshal Sholto-Douglas[1] spoke of T. E. Lawrence (Lawrence of Arabia): to the service, he was a nuisance.

Other members of No. 21 Course left during the year. Some like A.F.P.J. could not fit into service life while others failed to make the grade as pilots. One of the latter was Les Holten, who within a few months showed that he was useless as aircrew and left the course, transferring to the equipment branch where he finished as an air vice marshal in the permanent air force.

Another who was discharged for poor flying ability was Frank Graeme-Evans, who had learned to fly in Tasmania before joining the RAAF. He went to England anyway, joined the RAF pre-war and flew with that service with distinction, during and after the war. Years later he told me that he had failed at Point Cook because he had tried too hard; I believe Frank's flying work with the RAF seems to indicate that the judgement of the Point Cook hierarchy was not too good.

Frank Graeme-Evans was from Launceston, Tasmania and he became a member of No. 26 (Army Co-op) Squadron RAF flying Lysanders from 9 September 1939 to 2 August 1940. He served in France 1939–40, and flew fighter reconnaissance during the Battle of Britain and later in North Africa with 451 RAAF Squadron. He operated mostly from Sidi Barrani until his Hurricane was shot down and he was captured on 27 September 1941. After the war he remained in the RAF.

The severe system of training and discipline left most course members in constant fear of being dropped from the course, an attitude which tended to make them fail. I overcame this problem by doing my best and to hell with the consequences.

Stuart Beggs was one who became a victim of the pressure. He was the product of an old western district family and I think, had he lived, would have been Tammie Fraser's uncle.[2] He was rather spoilt and could not take the change to service discipline. After about nine months of trying, he borrowed my .303 rifle (each of us had a rifle on charge for drill purposes) and blew his brains out in a bathroom. There was a panic. CIB men came from Russell Street to investigate and the affair seemed to be hushed up.

The training course (flying, physical and academic) at Point Cook took twelve months, two terms of about six months each. A new course started every six months so that there was always a senior and a junior course. The custom was that the members of the senior course introduced those of the junior term into the system, which involved rather vicious initiation ceremonies and penalties for minor offences.

At our initiation we were made to strip and run naked across the drome to the hangars along the foreshore. There we were painted with colourful aeroplane dope – only on parts of us which could not be seen when we were in uniform. In this condition we were forced to walk the plank into the sea. One or two of us could not swim and nearly drowned. Then we had to take part in a race, pushing peanuts along the concrete tarmac with our noses. All rather stupid and childish, yet it was condoned by the senior staff as it was supposed to make us group together and bend to discipline.

The routine of the training course was rigid. We rose at a fixed time, showered, made our beds, tidied our quarters (these were inspected each day) breakfasted, did precision drill with rifles and attended academic lectures on service and technical subjects and law. Five-mile runs were a regular exercise for all except crafty ones such as A. F. P. James who usually avoided them by claiming to be suffering from some complaint or other, usually one that was difficult to diagnose. Early in the course we hardly saw the inside of an aircraft.

For the first three weeks we were not allowed away from the aerodrome. We began our flying training in Gypsy Moths, which were slow, stable and safe enough. We flew dual for about 10–12 hours before going solo. During our second term we did our flying training in Westland Wapitis, a heavier single-engine, twin-seater biplane. Both the Moth and the Wapiti were obsolescent at that time, the RAAF's equipment being years behind that of the RAF. We were extremely naive and thought of our instructors as gods, but later when we joined the RAF we learned that they were only average instructors. When being admitted to the RAF we were asked where we had learnt to fly and when we told them Point Cook, we were immediately posted to an advanced RAF flying training school for further instruction.

Flying training at Point Cook included aircraft handling on the ground as well as in the air, the usual tuition of take-offs and landings, cross-country flying, aerobatics, formation flying and some night flying. My instructor at the time on Wapitis was F/Lt J. R. 'Sammy' Balmer. I was told that as I took off on my first solo night flight he was heard to say to a friend, 'They will be alright'. When asked who 'they' were, he answered, 'French and Jesus Christ of course' – a good flying companion.

I think of Sammy Balmer as one of the better types I met in the pre-war RAAF. He was one of the few regular air force officers, including Brian 'Black Jack' Walker and Keith Parsons, who successfully escaped from the safe drudgery of the RAAF in Australia and flew operationally. Sammy owned a large sporty Vauxhall car in which he made record-breaking runs (Darwin–Adelaide, Perth–Adelaide and, I think, Perth–Melbourne) at a time when the highways were dirt tracks. He was eventually posted to 467 Squadron RAAF (Lancasters) in the UK where he was killed in action in 1944.

G/Capt J. R. 'Sammy' Balmer OBE DFC commanded No. 13 Squadron during 1940–41, Nos 7 and 100 Squadrons in 1942 and 467 Squadron 1943–44, all RAAF units. He failed to return from a mission to bomb a military camp in Belgium on the night of 11/12 May 1944. His Lancaster (LL792/PO-E) was attacked by a German night fighter and set on fire. It exploded moments later, killing all on board. He is buried in Heverlee War Cemetery.

G/Capt Brian 'Blackjack' Walker DSO was from South Australia and was a cadet at Point Cook in January 1935. After graduating in March 1936 he was posted to No. 1 Squadron at Laverton flying Bristol Bulldogs and later returned to Point Cook as a flying instructor for two years. He commanded No. 12 Squadron in 1941–42, then No. 30 Squadron, newly formed and equipped with Beaufighters, 1942–43 and was involved in the Battle of the Bismarck Sea. Next he commanded No. 5 OTU, went on loan to the de Havilland Co. as test pilot of the new Mosquito then being produced for the RAAF in 1944 and then sent to Darwin to command of No. 1 Fighter Wing RAAF, consisting of three Spitfire squadrons, 1944–45. He left the RAAF in January 1946 and became chief test pilot for de Havilland's at Bankstown for ten years where he tested numerous aircraft, including the first Australian-built Vampire jet. In 1957 he joined Bobby Gibbes in a flying venture in New Guinea. His flying career spanned fifty years (1935–1985) in total, and he flew over 130 aircraft types accumulating nearly 14,000 flying hours. He published his autobiography, *Blackjack*, in 1994 and died in 1997.

Air/Cdr K. R. J. Parsons CBE DSO DFC AFC RAAF (Ret'd) from Burnie, Tasmania, commanded No. 1 ATS 1941–42, No. 7 Squadron 1942–43, No. 5 EFTS 1944, 460 Squadron in England 1944, RAF Station Binbrook 1944–45 and RAF Station Gamston 1945.

In retrospect, after years of service with the RAF, I formed the opinion that the regular pre-war RAAF was of little use to Australia from a defence point of view. For example, after two years of war, when the first Japanese attack on Darwin took place, no RAAF aircraft took off to fight them, probably due to poor decisions years earlier by senior officers as to the types and quantities of aircraft required. The service did, however, perform good war work by taking part in the Empire Air Training Scheme (EATS), which produced thousands of aircrew badly needed during the war.

Towards the end of our flying training course at Point Cook, eight volunteers were called for who on graduation were to transfer to the RAF to serve five-year short service commissions with that force wherever in the world they might need us. This offered a chance to travel widely and to fly more up-to-date aircraft than were available in Australia.

Those who were finally selected for this transfer were T. H. Boylan (Tom), H. K. Gibson (Ken), A. E. Oakley (Bert), G. R. Taylor (Dick), B. E. Cremin (Dan), A. M. Young (Alf), P. J. Rowan (Perc) and myself. We, as civilians having been discharged from the RAAF, left Melbourne on 4 January 1938 on the P&O liner RMS *Orford* and steamed for England, fares paid.

By the end of his training at Point Cook in December 1937, Dereck had accumulated 131 hours in the air: 53 hours 25 minutes of dual instruction, 74 hours 10 minutes solo and 3 hours 25 minutes as an observer or passenger.

The years 1936–37 had seen the largest numbers of Point Cook-trained pilots going to the UK. This was in the face of growing criticism by some RAAF officers who argued that the RAF short service commission scheme resulted in Australia's best pilots being drained away from its home air force. Increasingly conscious of Japan's rapid and aggressive incursions in Asia, the RAAF could see a pressing need for its own programme for expansion. It would be far better for it to keep all of the pilots it could train, and so the arrangement with Britain was duly suspended. By July 1938, when the last eight Point Cook graduate pilots sailed for England, a total of 149 of them had transferred under the system.

Although the scheme had been suspended, it did not mean the end of the RAF's recruitment drives in Australia. Applications for RAF short service commissions continued to be advertised in the Australian press and regular intakes were made until mid-1939. The outbreak of war in September that year terminated the arrangement

Young men accepted through advertising after July 1938 came directly from civilian life, and were selected by a board of RAAF officers in each state. Unfortunately, they did not receive the benefit of an initial flying training course. Some of them had no flying experience at all when they boarded ship for England!

4

England

Our route was via the Suez Canal calling at Adelaide, Perth, Colombo, Aden, Suez, Port Said, Naples, Villefranche, Toulon, Gibraltar and Tilbury docks (London) on 10 February 1938. The voyage was a wonderful experience for us, we went ashore at each port of call and spent what little money we had seeing the sights.

On arrival in grey, foggy and damp London we went to Australia House where we met the Australian air liaison officer (ALO), G/Capt McNamara VC (an Australian Victoria Cross winner of the First World War originally from Rushworth) who presented each of us with £20 ($40) in cash to tide us over until our RAF pay came along. We were accommodated at RAF Uxbridge, in outer London, through which at that time all new recruits to the service were processed. The following day we were ordered onto the parade ground and given fifteen minutes of drill, after which we were told that we need never drill again – apparently this was a part of service life in which the RAAF had trained us well.

While at Uxbridge we were introduced to the system whereby RAF officers obtained their uniforms and other clothing. I was sent to the tailor Herbert Chappel of Conduit Street, London, where I was measured and fitted with a uniform for everyday use, mess kit for dinner nights, full evening dress and the accompanying bits and pieces. I was then introduced to the system of paying for them by means of a weekly payment of £1 ($2) by a banker's order from my bank, Lloyds. This arrangement suited us as it allowed us just enough money from our pay of £22 ($44) per month to pay our mess bills and the usual living expenses. We were usually nearly broke.

We were asked, about this time, where we had learned to fly and had gained our wings and when we told them of Point Cook Flying Training

School we were astounded to hear that that our training was considered inadequate and we should undergo further advanced flying training at an RAF establishment. To fill in time until the next flying training course commenced we were posted, with the idea of gaining further flying experience, to various small RAF units close to London. My posting, with Perc Rowan, Dan Cremin and Bert Oakley, was to Station Flight, Northolt, where we were under the scrutiny of S/Ldr Hamersley (we vaguely knew him to be an Australian, but always thought of him as a 'pom'; he was a nice chap and we had no idea he was an 'ace') and the immediate supervision of a flamboyant aerobatic ace, F/Lt Donaldson (English), who I believe was killed during the invasion of Norway. He introduced us to Hawker Hart and Miles Magister aircraft and to RAF flying procedure.

Harold Alan Hamersley was born in Guildford, Western Australia, on 6 February 1896. He was commissioned in the AIF and served on Gallipoli in 1915 after which he transferred to the RFC, and in September 1917 was posted to 60 Squadron. On 23 September that year he nearly became the forty-ninth victory of the German ace Werner Voss. In the early stages of the famous fight in which Voss was killed, Hamersley's SE5 was damaged by the German's fire. He was promoted to captain, received an MC, and claimed 13 enemy machines shot down before returning to England in May 1918. In the meantime, the RFC and RNAS (Royal Naval Air Service) had combined to become the Royal Air Force (RAF) on 1 April 1918. In 1920–22, Hamersley again flew with 60 Squadron, this time in India, and then for a time was test pilot at Avro; he held an altitude record in a machine powered by an Austin Seven engine. He became a squadron leader in March 1935, and in July went to Worthy Down for engineering duties. In 1938 he was CO of the University of London Air Squadron, and in 1940 commanded RAF Hullavington; he later became President of the Aircrew Selection Board in Scotland. G/Capt Hamersley retired from the RAF and died in December 1967.

S/Ldr John 'Baldy' Donaldson commanded 263 Squadron from 1939 to 8 June 1940. He scored a number of successes during the ill-fated campaign in Norway before he had to lead his remaining Gloster Gladiators to land on the aircraft carrier HMS *Glorious* during the British evacuation. Two days later, *Glorious* was sunk by the German battlecruisers *Scharnhorst* and *Gneisenau* with the loss of 1,207 lives, including Donaldson's.

At that time, Northolt was the home of No. III Squadron, an élite fighter squadron, being the first to be equipped with Hawker Hurricanes.

The Station Flight to which we belonged was equipped with easy-to-fly aircraft used mainly by flying types at the Air Ministry in London. A similar communication flight was at nearby Hendon to which Dick Taylor, Tom Boylan and the others of our party had been posted. It was a good way of introducing us to English flying conditions. Our work load was minimal: 900 hrs–1200 hours; lunch from 1200–1400 hours, then more work from 1400–1600 hours.

With the £20 ($40) each of us had received on arrival in the UK some of us bought cars, which at the time were unbelievably cheap owing to the recent introduction of a new Horse Power Tax on all vehicles. An almost new Ford V8 could be obtained for under £25 ($50). I bought a 1931 vintage 10 hp Standard Sedan for £17/10s ($35), which included tax and insurance. It was a sedate vehicle with a top speed of 45 mph (72 km/hr) and a fuel consumption of 25–40 miles (40–64 km) per gallon.

The first serious outing the car had in my ownership was a drive in the company of Dan Cremin to Somerset to visit my Hanham relations at Wincanton. I found them at Maperton Ridge, a group of smallish cottages built along a ridge. The name 'Maperton Ridge' was later used in Australia, when Susan Babstock McNair (née Hanham) used it to name her house at No. 1 Rose Street, Ivanhoe. I introduced myself to our Somerset connections as their Australian cousin, but at first was not believed. Eventually they thawed and became very hospitable – sherry, Somerset cider and talk of family trees and their wish to take me to see the family graves in the churchyard at Blackford. They were very nice, natural people.

Our stay at Northolt was for nearly two months during which time we gained a good knowledge of how the RAF operated, as well as valuable flying experience under English weather conditions, which were so different to those in Australia where one was seldom forced to fly through cloud. The end of this period, 19 April 1938, coincided with the commencement of the final stage of the RAF advanced flying training courses, to which we were posted. I went with Bert Oakley and Percy Rowan to No. 10 Flying Training School at RAF Ternhill in Shropshire. At the time we resented being posted back to a flying school as we thought we knew all there was to know about flying; and only later realised that our earlier flying training at Point Cook had not been as good as we had supposed. The attitude of the RAF instructors at Ternhill to us was rather overbearing, which caused me to make a note in my diary: 'Our fellow Australians, who came before seem to have left the wrong impression.' These would have been some of the twenty-five graduates from our senior (No. 20 Course) at Point Cook who had passed through Ternhill about six months before us. Among the trainees at Ternhill I met Merv Thomas, who had been a student at University High School when both Neil and I had been there. Merv later joined me in 50 Squadron at Waddington.

Being young and on our first journey out of Australia, life at Penrhos was rather wonderful. We behaved like tourists and enjoyed everything new to us: the North Wales scenery; the local culture; and the unique bird life. During our stay in that corner of the UK, Merv and I accepted a bet that we could complete a zigzag walk into north Wales from Shropshire and then go on to a party at Birmingham (on 4 June). We won the bet, walking 49 miles (79) km) in twenty-two hours, sleeping for an hour and a half under a hedge and then going on to the party. This was a typical part of our social life at that time – pub crawling, sightseeing, with plenty of leisure time on our hands.

Our fellow trainees included chaps from all parts of the Empire, Canada, New Zealand, Australia and the Argentine, many of whom came to grief in one way or another during the war. One character was Brian Carbury from New Zealand, who during the Battle of Britain was awarded a DFC & Bar. A few weeks later he was cashiered and discharged from the service because he had been unable to handle a chequebook and had written cheques which bounced.

Brian John George Carbury was the son of a veterinary surgeon in Wellington, New Zealand. Just before the outbreak of war he was attached to 603 Squadron to assist with Spitfire training, a temporary posting that became permanent late in September 1939. His claimed tally of 15½ enemy aircraft destroyed placed him among the five top-scoring pilots of Fighter Command at the time and he was one of the few who were awarded the DFC & Bar during the Battle of Britain. On 30 December 1940 he was posted to No. 58 OTU as an instructor. He did not fly operations again but served as an instructor until he left the RAF in 1944 as a flight lieutenant. He stayed in England after the war and died in July 1962.

Another good friend was Don Jacklin, an English Catholic who was later with me at Waddington flying Hampdens operationally, and in the Middle East in 1942 briefed me on how to fly Wellingtons. He survived the war, being awarded the DFC and Bar.

The training aircraft at Ternhill were a Hawker Hart and Hawker Audax, sedate single-engine, two-seater biplanes well suited for the bombing air gunnery and night flying exercises we practised. Part of the course was carried out at an RAF armament training school at Penrhos near Pwllheli in North Wales. This was a picturesque aerodrome perched on high cliffs on the coast. The local inhabitants were strongly anti-British and had three prices for everything – one for the local Welsh, another for British tourists, and a third, the highest, for the RAF. At one stage their Welsh Nationalist Movement reached a climax when they raided the aerodrome and burned a hangar.

These little annoyances did not prevent us enjoying the beauty of the area, studying the prolific bird life and exploring the places of historic interest, such as the castles at Harlech and Caernarvon and scaling the higher peaks such as Mount Snowdon. I found a beautiful place, Lake Vyrny, which was the water supply for Manchester. It had little else apart from a fine hotel where I was later to spend time relaxing to the full while on leave in the early war years. At that time it was managed by Australians (the Brooks).

We completed the Flying Training Course at Ternhill and received our next postings. Most of us were sent, with others, to form a group of twenty-six young pilots at Brough, on the River Humber near Hull. This was the aerodrome of the Blackburn aircraft factory, also used as a civilian flying school. Our party was under the control of Flight Lieutenant Harston, ex-RAF, who supervised our activities. We became known as 'Harston's Circus'. Our purpose was to gain air experience over the UK flying B. A. Swallow aircraft – slow, safe, single-engined, two-seater, open-cockpit monoplanes.[1]

We were allowed to fly anywhere in the country, calling at RAF stations for fuel and accommodation. We flew as pairs, wondering about visiting friends at different stations. It was a most beneficial experience, but it was abused by some. One couple, Dick Taylor and Ken Gibson, flew to spend the weekend in France, beyond our remit, and were in trouble when their landing fee charges came back to the Air Ministry for payment. Gibson continued to display a similar lack of discipline and was asked to resign his commission and return to Australia shortly before WW2 started.

The Swallow was a most safe aeroplane, although one chap, Dennis Baker, crashed one and killed himself. I was apparently the senior member of the 'Circus' so I was sent to identify the body for the local coroner. This was a horrible job as in the crash the engine had folded back into the face of the pilot.

At Brough were several Hawker Harts in which we were allowed to practise. I made a poor landing in one of these, finished without wheels and the nose of the aircraft stuck in the mud. It was a good lesson, the accident being due to careless overconfidence. I was more responsible in future.

After about three months of this wonderful touring we received postings to our various squadrons. Most of us went to Bomber Command units, some to fighters. Dick Taylor and I went to join No. 50 Squadron at

Waddington near Lincoln. Waddington at that time was one of the three permanent RAF stations of No. 5 Group, the others being Scampton and Hemswell. All of these operated Hawker Hind aircraft, single-engine, two-seater, open-cockpit biplanes which were cousins of the Hawker Hart and Hawker Audax aircraft on which we had been trained, so we soon became familiar with them.

From early 1938, Britain's Prime Minister, Neville Chamberlain, and the League of Nations followed a policy of appeasement in the hope that it would assure world peace. A pattern developed that was repeated over and over: Britain and the League of Nations would make concession after concession to the expanding Third Reich, and in return Chancellor Hitler would give assurances that the re-emerging Germany had no further territorial claims. His assurances were worthless. The German Army marched into Austria in March 1938; in September it threatened Czechoslovakia. The threat of open hostility was palpable. Would Britain and the League of Nations say stop, that's enough, no more? Chamberlain flew three times to Germany for talks with Hitler, and at Munich he took part in negotiating an agreement that weakly ceded Czechoslovakia's Sudetenland to Germany in return, of course, for more hollow assurances.

The immediate crisis was averted, but Chamberlain's assertions of 'peace for our time' as he held up a paper signed by the German government totally ignored what had been going on in Spain since 1936. Germany, Italy and the USSR were locked into the bloody struggle of the Spanish Civil War, a dress rehearsal for what lay ahead. Although the world breathed a sigh of relief, the reality of the international situation – an almost inevitable drift to war – was more widely realised.

In reality, for Britain to have opposed Germany in September 1938 would have been suicidal. What the crisis made abundantly clear was that Britain's armed forces, particularly the RAF, were not ready. Facing a *Luftwaffe* strike force of an estimated 1,200 modern bombers, RAF Fighter Command would have only been able to muster ninety-three of its new eight-gun monoplane fighters, including all reserves. The remainder of its aircraft were outdated biplanes. As for Bomber Command...

We carried out formation flying and cross-country flights [in Hawker Hind biplanes!] which were supposed to prepare us for war conditions. Our range was limited, so much so that at one time we were told that in the event of war we had enough range to reach and bomb Germany but could only return as far as the English Channel where we were to ditch and be picked up by the Royal Navy!

One interesting job we were asked to perform in these planes was to fly as a squadron to Scotland where we were detailed to drop 'poison gas' on vessels of the North Sea Fleet at anchor in the Firth of Forth. We did this in daylight and the exercise was said to have been a success, although if it had been done under war conditions none of the squadron would have survived. The accuracy of our gas dropping was judged by the numbers of droplets which fell on yellow cards spread about the decks of the ships.

Waddington had been a permanent RAF station since WWI and was well established with hangars and mess buildings, although at that time the landing ground was simply a large grassed paddock without any specific runways. As the fear of war developed this grassed area was disguised by painting thick black lines across it (soot and oil mixtures) to give the appearance of small fields divided by hedges. This was quite a good camouflage and had the effect of encouraging the growth of mushrooms along the make-believe hedges. It was situated on the old Roman north road (Ermin Street) and part of the aerodrome was said to have been the site of a Roman camp. On that particular area if one suffered an injury resulting in broken skin it was always likely that tetanus would develop. To combat this we always kept our anti-tetanus injections up-to-date.

Towards the end of 1938 the Squadron was gradually converted to handle twin-engine aircraft by learning to fly Bristol Blenheims. These were at that time a fairly common twin-engine medium bomber of the RAF and not really a true training type. Avro Ansons would have been more suitable. After we had mastered the Blenheims our Handley Page Hampdens began to arrive. We became fully equipped with these and thought that we were ready for war. Little did we know!

The Handley Page Hampden was one of a trio of 'heavy' bombers that formed the main equipment of RAF Bomber Command when war arrived, the others being the Vickers Wellington and the Armstrong Whitworth Whitley. Appropriately named after John Hampden, a seventeenth-century opponent of tyranny, the bomber was unique in several respects, not least of which was its distinctive appearance. It inspired an assortment of nicknames ranging from 'The Frying Pan' to 'The Flying Tadpole'. Its aerodynamic form was characterised by sharply tapering, slotted and flapped wings, and a deep, slab-sided narrow fuselage – the maximum width was only 3 feet (.9 m) – to which was affixed a slim boom carrying the tailplane. In load-carrying capacity and operating range, it lay more or less between its contemporaries, the Wellington and Whitley and the Blenheim medium bomber. Its performance compared closely with that of the Blenheim.

On its debut on 21 June 1936, the Hampden was one of the world's most advanced warplanes. It came from a distinguished line, tracing its ancestry back to the outstanding Handley Page 0/100 strategic bomber of 1915. It was the company's first monoplane bomber, and its low-drag wing incorporating the most advanced slot equipment enabled it to achieve a high maximum speed without sacrificing low-speed qualities. From the pilot's viewpoint its cockpit offered an excellent fighter-like field of vision, it was small enough to be highly manoeuvrable, and its ease of control made it an extremely pleasant, forgiving aeroplane to fly. The exceptionally slim, compact fuselage and long boom-like extension permitted the provision of dorsal and ventral defensive armament without incurring any serious penalty from drag. Four crew members were carried, and armament comprised of one fixed forward-firing .303-inch Browning machine-gun and three hand-held Vickers K guns of the same calibre. The first Hampden was delivered to the RAF on 8 August 1938, and manufacture proceeded rapidly. By the end of the year, No. 49 Squadron based at Scampton had received its full complement of machines, and Nos 50 and 83 Squadrons were in the process of re-equipping.

During February 1939 we flew as a squadron to Evanton, near Inverness in Scotland to take part in armament training, especially low-level bombing from a few feet. We used only small practice bombs and did not see or carry any live bombs until long after the outbreak of war.

Evanton was in beautiful Highland country, most being heavily timbered with pine forests; there were a few farms and very few people. We could drive for hours towards the west and not see a soul. The place was a fisherman's paradise. A local RAF chap took me fishing in the evenings to a brackish estuary, Bonar Bridge, where we caught both sea trout and brown trout. At this time of the year in this area twilight continued until nearly midnight, so there was plenty of time for fishing.

During our stay in Scotland I chanced to land in a Hampden at Leuchars near Edinburgh and was badly burnt on the face and head by the engine exhaust while starting up. This resulted in me being grounded and sent on sick leave, which I spent at the home of a fellow pilot, David Penman, in Edinburgh. While there I learned how dedicated the Scots were to golf: each afternoon after school, the children would take off with one club each and presumably a ball to practise with.

No. 50 Squadron had originally been formed at Dover as a home defence unit on 15 May 1916. It carried out defensive patrols from airfields in Kent until the end of the First World War, receiving Sopwith Camels in February 1918 to combat enemy bombers based in Belgium. The squadron disbanded on 13 June 1919. It was reformed at Waddington on 3 May 1937. Its official badge was an Australian dingo!

It became known as the Dingo Squadron during WW1 when it had many Australian pilots on its strength. TheSSquadron's recall signal at that time was, 'All Dingoes Rum.' (They were probably not teetotallers.)

During early 1939, we in 50 Squadron decided that the unit should have an official crest and designed one on which the main item was a winged dingo head. This we sent to Chester Herald, Inspector of Air Force Badges, College of Arms, for approval. The answer was that there was no such thing as an heraldic dingo and would we accept a crest which displayed a segment of the coat of arms of Dover, the port being where 50 Squadron had been formed in 1916. We humbly accepted this awful symbol, which is supposed to be a cloak being cut in half with a sword. Our reason for submitting the winged dingo head as a crest suggestion was that at the time, pre-war, the squadron had about twenty-three pilots, eight of whom were Australian. S/Ldr Duncan C. F. Good was one of these. He was a magnificent leader who, had he survived, would surely have become one of the leading bomber pilots. He was for a while my flight commander and a good one at that.

The Australians in 50 Squadron RAF at this time were: John 'Ferdinand' Bull; Bob Cosgrove; Dereck French; Duncan Good; Robert 'Dave' Reed; Dick Taylor; Mervin Thomas; and Bob Wawn.

During these pre-war days at Waddington, apart from our flying and other service duties, we were allowed sixty-two days' leave each year as well as all weekends and public holidays and so had more leisure time than we could afford. We used this time to visit the tourist centres. A favourite place was the Lake District, where we climbed all of the peaks and fells. London was always high on our list of places to visit, where we always made a point of seeing the latest theatre shows and the usual pubs and tourist haunts.

During June 1939, I attended a Blind Approach Training (BAT) Course (also known as Lorens Course) and VHF (Very High Frequency) Course at Mildenhall in suffolk. This took several weeks, was carried out in Avro Anson aircraft, and involved being taught to fly solely on instruments. The equipment required for blind approach, the beam and relevant beacons, was at that time available at few aerodromes, mainly in Bomber Command. The purpose of the training was to improve our general flying ability while at the same time form a group of pilots who were capable of carrying out 'nuisance' raids over Germany when weather conditions were so bad as to ground the Command in general. On these occasions our duty would be to fly independently over centre to centre of Germany dropping the odd bomb on each of them. The idea was to disrupt the life of each town and cause the people to go to the air raid shelters. The emphasis of the training was on our instrument flying, helped by many hours spent in the Link Trainer on the ground where we were again entirely dependent on our instruments. At the end of each course we were expected to be capable of taking off and landing without seeing the ground, being completely screened from the outside while a safety pilot sat beside us on guard.

At Mildenhall one day, while doing an approach to land, a safety pilot was disturbed to see that the approach meant crashing into a hangar. All flying was abandoned and scientists investigated the fault. It turned out that during a long spell of rather hot weather the beam (usually only a few metres wide) had widened to include the hangar. The fault was corrected. Later on in the war I repeated the course at Boscombe Downs and Waddington. In retrospect, I think that these three BAT courses had a great influence in my survival as a bomber pilot. There the weather conditions were so often atrocious and the ability to fly confidently on instruments was a lifesaver.

For us service life was interesting and easy, mainly due to the generous holidays we received. When not on duty, off the aerodrome we, as young officers, never wore uniform but always dressed in mufti, which allowed a greater opportunity to explore. During July, three of us decided to make a bicycle tour of France: George Sansom; Peter Wilcox of Palmerston North, New Zealand; and myself. George was a pukka English chap who was later shot down into the sea by our RAF fighters, then bombed by one of our bombers which had become lost, and finally sent up in a Halifax aircraft which lost a wing and finally finished George. Peter flew with me for ages, including a ferry trip to Egypt, but was killed fairly early in the war.

We drove to London, took a ferry to Calais and a train to Paris and established ourselves. George was a cosmopolitan gent who had been on the continent for a part of his education and spoke fairly good French, making our tour easy. After a few days seeing the sights of Paris we took a train to Brussels, mainly to visit the International Aero Exhibition. This included among the exhibits a Spitfire, a Wellington and a German *Stuka* dive bomber. At night over Brussels the Belgian Air Force put on an amazing flying show – Gloster Gladiators doing aerobatics in formation. Unforgettable!

After this we visited WWI battlefields at Ypres, Hill 60 and Menin Gate – all a bit gruesome as they were still digging up bodies from the war. By the time we arrived back in London, without even seeing a bicycle, we were almost broke having only three pence between us. We went into the Brass Arse, an RAF haunt on Piccadilly Circus, ordered three beers and then waited until an acquaintance came in and we were able to borrow a pound to get us back to Waddington. It was a ten-day break well spent!

As part of our service training we as junior officers had, from time to time, to perform administration duties as either squadron or station adjutants. This gave us an insight into the way the RAF was administered. While performing this duty as Station Adjutant I learned that a pilot was required to fly a Mk I Bristol Blenheim to Egypt, so I applied and got the job. The flight was to be made in August in company with two similar Blenheims, all three products of the newly developed 'shadow factory' system which was operating for the speedy expansion of the RAF as the threat of war became more acute.

Enlargement of the RAF had necessitated major reorganisation. The RAF expansion programme was a series of successive schemes, noted alphabetically, each the result of re-thinking future requirements in the light of changing circumstances. The first plan, Scheme 'A', was announced in July 1934. By February 1936, Scheme 'F' was being announced and, among other things, it called for an extensive increase in the RAF's strike power by replacing light bombers with medium bombers, plus the creation of much larger reserves.

All of this needed to be achieved within three years but there were huge practical problems. The aircraft industry itself was already in a state of flux. It was in the process of adapting itself to the radical change from biplanes to monoplanes and from fabric-covered fuselages to fuselages of stressed metal construction. It simply could not cope with the enormous, complex workload that Scheme 'F' demanded. To produce the new, more sophisticated modern aircraft, factories themselves needed to be restructured. Stocks of basic materials had to be changed, and the traditional small-scale production methods replaced by the techniques of mass production: jigs, dies, tools and fast new assembly lines. Not only that, workers had to be re-trained for their new tasks.

The far-sighted system known as the Shadow Factory Scheme was instituted in April 1936 to rectify the situation. Initially, this was introduced as a means of utilising the resources of Britain's motor vehicle industry to provide extra production capacity. It involved building new state-owned aero engine, airframe component and assembly factories which were equipped and run by such leading motor companies as Austin, Daimler, Rootes and Standard. They would turn out products designed by a 'parent' organisation within the aircraft industry. This scheme was quickly under way, and was complemented early in 1938 by an additional shadow scheme that provided for the erection of more state-owned factories managed by approved firms in the aircraft industry to further increase production.

There were teething problems, as Dereck found out when he inspected the aircraft that he and the others were required to take from Waddington to Egypt. They were Bristol Blenheim Mk Is. Dereck's machine was No. L8528, which had been manufactured by Rootes Securities Ltd, and the members of his crew were Sgt Wright, A/C Marshall and A/C Barrass.

The aircraft appeared to have been hastily assembled and were roughly finished. Many of the rivet holes along the fuselage were misaligned, the surplus holes being hidden with filler and paint which came away as the trip progressed giving the aircraft an airy colander effect. The engines (Mercury VIIIs) had a modified mixture control on the throttle which malfunctioned and left us very short of fuel on several hops. Valve springs broke frequently and caused trouble.

We were able to make use of these troubles later as an excuse to change our flight plan of Marseille to Malta to Marseille to Tunis, as our flight leader, a Canadian, F/Lt McKenzie, had been briefed by the RAF authorities to fake engine trouble and divert our planes to the nearest land – Tunis. He was to go there to investigate what the strength of the French Air Force was in that area.

Marseille was our first overnight stop after leaving the UK. We were met by an RAF liaison officer, S/Ldr Homer, the brother of Mike Homer, one of our pilots at Waddington. S/Ldr Homer took us under his care, arranged aircraft servicing facilities, fuel, accommodation for ourselves and our crews and then gave us a pep talk and issued everyone with visiting cards bearing the addresses of the most hygienic brothels in the town! The French Air Force here interested us; they seemed to lack the military style of the RAF. The general atmosphere was that of being an élite flying club where all the members lived off the aerodrome, coming along to fly from time to time.

Next day we started off for Malta and from our usual cruising height of about 10,000 feet (3,000 m) were able to see the mountains of North Africa. McKenzie then told us of his 'engine trouble' and we headed for Tunis. While we were at our cruising height my second pilot, Sgt Wright, produced a bottle of champagne he had acquired in Marseille. We demolished this using a service dixie as a cup, although a fair bit was lost in froth due to our altitude and the shaking up the bottle had suffered in transit. Champagne in a dixie at 10,000 feet!

The French Air Force at Tunis were most helpful to us, laying on accommodation, aircraft servicing facilities, entertainment and a flying display of their latest fighter plane, the Morane 406, the equivalent to our Hurricane. The flying display was magnificent, although the aircraft appeared to overheat in both the engine and the cockpit. The pilot wore only a tiny pair of swimming trunks under his flying suit and was dripping.

The crews of the three Blenheims totalled three officers and six NCOs and other ranks. The officers were accommodated at the luxurious Hotel Majestic and were supplied with a car, a driver and an interpreter for the period of the stay, while the rest were billeted at the aerodrome where they carried out the servicing and repairs to the planes. This they managed with some difficulty as the French Air Force maintained an endless supply of beer to them as they worked.

Our interpreter was Corporal Robert Petain, the grandson of Marshal Petain. Robert was serving two-year conscription duty with the French Air Force. All young French males performed this duty.

Henri Philippe Petain was the French general and statesman who led the Vichy French government. At age sixty he became a French national hero when he stopped the German advance at Verdun in 1916. He was appointed commander-in-chief in 1917 and restored morale in the weakened French army. During the 1920s he was responsible for the construction of the Maginot Line, fixed defences which proved disastrously easy for the German panzers to outflank in 1940. Petain retired in 1931 but his prestige was enough for him to enter politics. He briefly served as war minister in 1934 and he later became a central figure in right-wing politics. When France was on the point of defeat in June 1940 he was asked to form a government and negotiate peace with Germany. On 22 June the armistice was signed. Under it, France was divided into a German-occupied zone in the north and west, including the Atlantic coastline, and an unoccupied zone in the south with the Mediterranean coast. Petain became head of the new government in the south, which was set up on 10 July 1940 at Vichy. His principal aim was to keep France safe from the ravages of war as suffered in 1914–18. He was arrested in 1945 and tried for treason. A conviction followed and he was sentenced to military degradation and death. The sentence was commuted to life imprisonment and he died six years later. Was he an arch-traitor, or a hero who sacrificed everything to save France from suffering as she had in the First World War? Opinions remain divided to this day.

Robert took us (the three officers of the party) to various clubs, dinners and embassies where we met what might be called the 'élite' of Tunis. He also took us to visit a large brothel where the Madame proved to be Australian by marriage, having married an Australian digger during WWI and returned to Australia with him when the war ended. She wore as a brooch an Australian

'Rising Sun' hat badge. After three days, and despite the efforts of the French Air Force to sabotage our servicing efforts, our men managed to repair the aircraft and we were able to escape and make our way to Malta – away from the intense hospitality.

At take-off we 'shot up' the aerodrome and town of Tunis in formation. During these manoeuvres the toupee of one of our navigators, P/O Peter West of NZ, was sucked through the open cockpit hood of the plane. It slid down the wireless aerial and lodged on a protrusion on the front of the tailfin and remained there for the 300-mile (480-km) hop over the Mediterranean, falling to the runway as the aircraft stalled to land at Halfar, Malta. Later, in Egypt, the same toupee fell down a vent gap inside the Great Pyramid, when it was again recovered; this time by one of the Arab guides who led us through locked grilles and dusty passages into the lower bowels of the pyramid until we found it. I had been on leave with Peter during July of this year in Paris, when he had lost his virginity to a seductive French girl. He was a steady, good type of chap, who, while on the *Corfu* returning to the UK, developed a close friendship with an elusive, beautiful English girl, to whom he became engaged before we berthed at Liverpool. She had been visiting her brother, a member of the Palestinian Police Force in Palestine. They were soon married, but not for long, as Peter was soon to die on operations.

Our base at Malta was Halfar aerodrome where we remained idling for a week so that a build-up of ferried aircraft ahead of us in Egypt might be processed and dispersed. While on the island we swam, sunbathed, went sightseeing and caught an infection called 'Malta Dog', a severe form of dysentery. The cure for this was to go to bed and consume a large glass of brandy and port. It worked.

During our stay at Halfar more RAF aircraft passed through in transit to Egypt and Singapore. One Blenheim missed sighting the island yet flew directly above it on to the east, eventually performing a forced landing in the sea beside a steamer.

Take-off for our flight to Egypt was at 0645 on 21 August. The aerodrome at Mersa Matruh was without marked landing strips or boundary markers, just hard desert. I touched down a bit short of the aerodrome proper when a freshly dug ditch appeared ahead of us. Fortunately we still had sufficient flying speed to clear it and so land on the true aerodrome, where we refuelled from four-gallon (18-litre) tins. Our next hop was to Alexandria and up the Nile to Cairo and Heliopolis where we handed over the aircraft for delivery onward. The main rumour was that they were destined to go on to India, but I later heard that they became part of the Turkish Air Force. While waiting for further orders regarding our return to England we were given various station duties to keep us out of mischief, and we amused ourselves between times by seeing the tourist sights of Cairo.

One day, while acting as duty pilot, or station duty officer, I received a signal advising the scheduled arrival of an aircraft of the French Air Force piloted by someone of the rank of adjutant general. Not knowing the ranks of the French Air Force, I imagined the arrival of a very high ranker and acting accordingly roused the station commander to greet him. I felt a fool when I learned that the rank of a French adjutant general was equivalent to a RAF warrant officer. Apart from these odd station duties we had plenty of time for tourist runs to the Pyramids, the Sphinx, camel rides and most memorable of all, a visit to see the contents of the tomb of Tutankhamen. The beauty and craftsmanship of the gold work, the scarabs with their beautiful enamel inlay could never be forgotten.

Our main worry, at the time, was that we would not return to England fast enough for us to take part in any air action which would arise should war break out. Otherwise, should peace continue, we intended to get to England as soon as possible and then try to wangle a job ferrying Bristol Bombay Troop transport aircraft to the Middle East to replace the old 60-mph (95-km/hr) Vickers Valencia planes which were still in use there. The Valencia crews had promised free grog for a week to the first crew delivering a Bombay to them!

We awaited orders to return to UK by ship at Heliopolis on the outskirts of Cairo. Eventually we embarked from Port Said on the P&O liner *Corfu* and started for England. Aboard ship we were cut off from most news from the outside world, especially with regard to the growing tension arising out of the invasion of Poland. We went ashore briefly at Malta but learned nothing. Later at Marseille we heard talk of us going from there by train across France to reach our units sooner. Nothing came of this idea when we learned of the chaotic state of the French railways trying to cope with the general mobilisation of the French Forces.

Next day while steaming between Marseille and Gibraltar all service officers aboard were assembled in the ship's saloon where we were addressed by the senior British officer present. He was a pompous old Indian Army colonel who was on his way to the UK before retiring. He gave us a pep talk telling us that, 'War has been declared and England expects every officer to do his duty etc., etc.', real Lord Nelson stuff. I later heard that the old chap had, on arrival in the UK, been given an about-turn order and sent back to India.

Aboard the *Corfu* were the usual female passengers, the young and not so young ones of the so-called 'Fishing Fleet' who were returning home after visiting the Middle East, and some even India and the Far East, where they had been searching the outposts of the Empire for suitable husbands. This was traditional practice at the time.

There were more elderly ladies aboard, who we (being callous youths) said had been given free passage by the P&O Company to scare the seagulls from the boat. Once the declaration of war had become general knowledge this latter group donned their life jackets and refused to go below decks. They littered the decks wearing standard pattern cork filled life jackets; later we heard that people who jumped overboard wearing this model of jacket usually finished in the water with a broken neck. We were not torpedoed and eventually berthed safely at Liverpool.

5

Phoney War

Aboard the *Corfu* as we steamed towards England, our main thoughts were
of our squadrons; wondering whether they were busy on bombing raids and
what was happening. We, the aircrew, were most anxious to get back to
our units before the war was over, fearing we should miss out on what we
thought would be fun.

Having trained for years as bomber crews we felt that our destiny lay
in fulfilling that role. What we did not recognise then, however, were the
inadequacies of our aircraft, our lack of night flying experience and skill, our
poor navigational abilities and our general lack of true operational training
and experience. Our attitude to war was unreal. We had a 'Dawn Patrol'
image of war and air operations.

The *Dawn Patrol* referred to by Dereck was the 1938 remake of a 1930
film of the same name. It starred Errol Flynn, Basil Rathbone, and David
Niven as Royal Flying Corps fighter pilots in World War I. Both films were
based on 'The Flight Commander', a short story by John Monk Saunders.
The movie romanticised many aspects of the war in the air which
would become clichés: white scarves; the hard-drinking, hard-playing
fatalism of doomed airmen; the short life expectancy of new pilots;
esprit de corps; chivalry between combatants (woven around the legend
of the 'Red Baron'); and the desperate final mission. Its deeper underlying
theme was the severe burden of emotional stress on a military commander
who must constantly order his men to almost certain death. With another
world war looming, the remake was timely and successful.

Back at Waddington we soon learned that we had not missed much.
The squadrons had been on frequent stand-by for operations; one squadron
actually took off on a mission, only to be recalled to base soon after it was

airborne. On this occasion at take-off, the tarmac audience included local civilians, together with the barmaid from the local Horse and Jockey Inn. In the officer's mess, hilarious, drunken parties were the order of the day. We settled into the unreal world of a peacetime squadron routine, to which was added the panic of stand-by for operations, activities such as formation flying, ZZ approach training and air-to-air gunnery practice.

RAF policy at that time regarding junior officer pilots marrying was to discourage. Those who married before reaching the age of twenty-five or reaching the rank of squadron leader were not allowed the usual married officer's allowance, and if they were without adequate private means suffered financial hardship. The official attitude was put to us rather crudely when we were at Point Cook by an instructor, F/Lt Welters: 'Why keep a cow if you can buy milk.'

Later, as our casualties increased at a steady rate, the wives of aircrew were prohibited from living on or within a certain range of the home aerodrome. As it proved, probably 90 per cent of the original RAF bomber aircrews were off operations by mid-1941, having either crashed, been shot down, become POWs, or been killed or wounded.

Dereck's diary entry for 17 September was 'Slow war this', an attitude revealing his youthful frustration, but there were political and practical reasons why it was so. On the eve of war, President Franklin D. Roosevelt had cabled the leaders of the major European powers – Britain's Neville Chamberlain, France's Edouard Daladier and Germany's Adolf Hitler – seeking their assurances that they would exercise restraint in using their bombers by choosing targets where civilians would not be at risk. Britain and France immediately signalled their agreement, but with the fighting going on Poland, Germany delayed. Bearing this in mind, the British and French governments had to consider how the powerful Third Reich might react if they took the initiative against its western frontier. Would the *Luftwaffe* be used to retaliate by bombing French and British cities, and perhaps those of Belgium and Holland as well? Meanwhile, almost overnight, RAF Bomber Command had been seriously weakened. In August 1939, Bomber Command's strength had been fifty-five squadrons, organised as follows:

Headquarters Bomber Command was at Richings Park, Langley, Buckinghamshire, but a new location was being prepared at High Wycombe. The C-in-C was ACM Sir Edgar Ludlow-Hewitt.

No. 1 Group was commanded by AVM A. C. Wright; HQ at Abingdon, Berkshire; with Nos 12, 15, 40, 88, 103, 105, 142, 150, 218 and 226 Squadrons, all equipped with Fairey Battles.

No. 2 Group; HQ at Wyton; commanded by AVM AM C. T. Maclean; with Nos 21, 82, 101, 107, 110, 114 and 139 Squadrons, all with Bristol Blenheims.

No. 3 Group; HQ at Mildenhall; under AVM J. E. A. Baldwin; with Nos 9, 37, 38, 99, 115 and 149, 214 and 215 Squadrons, all with Vickers Wellingtons.

No. 4 Group. HQ at Linton-on-Ouse; commanded by Australian-born AVM A. Coningham; with Nos 10, 51, 58, 77, 78 and 102 Squadrons, all with Armstrong Whitworth Whitleys.

No. 5 Group; HQ at St Vincent's House, Grantham; under AVM W. B. Callaway; with Nos 44, 49, 50, 61, 83, 106, 144 and 185 Squadrons, all with Handley Page Hampdens.

No. 6 Training Group with Nos 7, 18, 35, 52, 57, 63, 75, 76, 90, 97, 98, 104, 108, 148, 166, and 207 Squadrons; and the New Zealand Flight with a mixture of aircraft including Ansons, Battles, Blenheims and Wellingtons.

The Whitleys of No. 4 Group could carry the heaviest bomb loads and had the greatest range, but they were slower than the others and therefore more vulnerable to fighter attack. For this reason the Whitley squadrons were trained exclusively for night operations. It was intended that the main bombing operations for Battles, Blenheims, Hampdens and Wellingtons would be carried out in daylight using tight, self-defending formations. The Battles and Blenheims were restricted by their limited range but the other three types could reach most of Germany from the UK except for the extreme east. These long-range bombers were situated on the aerodromes nearest Germany in the counties of East Anglia, Lincolnshire and Yorkshire.

The short-range light/medium bombers which were designated under Britain's war plans to go to France with the British Expeditionary Force (BEF) were based in the Oxfordshire/Berkshire area. When the Advanced Air Striking Force (AASF) did move to France with the BEF, the ten squadrons of Fairey Battles of Bomber Command's No. 1 Group were transferred from England to bases in the Rheims area. No. 1 Group ceased to exist.

The other main element of the RAF ordered to France with the BEF was the Air Component. Its job with its two squadrons of Blenheim bombers and Lysander army co-operation squadrons was to support and protect the British Army. The two Blenheim squadrons were taken from No. 2 Group. It had been planned for all the Blenheim squadrons to move to France but as there were not enough airfields available this was cancelled. The other units of No. 2 Group were dispersed around the British countryside ready for anti-shipping work and with a commitment to operate over the Low Countries if and when the Germans invaded. The AASF and Air Component would soon be combined into a separate command, the British Air Forces France (BAFF).

Bomber Command's remaining effective strength for missions that could be directed against Germany itself therefore rested on the shoulders of just eight squadrons of Hampdens, six squadrons of Whitleys and eight squadrons of Wellingtons. This was hardly enough, and if casualties were heavy at the outset, who was there to replace these professional, highly trained crews? Clearly the RAF was not ready for all-out war. It desperately needed time to build up reserves of men and machines before full-scale fighting began.

The 'panic' must have been on for within a month of the outbreak of war we were busy practice bombing, dropping 14-lb (6.35-kg) practice bombs from 1,000 feet (300 m) as well as doing a short session of night flying. This brought my night-flying experience – total hours in twin-engine aircraft – to 3 hours and 50 minutes; which was all I had when I started night operations in March 1940. I know of no other pilot of 50 Squadron who at the time had more night experience on twins, so it is no wonder we lost so many of our aircrew so early in the war. The cause of these losses was simply lack of night-flying experience and the fact that until we began operational bombing in March 1940 no one in the squadron had taken off in a Hampden with a full bomb load. In fact, none of us had dropped anything but the 14-lb practice bombs! We were woefully unprepared.

Our total flying hours for September 1939 came to about 16. Apart from our hours on duty, we relaxed with pictures, booze, roulette and dice, as well as enjoying a great amount of rough shooting. We had easy access to this shooting as our Waddington station commander, Group Captain Cocky, was a keen shot who encouraged it. The Air Ministry was at the time developing great tracts of rural land into new aerodromes, particularly in the flattish parts of Lincolnshire, and it was on this country that we were permitted to shoot as we wished before the bulldozers began on the construction of the runways. What became Skellingthorpe and Wigsley aerodromes were part of our shooting range. We shot fairly large bags of rabbits, hares, quail, pheasants, partridges and the odd woodcock, going out once or twice a week as time permitted.

On 22 October I went to Boscombe Downs on another VHF Course. This was the second of three such courses I was to complete. A few months pre-war I took the first of these at Mildenhall RAF station when I had been passed as being qualified to instruct in VHF blind approach training.

A month later, back at Waddington after the second course, three of us – F/O 'Dizzy' Ayres, P/O Merv Thomas and myself – were in a signal room of a 50 Squadron hangar on 23 November following the progress of an aircraft (a Hampden from Scampton) making a ZZ approach. The weather was bad, with cloud almost down to the ground; visibility was only a few hundred feet. During the exercise we heard the controller order the plane to do another circuit, so being curious we went out onto the tarmac to see the aircraft as it passed overhead. We heard it approaching with its engines at full revs but did not sight it until it roared into the top of the hangar above our heads.

It immediately exploded into flames, the hangar caught fire, burning bodies and parts of the plane and engines fell about us. One chap hit the ground, burning and in a running position. He continued to run until he was well out on the aerodrome when he keeled over and died. The station ambulance arrived but the crew appeared to be at an accident such as they had never experienced before and dithered, going from one body to the next but doing nothing useful. The Hampden was piloted by S/Ldr Watt of Scampton, a very experienced captain, who had on board six or seven wireless operators under training learning the ZZ drill. All were killed.

That evening the three of us, Ayres, Thomas and myself went to the cinema in Lincoln to see the film *Goodbye Mr. Chips*. I found that during an emotional part of the show all three of us were quietly weeping. It was probably a delayed action of the traumatic experience we had undergone that day, the most horrible crash we had witnessed to date. The cause of the accident was attributed to the plane's altimeter not being set correctly for the exercise.

Eyewitness accounts reported that the aircraft, Hampden L4034 from 49 Squadron, suddenly appeared from the gloom flying about 10 feet (3 m) above the ground heading directly towards Waddington's Watch Office. Then it banked steeply to starboard and tried to climb away. As it did so it collided with one of the hangars, killing the entire crew and a number of airmen, some from 50 Squadron who were working in the hangar and were crushed when one of the engines plunged through the roof. The known casualties were S/Ldr Peter McGregor Watt, Cpl Thomas Alexander Keating, AC1 Stanley Taylor, AC2 Frank Leslie Talbot, AC1 Leslie McGarvie, LAC Walter Gerald Kelly and Cpl A. Cooke, all of 49 Squadron; plus 50 Squadron's Cpl Archibald McDonald Henderson and AC2 M. Bastow. All were killed except Aircraftsman Bastow, who was injured. How many suffered minor injuries is not known.

Dizzy Ayres, was soon to fall victim to the blind approach system, when on 16 March 1940 while returning from a night trip he was told to descend through cloud and land. He obeyed orders, came down through the cloud and crashed into a mountainside in Scotland, 150 miles (240 km) north of where he was supposed to be. It was an unexplained casualty about which we never learned the cause. The controller in this case, F/O Goodfellow, a good friend of Ayres, took responsibility for the tragedy, assuming the role of the guilty one, and was eventually posted from his air traffic controller duties.

Killed or missing in this later incident were F/O Vivian Howard 'Dizzy' Ayres, P/O Peter Aubrey Forrester Addie, Sgt George Albert Rowling and LAC Allan Vincent Wallace. The aircraft, Hampden L5063, crashed into high ground at Cocklaw Foot in the Cheviot Hills, 12 miles (19 km) from Kirk Yetholm, Roxburgh, Scotland. The bodies of Sgt Rowling and LAC Wallace were not found and their names are listed on the Runnymede Memorial. Faulty direction-finding equipment at Waddington which resulted in the transmission of incorrect information was said to be a contributing factor to the accident.

On 24 November, our squadron flew to Wick, the most northerly aerodrome in Scotland at the time, so that we might be on hand should the German pocket battleship *Deutschland* be located. It was said to be at large in the North Sea. Operationally, our stay at Wick was a washout. The ship was not sighted although Anson aircraft carried out searching sweeps towards Norway, being backed by Skua aircraft from the Fleet Air Arm. The weather was wild. A partially built hangar was completely demolished by the wind. Our Hampdens were dispersed, being pegged down facing into the prevailing wind which at times was so strong as to cause the propellers of 980 hp Bristol Pegasus engines to slowly rotate.

The officers of our detachment were very well accommodated at Mackay's Hotel in Wick, which was very well run by two dear old souls who really mothered us and who were determined that the 'colonials' in the group should have a taste of true Scottish hospitality in the form of a genuine haggis. They made the haggis but before it was ready to be consumed the squadron received orders to fly back to Waddington. This resulted in us being chased across Scotland and England by a haggis. It eventually caught up with us when we had an official dinner, during which it was piped into the mess and consumed.

While our billets were excellent at MacKay's, the other ranks had a bad time, sleeping and eating at the local school, which had been requisitioned for that purpose. The building had cold concrete floors on which our chaps had to lay their straw palliases to sleep; unfortunately we could not buy any dry straw to fill the palliases locally and finally had to go to England, just south of the Scottish border, to obtain some. Wick was a rugged and beautiful place which we enjoyed to the full when we were off duty. Many farms seemed to grow oats almost to the edge of the sea. We saw many seals hunting and playing just beyond the surf.

Back at Waddington we did little flying, partly because of bad weather and also because of Air Ministry policy at the time of 'saving engine hours!' During the war, we had periods when we had available more pilots than aircraft, or more engines than airframes, or more aircraft than pilots, depending on which production line had achieved greatest efficiency. At this time we were ahead in the supply of pilots and airframes and lagging in the production of engines. Because of this I flew only 2 hours 15 minutes during December.

We were into the early stages of the 'Phoney War', which can be compared to a boxing match where the contestants spar, prance around, yet hardly make contact. We saved engine hours as the Air Ministry planned and became involved in schemes to keep us busy in other ways. One such scheme was an arrangement whereby two colonial officers were sent each week to spend a few days as guests at the Gawdy Hall estate in Norfolk of Jean and Adeline Tresfon, old friends of our AOC, AVM Harris. [AVM Arthur Harris had taken charge of No. 5 Group on 11 September 1939, replacing AVM Callaway.]

Jean was Dutch and a director of Boulton & Paul aircraft manufacturers. One weekend this chore fell to Merv Thomas and myself. We were more or less ordered to go and were a bit apprehensive about the visit, but then found that we had to put up with a couple of days of fascinating conversation, fabulous food and excellent shooting. Adeline was a very attractive woman who could have been Jean's wife, daughter or mistress. She handled a 20-bore shotgun better than any of her guests, cooked imaginatively, spoke umpteen languages and was a perfect hostess. We never found out the true status of this delightful person. The residence was very old but had been luxuriously renovated, being superbly fitted with mementoes of their travels. My room was carpeted wall to wall with springbok skins.

Mervyn Thomas had joined 50 Squadron the previous year as a direct entry short service commission officer. He had been at University High School in Melbourne with me years before. My last memory of him at UHS was at a school assembly when he was ordered onto the stage before the whole school and asked to apologise to the headmaster (representing the staff) and to the head prefect (representing the pupils) for having smoked at a school social. The alternative to the apology was expulsion. He apologised. Merv was a good friend and I was to miss him when he was shot down with many more of our 50 Squadron chaps into the Skagerrak off Norway on the 12 April 1940.

During December 1939, we did little flying, quite a lot of game shooting, a lot of drinking, and in general were frustrated with the inactivity. The frustration of this 'Phoney War' period was so bad that my second pilot, South African P/O Bill (Slug) Mulloy, and I decided to see a bit of action and wrote to the Finnish Aid Bureau offering our services as pilots to fly against the Russians who were attacking Finland at the time.

Despite the Nazi–Soviet Pact of August 1939, neither Stalin nor Hitler actually trusted each other. Following the division of Poland between Russia and Germany in October, the Soviets began consolidating a sphere of interest in the Baltic to provide a buffer zone against any future German expansion. Poland was not the only country that had featured in the secret clauses of the Nazi–Soviet Pact. These also concerned the Baltic republics, placing them all 'within the sphere of Soviet interest'. Faced with the spectre of Nazi conquest on one hand and intimidating pressure from Stalin's USSR on the other, Lithuania, Latvia and Estonia were quickly persuaded to sign treaties of friendship which gave Russia the right to establish garrisons and bases within their borders. They were bloodless coups resulting in Soviet occupation. A similar agreement was demanded of Finland; however, Finland was not so easily coerced.

After two months withstanding bullying Soviet 'diplomacy', Finland rejected the demands, mobilised her 200,000-strong army and deployed it along her frontier. On 28 November, the Russians broke off negotiations and demanded the immediate withdrawal of Finnish troops from their new positions. On the last day of the month, Soviet armies totalling nearly one million men advanced on Finland from the east and south-east, while an air attack initiated hostilities without a declaration of war. The Finnish Army could only muster sixteen divisions, which were short of all types of military equipment, and it had no armour at all. What chance did it have? Finland appealed to the League of Nations for backing against Russian aggression on 2 December and the Soviet Union was expelled from the League of Nations on the 14th, but this did not seem to worry the Soviet dictator.

During that December, contrary to the expectations of the Russians and the watching world, the Finns were not overwhelmed. Heavy snows and subzero temperatures had little effect on Finland's troops or their mobility. They were all skiers and warmly clad. Russian columns moving along narrow roads surrounded by woods were impeded by deep snow and plummeting temperatures. These men fresh from Ukraine lacked arctic clothing. On their flanks, Finnish civil guard units in white smocks swooped silently on skis, sniping at supply vehicles and field kitchens. From the Vuoksi to Lake Ladoga, their accurate rifle and machine-gun fire combined with heroic attacks on Russian tanks with petrol bombs proved so successful at causing huge losses that on 22 December the remnants of the Russian 17th and 13th Armies broke off the action and fled. Of huge concern to Stalin was the fact that the world had witnessed the humiliating failure of Russian arms in what should have been a crushing victory. By now Finland was advertising for adventurous volunteers in the world's press. Two skills were required: volunteers had to be able to ski and use firearms, to the disappointment of Dereck and many others like him.

Our offers were rejected on the grounds that we were serving officers of the RAF and so not free for such duty. The British government later removed any such restriction and some RAF crews flew Blenheim aircraft to Finland. The fighting there soon fizzled out and we heard no more of those crews.

Some Blenheim bombers were given belly packs of four .303 Browning machine-guns and converted into fighters, then they were dispatched to Finland to fight the Russians, but it was a case of too little, too late. Reorganised and reinforced, the Russians launched overwhelming new assaults early in 1940, which obliged Finland to capitulate in March.

No. 44 Squadron shared Waddington with 50 Squadron, both being equipped with Hampdens and sometimes joined forces for special operations. On 21 December, 44 Squadron's Hampdens were returning to the UK from a daylight sweep of the North Sea where they had been searching for enemy shipping and expected to make landfall at about the Firth of Forth in Scotland. As they approached land they were mistakenly attacked by our own RAF fighters from Drem, Scotland. Two of our Hampdens were shot down into the sea while the remainder flew on to Drem where they spent the night. Relations between the fighter and bomber boys at Drem that night were poor.

One of the Hampdens to be shot down was piloted by a good friend of mine, F/O George Sansom, who had been the third member of our group to visit Paris just pre-war. George was a well-educated, much-travelled Englishman. He spoke good French and although he was a pilot he was soon to become one of the leading navigators of the RAF. He had a certain deadly charm for women, and even in Paris he had an earlier French girlfriend, Denise, who was then engaged to a Yank, slip away from her fiancé each evening to stay with him. George later achieved a certain fame when after being bombed at Bassingbourne by one of our RAF bombers (who had become lost thinking he was over France) and also shot down by our own fighters. While he was carrying out a navigational exercise in a Halifax the wing fell off and that was the end of George. A sad loss.

During November and December 1939, our lives became more complicated with the arrival of WAAF personnel who freed many of our male cooks for other duties. They became stewards, drivers and signal and cipher operators, in fact they occupied nearly every muster except that of aircrew. Women did, however, serve as pilots with the ATA (Air Transport Auxiliary), delivering all types of aircraft to the RAF units. The aviatrix Amy Johnson (Mollison) lost her life in the Thames Estuary while ferrying an aircraft. The ATA did a magnificent job, but did not receive the recognition or the acclaim it warranted, being overshadowed by the great work done by the WAAFs who were more in the public eye.

It was amusing on the morning that WAAFs first appeared as stewards in the Officers Mess at Waddington. Some officers looked up from their breakfasts to find that they were being served by the same girls they had been out with in Lincoln the previous night. They were a wonderful asset to our service.

Winter was truly with us and it was a terrible one, bringing flying almost to a stop and a car trip to Lincoln, only a few miles away, was a real hazard over the frozen roads. Car engines froze and glycol was a necessity. We prayed for the thaw.

The end of 1939 in Britain saw snow, frost, fog, and heavy rain. In Lancashire, showers of sleet held up trains. On the Yorkshire hills between Burnley and Harrogate the snow was so deep that a snow-plough had to clear the roads. With the New Year, the coldest winter for more than forty years crept over the country. Pipes froze and burst and the population shivered beside modest fires of rationed coal.

At night, heavy mists and the blackout made normally familiar city streets dark and menacing and posters everywhere warned the public: 'Children are safer in the country. Keep them there.' Early in January, rumours of a Nazi invasion of Holland because her water defences were frozen startled Europe for several days. The 21st was said to be the coldest day England ever recorded. In London, the snow fell and lay deep, as hard as iron beneath heavy frost. The River Thames froze over at Kingston and for 8 miles (13 km) between Teddington and Sunbury. Some 12 inches (30 cm) of ice covered lakes and reservoirs, and in Hyde Park people went skating on the Serpentine. Snow was still falling in mid-February.

Every night nationwide an inky blackness descended over the country. The imposed blackouts were far more rigorously enforced than those of the 1914–18 war, and the combination of blackout and snow made life difficult. In the cities, vehicles crept their way through the streets with masked headlights. Ministry of War Transport road accident reports in January showed that 4,133 people were killed in the last four months of 1939 compared with 2,497 over the same period in 1938, and in December alone there were 1,155 fatalities, mostly pedestrians, the highest ever recorded. With their social lives hampered in the evenings by blackouts and the weather, most Britons tended to stay home and listen to the radio. Meanwhile, on 11 January 1940 Dereck carried out his first nickel raid.

'Nickel' was the code for operations over enemy territory dropping propaganda leaflets. These trips were usually short, simple ones and were later commonly used to give fresh crews experience of a not too hazardous nature and so break them into operational work gently. Sometimes, however, Nickel raids went over the Alps to Italy and these long trips resulted in quite a few casualties. Whitley aircraft were commonly used on these long Italian trips and later the larger bombers that came into service were also employed in this way.

We, in Hampdens, usually dropped leaflets in bundles from long narrow containers slung in the bomb bay, which operated as on a normal bombing drop with the leaflets being released from the SBC (Small Bomb Container) that remained with the aircraft. These SBCs were also used to drop incendiary bombs and other small explosives.

On one occasion, being short of SBCs, we loaded thousands of leaflets through the floor of the plane into the bomb bay, the bomb bay doors being tightly closed. The idea worked perfectly until the take-off run started when the bomb doors started to sag, just a fraction, and the leaflets slipped out over Lincolnshire like a mad paper chase. We did not try it a second time.

On 10 February we carried out a North Sea sweep (in Hampden L4063) for three hours. This was our first operation, being a daylight trip from Lossiemouth in Scotland towards Norway in search of enemy shipping. We found nothing, which was perhaps fortunate, because although we carried bombs it was ordered that should we find any shipping we were not to attack in any way unless fired on first. The British 'powers that be' were afraid that one of us might do the wrong thing by bombing the wrong target or causing harm to a civilian ashore and so give the Germans an excuse to escalate the war.

While we were stationed at Lossiemouth, most evenings we watched the fishing boats of the port return with their catch of the day. Usually they spent days at sea before returning but under war conditions they had orders to be in port overnight. After tying up at the stone quay, their catches, mainly 10- to 18-lb (4.5- to 8-kg) cod, were lined up in heaps and auctioned. One evening among the catch was a conger eel, about 7 feet (2.1 m) long, which sold for £1.

Leave came frequently. On returning to Waddington from Lossiemouth I went on leave with 'Dizzy' Ayres to Cumberland for a week, walking from

Penrith over Helvelyn and Scawfell, staying overnight at the Dungeon Ghyll Hotel, a snug pub at Ambleside. It was a wonderful leave.

On 1 March, Dereck flew his second wartime mission. It was a security patrol in the area of Borkum-Sylt lasting six hours and 35 minutes in Hampden L4077. His crew, as usual, consisted of P/O Mulloy, Sgt Hyland and LAC Barrass.

Once again the restrictions imposed on us regarding any attack on enemy shipping applied and we tackled the job in a frustrated manner, although we realised that we were gaining much-needed night-flying experience. If we got to the target area and back we considered we had learned something. The weather conditions over the North Sea were usually horrible and most of our losses at that time were caused by the weather.

A week later, a chain of events led British leaders to order the deliberate bombing of a German land target for the first time. The war was about to escalate…

6

Sylt

In October 1939, a new secret weapon appeared: the magnetic mine. They were laid close inshore by German submarines to block shipping ports along Britain's east coast and in the English Channel. At first, the campaign was slow to gain momentum, mainly because there was a shortage of mines. These had not been mass-produced and stockpiled before war broke out, but it did not take long for German industry to catch up.

Germany's magnetic mining campaign reached full stride during November when surface ships and aircraft joined the effort. Using the cover of darkness provided by the longer nights as winter approached, surface vessels criss-crossed the North Sea and laid over 500 mines. In separate missions over three nights, *Luftwaffe* aircraft parachuted forty-one mines into the mouth of the River Thames, off the Humber, and at Harwich. One such mine was misplaced. It fell on mudflats at Shoeburyness and British experts recovered it intact. They immediately pulled it apart and quickly set about analysing it. An urgent programme was initiated to develop countermeasures and put them into practice.

While this was being done, the German mine offensive was proving highly effective. Within three months over a quarter of a million tons of shipping was sunk by this method alone. It severely restricted ship movements and obliged the British to close down numerous east coast and Channel ports. At the time, the psychological impact of these mines was as great as, or even greater than, the losses caused by U-boats.

Seeking to calm the shaken British population and to censure Hitler for employing such a 'sinister and barbaric weapon', the Chamberlain government was quick to reveal the magnetic mine's secrets. It was 'an amazing new invention', one British official said, promising that 'science and intelligence' would deal with it as effectively as it had dealt with the U-boat menace (which at this stage of the war was seemingly almost under control).

Meanwhile, the RAF joined the Royal Navy in trying to minimise shipping losses. On the defensive side, the first CHL (Chain Home Low) radar unit became operational in November and was positioned to cover the Thames Estuary where low-flying German planes were already laying mines. Balloon Command put up a barrage above the Thames Estuary from barges and lighters. Fighter Command carried out night patrols, despite inexperience causing some serious crashes.

Besides patrolling the east-coast estuaries by moonlight, Coastal Command formed special flights of Tiger Moth and Hornet Moth biplane trainers to do the same in the north and west. This was done in the belief that the sight and sound of *any* aircraft would scare mine-laying U-boats into remaining under the surface. It was a bluff that seemed to work.

Bomber Command's part in the campaign against the magnetic mines consisted of trying to prevent mine-laying He115 seaplanes from taking off from their bases on the islands of Börkum, Norderney and Sylt. Beginning on 12 December 1939, patrols were flown nightly by Whitleys working in relays over these bases. Any lights put on the water to help seaplanes take off in the dark were systematically bombed. The idea was to impose a blackout, but the bombs were only allowed to be dropped in the water! This was to comply with US President Roosevelt's special appeal for the combatants to avoid the risk of causing civilian casualties. Success during the five nights of 12–16 December was gauged from the fact that only one enemy aircraft was reported carrying out mine-laying. The patrols were sent out whenever possible, forty-two sorties over Sylt and forty-one to Börkum being made between 12 December and New Year's Eve. Leaflet raids and seaplane-base patrols continued thereafter with Wellingtons and Hampdens increasingly joining Whitleys in the leaflet raids and Hampdens taking over the patrols of the seaplane base.

During the night of 16/17 March while attacking Royal Navy ships in Scapa Flow, German aircraft dropped bombs on British soil for the first time. A civilian, Mr James Isbister, was killed as he stepped outside his home at Bridge of Waithe to help a neighbour. Seven other people were wounded. It was this raid that led to Britain's leaders deciding to deliberately bomb a German land target for the first time. A reprisal raid was ordered on the German seaplane base at Hörnum, on the southernmost tip of the North Frisian island of Sylt.

Sylt lies off the border between Germany and Denmark. Its civilian population had been evacuated at the outbreak of the war so there were no civilians in houses nearby. It is nearly 30 miles (50 km) long and is connected to the mainland by the Hindenburg Dam. The average distance from the English coastline of Norfolk is 325 miles (525 km).

Thirty Whitleys and twenty Hampdens were allocated the task of carrying out the first RAF bombing attack on a designated land target after more than six months of war. It was scheduled for the night of 19/20 March.

At RAF Hemswell in Lincolnshire, the intelligence room filled with eager young men: the Hampden pilots and aircrews for the mission. They gathered around while the officers pointed out the long thin shape of the island of Sylt on a map, and explained that the seaplane station at Hörnum was one of the main bases used by German mine-laying aircraft – mines that were a serious threat to British shipping in the North Sea. Alex Gould of 61 Squadron recalled that AVM Arthur Harris himself, at that time in command of No. 5 Group, was next to deliver a pep talk. For Bomber Command this was a long-awaited occasion, he said, the first chance to show what it could really do. They were about to make history.

On the way over the North Sea the weather was poor (as usual) with a great deal of fog, but in the target area they found moonlight. The Whitleys started proceedings and bombed first. Over the next four hours, twenty-six Whitley crews claimed to have found the target in clear visibility and bombed accurately. The Hampdens followed up and over another two-hour period fifteen of the twenty crews claimed to have bombed accurately.

At midnight in London, the House of Commons was still sitting in late session. When Prime Minister Neville Chamberlain announced that the recent German air-raid on Scapa Flow was being avenged, the members cheered. As he spoke, he said, British bombs were obliterating the main enemy air base at Sylt. He explained that this information had come 400 miles (640 km) from across the North Sea transmitted by the leading aircraft as it still directed the attack. The message had been decoded and sent straight on to him so he could announce the news while the raid was still in progress, an event 'probably without precedent in the history of warfare'.

Well-known aviation writer A/Cdr L. E. O. Charlton CB GMC DSO, in his very patriotic book *Deeds that Held the Empire by Air*, gave an enthusiastic description of the raid. Because it was published late in 1940, for obvious security reasons the names of the participating RAF bomber crews were not included in his account:

A young Dominion pilot gave an exhibition of coolness and calmness which is probably unprecedented in action from the air. His was one of the last flights of the raid, and he was greeted, on that account, with a more than ordinary intensity of fire. For this reason, in all probability, his bomb-sighter lost his bearings for a moment just as he was approaching the objective. The pilot was duly notified that it was a 'dummy run' and immediately turned back for a second approach, just as if he had been over a practice ground at home, letting go a salvo of three large bombs with gratifying effect.

The 'young Dominion pilot' was Dereck French. That night Dereck was at the controls of Hampden L4077 flying his third combat operation. His description of the 'dummy run' was a little different:

Hampdens at that time carried a crew of four, the captain or first pilot, the second pilot who also acted as navigator and bomb aimer, the wireless operator and the rear gunner. P/O Mulloy was my second pilot on this trip and was found to be wanting in that he did not have a full working knowledge of the bomb-release gear. This operated electrically, the bombs being released in turn as a rotating metal arm made contact with a series of terminals. We had never dropped true live bombs before and Mulloy did not know that the rotating arm was fitted with a safety catch. We carefully made our first run on to the target at 1,000 feet (300 m), being initiated into a great variety of AA as we did so. It was then that 'Slug' discovered how the gear worked and we had to carry on and make a second run through the flak, and drop our load of bombs.

Dick Taylor in Hampden L4076 was also 'Shovelling bombs on Sylt', as he noted later in his log book. He bombed at 0230 hours, dropping four 250-lb GP bombs and a container of incendiaries. Over the target too was Tasmanian, F/Lt Bob Cosgrove, who reported: 'Shells and yellow tracer bullets began shooting up everywhere and red shells burst below but we got on our mark, and I heard the crew shout "We've hit 'em, sir!" I was too busy to look back, but when I turned the machine and came back over the objective we saw the hangars were in flames.'

Altogether, 20 tons (20,320 kg) of high explosive and 1,200 incendiary bombs were dropped. Many crews reported accurate bombing and just one Whitley from 51 Squadron was shot down by flak. In his account of the raid, A/Cdr Charlton added:

Here is the testimony of an impartial witness. It is from an innkeeper living on the adjacent Danish island of Roemo, very little more than a mile from the northern tip of Sylt. He watched the whole performance in security, and noted the dropping of 85 bombs up to 11 p.m. when he lost count. He saw columns of flame and smoke belch forth and mount to great heights, especially remarking one violent explosion and flash which lit up a wide surrounding space, and which he very rightly put down to a munitions depot going up. He describes the regularity with which our bombers came and went, observable in pairs or singly, and how the noises and flashes of explosion followed each other at short intervals, so spread about that no part of Sylt could have escaped some of the consequences of the violent onslaught. Roemo lies but a step from shore and all along the mainland road the Danes were out to stand and watch the demonstration of air power so near to themselves.

When the bombers returned, the crew debriefings went on for hours before the reports went off to group headquarters. The raid was a wonderful success, though the accounts were not as dramatic as AVM Harris would have liked. Nevertheless, it was just what the bomber crews needed to boost their self-esteem and the country's morale. Newspaper headlines in the morning blazed out:

LAND TARGET AT LAST FOR THE RAF;
TONS OF BOMBS DROPPED;
SIX HOURS' ATTACK ON SYLT;
HANGARS AND OIL TANKS ABLAZE;
ADMIRATION IN U.S.;
NIGHT SKY LIT UP!

Reports on the BBC described it as a heavy raid and claimed extensive damage, but the story was told differently in Germany. Berlin's newspapers carried the headline: 'British Bomb Denmark!'

The German High Command claimed that no damage had been caused despite the bombing going on continuously for nearly seven hours. It seems that during the attack on the seaplane base a couple of bombs did fall on Danish territory, and on orders from Dr Goebbels this was how it was reported. At noon, to prove its claim, the German government offered to fly neutral reporters working in Berlin up to Sylt to see for themselves. American correspondent William L. Shirer mentioned the German offer in his scheduled broadcast to the US but even as he was speaking on air he was informed that the trip had been cancelled. He announced this change at the end of his talk. Later the Germans had another change of heart, as Shirer noted in his book *Berlin Diary*:

March 21. They took the American correspondents up to Sylt after all to-day, but I was not invited. They telephoned Berlin tonight that they had not seen much damage at the chief seaplane base at Hörnum, which was the only one they were shown – a fact I pointed out in my broadcast to-night. The Nazi press has been ordered to make a terrific play

tomorrow morning of the reports of these American correspondents...
The American correspondents were not shown all of Sylt. This afternoon
the High Command was very angry with me for having mentioned this.

It was Good Friday. Later, there was another change of heart: 'Radio
people called up. They will fly Irwin and me to Sylt tomorrow to inspect
the northern part of the island.' The on-again, off-again trip was then
called off once more: 'At midnight last night the RRG phoned to say our
trip to Sylt could not be arranged after all. What did the British do on the
northern end of the island that the *Luftwaffe* does not want Irwin and me
to see?' A/Cdr Charlton's account concluded:

Such is the story of the raid on Sylt, during which 50 British bombers
dropped some 45 tons of high explosive consisting of 500-lb and
250-lb bombs. The enemy was at pains to draw a balance sheet of the
damage done at Scapa Flow and the destruction wrought at Sylt, having
previously conducted a party of journalists from neutral countries
to take note for themselves at such places which had not been much
affected. As against the £34,230,550 which their raid on Scapa Flow had
cost us, they had the brazen audacity to state their own net loss at £97,
this sum being made up of £60 for a damaged house roof, £9 for the
repair of a rifle range, and an estimated sum of £28 for the replacement
of window-panes.

Who should you believe?

After the raid, the weather in the area had closed in again. It was
not until 21 March, two days after the attack, that a Blenheim from 82
Squadron was sent to photograph the target so that bomb damage could be
assessed. Unfortunately, the photographs were reportedly of poor quality
and inconclusive but they seemed to show that little or no damage had been
inflicted, despite the claims of the bomber crews. Next day a request was
made to send a PDU Spitfire to obtain more detailed coverage. It took off
for Sylt that afternoon but the pilot was not able to find the target because
cloud totally obscured the area. It was not until 6 April that photographic
coverage of Sylt was eventually secured. To Bomber Command's annoyance
the photographs revealed only slight damage to the seaplane base – certainly
not enough to restrict the German mine-laying operations. Seventeen days
had passed since the raid, and it was tempting to ask how much repair work
and window dressing could have been done in that time.

After each sortie, at that time, we had to write out and sign an 'Operational
personal experience report'. My report for this trip clearly shows how naive

we were in those days when I report that I consider the colourful HE (high explosive) shell fire to be fireworks. Later we were to learn how wrong we were. All of the Hampdens returned safely and we told our stories. I remember I could hardly wait for daylight to see how many holes we had collected in our aircraft and we could not believe our eyes when we found that we had not been hit.

PERSONAL EXPERIENCE REPORT
No. 50 Squadron
Waddington
25th March 1940

<u>Bomb Raid on Hornum Seaplane Base on night of 19-3-40.</u>

Aircraft –	Hampden L.4077.	
Crew –	F/O D. J. French.	(Captain).
	P/O. W. A. C. Mulloy.	(Navigator)
	Sgt. Horsfall.	(Observer).
	Lac. Barrass.	(W/Optr).
Bombs.	Bombs.	4. 550 lb. G.P.
	3 containers of Incendiary.	

The aircraft took off on time at 1130 hours and on receipt of the W/T signal 'GO' set course for SKEGNESS. From SKEGNESS the aircraft was navigated by D/R to a point 85 miles North of ESBJERG. Weather conditions encountered on this track were bad due to increasing cloud with a base at 600'–1500'. Cloud base on the DANISH Coast was 1000' and caused difficulty in identifying the position. When position had been definitely established course was set for SYLT.

The northern end of the inland was reached at 0230 hours. The cloud was then 1/10–9/10 at 3000'. A track was made good at 1000', parallel to the coast of SYLT and about ¾ mile out to sea. Searchlights appeared along the coast but were mainly above and behind the aircraft. The aircraft was caught only once on this track by a searchlight but was not held. These lights were accompanied by A.A. fire of red tracer type which appeared to be fired from batteries placed evenly along the WEST coast of the island and all firing at the same elevation. The fire was in general behind the aircraft.

The target was identified and a dive attack from 3500' to 1000' was made from a few degrees south of east.

The aircraft was caught in several search lights and was subject to intensive A.A. fire. The A.A. fire was of the red and blue tracer type accompanied by something which exploded in the form of a white star.

The fire was so intensive and colourful that with, a view to the lack of damage sustained by our Squadron aircraft the impression might be formed that a large percentage of so called A.A. fire was in reality only pyrotechnics.

The attack was made at 0340 hours but no bombs were dropped due to the catch on the 'Mickey Mouse' bomb release being in a locked position. The Aircraft proceeded to sea level after attack until clear of A.A. fire and searchlights and then climbed to 3000' for a second attack.

The second attack was made at 0243 hours in a dive from the West I.A.S. was approximately 350 mph. The attack was obviously a surprise for the enemy as very few searchlights and little A.A. fire was encountered until actually reaching the target. All bombs were dropped from 1,000', all of which fell on land, on or near the target.

The attack dive was continued to sea level and when clear of A.A. fire and searchlights a course was set for BASE. White-burning fires, apparently of incendiary origin, were distinctly visible from over 30 miles.

No fighter opposition was encountered. Searchlights were in all cases of blue-white light and of high strength.

On track to Base several D/F fixes were obtained and identification signals sent. Aircraft homed on GRANTHAM [?] and landed at Base at 0605 hours.

Signed. D. J. French Flying Officer

We were soon told that 50 Squadron was to be honoured for its part in the raid by being awarded a DFC (Distinguished Flying Cross). It was decided that this should be awarded to the most senior squadron pilot who had taken part and in this case it went to F/O. J. J. Bennett and everyone was happy for a few days. By then the navigational experts had been checking the navigation logs of the night and decided that Bennett had not been near Sylt but had bombed Esbjerg, north of Sylt, in Denmark!

Compensation was claimed by the Danish government for loss of life and damage done at the time, and was duly paid. Bennett retained his DFC, which award he truly earned many times in the operations to come. I believe he survived the war and ran a pub in Lincolnshire.

At this time other decorations were awarded on the principle that the highest award went to the most senior officer to get back to base. Even in the case of the Dortmund-Ems canal raid in August 1940, a VC went to F/O Learoyd. Later the system became more equitable and aircrews of all ranks were considered for the award of decorations on completion of an operational tour. -

Operational bombing was in its infancy at this stage of the war and with no past examples of aerial bombing to study (apart from the small example during the Spanish Civil War) we had to learn as we operated. Some of the WWI pilots with us had memories of conditions towards the end of that war and rambled on about 'archie' and 'flaming onions'... I still do not know to what they were referring.

Meanwhile, the first consignment of new magnetic mine countermeasures had been delivered back on 18 January. This consisted of copious lengths of buoyant electrical cable. It was part of a very significant order issued by the Admiralty. In operation, the cable was towed behind a wooden trawler while an electrical current was generated from the ship. The resulting magnetic field produced around the cable was enough to detonate the mines. As soon as any threatening minefields were discovered in areas around the coast, the cable-equipped trawlers went to work.

It was found that magnetic mines could be exploded from the air too. Coastal Command operated special DWI (Directional Wireless Installation) Wellingtons. These aircraft evolved out of a joint endeavour by the Admiralty and the RAE. Fitted underneath with a huge hoop containing a magnetic coil which was turned on by an auxiliary motor inside the fuselage, DWI Wellingtons carried out sweeps at heights ranging from 25 to 40 feet (7.6–12 m) above areas where mines were suspected. Anything from a slight tremor to a heavy bump with bits and pieces flying off the aircraft revealed to the crews that another mine had been detonated, adding to their score. Beginning operations in January 1940, the half a dozen or so aircraft that were engaged on this task detonated one-eighth of all the magnetic mines swept or exploded in the period from November 1939 to May 1940.

Other, more momentous events were about to take place. With the coming of spring it was obvious that the forces of the Third Reich would soon make another decisive move. None of the anticipated large-scale air raids on Britain had materialised so far, but German troops were known to have massed along the borders of France and the neutral Low Countries. However, there was another area of concern for Hitler and the Allies – Scandinavia.

Germany's war industry depended heavily on the supply of iron ore from Sweden. Much of this was transported by rail down through Norway and then across to Germany by ship. Both of these Scandinavian countries were declared neutrals and as such they conducted their normal peacetime commerce – which was now very lucrative. If this traffic of iron ore could be blocked, there would be a detrimental effect on the ability of the Third Reich to wage war.

On 5 April, the British and French governments delivered diplomatic notes informing Sweden and Norway that their interpretation of neutrality was damaging to Allied interests. Britain and France had come to an agreement that the Royal Navy should lay mines across the sea lanes between southern Norway and Germany's ports.

RAF reconnaissance aircraft kept a watchful eye on the German harbours to spot any reaction to the pressure the Allies were putting on the Scandinavian governments. Before long, high-flying PDU Spitfires brought back evidence of the presence of warships. Later identified among them in the port of Wilhelmshaven was the cruiser *Admiral Hipper* and the battlecruisers *Scharnhorst* and *Gneisenau*, together with numerous other vessels. Next evening, 6 April, Dereck in Hampden L4077 flew his fourth operation. It was a reconnaissance sweep across the North Sea. Returning from this Reco 'E' trip to the Elbe estuary they saw a fleet steaming north, with all lights on, heading for Heligoland. It fired at them. This subsequently proved to be the German fleet on its way to invade Norway. The Sylt raid, and the controversy surrounding it, was about to be overshadowed and more or less forgotten.

7

God Help 50 Squadron!

Squadron Leader Duncan Good and his crew came back – but none of the others did. His badly shot-up Hampden was the only one out of five to survive.

Preliminary studies on the possibility of invading Norway had been under way in Germany since mid-December when Admiral Erich Raeder stressed to the *Führer* the advantages of controlling the area. During the opening months of the war, Sweden and Norway supplied two-thirds of Germany's iron ore. Sweden's iron-ore deposits were located in two widely separated areas: one around Grangesberg within easy access of Stockholm, and the other around Kiruna and Gallivare in the extreme north. The export of ore from Kiruna and Gallivare was via the port of Lulea after being transported there by rail, but from mid-December to mid-May Lulea was icebound and unusable. To maintain a constant export flow, the ore was moved by the single-track railway line through the mountains to the Norwegian port of Narvik, which remained open throughout the year. From there it went by sea to various destinations, but mainly to Germany.

It was therefore vital to the Third Reich that these resources be protected. Scandinavian neutrality was not enough of a guarantee. German planning for an invasion was under the direction of General Wilhelm Keitel, Chief of the High Command of the Armed Forces. The architect of the plan was General Niklaus von Falkenhorst, who had taken part in the German campaign in Finland back in 1918. Planning proceeded with increased urgency in mid-February after the widely publicised '*Altmark* Incident'.

The *Altmark* was a German auxiliary supply ship assigned to the pocket battleship *Admiral Graf Spee*. The two vessels had met for what proved to be the last time in the South Atlantic on 7 December 1939 when *Graf Spee* offloaded prisoners from five Allied merchant ships she had sunk.

Graf Spee was hunted down by the Royal Navy less than a week later off the south-east coast of South America. Engaged by the cruisers *Exeter*, *Ajax* and *Achilles* (NZ) on 13 December, the damaged pocket battleship sought refuge in Montevideo Harbour, Uruguay. Under international law, a warship was permitted to remain in a neutral port for emergency repairs for 24 hours, but if she did not depart after that time she could be interned. Rather than that, or risk running the gauntlet of blockading British warships believed to be waiting outside in international waters, just before sunset on 17 December, the *Graf Spee* moved out of the harbour into the main channel of the River Plate Estuary and was blown up by her crew.

Altmark's task was to take the off-loaded prisoners back to Germany. On 16 February, she was sighted off the coast of Norway on her way home by Lockheed Hudsons from RAF Coastal Command. She slipped into the nearby Josenfjord at the very south of the Norwegian coast to hide. Despite this being in Scandinavian territorial waters, the RN destroyer HMS *Cossack* entered the fjord. When the ships were 8 feet (2.5 m) apart, grappling irons were thrown onto the auxiliary and a British boarding party sprang aboard. *Altmark*'s bridge was seized at pistol point and the 299 prisoners were found under battened-down hatches, locked in storerooms and even in an empty oil tank. They were released, taken aboard the destroyer and transported to the port of Leith in Scotland. *Altmark* was left to complete her voyage to Germany.

The event had international repercussions. Germany, Norway and Britain argued over the legality of the whole incident. To mount the rescue, *Cossack* had needed to violate Norwegian territorial waters, but most Britons felt that this action had been justified. Naturally, those in Germany and Norway did not think so. Norway's protests tended to fade away, however, when Britain presented proof that *Altmark* was an armed vessel which had been allowed to take refuge in Norwegian waters contrary to international law. Winston Churchill, at this time First Lord of the Admiralty, revealed that that not only did *Altmark* have the prisoners but she was also armed with two pom-poms and four machine guns. Churchill took the opportunity to restate an earlier proposal to plant mines in Norwegian waters, with the result that Britain's Cabinet authorised him to begin preliminary measures for mine-laying operations.

Honouring Scandinavian neutrality did not benefit the Allies. Because of this, from the end of November 1939, when the Russians invaded Finland, the British Government had been considering sending a force to Norway. The Finns had appealed for help, but in order to reach their country Allied intervention would have to come via Scandinavia (defined as Denmark, Sweden and Norway). Allied planners realised that

Bomber Boy: My Life as a Bomber Pilot

if a military presence could be established in Scandinavia under the guise of sending aid through to Finland, there could be a real opportunity to sever Norway's railway line or block the iron ore ports, though this could only be achieved if Norway and Sweden agreed to allow the passage of Allied troops through their territory. They refused.

For Hitler, the British navy's provocative behaviour underlined the necessity for Germany to take action as soon as possible. He had to act quickly in case Britain and France launched an invasion anyway, despite Norway's refusal. A force had in fact been assembled in Britain for this purpose, but after Finland surrendered to Russia at the beginning of March, the pretext was gone. Troops in the force were actually beginning to be dispersed. Early in April, Churchill issued the go-ahead for mines to be laid in Norway's territorial waters. When Royal Navy destroyers approached the Norwegian coast they encountered German naval vessels on the move. They were convoying troop transports and warships toward Kristiansand, Stavanger, Bergen, Trondheim and Narvik. It was one of these convoys that Dereck and his crew had spotted.

Several violent engagements took place in which the German warships successfully protected their convoys but suffered losses. When cornered, destroyer HMS *Glowworm* deliberately rammed the heavy German cruiser *Hipper*, causing severe damage, but was herself lost. In a running battle between battlecruisers, HMS *Renown* badly damaged the *Gneisenau*. Two other German warships were sunk, and the pocket battleship *Lützow* was damaged near Oslo. Despite these clashes, all the German convoys reached their objectives.

'D-Day', 9 April 1940. German troops dashed across the border into Denmark. At the same time, a battalion of infantry hidden on a merchant ship moored in Copenhagen Harbour was landed ashore to seize the king and government. Denmark fell quickly, almost without bloodshed. That same day, the Germans made simultaneous landings along the coast of Norway while parachute assaults at Oslo and Stavanger tried to seize the king and government by surprise, as in Denmark. This would have paralysed the nation but the Norwegian armed forces, which were about 12,000 strong, were more substantial and better prepared than the Danes, and had the brief warning provided by distance and size. In Britain, it was almost impossible to find out what was going on.

On the morning of 9/4/40 a detachment of Hampdens of 44 Squadron at Waddington were briefed and sent off in daylight to find and attack German Naval Forces invading Norway. These aircraft were soon recalled when doubts were raised in Parliament or at the War Council of the possible consequences should any damage be done on the Norwegian mainland.

Later that day after further discussion of the situation, No. 50 Squadron was detailed, with little or no briefing, to carry out the same mission. I personally was not briefed in any way for the raid and did not even know what our target was until it was located by our flight leader. It proved to be a cruiser and two destroyers in a fjord south-west of Bergen.

The flight broke formation and climbed from 4,000 feet to 10,000 feet (1,200–3,000 m) to carry out individual attacks. We dropped a stick of four 500-lb (227-kg) SAP (Semi Armour Piercing) bombs, one of which was seen to hit the cruiser. This type of bomb was really only suitable for use against this type of target when dropped from this height or higher. During the bombing run we ran the gauntlet of AA from the ships but were not hit. We had lost sight of the other Hampdens by then and headed back for the UK, landing at Leuchars in Scotland.

PERSONAL EXPERIENCE REPORT
RAID ON GERMAN FLEET OFF BERGEN ON 9/4/40.

AIRCRAFT HAMPDEN L.4077.
Crew F/O FRENCH, Capt.
P/O MULLOY, Navigator,
Sgt HORSFALL. Observer.
qCpl BARRASS, W/Op.
Bombs 4 x 500-lb SAP ON STICK RELEASE.

Aircraft took off in formation and set course for BERGEN at 1605 hrs.
At 1930 hrs formation altered course to 090° M and made landfall approximately 50 miles SOUTH of BERGEN at 1945 hrs.
Formation followed the coast North at 4,000 feet and located the target (1 Cruiser 'K' Class at anchor, and 2 Destroyers) in a FJORD SOUTH WEST of BERGEN at 2010 hrs.
Heavy anti-aircraft fire of pom-pom, red-tracer, and white star-shell types was encountered from the target. Avoiding action was taken by the formation, which climbed to 10,000 feet, and broke up.
At 3020 hrs aircraft L.4077 approached the target from the South. The Cruiser was then under way moving south, and opened fire with A.A. The run was continued over the target, and all bombs were dropped at 2021 hrs.
The third bomb was seen to land 50 yards in front of the Cruiser, the fourth bomb was a direct hit.
After turning away, thick black smoke was seen to issue from the Cruiser, and continued until the cruiser was out of vision.[1]
Course was set for PETERHEAD at 2022 hrs.
D/R position at 2121 hrs was 58°42' North 01°10' East.

Aircraft requested D/F aid from LEUCHARS at 2210 hrs, when approximately 30 miles South of PETERHEAD by D/R.

During the following 30 minutes, Q.D.M's of approximately 124° M. were obtained. These Q.D.M's appeared to take the aircraft out to sea, and a check was requested from LEUCHARS. New Q.D.M's were given of approximately 310° M. These seemed correct and homed aircraft, which sighted LEUCHARS at 0030 hrs.

Aircraft landed at 0040 hrs.

Signed D. J. French P/O

Next day we returned to Waddington where we were told that 'Slug' Mulloy and I were each to receive a DFC for our efforts. This came as a surprise to us as we felt that we had done little to earn the awards. Congratulations came in from around the world! This was mainly because these DFCs were said to be the first such awards to South Africans and Australians in WW2.

What really interested us was the talk we heard from WWI chaps of 'prize money' for such jobs. In earlier wars when enemy vessels were either captured or sunk the successful crew shared an award of prize money. After hearing this talk we thought that we too should collect and started to spend and have a series of parties. It was then that we found that the practice of awarding prize money had been stopped and we were left with large mess bills.

The station commander at Waddington at the time was a WWI pilot, Group Captain Anderson, a strange character who was rumoured to be a genius who periodically spent his time in psychiatric hospitals. He was credited with having originated the RAFVR (Volunteer Reserve) scheme which gave the RAF a supply of trained aircrew personnel who could be called upon as required.

Anderson was a personal friend of Winston Churchill (Minister of the Navy at that time) and had him to lunch with us in the mess a few days after the Bergen show. In preparation for the visit special champagne and large cigars were on hand for the great visitor, who did not touch the champagne and smoked his own cigars. We had to foot the bill for this preparation, and in the months to come had mess bills larger than usual.

Mulloy and I were the 'flavour of the month' after the Bergen show so G/C Anderson had us sit with Churchill for the luncheon party. He told us that he had hidden away on Mulloy's family farm in South Africa during the Boer War when he had escaped from Boers. We doubted the truth of the yarn. The only thing I learned from the lunch was that Churchill, sensibly, ate his peas from the flat of his fork and not in the polite way, from the back.

Anderson had strange ways. At an operational briefing one day he offered to any of the aircrew present a fountain pen with which Winston Churchill had just written a very important speech. No one seemed to want it. Earlier that year one evening, while I was sitting in the mess lounge filling in time before I became due to take off on operations, he came up and sat beside me and proceeded to cheer me up by telling me, 'You will soon get used to this killing business.' Of course, he was correct, but that was hardly the time and place to say so.

General policy regarding air crew formation and changes was that after a 2nd pilot/navigator/bomb aimer had completed a few successful raids in that role he was given a crew of his own and flew as aircraft captain. Bill Mulloy had been agitating for a captaincy for some time without success; one night, however, to prove his point he left the trap door in the nose of the aircraft open as we roared down the runway on our take-off. His flight plans and maps for the trip were sucked out and littered the aerodrome and by the time we had gathered them together it was too late in the night to take part in the raid.

He proved his point and became a captain, but not for long. As he was coming home one night from a mission with only one engine still in action he tried to land on what he thought to be a sandy beach near Newcastle. It turned out to be a reef of rocks so that Bill and all his crew were killed. We buried him with service honours at Doncaster Cemetery. I was detailed to look after Bill's sister, Margot, at the funeral; a lousy duty which I dreaded, yet which turned out to be not too bad because of Margot's realism. She was a fantastic girl, older than Bill. She drove an ambulance during the London Blitz and later became a quality inspector in an aircraft factory. Later she married a member of the RAF ground staff. He re-mustered, becoming aircrew, and he, too, was soon killed on operations. At the end of the war she went to live in the Channel Islands where she adopted a little girl, Jocelyn Felicity. J. F. grew up, married, had children and then developed multiple sclerosis, and so the sad saga continued. Margot died in the 1980s.

I remember staying with Margot at her flat in London one night of the Blitz when there was a heavy raid in progress. The flat was on the top floor of a terrace from where we watched and listened to the din of the AA guns and the rattle of shell fragments raining down on the roof while drinking a bottle of Scotch to cheer us up. She remained quite unperturbed through it all. At Bill's death she gave me his No. 1 RAF uniform (a perfect fit) and a set of silver hair brushes she had just had engraved for him for his twenty-first birthday present. I finally passed these on to her niece Jenny Field of Canberra in the 1980s.

Our wireless operator, the quiet Englishman Sgt Alan Horsfall, was with us for most of the trips of early 1940. His work could not be faulted, and continued until 9 June 1940 when I was wounded and hospitalised. He was then transferred to another crew but was soon killed. His father came to see me after his loss and wept as he thanked me for looking after his son, who he said had told his parents that if he could remain in my crew he would survive the war. I found this type of incident hard to take.

It was repeated soon after when I received a visit from the father of our rear gunner LAC, later Corporal, Barrass. Alexander Barrass had flown with me for years. He was our gunner when we took the Blenheim to Egypt and had taken part in all of our early missions. He died with so many others of 50 Squadron off Norway on 12 April. These visits from bereaved parents were ones I would have preferred not to experience.

At the outbreak of war, aircraft captains, pilots and navigators were usually officers or senior NCOs, while the wireless operators and air gunners held the ranks of LAC (leading aircraftsman) or corporal. These LACs and corporals did general maintenance work in the squadron, flying only when called upon to complete an aircrew. For this duty they received a few extra pence flying pay. As the war progressed and our casualties grew, it was deemed proper that all flying personnel be mustered purely as aircrew and be the rank of sergeant or higher. This made things easier for the crews and also for the next of kin of those who were either killed or became prisoners of war. Corporal Barrass did not last long enough to benefit by this change of rank/mustering policy.

We had many losses and deaths of air crew, most of whom simply went out on raids and failed to return. Apart from these we had losses from crashes on take-off or crash landing after returning from raids, as in Bill Mulloy's case. General policy in the UK at that time regarding funerals was that squadron aircrew personnel did not take part in the ceremony, except perhaps to have a squadron representative attend, as I did in the case of Bill Mulloy. Seemingly the RAF had available a unit employed in nothing but performing service funerals as required – really, a good idea.

Friday, 12 April, was the first of 50 Squadron's disastrous days. What happened prompted Dereck to lament in his log book: 'God help 50 Squadron.' Twelve Hampden crews, five from 50 Squadron and seven from 44 Squadron, were ordered to attack German shipping off Kristiansand, in particular a battlecruiser and a cruiser expected to be in the area by 1100 hours. It was a daylight operation with all of its inherent dangers.

They took off from Waddington at 0820 hours, each aircraft carrying four 500-lb (227-kg) SAP bombs. S/Ldr J. J. Watts of 44 Squadron was leading and in overall command. S/Ldr Duncan Good headed the contingent from 50 Squadron, which fortunately for Dereck did not include him. Those other Australians on the mission were Mervyn Thomas and P/O Johnny Bull. Merv Thomas had been at University High

School with Dereck years earlier in Melbourne and later joined him in 50 Squadron. Johnny Bull was from Adelaide. He had been nicknamed 'Ferdinand the Bull' after a well-known cartoon character, a huge creature bred for bullfighting. Though fearsome in appearance, Ferdinand's nature was so gentle that all he wanted to do was live peacefully and smell the flowers in the fields.

Heading towards Norway, the bombers encountered heavy rain and 10/10ths low cloud, which forced the formation to fly at sea level. As they approached the Norwegian coast at 1130 hours, the weather suddenly changed. There was clear sky with no low cloud and visibility ranging out to about 50 miles (80 km). Shipping in Kristiansand Bay could be seen 12 miles (19 km) ahead. Over the R/T, S/Ldr Watts ordered the formation to gain height for a high-level bombing attack from 9,000 feet (2,700 m) flying in sections of three in line astern.

With 44 Squadron leading, each section followed the one in front towards the target on the same heading and at the same height. During the run-in, AA guns ashore and on the ships began firing. Watts' section of three Hampdens bombed through the flak and immediately afterwards enemy fighters arrived on the scene. Watts dived to sea level ready to race for home accompanied by his two 44 Squadron wingmen.

As successive sections made their bombing runs, always flying in from the same direction and at the same height, the flak gunners soon found the range and became increasingly accurate. One Hampden in the second section of three, also a 44 Squadron aircraft, was hit and fell behind the others. The fighters pounced and sent it crashing down into the sea in flames. The upper gunner was seen to be still firing his guns as the blazing machine hit the water.

A second Hampden was badly damaged by the attacking Me109s.[2] One cannon shell blew a large hole in the starboard wing and another exploded in the oil tank of the port engine. Machine gun bullets punched holes in the wings and fuselage, as well as causing damage to the Perspex nose. Nevertheless, the 109s did not have things all their own way. The wireless operator/upper gunner shot down one of the attacking fighters but the Hampden's port engine began to overheat as the pilot nursed the bomber back across the North Sea.

All the aircraft in the third section led by Duncan Good came through the flak without any obvious damage, but as they dived towards the sea the fighters rushed in. One Messerschmitt made the mistake of flying right over the top of Good's plane. Its sky blue belly presented a perfect target for Good's wireless operator/upper gunner, Cpl Wallace, who promptly shot it down, amid great excitement. On reaching sea level they raced to join up and close ranks with the leading section, but Good's No. 2

Hampden was hit and set on fire. Flames gushed from the upper and lower gun positions and over the fuselage as the stricken bomber fell behind and then plunged into the water.

Some of the fighters made their attacks by flying parallel to the bombers until slightly ahead and then turning in to fire. None of the Hampdens' guns could be brought to bear as they made these beam attacks. The lower gunners could not fire anyway because the bombers were flying so low. Hampden L4064, the No. 3 aircraft of Duncan Good's section and piloted by Johnny Bull, took hits and was damaged. For the moment Ferdinand the Bull was keeping up with Good's machine but his petrol tanks had been holed and he was losing fuel at an alarming rate. His chances of reaching home were slim, but he was determined.

None of the aircraft of the fourth section came through unscathed. Flak hit one and it was seen plummeting down in a vertical dive. Another fell victim to the fighters as it tried to catch up with the main formation. Which of these aircraft was Hampden L4081, the machine piloted by Merv Thomas, remains uncertain. No crewmembers of either plane survived. Alex Barrass, Dereck's usual gunner, was flying with Thomas and his crew.

Meanwhile, the last Hampden in this section was unable to close the gap between it and the main group despite the pilot pushing his throttles to full emergency power. Inevitably, it attracted the concentrated attention of the 109s. Their attacks transformed the Hampden into a blazing wreck but the pilot managed to make a crash-landing on a small island off Tregve on the Norwegian coast.

The chase out over the water continued and it seemed that it would only be a matter of time before all of the Hampdens were caught and shot down. Then abruptly, and mercifully, after twenty-five minutes, it was all over. At 60 miles (95 km) out the fighters were running short of fuel and ammunition and had to abandon their pursuit. Seven Hampdens were still in the air. One of them, the machine with the overheating port engine, altered course to head for Scotland to land at Acklington, which was closer. That left six, but two more fell behind, leaving only four Hampdens flying together towards Waddington. The two lagging bombers were those of Duncan Good and Johnny Bull. Dereck later recorded what happened.

A combined formation of Hampdens from 44 and 50 Squadrons had taken off in daylight to carry out a sweep of the Skagerrak between Norway and Denmark in search of enemy shipping. They had orders to remain close to cloud cover in case they were located by enemy fighters. They failed to obey this order and when they were attacked Me109s could do nothing but try to fight them off. We had always been assured by our armament experts, who were supposed to know, that the Me109 could not and would not attack from the beam; against which form of attack we had no defence.

All the attacks were made from the beam and six of the twelve Hampdens went into the sea. Lacking self-sealing fuel tanks some pilots with holed tanks tried to make a landing in England before their petrol ran out. One such, P/O Johnny Bull of Adelaide, got to within about 100 miles (160 km) due east of Newcastle before he was forced to ditch. Some of the surviving aircrews watched him ditch successfully and take to their dinghy; these survivors then pinpointed the position and returned to Waddington.

In those days the RAF had no such thing as Air Sea Rescue units. Coastal Command could not, or would not, help out with a flying boat so the Royal Navy sent a vessel to rescue the crew, without success. We heard that this attempt came to naught when the skipper of the boat lost his nerve and returned to port when he found himself in the middle of a minefield. We later heard that he was court martialled. Our Hampdens from Waddington went out each day, sometimes finding the dinghy and crew, sometimes not...

On this sad operation the flight of 50 Squadron Hampdens had been led by Squadron Leader D. C. F. Good DFC of Adelaide, ex-Point Cook 1936. Good was a remarkably able, unassuming, likeable and efficient flight commander who would have certainly made history had he survived. On this operation during the attack by the Me109s the wireless Morse key had been shot to pieces so his wireless operator, Sgt Bates, sent the necessary identification signals by tapping a bare wire on the fuselage in Morse – or so the story goes.

Duncan Good and his crew were lucky. They came back – but none of the others from 50 Squadron did. Good's Hampden had been severely damaged. An inspection after landing showed that something almost unbelievable had happened. The fuel tank had been pierced and the petrol had ignited. The tank itself was badly blistered and there was an area of the wing some 5 feet (1.5 m) long by 4 feet (1.2 m) wide that was scorched and burnt. Somehow, the blaze had put itself out: the first instance they knew of a fuel tank catching fire and going out again. It was a good argument for the installation of self-sealing fuel tanks!

This day, 12 April 1940, marked the end of the RAF's pre-war daylight bombing strategy. The theory that bomber formations could successfully defend themselves from attacking fighters clearly no longer applied. The RAF could not afford such heavy losses any longer. Except for a very few special occasions, Hampdens and Wellingtons from now on would operate only at night, and night bombing would remain the strategy for the British 'heavy' bomber force for the next four years. It was a significant turning-point in Bomber Command's war.

Attempts to find and rescue Johnny Bull and his crew began immediately but in these early months of the war the RAF had no properly organised air-sea service. Dereck and others in 50 Squadron went out searching until they were obliged to return because of fading light or poor weather. They could not find them. The dinghy was a very small object on a wide, wide sea. Dereck landed back at Waddington after six frustrating, fruitless hours.

Next day, the search was taken up by Lockheed Hudsons from Coastal Command as well as Hampdens and Avro Ansons from Nos 44 and 50 Squadrons. The Ansons were normally used for general non-operational flying. They were slow and did not have the range or endurance of Hampdens or Hudsons. Dick Taylor used 50 Squadron's Anson, N9829, and was out for 4 hours 40 minutes without success. He could only note in his log book: 'Search for Ferdinand the Bull' without a result. Bob Wawn took out Anson N5193, but he misjudged the amount of time he spent searching. After being in the air for over five hours, he ran short of fuel and had to crash-land near Grimsby. The Anson was a write-off and all on board suffered injuries.

It was a Hudson from 220 Squadron that found Ferdinand the Bull and his crew. It stayed over the dinghy all morning, circling helplessly until midday came and went. Then reluctantly, with its own fuel situation becoming critical, it had to depart leaving the men in the dinghy to the mercy of the weather and the sea. Johnny Bull and his crew were never seen alive again.

The dinghy was located once more a few days later. It was still floating 100 miles (160 km) east of Flamborough Head, but it was empty. The body of the observer/lower gunner, Sgt William Nevinson, was discovered afterwards. He was buried in Kiel War Cemetery, but his three companions were never found. Their names are recorded on the magnificent memorial at Runnymede.

Hatred for the 'powers that be' who had permitted this to happen was at a high level at Waddington and continued until further operations and further losses dimmed the memory. The losses on 12 April 1940 provided one small crumb of comfort, in that they engendered the development of an air-sea rescue aid which could be dropped to ditched aircrew and the creation of an efficient Air Sea Rescue Service.

The device we developed was known as the 'Lindholme Dinghy', Lindholme being the aerodrome from which 50 Squadron was operating when it was first used. It consisted of about six heavy paperboard cylinders (which had originally contained bombs or bomb-fins for delivery) fastened at long intervals along a long rope, each cylinder being slung like a bomb in the bomb bay. They were dropped in the same way as a stick of bombs, being dropped at low level upwind of the ditched crew and would float down towards them. Each container carried emergency gear, food, clothing and even a spare dinghy. It worked…

It did not take long for 'further losses' to occur.

The Hampden was at that time the only RAF bomber with a bomb-bay suitable for easy alteration to carry sea mines and so No. 5 Group became the pioneers of mine-laying in Bomber Command. These operations began on 13 April 1940; they carried the code name 'Gardening' with different areas being known by their relevant code. The Elbe area was coded 'Eglantine' while Oslo was known as 'Onion'. The mines used were like a large cylindrical can about 10 feet (4 m) long and about 18 inches (46 cm) in diameter, with a parachute fitted into one end and an anchor into the other. They weighed approximately 1,500 lbs (680 kg). Mine-laying involved very accurate flying which was emphasised by the naval officers who briefed us before each trip. They explained the tides, the currents and the exact position of the drop. They also attended to the fusing and defusing of the mines; these could be set to explode when any number of vessels – up to six – had passed overhead. This made the task of sweeping them very difficult.

We usually flew to the dropping area then descended to 500 feet (150 m), the precise height required for the job, reduced speed to 150 mph (240 km/hr), the speed required, and then having pinpointed our position by making use of a prevalent landmark such as a cape or the bend of a river, flew to the target area and dropped the mine. Correct positioning was essential. When dropped the mine sank to the bottom where after a while the salt water dissolved a capsule which held the mine body to the anchor. The mine body then floated to the limit of a cable from the anchor and remained swaying in the current until a victim arrived. If dropped in too great a depth of water the mine would be ineffective. In those days mine laying was an exacting task, especially when the Germans sited AA guns and flak-ships in our popular target areas. I understand that when our four-engine bombers came into service they carried up to four mines and dropped them from about 3,000 feet (900 m) – much safer.

The Germans reacted quickly to meet the threat of RAF aircraft laying mines. As they conquered more and more territory, they set up AA batteries on the shores of estuaries, along the sides of the Norwegian fjords and on numerous islands in the Baltic seaways. Patrol boats in more open waters stood by to alert the defences by reporting approaching aircraft, and larger fishing trawlers began to be outfitted as mobile flak ships.

On the night of 13/14 April, fifteen Hampdens took off from Waddington to carry out the RAF's first mine-laying operation of the war. Fourteen aircraft are known to have laid mines in the sea lanes off Denmark between the German ports and Norway. One bomber was lost, Hampden L4065 from 50 Squadron. Its pilot was F/Lt Bob Cosgrove. Apparently he and his crew also completed their mission. The aircraft was detected by RDF (radar) approaching Mablethorpe as it returned but then it disappeared without trace, never to reach the coast.

Squadron Leader Bob Cosgrove was the Flight Commander of A Flight of 50 Squadron. He had trained at Point Cook with S/Ldr Good before transferring to the RAF. His father was the Premier (Labor) of Tasmania, Sir Robert Cosgrove. When I returned to Australia in 1944, I received a letter from him, via his secretary, asking what I knew about the death of his son. I felt that I could hardly tell him the truth – that he should shoulder part of the blame for the loss of his son himself – for Labor policy at the time put defence spending at the bottom of the list of government expenditure, with the result that when we started to fight the war, we were poorly trained and poorly armed. I answered his secretary's letter politically – saying nothing...

Mine dropping properly done was an exacting task. Our mine drop in the Elbe on 21 April 1940 was an interesting one, for when we came to 'plant' it we found we had to do so between two ships at anchor! I sometimes wonder which ship moved first and what happened.

The effectiveness of air mine laying cannot be disputed. After the war when records were checked, it was found that of the 1,120 enemy vessels sunk worldwide by mines, 940 of these had been laid from the air.[3]

Dereck's diary entry for 4 May 1940 reads: 'Gardening "O". S/Ldr Good gets shot up. Kinloss.' His log book shows that he was flying Hampden P1231 with F/O Lowe, Sgt Horsfall and Cpl Ashmore. 'Gardening "O" – Mining Oslo Fjord. 6 hours 20 minutes.'

This was a very interesting trip; about five Hampdens were detailed to plant mines in the fiord that leads to Oslo. This involved flying at 500 feet (150 m), at night, up the fjord towards the town, having high country on each side and a large mountain ahead, beyond the city. We knew about these hazards but did not know the extent of the defences along the fjord.

Squadron Leader Good went in ahead of me to plant his mine and I was able to watch his progress up the fjord as he became coned by tracer fire, AA and searchlights from both sides. I followed him and we too were soon caught by the searchlights and AA. The searchlights were blinding to the extent that I became completely disorientated and unable to see my instrument panel and the aircraft became inverted. How we got back to a normal flying position I shall never know, but we did and continued our run-in to drop the mine and then get the hell out of the place as fast as we could. When we landed at Kinloss in Scotland it was proved that we had certainly been upside down on our dropping run. Some of the inspection plates from the floor of the plane had come adrift, hit the roof and had finally come to rest jammed behind our throttles.

At Kinloss we found S/Ldr Good and his crew. When we had seen him last he had been held by searchlights when he was struck by several 40 mm cannon shells, one of which exploded across the cockpit. Good was shot through both arms and his face, some of his teeth being knocked out. His 2nd pilot/navigator/bomb-aimer P/O Gardner saw blood trickling down the control column and realised Good had been hit. He crawled up behind the pilot's seat, pulled Good out of the cockpit and took over, flying to Kinloss where we met up with them. The whole incident was remarkable, considering it happened at night, at less than 500 feet, in the confined limits of the fjord and in a Hampden where there was little space to move about. An amazing feat. Both S/Ldr Good and P/O Gardiner were awarded DFCs – awards too low for the deeds performed…

It *had* to be done if the pilot was dead or disabled. Duncan Good had made sure his crew had practised the routine in case something like that happened. It was vital that they knew exactly what to do. All of their lives depended upon it.

The fuselage of the Handley Page Hampden was very narrow, only 3 feet (0.9 m) wide. There was little space to move about. It was almost impossible for crewmen to pass each other inside the plane, so what would happen if the pilot was hit and he could no longer work the controls? Someone else would need to take over. That man would have to be the navigator, who was usually a newly trained pilot gaining operational experience before being given captaincy of his own aircraft and crew. In Duncan Good's crew that night it was P/O Walter George Gardiner; but how was it done?

Gardiner had to crawl back from his front position, through the space under the pilot and stand up behind the pilot's seat. He then had to unbuckle the pilot's parachute harness and undo the straps holding him in the seat. This enabled the back of the seat to be pulled down but it could not be done if the pilot was strapped in with his feet in the pedals. When down, the back of the pilot's seat rested on the padded top of the main spar. Gardiner then wriggled over the inert man to grasp the controls while the wireless operator, with the aid of the rear-gunner, slid the disabled pilot beneath him back out of the seat. This done, the back of the pilot's seat had to be raised again with the navigator now in position to fly the plane. That was the drill, but even in practice on the ground the task was not easy. Needing to do it in the air while under fire would be something else again.

But pause for a moment to consider the drama of Dereck's own predicament, which he himself understated, and which was overshadowed by what happened to Duncan Good. Dereck and his crew, three men whose lives depended on him, found themselves upside-down in the dark, just 500 feet (150 m) above the water, hurtling along at about 150 mph (240 km/hr) within the narrow confines of the walls of a winding fjord in a large twin-engined aircraft weighing around 8¼ tons (about 8,400 kg) while carrying a large mine weighing nearly another ¾ ton (680 kg) in its belly, with dazzling searchlights probing after them and anti-aircraft guns blazing at them! He had already seen his leader 'coned by tracer fire, AA and searchlights from both sides' just before becoming completely disorientated and unable to see his own instrument panel directly in front of him.

What were their odds of survival in such circumstances? Dereck was an experienced flier by now, with over 600 flying hours in his log book, but by 4 May 1940 less than 38½ of these hours had been spent piloting multi-engined aircraft in the dark. What if he, like Duncan Good, had been hit? What if one of the bomber's wings had touched the water, or it had lost direction within the confines of the fiord as Dereck was rolling it back upright?

Despite the odds, Dereck did manage to control the plane. He levelled out and flew on to complete the mission. At the very least, it was an outstanding example of exceptionally good luck, remarkable courage, and astonishingly good flying.

S/Ldr Good had trained at Point Cook with S/Ldr Cosgrove in 1936. He was a born leader who would have achieved great things had he survived a bit longer. After the Oslo raid he was sent to the RAF Officers' convalescent hospital at Torquay, where he was patched up and acquired a new set of false teeth and a wife. He was keen to resume operations and was back with us sooner than he should have been, flying with his wrists still in plaster.

Good, when mine laying, made a practice of descending to sea level at the target area to reset his altimeter to ensure a more accurate planting of the mine, which had to be dropped at exactly 500 feet (150 m). He did this once too often and apparently went into the sea off Lorient, France, on 28 April 1941, his body being washed up later.

Duncan Good was flying Hampden AD728 on a mission to lay mines off La Rochelle on 28/29 April 1941, the night he was killed. The bodies of his crewmen were recovered and buried at various places along the French coast, but the Australian's body was never found. S/Ldr Duncan Charles Frederick Good DFC has his name recorded on the Runnymede memorial in Britain, as do F/Lt Robert James Cosgrove, P/O John Bartlett Bull, P/O Mervyn Thomas and Cpl Alexander Scougal Gibson Barrass. Sgt Alan Albert Horsfall, who was killed on 30 August 1940, is buried in Groesbeck Cemetery at Nijmegen in the Netherlands.

While visiting the Australian War Memorial in Canberra about fifteen years after the war ended, I was amazed to find no record of S/Ldr Good and hundreds of other Australians who had died flying with the RAF. The War Memorial Authorities at the time maintained that the Honour Roll was only for chaps with Australian service numbers. I believed that a few years after this policy was changed and some RAF Australian casualties were recorded.

As can be imagined, these circumstances generated a great deal of bitterness among the Australian RAF veterans and their families, especially by those whose pathway into the RAF had been via the RAAF in the first place. Happily, after many years, the policy did change. More on this later.

8

Target Eindhoven

I went to be invested by the king with the DFC. I was hardly lonely as Bill Mulloy and Mike Homer from Waddington were there for the same purpose. We lined up in order of the seniority of the award to be received and when instructed walked up to the king and queen, from whom we received a few words, the 'gong' and a handshake, about turn and away. All so simple.

The first chap to be decorated on this occasion was Wing Commander Basil Embry, who received a Bar to his DSO. He looked after us at the palace and later took us for drinks at the Air Force Club. He was a fabulous leader, became quite famous, being knighted and rising to the rank of air marshal. After leaving the RAF, he farmed in western Australia.

While standing before the king I noticed him to be heavily made up with a pinkish-tan shade of face cream. It may have been for photographic purposes. Who knows?

After the show, Bill Mulloy, Mike Homer and I were photographed as a group. The picture appeared in a few magazines and papers where it caught the eye of an old air vice marshal who wrote letters to the Air Ministry and to our station commander protesting about the angle at which we wore our service caps. A file was started on the subject and grew in size until both Bill Mulloy and Mike Homer had been killed, when it too died.

Mike Homer, a good type of Englishman, completed a tour of operation (30–35 trips) with us on Hampdens and then, by way of a rest, joined Fighter Command but did not last long, being killed during the Battle of Britain. He was the brother of the RAF Air Liaison Officer with the French Air Force at Marseille who had helped us on our way when we were ferrying to the East.

Michael Homer, who was from Dorset, was with 44 Squadron, 50 Squadron's sister unit at Waddington, and was one of those involved in the vicious air battle on 12 April when Merv Thomas and Johnny Bull and their crews failed to return. He survived the anti-aircraft fire and attacks by Me109s, one of which his air gunner shot down, and brought his damaged Hampden safely back to base. It was for this operation that he was awarded the DFC. In August, he volunteered for Fighter Command and joined No. 1 Squadron at Northolt early in September. On the 7th, he damaged a Dornier Do17. A posting to 242 Squadron, Douglas Bader's Hurricane unit, at Coltishall followed on 21 September, but he was shot down and killed just six days later.

The arrival of the warmer weather meant the Germans were likely to very soon launch their long-anticipated invasion of France. They had taken Denmark already and fighting was continuing in Norway with increasing intensity. That might keep them busy for a while but it was only a matter of time. In Norway, with all their initial objectives taken, German troops had spread out over the countryside while a concentrated airlift brought in a flow of reinforcements from Germany. At the same time, *Luftwaffe* units that had relocated to Norway's airfields attacked British warships off the coast. For three weeks the Norwegians tried to hold on to south-central Norway, but the Germans overwhelmed them or drove them northwards. A small 'fifth column' led by Norwegian traitor Vidkun Quisling gave the invaders support.

Even before the war, Quisling had approached Hitler with a proposal for a *coup d'état* in Norway. After the invasion, Quisling set himself up to rule conquered Norway but his regime only lasted a week because few Norwegians would work with him. He remained head of the *Samling*, the only political party permitted, but the Germans ignored him and from September 1940 to February 1942 deprived him of all powers. The Germans restored him nominally to office as 'minister president', but he had no authority. Taken prisoner after the war, he was tried for treason and executed on 24 November 1945. His name did give a new word to the English language: a 'quisling' is a traitor serving a foreign occupying power in his own country.

The roughly 10,000 French and British troops who had already been assembled in British ports for a possible attempt to aid Finland were hastily embarked and made landings at Namsos and Andalsnes. Their task was to try and take Trondheim and retain some sort of foothold in the country. Another smaller force landed near Narvik. The Germans at Trondheim held the Allies off while reinforcements were rushed from Oslo.

Fighting so far away from home, the British and French were at a huge disadvantage. In continuous violent attacks, the *Luftwaffe* assailed the Allied troops, landing areas and support ships. Unable to fight effectively and without proper fighter air cover, at the beginning of May the Allies had to evacuate Namsos and Andalsnes. In the meantime, Norway's King Haakon VII and the Norwegian government were obliged to relocate to northern Norway.

At this stage, the spotlight shifted away from the Scandinavian countries. By midnight on 9/10 May, Germany had assembled some two and a half million men along its western borders with France, Luxembourg, Belgium and the Netherlands. There were 104 infantry divisions, nine motorised divisions and ten armoured divisions organised into three army groups. On the northern flank from the North Sea to Aachen was German Army Group B, comprising two armies. In the centre was the main force, Army Group A under General Gerd von Rundstedt, which consisted of four armies and a strong armoured (Panzer) group, concentrated in a relatively narrow zone between Aachen and Sarrebourg. Most of the *Reich*'s 2,574 tanks were in this command. Army Group C consisted of two armies facing the French defences in eastern Lorraine and along the Rhine.

The storm broke in the early hours of 10 May. Following predawn bombardments of all major Dutch and Belgian airfields, German Army Groups A and B crossed the Belgian and Dutch frontiers. As planned, the main initial effort was on the right in the Netherlands by Army Group B. Drops of parachute troops in the vicinity of Rotterdam, The Hague, Moerdijk and Dortrecht quickly paralysed the interior of the Netherlands.

Glider and parachute units landed on the top of the powerful Fort Eban Emael, northern anchor of the main Belgian defence line, and neutralised it at the same time as other German troops crossed the Albert Canal. The violence and success of these initial German attacks, combined with the bombing of the interior of both countries, threw the general populace into panic and confusion.

To French Army GHQ, the main German attack appeared to be in the direction of Maastricht, Tongres and Gembloux, but some reports of German army movements in the Ardennes were received during the early hours of the morning. Amid the confusion, little attention was paid to this new intelligence. The Allies anticipated a German offensive would be mounted through Belgium as in 1914 and had prepared plans to move French army units and most of the British Expeditionary Force (BEF) into Belgium to meet this threat – without Belgian permission. Because of the declared neutrality of Belgium and Holland, there had been no co-operation of any kind with the Allies from either country. The result of this was that no co-ordinated defence plan existed. A chain is only as strong as its weakest link, but in 1940 the truth was that there was not even a chain along the German frontier – only a series of links that were not even connected!

At 0800 hours, in the Ardennes, Panzer units of Army Group A moved forward as French troops and the BEF moved across the frontier into Belgium to take up positions along the River Dyle. French reservists were left to hold the Ardennes frontier. But Army Group A's initial thrust was a feint. With the Allies committed to moving into Belgium, it changed direction and pushed south through the Ardennes to outflank the overrated Maginot Line. The trap was sprung. *Blitzkreig*, violent mobile warfare, was unleashed.

Holland fell within days and the Belgian army, BEF and French troops in Belgium were steadily pressed back. A brilliantly executed German breakthrough resulted in an armoured drive that reached the French coast of the English Channel towards the end of May. The combined Allied armies were split in two and those trapped north of the breakthrough were eventually encircled with their backs to the sea at Dunkirk.

Under the code name of *Operation Dynamo*, and the command of Vice-Admiral Bertram Ramsay, the Royal Navy and a host of private boats manned by civilian volunteers began to evacuate those who were trapped on the beaches. When the Belgian surrender became effective from 11.00 a.m. on the 28th, British and French troops just managed to block the gap they left in the defence perimeter in time to prevent the Germans reaching the beaches. Meanwhile, Herman Göring boastfully declared that his *Luftwaffe* would destroy the trapped troops before they could be evacuated.

Before 10 May, RAF Bomber Command had not carried out bombing of any kind on the German homeland to hinder the Reich's build-up of forces. It just continued dropping propaganda leaflets over the Third Reich right up to the end, despite all the daily reconnaissance flights and the telltale warning signs of the preparations for invasion. Afterwards, the entire RAF bomber effort focused on this new, closer and much more threatening land battle rather than on the campaign still being waged in Norway.

Blenheims of Bomber Command's No. 2 Group operating by day from their airfields in England sometimes suffered heavy casualties, as did the Fairey Battle squadrons of the AASF. Meanwhile, the longer-ranging Hampdens, Wellingtons and Whitleys, which were at last released for the actual bombing of enemy land targets, operated by night. In the darkness they faced the seemingly almost insoluble problems associated with achieving accurate navigation, target-finding and bomb-aiming.

We continued mine-laying with our Hampdens, sometimes going far into the Baltic, but when the invasion came we mainly kept battering away at Hamburg, Frankfurt and the Ruhr. We carried about 2,500 lbs (1,130 kg) of bombs which we dropped from 8,000 to 10,000 feet (2,500–3,000 m), showing that we had quickly learned to respect the German defences. Later in the war many Lancaster crews did a tour of operations without ever bombing from lower than 20,000 feet (6,000 m). We could not fly a loaded Hampden above 15,500 feet (4,700 m).

Dereck noted in his diary for 30 May 1940, '9 trips this month.' He commented later: 'This speaks for itself – we were very busy.' Busy he was, and intense it was, as his log book clearly shows. In one month, he more than doubled the number of combat operations he had flown since hostilities had begun. It also shows the nature of the rapidly and dramatically changing war.

On the 1st, he was 'gardening' – mining – in the Elbe area in Hampden P1237 (his 9th mission of the war);

On the 4th, mining in Oslo Fjord in Hampden P1237 (this was the operation in which Duncan Good was wounded);

On the 9th, mining near Lubeck in Hampden P1327;

On the 14th, mining Langlande (Kiel Canal) in Hampden P1327;

On the 17th, bombing 3,000 feet (900 m) over Yvior, Belgium, in Hampden P1327;

On the 19th, bombing Salzbergen from 9,000 feet (2,750 m) in Hampden P1327;

On the 23rd, bombing German railways from 1,500 feet (450 m) at Eindhoven in Hampden P1327;

On the 27th, bombing Hamburg from 10,000 feet (3,000 m) in Hampden P4289; and

On the 30th, bombing Hamburg again, this time from 9,000 feet (2,750 m) in Hampden P1327 (his seventeenth operation).

These were, at the very least, long, energy-sapping flights usually lasting more than five hours, the longest being 6 hours and 45 minutes. Each was a potentially deadly mixture of anticipation, tension, excitement and heart-pumping adrenalin, combined with waves of extreme fatigue that could induce sudden and total exhaustion in the darkness.

Within the confines of the narrow cockpit, Hampden pilots had no opportunity to take a comfort break.

This was one of the main disadvantages of the Hampden, apart from the general lack of space and restriction of movement by any crew member. It caused one to hold one's water for eight hours or more, or make other arrangements. The worst restricted in this regard was the pilot, who tried various devices both official and unofficial. One unofficial idea was to use a condom as a container for the urine. This worked quite well until the condom became full when it usually touched against a sharp part of the cockpit and burst showering the contents over the second pilot/navigator/bomb aimer who worked below in the nose of the plane. Bill Mulloy suffered this fate once. The official gear was a rubber funnel and drain tube contraption one strapped on beneath one's clothes. This sometimes worked satisfactorily, but if one missed the funnel the balance of the trip was done with a damp seat or wet flying boots.

The German forces were now moving towards the English Channel and we were given as targets strategic railway junctions and prime industrial and shipping centres such as Hamburg, which was attacked dozens of times during 1940. I took part in seven bombing raids to it and learned something new each time. We usually pinpointed it by first locating a nearby lake, which was easy enough to pick up most nights. The Germans soon became aware of this landmark and, after covering it, constructed a dummy replica further away, which led us astray for a while. Their defences were very good and one was often 'coned' by searchlights and anti-aircraft fire. It was fascinating to watch an aircraft caught in the cone, but not so good to be the victim oneself.

We tried many different tactics to destroy Hamburg, sometimes carrying out a series of raids, dropping nothing but HE bombs which we followed with raids dropping nothing but incendiary bombs. The idea was good but did not achieve much until the massive raids of July–August 1943 took place, when 6,000 acres (2,430 hectares) of the town were destroyed and some 70,000 people killed. This result was only possible because conditions were 'right': the humidity was very low, allowing fires to start and keep burning while the city had a building density which was suited for a mass conflagration. In cities where the ratio of roof area to ground area is between 30 and 40 per cent fire-storm conditions may be created.

When we were not on operations, we spent our time at the pictures or in the pubs. On one such pub night I had been to Nottingham with our station accounting officer, F/O Petchell Burtt. He was a wealthy, regular officer who had been at Waddington for years. His home was in a nearby village of Wellingore, in the vicinity of which he frequently arranged game shooting for us at the local farms. He was a fine shot.

While in Nottingham we had bought a large scale wall map of Europe with a large number of flags and symbols of the different warring nations to mark the progress of the war front. The night out had been a good one and we were still intent on a little fun when we got back to the mess at Waddington in the early hours of the morning. We had a feed and, seeing all the tables set for breakfast, set a stick-on swastika symbol in the centre of each breakfast plate and then went to bed.

Next day, when we finally surfaced, we noticed a distinctly tense atmosphere about the place and then found that a search was on for a Fifth Columnist responsible for the swastikas. The night duty cook, a Cypriot, had been interrogated and was still under suspicion so Petchell and I decided to confess. We fronted up to the station commander and told our story; he was not amused and gave each of us a severe reprimand.

Petchell had permanent security in his mustering as accountant, but he envied the flying types their job and the fun and games we got up to. Unofficially, he sometimes flew with us on operations. When I finally left England for the Middle East in 1942, Petchell undertook to store my surplus gear and trunks at his home at Wellingore until I could reclaim them. When I arrived back in Australia in 1944, I wrote to Petchell and asked him to arrange to send the gear to me in Australia. Eventually I received a reply from his mother who told me that Petchell had thrown in his permanent commission with the rank of squadron leader and had re-mustered as aircrew as a pilot officer. He had been killed over Berlin shortly after.

When I remember the quote 'All Poms are bums', I think of the exceptions – one was Petchell Burtt.

F/Lt Robert Petchell Burtt, who was still with 50 Squadron RAF, was flying Lancaster III LN428/VN-O during an attack on Berlin on 28/29 January 1944 when the aircraft crashed at Steinberg. All on board were killed. They were at first buried at Steinberg, but their graves are now in the Berlin 1939–1945 War Cemetery.

Regarding the Handley Page Hampden, those of us who flew them thought they were good aircraft, probably because we had not flown anything better. In No. 50 Squadron, the Hampden had replaced the Hawker Hind, a single-engine open-cockpit biplane light bomber with which we had been equipped during the 1938 Munich panic when Neville Chamberlain had stalled Hitler and German confrontation and gained twelve months reprieve for us, and for Britain. As mentioned earlier, at this time we had been told that the aircraft range of the Hind would allow it to bomb just into Germany and leave enough fuel to return to the English Channel where we would ditch and be picked up by ships of the Royal Navy. Thank Heavens for Mr Chamberlain. By comparing the Hind and the Hampden we were satisfied and happy with the Hampden. Similarly, we felt we were bettering ourselves when we first flew Manchesters.

The Hampden unladen could stagger up to about 24,000 feet (7,300 m), but with our usual bomb load of about 2,000 lb (900 kg) the ceiling was from 15,000 to 16,000 feet (4,570–4,870 m) depending on the condition of the engines and how much extra gear, such as armour plate, had been fitted.

This 15,000-foot (4,570 m) ceiling was a great embarrassment to us, in that on most nights the tops of the cloud layer were at that level, making flying difficult, usually with severe icing problems. Our confidence in the Hampden was, I think engendered by the great reliability of the Bristol Pegasus engines which hardly ever gave trouble. We had troubles, but engines were low on the list.

Mist and low cloud hung over Dunkirk when dawn broke on 1 June, but it dispersed as the sun rose. A series of vicious *Luftwaffe* attacks developed against the shipping off shore until, mercifully, clouds rolled over again and the German effort dwindled away. But within that time, great damage had been done. This day marked the nadir of the Dunkirk evacuation. Amid the carnage, ten vessels were sunk including three RN destroyers and several others had suffered serious damage. Worse, German artillery was now in range and covering the Royal Navy's central route to Dunkirk, which was newly cleared of mines, as well as the direct and the eastern approaches. Confronted with the prospect of heavy losses from enemy aircraft and the guns, Vice Admiral Ramsay was obliged to call a halt to daylight evacuations. From then on the work had to be done only at night.

On 2 June, the embarkation of troops ceased at first light. Overnight, although the beaches were shelled and a trawler sunk in the harbour, loading continued according to plan. Early morning haze helped to cover the departure of the ships and the *Luftwaffe* did not arrive until 8.00 a.m. when it ran into five squadrons of RAF fighters. The Germans were kept much too busy fighting for their own survival to seriously molest the ships.

However, what had seemed at first to be a disastrous turn of events proved to have unforeseen advantages. It was realised that if the troops were lifted off only during the night, the demand for continuous air cover could be relaxed. The RAF could concentrate its fighters over the evacuation area in great strength during the two critical periods of the day, dawn and dusk, when the ships were leaving and approaching Dunkirk.

Under these circumstances, the soldiers waiting in the sand dunes were in the safest possible place because the soft sand dampened the concussion of exploding bombs. Being sprayed by grains sand was far less dangerous than being sprayed by shards of rock and metal from bombs dropped on a rocky shoreline.

Throughout that day no ships were sunk and only two were damaged, apart from hospital vessels which had courageously but rashly approached the harbour in daylight. Before midnight, although the embarkation of the French allies was going slowly because they failed to organise a continuous flow of men, a very welcome signal was sent to Vice Admiral Ramsay stating briefly: 'BEF evacuated.'

It was not yet over. French troops were still holding the shrinking perimeter and waiting in their thousands for rescue. For two more nights the heroic rescue continued. On 3 June, as on the 2nd, embarkation ceased at first light and began again during the evening. Once more the fighter patrols were concentrated at the dawn period, but the mist was heavy and the *Luftwaffe* stayed away. Around 7.30 a.m., there was a brush with some *Stuka* dive-bombers and then, thankfully, the weather closed in completely for the day.

In the early hours of 4 June, Major-General Harold Alexander patrolled along the shoreline of the port in a fast motor boat to ensure that there were no British soldiers still waiting to be lifted off. On returning to the quayside he boarded ship for Dover, the last Allied soldier to depart. He left behind a backdrop of thick oily smoke rising from burning vehicles and stores and several thousand Frenchmen in a rearguard that continued the fight to cover the withdrawal. Fighting continued in the contracting bridgehead until the Germans were in the outskirts of the town and there was no other choice but to surrender. That morning, 26,175 Frenchmen that did escape were landed in England. Finally, at 2.23 p.m. on 4 June, the Admiralty, with the agreement of French authorities, announced that Operation *Dynamo* was over.[1]

In seven days 338,226 men had been evacuated from under relentless enemy air attacks.[2] Although the 112,000 Allied troops brought back were mainly French, there were also Belgian soldiers and some civilians. Casualties numbered 68,000 killed, wounded or missing. A total of 222 RN ships had been involved plus around 800 civilian craft; six destroyers and 243 other vessels were sunk. Meanwhile, 40,000 French troops who had fought the valiant rearguard actions on the perimeter were marched into captivity.

Dereck's next sortie, his eighteenth and his first for June, was to bomb Frankfurt on the 3rd. That night saw the largest RAF effort in the war so far with 142 aircraft in the air. From Frankfurt to Hamburg, a range of industrial and communications targets were attacked. Two Hampdens were lost. One of them was from Waddington, a 44 Squadron aircraft that collided with the cable of a barrage balloon over Essex. The other, which crashed in Germany, was from 83 Squadron based at Lossiemouth.

The Germans began their major assault on the remainder of the French Army south of the Somme on 5 June and that night ninety-two RAF bombers were launched. For Dereck and his crew the target was Hamburg again, and this time he unloaded from 8,000 feet (2,500 m) in a mission that lasted 5 hours 40 minutes.

Dereck's most recent co-pilot gaining experience before becoming an aircraft captain, P/O Ken Smettem, was landing a Hampden at Hemswell on the 8th when he crashed. The first mission he had flown with Dereck had been less than two weeks earlier, to Hamburg back on 27 May. The crash did not do the aircraft much good but fortunately Ken Smettem was uninjured. Dereck picked him up in his usual aircraft, Hampden P1327, and brought him back to Waddington.

The primary target for the Hampden bombers of 50 Squadron on the night of 9/10 June 1940 was the marshalling yards at Eindhoven in Holland. This was the main railway junction for traffic coming into the Netherlands from the east. The important Philips (Light globe) factory was located there too. Dereck and his crew – Sgt Ashmore, P/O Smettem and Sgt Horsfall – were flying Hampden P1327 as usual. Visibility was appalling as they searched for their target in the darkness until they came to the realisation they were lost. They were having difficulty pin-pointing their position. Flares were dropped at intervals in the hope of finding a landmark.

Visibility was poor and we had trouble pin-pointing our position, so we dropped flares at intervals in the hope of finding a landmark, gradually losing height after each flare drop. We had maintained an easterly course during our search and were at about 1,000 feet (300 m) when we released another flare. All was quiet until this ignited when all hell broke loose; we were over a heavily built-up area of a town dotted with anti-aircraft guns that hosed streams of projectiles of all colours of tracer towards us, coming from all directions, including head on.

Finally a shell hit us, just to the right and slightly to the rear of the pilot's seat. It blew a hole in the side of the plane, destroying the hydraulic gear (this controls the operation of the undercarriage, the bomb-doors and the landing flaps); shell fragments went past me into the instrument panel, some lodged in my upper right arm but most of it hit the armour plate behind the pilot's seat. This armour plate was a new crew-saving device which had been fitted only a few days earlier. Thank heavens for this, or I should have been cut in half!

The only way out of the trouble was to get as low as possible as soon as possible and so I dived to almost ground level amongst the flak. At one time we were flying along a fairly large river with multi-storied buildings like warehouses above us on each side. At this height we could not be sighted with any accuracy by the AA, if at all. Eventually we were clear of the AA and the town and set a course for Waddington. The crew tied a tourniquet near the shoulder of my damaged right arm.

The AA damage to the aircraft was such that we were unable to release our bombs and had to carry them back to base. With the hydraulic pipe severed, warm oil under pressure spurted about the cockpit, some of which ran down into my flying boots. This really made me worry for knowing I had been hit I thought that I was bleeding at such a rate as to nearly fill my boots with blood. A taste of the mess in my boots gave the truth – oil – and the panic was over.

With the hydraulics unserviceable, I had a problem when we arrived at base. The Hampden carried a high-pressure air bottle piped into the hydraulic system for use in such an emergency. It could be used only once; which meant that we had the choice of either using it to open the bomb doors and drop the bombs, or to lower the undercarriage and do a normal landing, with a full bomb load aboard and without the aid of landing flaps. I took the latter option.

I could at this stage of the flight have handed over the control of the aircraft to Smettem to take us home but decided against the idea. On the previous evening he had been delivering a Hampden to one of our satellite aerodromes for dispersal, when he had crashed it from about 600 feet (180 m) so I considered that we had a better chance of getting back in one piece if I flew myself. I still think that it was his poor navigation earlier that night that caused us to get into the trouble we did. I felt sorry for him and think that he, like many other young chaps, was pushed into rank and responsibility far beyond his capacity. He was killed soon after this.

P/O Kenneth Richard Killey Smettem was killed on the night of 30/31 August 1940. His aircraft, Hampden L4079, crashed about 9 miles (14 km) northwest of Arnhem, Holland. All on board were killed. They are all buried in the Groesbeek Canadian War Cemetery at Nijmegen.

The trip back to England was fairly normal until we reached the Lincoln area and passed near Scampton aerodrome where we had a very difficult time being caught and held by our own searchlights. We eventually landed at Waddington. I taxied to the tarmac, climbed down from the aircraft, and gracefully passed out...

9

Operations

When Dereck regained consciousness after passing out so 'gracefully', he found that his wounds were now very painful, although they were not deemed to be serious. It was not until afterwards that they realised they had strayed over Dusseldorf.

I received a brief medical check-up and so to bed until the following morning when I went with our station medico, Dr Cullinan, to the operating theatre at RAF Cranwell where, using X rays, most of the shrapnel was removed from my arm. On the journey home to Waddington after this, Dr Cullinan insisted on stopping at our local pub for a long session of drinking. Doc Cullinan was a fine South African type, who claimed to be related to the finder of the famous Cullinan Diamond (part of the Crown Jewels). He was more than a diamond to us, for he kept us supplied with biltong (dried meat) which we ate on pub sessions and on long operational flights.

Next day I was ordered to report to the station commander, the strange G/Capt Anderson, who abused and reprimanded me for flying too low over enemy territory! Of interest is the fact that when I was hit, I was aware of having been wounded but suffered no excessive pain and was able to carry on. The pain became acute only after I had landed. In discussing this pain or lack of it at the time of being struck with other chaps who were similarly wounded, all agreed that they had been capable of being in control until they were out of immediate danger.

On joining the RAF, we had been told that ex-RAAF chaps could continue to wear, for general duties, their old Australian uniforms until they were worn out; the RAF blue being worn on special occasions. We preferred to wear the RAAF blue and made sure it never wore out. This was fairly easy with the large number of ex-RAAF chaps with the RAF, as when one was killed his best Australian uniform usually came into the possession of one of his mates.

It was the custom in the RAF at the time to sell at auction the effects of a deceased officer. This was done in the mess. When the deceased had left a widow, unreal amounts were paid for odd bits of rubbish offered and so his estate would be bolstered. If he was unmarried, the financial result of the auction would not be important and the auction bids would be normal. By this system of buying old uniforms the ex-RAAF chaps continued to wear Aussie blue for a little bit longer. I remember that when S/Ldr Good was wounded, his old Australian uniform was badly damaged and I was able to get him a replacement one at a mess auction when the estate of Bill Kinane, another ex-RAAF chap, was offered for sale.

F/O William Kinane was a member of 218 Squadron, which was equipped with Fairey Battles and located at Boscombe Down, Wiltshire. He had graduated from Point Cook in December 1936 and was reportedly killed in a flying accident in August 1939 before hostilities broke out.

After I was wounded I had to get a certificate from our friendly doctor stating that he had been compelled to cut my uniform before he could treat me, before the Air Ministry would consider my claim for a replacement. My pay at the time was approximately £22 per month, which barely covered the cost of my mess bill, uniforms (we had to buy our own), run a car and general living expenses. At this time, casual Irish labourers working on the aerodrome received £12 per week.

Soon after my visit to the operating theatre at Cranwell, I was sent to recuperate at the RAF Officers' Hospital at Torquay in Devon. Policy here was to cure our ills and return us to our units as quickly as possible, without worrying us in any way with too much unnecessary discipline. Ambulant patients, like myself, had their wounds treated in the morning and were then free to go out and do as we wished until evening. Those with fairly simple shrapnel wounds, such as mine, were given ultra-violet ray treatment which appeared to heal the damage very quickly on the surface but made no allowance for the umpteen germs on bits of uniform and other foreign bodies which were carried into our wounds with the shrapnel. As a result the wounds generally healed beautifully on the surface of the damaged area but then a few weeks later the infection broke out elsewhere.

This happened to a New Zealand friend, P/O Pownall, who had been shot through the shoulder while on operations in a Wellington, and also to myself. I had been back with No. 50 Squadron for only a few days when the infection surfaced lower down my arm and I was once again sent to hospital, this time to Rauceby in Lincolnshire, a service hospital which had in peacetime been a psychiatric hospital and which a padded cell at the end of each ward. It catered for flying and non-flying types and lacked the character and happy atmosphere of Torquay.

At Torquay there had been some interesting cases. One was a Hampden pilot who had suffered extensive burns in a crash. He was seated, in bed, with his arms and his face completely bandaged. One side of his body was being treated with the usual burn treatment of the time, tannic acid jelly, while the other side received eucalyptus oil jelly. In this case, the eucalyptus oil treatment proved to heal faster, and with less scarring, than the tannic acid. Another victim, a fighter pilot, had been shot through both testicles during a beam attack. We puzzled over this case and concluded that he must have been in a very relaxed state when he was shot!

Sharing my room at the hospital was a strangely quiet English Hampden pilot. He wore a DFM but was almost non-committal regarding his past flying life. This lasted until one evening he returned from Torquay town very drunk and very talkative, to the extent that I could not shut him up until he had told me his story. He had been an experienced Imperial Airways pilot pre-war, with bags of flying hours to his credit. Somehow or other he became a Hampden pilot with No. 5 Group and was one of those shot down by our own RAF fighters into the Firth of Forth in December 1939. Later in early 1940, he was once again shot down by our own defences, this time into the Thames Estuary, when all his exposed parts, face, wrists and ankles had been badly burned. It was then that he said he had been awarded the DFM, which he referred to as a 'Gob stopper', to buy his silence after being downed twice by our defences.

Although Dereck does not name him, his companion at Torquay was most likely Sgt Tony Reid, formerly of 44 Squadron. On 21 December 1939, two of 44 Squadron's Hampdens had the misfortune to be shot down into the sea by Spitfires of 602 Squadron in a friendly fire incident off North Berwick, Scotland. Reid was the 2nd pilot/navigator of Hampden L4090 and one member of his crew was killed. Reid and the others were all rescued by a local fishing boat. Afterwards he joined the Photographic Development Unit (PDU) based at Heston in Middlesex. Tragedy struck him again on 3 March 1940, when he was co-pilot of a Lockheed Hudson assigned to take aerial photographs of RAF airfields in south-east England to assess the effectiveness of their camouflage. The Hudson was intercepted by Hurricanes from 32 Squadron and shot down in flames. This time Tony Reid was the only survivor. He was badly burned before he managed to bail out of the blazing aircraft. He had to spend four months in hospital undergoing skin grafts and recuperating before returning to duty.

While at Torquay I realised how lucky I had been to be wounded when I had been, for things operationally became more hectic and dangerous as we approached the period of the Battle of Britain with Bomber Command flat out battering targets such as railway junctions and ports that could be of importance to the Germans in the event of an invasion.

Events had indeed moved rapidly, the war situation accelerating from bad to worse. In Norway, with the army's circumstances untenable, the Royal Navy had to evacuate the British and Allied forces that would have been overwhelmed, but it suffered serious losses in the process. On 8 June, the German battle cruisers *Scharnhorst* and *Gneisenau* encountered the aircraft carrier HMS *Glorious* and her escort vessels *Ardent* and *Acasta*. The British carrier, unable to launch her own aircraft because her deck was overloaded with other aircraft flown out of Norway, was a sitting duck. *Scharnhorst* scored direct hits from a range of 15 miles (24 km) and sank her. Although outgunned, *Ardent* and *Acasta* attacked the German ships and they too were sunk, but not before *Scharnhorst* was damaged by torpedoes from *Acasta*. Over 1,500 RN and RAF personnel were lost, but it was a sacrifice that prevented an even greater disaster from happening. The German ships withdrew for repairs and so could not locate and attack the vulnerable ships of the evacuation convoy to the north.

Meanwhile, closer to home across the English Channel immediately after Dunkirk, the German Panzer divisions renewed their invasion into France by bursting across the Somme and the Aisne Rivers and sweeping south on 5 June. General Maxime Weygand had replaced General Gamelin as Allied Supreme Commander, but it was already too late to stem the advancing tide of the enemy's *blitzkrieg*. Worse followed when, on 10 June, Italy declared war on France and Britain with effect from the 11th. On 14 June, the Germans entered Paris. Next day, the remnants of the AASF's Fairey Battle squadrons were flown out of France back to England, and by the 17th the French armies had been broken and were in full flight.

British units still remaining on the Continent fell back to the ports of southern France to be evacuated. Close to disarray, they withdrew to La Pallice and La Rochelle, to Nantes and St Nazaire, to Le Havre and Brest, and to St Malo and Cherbourg. To protect them from the marauding *Luftwaffe* bombers the AASF had only anti-aircraft batteries and its last five squadrons of Hurricanes. These at first flew from French airfields before they were in danger of being overrun, then from the Channel Islands. Fighter aircraft from southern England also helped over Cherbourg.

Meagre though these defences were, for the most part they were effective. Only off St Nazaire was there a major disaster. On the afternoon of 17 June, German bombers managed to elude patrolling

Hurricanes and sink the *Lancastria* with 5,000 troops and many RAF personnel aboard. Such was the seriousness of this tragedy that news of it was not revealed to the British public until after the war. Nevertheless, by the afternoon of the 18th the remaining British forces had made good their escape. Nearly 200,000 men, mostly British, were evacuated to England. The Hurricane fighter pilots, most of whom had flown six sorties the previous day, could also now depart in whatever aircraft were still able to fly. As at Dunkirk, large quantities of equipment and stores were destroyed or left behind.

Meanwhile, the new French Prime Minister, Marshal Henri Philippe Pétain, made a plea for peace. In the Forest of Compiègne on 22 June, in the same railway carriage that had been used for signing the Armistice of 1918, the treaty with Nazi Germany was signed. France had been defeated and Germany was now the master of western Europe.

Winston Churchill had only been Britain's Prime Minister for just over a month when he announced on 18 June, 'What General Weygand called the Battle of France is over. I expect that the Battle of Britain is about to begin... The whole fury and might of the enemy must very soon be turned on us. Hitler knows that he will have to break us in this island or lose the war.'

Nearly a month later, on 16 July, three days before a bogus offer of peace, Adolf Hitler issued his top-secret Directive No. 16, 'Preparations for a Landing Operation against England'. Code-named *Seelöwe* (Sea Lion), it was to be an ambitious combined operation involving the German navy, army and air force. In his directive the *Führer* said, 'The aim of this operation is to eliminate Great Britain as a base from which the war against Germany can be continued, and, should it be necessary, to occupy the country completely.'

The landing area was to be on a broad 200-mile (320-km) front along England's south and south-east coast. The army was to assemble and train the invasion troops. The navy was to sweep the English Channel free of mines and lay a protective minefield on each side of the path of the invasion fleet. It was also to ferry the army and its supplies across the Channel to the beaches at Ramsgate and Folkestone, Hastings, Brighton, Worthing and the Isle of Wight, and as far away as Lyme Bay in Dorset. This huge, widespread task was, in reality, far beyond the German navy's capability, particularly with the Royal Navy and Royal Air Force still intact. Hitler's admirals made more practical counterproposals for landings on a narrow front only to be carried out under the security of an air umbrella.

The success of any such operation depended on *Reichsmarschall* Herman Göring's *Luftwaffe*. The *Luftwaffe* had to wipe out the RAF as it had wiped out the air forces of Poland, Norway, Holland, Belgium and France, or at the very least it had to maintain air supremacy over portion of England's south or south-east coast to cover the landings. The admirals emphasised as well that the only vessels available to transfer troops across the English Channel were slow canal barges and river barges, commandeered from Holland and France. Tugs and motor-boats would be needed to tow them across the open sea and push them onto the beaches.

In July, barges began to be moved in large numbers along the rivers and canals of western Europe towards the English Channel and North Sea ports: Dunkirk, Calais, Boulogne, Le Havre and Cherbourg on the French coast; Antwerp and Ostend in Belgium; and Rotterdam in Holland. On reaching their destinations their bows were removed, concrete floors were laid in their hulls and ramps were attached so that vehicles could be driven on and off. Meanwhile, workmen busily repaired the roads and railways, cleared the canals and built storehouses for the enormous quantities of ammunition and supplies that were needed. Operation *Seelöwe* was swiftly turning into a real possibility. On the *Führer*'s orders, the invasion fleet had to be ready to be launched by 15 August.

Also in July, aerial activity increased sharply over the English Channel as the *Luftwaffe* strove to close this vital shipping lane to England by sinking the vessels sailing on it and smashing harbours from Dover to Southampton. This was also to draw the RAF's defending fighters into action. The destruction of Fighter Command was essential for obtaining air superiority prior to any invasion attempt. By drawing the Hurricanes and Spitfires up to intercept attacks against shipping, RAF casualties began to mount. Attrition had begun.

Losses escalated on both sides. This was a matter of grave concern to the officer in charge of Fighter Command, Air Chief Marshal Sir Hugh Dowding. He was fully aware that he could not afford to fritter away his fighters before the heavy assaults which would obviously come in the near future. He needed every plane and pilot and only grudgingly committed them to battle. His instructions were that fighter formations were not to be heavily engaged, the main defence measures were to be directed against the bombers, and RAF fighter pilots were forbidden to fly across the Channel over France.

At the same time, Bomber Command, the RAF's offensive arm, never stopped operating over the Continent. As well as continuing to maintain pressure on German industry, its immediate role now was to disrupt Hitler's preparations for invasion by destroying barges and stores, blocking railways and canals, and raiding ports and supply lines. In one daring low-level precision attack on the night of 12/13 August, five RAF Hampdens successfully breached the vital Dortmund/Ems Canal. In command, F/Lt Roderick 'Babe' Learoyd was afterwards awarded the Victoria Cross. Anti-aircraft fire claimed two Hampdens, both flown by Australians, and the other planes were heavily damaged. Killed were F/O Ellis 'Rossy' Ross DFC and his crew in Hampden P4410/OL-H while F/Lt Allen 'Mull' Mulligan and his crew, flying P4340, were shot down and captured. Meanwhile, Dereck's diary entry for 24/6/40 reads: 'Torquay. S/Ldr Watts, S/Ldr Crockart, P/O Todd, P/O Luxmore written off. *C'est la Geurre.*'

Flying Hampden P4345 on the night of 12/13 June, W/Cdr Joseph Watts DSO and his crew of 144 Squadron had collided with a barrage balloon cable near Ipswich and crashed nearby onto a flour mill at Felixstowe in Suffolk. Joseph Watts, his entire crew – P/O John Andrews from Canada, Sgt Alex Winstanley and Sgt Ron Jolly DFM – and an employee of the mill were all killed.

Norman Crockart and Anthony Luxmoore were both from 50 Squadron, and both failed to return on 26/27 June. Their targets were in Hannover. Norm Crockart and his crew took off from Waddington at 10.15 p.m. in Hampden P1329. They crashed into the sea at about 4.00 a.m. after transmitting in plain language, 'Going down.' They had already sent an earlier signal in code indicating that their plane was flying on one engine. Two bodies were eventually recovered. Norm Crockart was buried at Callantsoog in Holland, and his gunner, Sgt Allen Ingram, was laid to rest in Haurvig Churchyard, Denmark. The names of the others, F/Sgt William Southey and Sgt Eric McKenzie Turner, were recorded on the Runnymede Memorial.

New Zealander Tony Luxmoore and his crew took off in Hampden L4078 two minutes after Norman Crockart had departed. Their instructions were to attack the aerodrome at Langen Hagen but nothing more was heard from them. Luxmoore and his crew, Sgt Walter Harding, Sgt Gerald Nichols and Sgt Arthur Smith, were buried in the Hannover War Cemetery.

Desmond Todd of 44 Squadron left Waddington on 3/4 July to plant mines off Denmark but his aircraft, Hampden P4352, came down in the North Sea. The members of his crew were Sgt Eric Apperson, Sgt Arthur Baird and F/Lt William Bull, who was apparently acting in the role of lower gunner. The body of F/Lt Bull was washed ashore at Strandlehen on the west coast of Denmark and he was buried in Lyngvig Churchyard. The others have been honoured on the memorial at Runnymede.

Although the entry in Dereck's diary concerning 'Watts, Crockart, Todd, and Luxmore' was for 24 June, it must have been written in after this date for them to be mentioned. He added: 'These losses were all old Waddington identities which really made us at Torquay appreciate how lucky we had been to be merely wounded. The war was no longer "phoney".' Dereck returned to the squadron early in July and wrote: '8/7/40. Waddington. Not so good – Too many new faces and old memories.'

I rejoined No. 50 Squadron at Waddington and made the 8/7/40 entry in my diary. Most of my old friends had gone during the month I had been away. A few days later, the squadron moved to a new drome at Hatfield-Woodhouse near Doncaster. This aerodrome became known as Lindholme. It was after only a few days here that my wound festered and broke out lower down the arm so I was admitted to Rauceby hospital, near Cranwell in Lincolnshire, for repairs. While I was there 50 Squadron was busy, mining, bombing the Ruhr, railway junction targets and attacking the build-up of invasion barges at the channel ports, and losing more good aircrews.

On leaving Rauceby, I was granted a week of sick leave which I spent walking in Cumberland for a few days and the rest of the time doing the shows in London, arriving back at Lindholme to find that my old friend Bill Mulloy had been killed returning from an operation.

P/O William Arthur Coote Mulloy DFC and his crew were killed on the night of 25/26 July. His aircraft, Hampden P1321, was damaged, apparently by enemy action. At 2.15 a.m., Mulloy reported over the w/t that the port engine had failed over Cuxhaven and they were heading towards Calais. Then, 45 minutes later later, the Hampden crashed on a beach 12 miles (19 km) south-east of Cromer in Norfolk.[1] There were no survivors.

Early in August the squadron spent some days searching for the crew of one of our Hampdens (P/O Bell) who had ditched. This was arduous work but in this case was of particular importance. It was the first time we carried the Lindholme Dinghy air-sea rescue device which was developed as the result of the 12 April 1940 operation and the loss of Johnny Bull and crew. Later, air-sea rescue was developed to the stage when small life boats were carried and dropped from aircraft to ditched crews.

Unfortunately, all the searching was to no avail. P/O Brian Bell was a Canadian in 50 Squadron. He and his crew had taken off from Lindholme in Hampden P4383 on the night of 31 July/1 August at 9.13 p.m. They were on a mining mission, but contact with them was lost at 4.10 a.m. It was presumed that they had ditched 40–45 miles (64–72 km) east of Flamborough Head, and this was where the searches were concentrated. Six weeks later, Brian Bell's body was washed up on the Dutch coast and he was buried in Bergen op Zoom War Cemetery. His three companions were never found and they were commemorated on the Runnymede Memorial. Dereck's diary entry for 29 July read in part, '... A1.B1 at last.' He explained: 'A1.B1 was a medical standard or classification required to be achieved by aircrew certifying us as being fit for flying duties.'

Dereck's log book shows that he took part in the fruitless search for Brian Bell and his crew on the first day of August. Then, his diary recorded for 5 August, 'Start Ops – rather shattering – Hamburg.' His log book showed more details: 'Bombed Hamburg again this time from 11,000 feet (3,350 m) in Hampden L4149, the mission lasting 7 hours 15 minutes.'

Bomber Command sent eighty-five Hampdens, Wellingtons and Whitleys to bomb targets in Hamburg, Kiel, Wilhelmshaven and Wismar that night, and airfields in Holland were also attacked. At Hamburg the primary target was the *Tirpitz*. Dereck arrived over the area at 12.22 a.m. but he and his crew were unable to locate the German capital ship because of darkness and haze. He decided instead to bomb the neighbouring docks but because of the haze the results were hidden from view. Wilhelmshaven was the base for another capital ship, the *Bismarck*. Crews bombing there were equally frustrated by darkness, searchlights and the intense anti-aircraft fire. Such targets were always heavily defended. On the 10th, over the Ruhr in Hampden L4395, Dereck bombed from 11,000 feet (3,350 m), the mission lasting 5 hours 5 minutes.

For nine Hampdens from 50 Squadron the target was the synthetic oil plant at Homberg, south-west of Hamburg. Dereck was first over the area at 11.30 a.m. and he dropped four bombs, but again was unable to see the results because of haze and cloud.

These early entries show that I was apparently a trifle apprehensive at returning to operational work and I find that for the first two trips I bombed from 11,000 feet (3,350 m); higher than I had generally bombed before being wounded. This apprehension soon passed and I once again got into my stride, taking part in seven bombing and mining sorties during the month.

On the 13th, he took off for an operation in Hampden P4417 but had to abort because the radio was u/s. He landed after 20 minutes. On the 14th, he bombed targets near Bordeaux in Hampden P4417 from 5,500 feet (1,675 m), the mission lasting 8 hours.

We had one very easy trip. When the BEF (British Expeditionary Force) left France, they did so in a hurry and neglected to destroy much that was to be of value to the enemy, including much fuel in storage tanks near Bordeaux. The RAF was asked to remedy this by bombing the tanks, our unit being briefed to take part in the operation very late in the programme. We had no difficulty locating the target as we could see the flames of the blazing fuel tanks from 150 miles (240 km) away. Anti-aircraft fire and searchlights were barely in evidence so the trip was really easy, but for the discomfort and inconvenience of being strapped into the cockpit for eight hours. It is not to be wondered that we welcomed the arrival of the new, more spacious Manchesters.

On the 17th, Dereck bombed Leuna/Merseburg in Hampden P4417, the mission lasting 7 hours 15 minutes. By 12.50 a.m. that night Dereck was encountering intense flak as he made his bomb-run across the synthetic oil plant at Merseburg. He dropped his four bombs but his Hampden then ran into trouble. The starboard engine started spluttering so he did not stay around to watch the results of his bombing. He reached home after a very tense 3½-hour flight. No. 50 Squadron had detailed eleven aircraft to attack this synthetic oil plant. Dick Taylor made a low-level attack ten minutes after Dereck and he found that the hydrogenation plant was already in flames. It seems highly likely that Dereck's bombs had indeed been very effective. Taylor's first bomb run was unsuccessful because the bombs did not release, so he brought the Hampden around to try again. This time he scored a direct hit. He and his crew also noticed incendiaries bursting nearby, which started another fire.

On the 21st, Dereck bombed Magdeburg from 9,000 feet (2,750 m) in Hampden P4408, the sortie lasting 6 hours 25 minutes. This mission was Dereck's twenty-sixth. He encountered bad weather on the way to Magdeburg's synthetic oil plant and over the target. Anti-aircraft fire was intense but he pressed his attack home and explosions were seen in the target area. Despite the inclement weather, the operation went smoothly for the most part except for the aircraft's air speed indicator malfunctioning. He and his crew returned safely to Lindholme.

His next operation was on the 24th. Dereck went to La Rochelle 'Gardening' again flying Hampden P4417. At the same time as Dereck was planting his mine at La Rochelle, some *Luftwaffe* bomber crews who had been instructed to bomb the Thameshaven oil tanks strayed unintentionally over the city of London. For the first time since 1918, they dropped their bombs on the British capital. Hitler had specially ordered that London was not to be bombed. He was furious. This mistake set in motion a chain of events that altered the course of the Battle of Britain.

On his own initiative, Prime Minister Winston Churchill ordered a hastily organised reprisal raid on the German capital for the next night. Accordingly, on 25/26 August, a total of 103 Bomber

Command aircraft raided France and Germany, forty-three of them with instructions to head for Berlin. Dereck was not rostered for the Berlin mission as he had flown the previous night. The bomber crews found Berlin covered by thick clouds and because of this very few bombs were actually dropped within the city limits. Many fell on large farming areas south of the city. Just two people were recorded injured. However, like the bombing of London, despite the raid's lack of success in terms of damage caused and casualties inflicted, its strategic consequences proved far-reaching.

Operating at maximum range and encountering strong headwinds while returning, six Hampden bombers were lost because they ran out of fuel. Three of the missing Hampdens had to ditch into the sea with their fuel tanks empty. The night was costly for 50 Squadron because Hampden P2070, flown by P/O Bob Wawn, failed to return. A w/t message asking for a compass bearing was heard from the aircraft at 4.12 a.m. This was given but apparently Wawn then inexplicably flew 180° in the wrong direction! Over two hours later the Hampden force-landed near Lautersheim in Germany. Bob Wawn and his crew were taken prisoner.

Wawn was not the only Australian lost to 50 Squadron that night. The other was F/Lt Dick Taylor in Hampden L4062, but he was not a casualty. Five Hampdens from 50 Squadron had been detailed to attack one of Berlin's electricity power stations. By 1.15 a.m., Taylor was flying over the extensive cloud cover which blanketed the German capital. At 1.23 a.m. his bomb-aimer released the Hampden's load of eight bombs but no results could be seen through the murk below. After struggling against the headwinds on the way back, he landed back at Lindholme at 6.28 a.m., an exhausting 8 hours and 38 minutes after takeoff. His safe return was cause for celebration. This was Dick Taylor's thirty-fifth combat mission – the last of his first tour of operations. It was time for him to be 'rested'.

When we began to fly operationally there was no such thing as an operational tour. The station commander at Waddington at the time (Anderson) told us then that after we had completed six operational flights we would get six months leave and a trip back to Australia, if we wanted it. The accent on Australia was because at that time eight of the twenty-three pilots in 50 Squadron were Australian. We carried out the six sorties and were then told 'make it twenty trips' and so on until the magic figure of thirty-five was decided upon as the final figure for a tour.

In those early war days, the whole idea of an operational tour was loose. When I had been wounded and was in hospital, I received a letter from HQ No. 5 Group on behalf of the AOC, AVM Harris, suggesting that I had done enough flying for the time being and I should have a rest from operations by changing places with a flight lieutenant at the OTU at Finningley. It also guaranteed my eventual return to 50 Squadron. The choice was mine, but I declined the offer. This type of personal approach to the original aircrew on posting matters was the method used by the staff handling personnel movements at that time. AVM Harris was seldom, or never, seen by any of his aircrew, yet he knew everything about those under his command, looking out for their welfare and suggesting when they should have a rest, a posting or whatever.

To firmly establish a fixed meaning for the term 'Operational Tour' took years and is best described by John Terraine's, *The Right of the Line*, pages 522-527, précised here:

> In the RAF at the end of 1940 it was clear that operational flying must be broken up into manageable portions of time, and that these must offer a reasonable chance of survival. This was known as the 'datum line', it was generally accepted that it should be drawn at a point which offered a 50-50 chance. Conferences were held at the end of 1940 and came up with 30 sorties; not exceeding 200 hours as a tour … this was not officially agreed upon until August 1942 when Bomber Groups were instructed that a tour of operations consist of a maximum of 30 sorties. Less than 30 sorties can count as a tour if the Commanding Officer considers the pilot of the crew has carried out his duties satisfactorily but is in need of a rest. This was not completely official until January 1943 when after more conferences, and finally ruled in May 1943, the first tour was set at 30 sorties with a 9-month rest at OTU followed by a second tour of 20 sorties. A total of 50 sorties. These figures applied only to Bomber Command; Fighter Command, Coastal Command and Pathfinders had different tours.[2]

On the 26th, Dereck bombed Leipzig from 9,000 feet (3,000 m) in Hampden P4408, the mission lasting 7 hours 40 minutes. That night the specific target for 50 Squadron was Leipzig-Mockau aerodrome and the adjoining aircraft component parts factory. Six aircraft were involved. Dereck was over the target area just after 11.30 p.m. in overcast weather. He was able to drop six bombs and incendiaries but because of the cloud cover his crew could not observe their bombing results. Except for his trip to Hamburg on the 5th, the regular members of his crew for the month of August were Sgt Wappett, Sgt Kelly and Sgt Doyle. Sgt Doyle had replaced Sgt Skinner as gunner beginning with the mission to the Ruhr on the 10th.

When we operated at night, we usually drove our cars to the flight office and parked them there until we returned; always finding our petrol tanks full. One night, however, we found that our tanks had not been topped up and later learned why. The good fairy that had been doing this topping up proved to be the airman responsible for the petrol tankers and the refuelling of planes. On this night, he had started his good work and attached his tractor to the tow hitch of a petrol tanker. As he reversed, he was apparently trying to pick up the trailer hitch when his foot slipped off the clutch and he was forced back and down between the tractor and the trailer and crushed to death. He was a war casualty – but a horrible way to die. We got no more free petrol.

The weather – an important factor in the success or failure of our operations – at Lindholme during August/September was fairly good with the result that we were able to carry out our missions with little worry about being recalled or diverted away from our base due to sudden weather deterioration. Also the uncertainty as to whether or not operations each night would proceed was reduced. Sir Maurice Dean in his book *The Royal Air Force and Two World Wars* stated:

> The Command's principal enemy at this stage was the weather. The winter of 1939/40 was hard and the available bombers were poorly equipped to cope with it. There were serious problems of icing, navigation and crew comfort. The operations of the Command in this phase were mainly valuable for the experience they afforded the crews and technical men; of the problems to be faced in operating over enemy territory in blackout conditions and in bad weather.[3]

No. 5 Group employed a remarkable civilian meteorologist, Mr Matthews, who briefed us on the weather conditions we could expect to encounter on each trip. His reports were precise and usually most accurate, so we came to rely on him. Considering the limited amount of meteorological information he was receiving, his forecasting was uncanny. (Later, when in India with 215 Squadron, our meteorological officers were Indians who, when briefing us on the weather conditions we might expect on operations, always gave us forecasts they thought we would like to hear, without giving any regard to the actual weather conditions that prevailed, usually with disastrous results.)

Dereck's tally of operations had now quickly reached twenty-eight, and it was time for him to have the usual obligatory short rest break. Towards the end of the month he was instructed to take leave and spend a few days as a guest at Woodborough Hall, starting on the 30th.

My host at Woodborough Hall was Air Vice Marshal Leigh-Mallory, who commanded No. 12 Group (the fighter squadrons of central England) at the time. Group headquarters was nearby near RAF Hucknall in Nottingham. I did not relish the idea of spending my leave at Woodborough Hall as all I knew about the Air Vice Marshal was that he was a rather tough, dedicated career officer with a long and reputable service history. I went along, having been persuaded to do so by his daughter, Jacqui, who was a WAAF officer at Waddington. The visit proved to be a truly wonderful experience.

I arrived in my battered old Ford 10, which I left in the driveway of the estate, only to find after I had been received that the car had been moved to the rear of the main building where it had been washed and polished (for the first time). My case had been placed in my room and carefully unpacked, except for a copy of *No Orchids for Miss Blandish* and a packet of condoms. So much for English hospitality!

At dinner one evening while discussing bomber operations, I told AVM Leigh-Mallory that we seldom found our targets in Germany on nights of no moon when the searchlights and anti-aircraft were not active, as we tended to pinpoint ourselves from our knowledge of various belts of lights and guns. Later that evening the Air Vice Marshal went on duty to his Group HQ. It was a night of no moon, so he decided to test the idea and issued an order that all AA batteries and searchlights in his sector of England remain inactive. This it was hoped would confuse any German intruders who might come over. Next morning he told me that the idea had been a failure for soon after his order of defence inactivity had gone out to his units, a counter order had gone out from his own HQ telling all units to carry on as usual. He was furious. He never heard how the counter order originated but it appeared that a fifth columnist, presumably of fairly high rank, was in the HQ office.

A piece of personal advice (which I did not accept) was given to me by the Air Vice Marshal during my stay. It was that I should remain in the service after the war and so be in a position to be of use when World War 3 broke out. Another idea he expressed, which rather seemed to be against service life, was that no matter how senior one became in the service, one always had some one of senior rank above one, meaning the monarch.

Later in the war, he, with his gracious wife and staff, disappeared while flying to India where he was to take command of the air forces in that theatre of war. They were later found to have crashed in the Alps, all being killed.[4]

Dereck's visit to Woodborough Hall took place at a crucial time. At the end of August and beginning of September the Battle of Britain was at crisis point. RAF Fighter Command was divided into four groups. Covering south-east England and bearing the brunt of the *Luftwaffe*'s attacks was 11 Group, commanded by the resourceful New Zealander AVM Keith Park. Behind 11 Group, covering the Midlands, was Leigh-Mallory's 12 Group. Covering half of the southern coast and Wales was 10 Group under AVM Sir Quinton Brand, and finally, to meet the threat from Norway and Denmark, AVM Richard Saul's 13 Group defended northern England and Scotland. After a month of attacking British coastal shipping and ports throughout July, early in August the Germans launched the first of a series of mass daylight air raids on airfields and the coastal defences in south-east England.

By the end of the month, Keith Park's No. 11 Group was fighting for its life – and losing. It was being battered into submission. Leigh-Mallory's No. 12 Group was the back-up group, but Park and Leigh-Mallory were constantly at loggerheads over tactics. Leigh-Mallory advocated employing 'Big Wings' consisting of three to five squadrons of Hurricanes and Spitfires against the enemy formations, but it took time for all the fighters to take off and assemble. In south-east England time was a luxury Park did not have – the enemy was much too close, just across the English Channel. His squadrons had to scramble singly or in pairs within minutes and claw for height before the *Luftwaffe* arrived to bomb their airfields. Leigh-Mallory's fighters were supposed to come south on request to cover these airfields but they were often too late and sometimes did not arrive at all. The two groups were operating under completely different conditions, and the daily *Luftwaffe* raids allowed no respite.

By the evening of 6 September, the situation was grim. Between 24 August and 6 September, Fighter Command had lost 295 fighters and 171 were badly damaged. Only 269 new and repaired Hurricanes and Spitfires had come on strength. At the same time, 103 fighter pilots had been killed and 128 wounded, resulting in the average number of pilots per squadron sinking from twenty-six to sixteen. So dire were the circumstances that HQ Home Forces issued its Alert No. 3: 'Invasion probable within three days.'

Next day, anticipating the usual airfield attacks, the British defences were taken completely by surprise when the *Luftwaffe* launched a massive daylight assault against London. The docks, warehouses and London's East End were set ablaze and the sky was prematurely darkened by a massive pall of smoke. As night fell, the first of 318 German bombers approached, guided by the fires. By morning, 306 civilians were dead and 1,337 badly injured. It was the beginning a series of violent attacks on London over the next fifty-seven consecutive nights – the Blitz had begun.

Overnight, the British Chiefs of Staff (COS) issued the code word 'Cromwell' for Alert No. 1: 'Invasion imminent and probable within twelve hours.' It was received in some places with panic. Numerous Home Guard and army units ordered the ringing of church bells, the signal that an invasion had already started! Meanwhile, Bomber Command concentrated on German invasion barges in ports on the Channel Coast.

In Germany on 8 September, the Berlin Sunday newspapers reported: 'BIG ATTACK ON LONDON AS REPRISAL.' Bomber Command's raids on the German capital had provoked Adolf Hitler into ordering the *Luftwaffe* to switch its attacks away from targeting airfields in south-east England to the British capital. Dereck noted in his diary: 'Lindholme becomes my home. London stops a packet of bombs. Where will this bombing end? It all seems so futile.' About Lindholme itself he wrote: 'Life at Lindholme was a rather happy one with bags of time off for poaching (fishing and shooting).'

Actually, Lindholme was a dreary place set in a low, swampy area. Nearby was our bombing range, set in a fen of peat which was set on fire by one of our practice bombs months before. It continued to burn and the glow from the fire was a Godsend to us as it attracted stray German bombers who usually unloaded their bombs onto it. The range was where we did most of our game shooting, bagging everything from partridges to foxes, which were commonly shot in this part of England.

These casual remarks gave no indication of what Dereck was doing at night when he was not at leisure. His log book revealed the other side of the story. On 4 September, he bombed Stettin from 10,000 feet (3,000 m) in Hampden P4408, the mission lasting 7 hours 15 minutes; his crewmembers were Sgt Wappett, Sgt Kelly and Sgt Doyle: 'Stettin was beyond Berlin and to the north, a long trip in a Hampden. Up to that time this was the furthest we had flown to bomb.'

Dereck and his companions in Hampden P4408 were one of four crews from 50 Squadron ordered to bomb Stettin's oil refinery. Their course to the target took them north of Heligoland and south of Kiel. Over Denmark they encountered 'troublesome' searchlights and accurate AA fire, and between Brunsbruttel and the target, numerous flares – presumably dropped by German night fighters – were seen floating in the air. Visibility remained good all the way. They found Stettin easily but the flak put up by the defences was intense. Dereck made his bomb run at 12.27 a.m., unloading four bombs and incendiaries. Three direct hits were seen that caused bright explosions with white flames. Bomber Command had despatched eighty-two aircraft to targets ranging from Stettin to Turin in Italy that night, and Berlin was raided again for two hours. Three Hampdens and one Wellington were lost.

On the 8th it was back to Hamburg again, this time bombing from 10,000 feet (3,000 m) in Hampden P4408, the mission lasting 7 hours; his crewmembers were Sgt Wappett, Sgt Ashmore and Sgt Bailey. This was actually a heavy raid by forty-nine Hampdens from various squadrons on Hamburg's Blohm and Voss Shipyard, six of them, including Dereck, coming from 50 Squadron. Out of the forty-nine, one Hampden was lost: it was in fact an aircraft from 50 Squadron flown by S/Ldr Willan and crew. A radio signal was received indicating they were bailing out and in due course news came that they were all POWs. On the 10th, Dereck bombed Duisburg from 10,000 feet (3,000 m) in Hampden P4408, the mission lasting 5 hours 30 minutes; his crewmembers were Sgt Ormonroyd, Sgt Ashmore and Sgt Doyle; there was poor weather over Ostend.

Again most of Bomber Command's effort was directed at the invasion barges in the Channel coast ports, but a small force of Whitleys also attacked the Potsdamer Station in Berlin. Two Hampdens from 50 Squadron were assigned to bomb the barges in Ostend Harbour. Both were piloted by Australians: Dereck and Bob 'Dave' Reed, who was flying Hampden L4097. Over Ostend Dereck encountered poor weather so he diverted to a secondary target and bombed Duisburg instead. Bob Reed and his crew never returned; they simply disappeared. F/Lt Robert James Reed was one of the Australians from Bomber Command whose name was listed on the Battle of Britain Roll of Honour in Westminster Abbey. His Hampden was one of two lost during the night. Two Whitleys on the Berlin raid were also lost, but for the first time the Germans had to admit that considerable damage had been caused to their capital.

On the 15th, Dereck bombed Mannheim from 11,000 feet (3,350 m) in Hampden P4408, the sortie lasting 6 hours 10 minutes; his crewmembers were Sgt Wappett, Sgt Ashmore and Sgt Doyle; barrage balloons were encountered and AA fire reached as high as 13,000 feet (4,000 m); the weather was violent with lightning and icing conditions. As usual, Dereck's log book entry only hinted at the full extent of the drama that took place. His target was the railway marshalling yard at Mannheim, which he reached after a three-hour flight. The area was alive with flak and searchlights, and as he flew across the marshalling yard about twenty-four barrage balloons were spotted nearby. His gunners fired on them as he continued his bombing run and one was seen to collapse. It was 10.44 p.m. when the aircraft's four bombs were dropped, but because of the searchlights it was impossible to observe the results. The return to Lindholme was eventful too. The autopilot became unusable and Dereck had to fly the Hampden through a snowstorm during which the starboard engine cut out. Despite all of this, he landed safely back at Lindholme at 1.59 a.m. Bomber Command's losses for the night were two Whitleys.

On the 17th, Dereck bombed Antwerp from 9,000 feet (3,000 m) in Hampden X2919, the mission lasting 3 hours 55 minutes; his crewmembers were Sgt Doyle, Sgt Ashmore and Sgt Bushnall. It was 12.30 a.m.

when Dereck approached Antwerp in gloomy weather. There was no anti-aircraft fire, only a few searchlights that merely served to betray the exact position of the target to the incoming bombers. Five minutes later he flew across the area, dropping his bombs in a long stick over the docks where barges were reported to be tied. Disappointingly, no explosions were seen. In the morning, PRU flights showed that more than 150 barges had been destroyed by Bomber Command overnight. The dock areas at Dunkirk and Antwerp had also suffered considerable damage. Two Hampdens failed to return.

On the 19th, Dereck bombed Bergen Op Zoom from 3,000 feet (900 m) in Hampden X2919, the mission lasting 3 hours 55 minutes; his crewmembers were Sgt Wappett, Sgt Doyle and Sgt Kelly. It was in the very dark early morning hours of Friday, 20 September that the twelve Hampdens from 50 Squadron set out to bomb German barge concentrations at Flushing. Out over the North Sea the crews ran into heavy rain and cloud that seemed never-ending. On making landfall over the Dutch coast and finding no improvement in conditions, Dereck and his crew became frustrated when they could not locate the target. They were reluctant to go home with their bombs. After searching for some other suitable objective, they found Bergen Op Zoom aerodrome where they unloaded their deadly cargo.

On Monday 23 September, Dereck bombed Flushing from 8,000 feet (2,400 m) in Hampden P4408, the sortie lasting 3 hours 10 minutes; his crewmembers were Sgt Wappett, Sgt Wallace DFM and Sgt Doyle.

Overnight ninety-five Blenheims, Hampdens and Wellingtons raided the Channel ports and nine Whitleys bombed a factory near Dresden. Dereck's Hampden was one of four aircraft from 50 Squadron assigned to bomb the German barges at Antwerp. It was 4.10 a.m. when he and his crew made their bomb run and unloaded seven of their eight bombs across Inner Haven Wess and the harbour works. One bomb failed to release. Afterwards, they managed to drop the 'hung up' bomb on the aerodrome at Vlissinger.

For many, coming home proved to be the most hazardous part of the trip as German bombers were still active over England. Some of these mingled with the returning British planes to try and sneak through the defences and make attacks on the airfields in Lincolnshire – without success, as it turned out. All of 50 Squadron's aircraft returned safely. It was Dereck's thirty-fifth mission – his last. He wrote in his notes afterwards, 'This marked the end of my first tour of operations.'

Out of the original eight Australians in 50 Squadron when the war started, only two, Dick Taylor and Dereck French, succeeded in finishing their first tour. John 'Ferdinand' Bull was missing, believed drowned; Bob Cosgrove was missing, believed killed; Duncan Good was badly wounded; Robert 'Dave' Reed was missing, fate as yet unknown; Mervin Thomas had been killed in action; and Bob Wawn was missing, fate as yet unknown.

Nevertheless, it did not mean the end of the well known 'Ye Olde Dingo Flight'. No. 50 Squadron would continue to have a worthy Australian contingent as newcomers such as Pilot Officers Ron Ash, Geoff Cornish, Pat Macrossan, Philip 'Micky' Moore and Bill Preece were posted in fresh from operational training units. They too would become part of the squadron's proud history. Meanwhile, Dick Taylor was now at No. 16 OTU at Upper Heyford in Oxfordshire, helping in the training of new young pilots and preparing them for war.

It was time now for Dereck to leave Lindholme and 50 Squadron. But the squadron had been his 'home' since October 1938, and he was not particularly happy about going...

10

Wittering

Having completed thirty-five operations I was posted, by way of a rest, to join 106 Squadron at Finningley. This squadron was at that time non-operational and was an OTU (Operational Training Unit) where fledglings from flying schools came together as crews and learned to work as a unit, flying generally over the UK both by day and night before joining operational squadrons. Time-expired operational crews, like myself, hated being posted to units of this nature and did everything possible to avoid it. Wing Commander Guy Gibson VC DSO DFC says in his book *Enemy Coast Ahead*, 'And now I was having to go to an OTU. The idea was extremely distasteful and I felt sorry for myself.'

Guy Gibson of course gained renown as the leader of the famous successful raid on the dams by 617 (Lancaster) Squadron using 'bouncing bombs' designed by Barnes Wallis. He led the raid on the night of 16/17 May 1943, and he was subsequently awarded the Victoria Cross. He was then taken off operations and given 'desk jobs', but during this time he wrote his autobigraphy, *Enemy Coast Ahead*. This was not published until 1946, well after his death. The book is regarded as a classic of its genre. Gibson pestered authorities for further operational flying, and he acted as a master bomber for a raid on Rheydt on the night of 19/20 September 1944 from which he failed to return.

Back in August 1939, RAF Bomber Command had consisted of five operational formations (Nos 1, 2, 3, 4 and 5 Bomber Groups) plus No. 6 (Training) Group, but in reality this was a force without sufficient reserves, despite the existence of the Royal Auxiliary Air Force (RAuxAF). On the outbreak of war its training organisation was inadequate. From the outset, it was obvious that any sustained campaign with its inevitable casualties could very quickly bring the Command to the end of its small supply of trained crews; the trained and experienced crews were the very ones that were committed to battle and being lost.

When No. 1 Group's ten squadrons of Fairey Battles transferred to France on 2 September, and several Blenheim units departed bound for there too, the number of operational squadrons remaining in Britain was reduced accordingly. The opposite was required. An organisation had to be built up for the inevitable bombing offensive of the future. A substantial, continuous flow of new pilots and crews was essential. To cater for the influx of new men that had to come to boost the command's strength, instructors, aircraft, and specialised training units were needed. Only the most experienced pilots and other aircrew were suitable to serve as instructors, but the men gaining the real experience were all in the front line.

To create a pool of reserves quickly, Bomber Command's offensive capability had to be reduced yet again, down to only twenty-three operational squadrons: six squadrons each of Wellingtons, Hampdens and Blenheims, plus five squadrons of Whitleys. Of the remainder, fourteen squadrons had to be assigned to a training role under the authority of No. 6 Group, and six others were set aside to become Group Pool training squadrons.

Fortunately for Bomber Command, this all happened during the 'Phoney War'. For the rest of 1939, more aircraft were written off in training accidents and in other non-operational mishaps than were lost during Bomber Command's missions, although there were some heavy losses in several daylight operations. That was before the disastrous Wellington losses in December and the dreadful Hampden losses in daylight missions in the early months of 1940. Aircraft could be replaced, but it was harder to replace the people needed to maintain them and fly them. It took valuable time, normally a couple of years, to train new pilots. The call for replacement pilots and crews increased daily and those capable of training the newcomers properly had to come from somewhere.

The standard practice was for pilots and aircrew who had finished their operational tours to 'rest' by taking on the role of instructing the newcomers. Many did not like it. Some veterans felt that this gave their nerves no real rest at all – placing their lives into the hands of clumsy novices could be just as dangerous as flying missions! But a deep-rooted resentment existed too, as Dereck explained:

The reasons for this attitude were many, but in general they [the veterans] did not like the more-or-less permanent personnel who comprised such units. These types were keen to see the war out as non-combatants. The thinking of the permanent OTU officer is best portrayed by the following true story. While with 106 Squadron, I attended a conference about some matter or other when the CO of 106 Squadron, W/Cdr Lionel Stubbs, was asked by the Station Commander G/Capt Foden (a not so nice Australian) his opinion on a certain point of dispute. Stubbs came back with the classic answer: 'I think what you think, sir. What do you think?'

Dereck's initial flying at Finningley began on 4 October and over the next few days he was checked out on a variety of aircraft types other than the Hampden. These included the Avro Anson, Vickers Wellington, Armstrong Whitworth Whitley and Miles Magister. They were all short daylight flights.

I had been at Finningley only a short time when I noticed a signal on the adjutant's desk asking for a pilot to carry out experimental, co-operation work with our RAF night fighters and Army Search Light units in central England. This was a chance to get away from the unreal atmosphere of the OTU, so I applied for and got the job, which involved taking a Hampden and crew on detachment to Wittering, a fighter station.

The aircraft selected for the co-op tests seems to have been Hampden X2968, which he flew to Wittering on the 14th.[1] The exercise began with a series of R/T tests.

The Hampden was modified, in that it was completely painted with a matt black non-reflective paint and was fitted with a wireless set similar to those used in fighters, so that I could keep in touch with both the fighter operations control room and the night fighters I was supposed to be co-operating with. My job was to fly into various groups of searchlights at different heights, when I was supposed to be intercepted by Blenheim night fighters of 29 Squadron.

Wittering airfield was in Northamptonshire about 10 miles (16 km) west-northwest of Peterborough. No. 29 Squadron was stationed around 60 miles (96 km) away at Digby in Lincolnshire, 10 miles south-east of the city of Lincoln. As the Second World War approached, No. 29 had received Bristol Blenheim IFs and it was declared operational in October 1939. It had started intensive night-flying training from the outset and was at 'readiness' each night.

The squadron's Blenheim Mk IFs were actually modified Blenheim Mk I bombers changed by the addition of a belly pack of four .303 inch Browning machine-guns. These were bolted on under each aircraft's bomb bay, which now stored four belts of ammunition containing 500 rounds each. They were capable of 20 seconds of continuous firing. A similar conversion was made to the later 'long-nosed' Blenheim Mk IV bombers to turn them into Mk IVF fighters. Both these machines were stop-gaps, lacking the speed necessary for the assigned task.

The squadron experimented with all sorts of ideas for flying and fighting at night. It was then using Fairey Battles to drop flares close to enemy aircraft flying in the darkness in an effort to expose them for attack. So far this idea had not met with any success.

No. 29 Squadron also had its own single-seat fighter, Hawker Hurricane P3201, which the CO, S/Ldr Stanley Widdows, was using for night-fighting trials.[2] Anti-glare panels were bolted to the Hurricane's engine cowling just in front of the cockpit so the pilot's night vision would not be affected by flaring from the engine exhaust stacks.

Night defence was the Achilles' heel of both the RAF and the *Luftwaffe*. At this stage of the war, night bombers could wander almost at will over enemy territory without suffering the prohibitive losses that plagued attacks in daylight. The RAF had learnt this early in the war and so had the *Luftwaffe* during the Battle of Britain. The night blitz on London had started on 7/8 September 1940 and it was currently going on every night that the weather permitted.

Showing far more promise was 29 Squadron's first Bristol Beaufighter, recently received. S/Ldr Widdows flew it operationally for the first time on the 17th. Powered by two big Bristol Hercules radial engines and carrying an armament of four 20 mm cannons and six .303 machine guns, it had a maximum speed well over 300 mph, fast enough to catch any German bomber. A few more of these lethal, twin-engined machines were starting to arrive and they were equipped with the completely new, top-secret 'Magic Mirrors' – radar sets fitted inside the aircraft.

In parallel developments at the University of Birmingham, research teams under Professor Marcus Oliphant, formerly from Adelaide, had experimented with a special valve called a Klystron and also created a separate prototype 'Cavity Magnetron'. The latter device was switched on for the first time on 21 February 1940 – and it worked! In the long run it would lift radar technology out of the electronic Stone Age and give the Allies an almost unassailable lead in the field of airborne radar (AI radar). It was a vital new start, but before the magnetron could be used operationally a huge amount of developmental work had to be done. The challenge for the scientists and the RAF was to have something ready in time to combat a looming assault on Britain by night.

As the year advanced towards the crucial summer of 1940, discounting the experimental AI Mk I and AI Mk II sets, for practical purposes the RAF had two generations of AI radar coming on line, the AI Mk III and AI Mk IV. These were separated in development by weeks rather than years, yet they were dissimilar. AI Mk III was primitive and lacked reliability, but it was the first that could be supplied to the air force for the task ahead. RAF crews referred to the sets as 'Magic Mirrors', or the 'Magic Box', but the newly trained service operators were not finding them easy to use.

Apart for the aerials, the other AI Mk IV set had little in common with the older AI Mk III. AI Mk IV was the first airborne radar that gave results which were reliable in the hands of proficient operators. Initially following directions from a radar (RDF) operator on the ground, the night fighter pilot manoeuvred his plane into a position somewhere behind an enemy bomber so his airborne radar operator could locate it on his AI set. Provided the target was within a 40° cone ahead of the night fighter, its direction could be indicated unambiguously within 10°. The pilot then followed his operator's instructions to close in until he could see the enemy bomber and attack. The system was better, but it still had inherent shortcomings.

At the same time, other experiments were being carried out to keep the RAF bombers 'invisible' in the night skies over Germany, and this was where Dereck and his modified Hampden painted with matt black non-reflective paint became involved.

Because of bad weather conditions the tests dragged on for weeks and when we did fly the only time the fighters sighted us was when we turned on our navigation lights to help them. The non-reflective paint certainly was a success, but during daylight hours it absorbed so much solar heat that to work inside the plane became almost impossible.

One night when they were carrying out these tests at about 20,000 feet (6,100 m) – very high for a Hampden – a German air raid started at the same time as our fighter wireless set ceased to function, leaving us more or less lost over central England. The searchlight boys realised what had happened and came to our help and directed all searchlights in the mid-east of England to be pointed at their lowest setting – almost along the ground – directed towards Wittering. We were able to follow these to their focal point and land at the first aerodrome we saw. We did this and found that we were not at Wittering but at its satellite about 5 miles away. We were grateful to be down in one piece.

At this time Wittering was commanded by Group Captain Broadhurst, a magnificent character who kept a 'tame' Hurricane on the tarmac for his own use against intruding German aircraft. At a mess party one evening I met his wife, who in her pre-marriage days had been Miss French. She was a charmer.

Born on 28 October 1905 at Frimley in Surrey, Harry Broadhurst had joined the British Army at first and was commissioned as a 2nd lieutenant in the Royal Artillery. In 1926 he transferred to the RAF and served in India on the North-West Frontier where he received a Mention in Despatches. In January 1940, while commanding 111 Squadron, he was awarded a DFC for taking off alone in extremely bad weather to intercept and shoot down an enemy aircraft. During the Battle of Britain he flew sorties with 1 Squadron, thus qualifying for the clasp. After Wittering, he took command of RAF Hornchurch on 23 December 1940 where he was until May 1942. He was awarded the DSO & Bar, the citation for the latter crediting him with 12 enemy aircraft destroyed and 4 probables. For his actions during the Dieppe Raid of August 1942 he was awarded a Bar to the DFC. Posted to the Middle East as SASO to AOC Western Desert in late 1942, Broadhurst took over as AOC Allied Air Forces, Western Desert in 1943. He commanded 83 Group Allied Expeditionary Air Force in 1944–45. Harry Broadhurst retired from the RAF on 1 March 1961 as an Air Chief Marshal, after a distinguished career spanning thirty-five years. As well as his gallantry awards, he was a GCB (1960), KCB (1955), CB (1944), KBE (1945), Knight Grand Cross of the Order of Orange Nassau, and Legion of Merit (US).

Broadhurst was determined that as I flew only by night, I should be gainfully employed and kept out of mischief during the day and accordingly gave me the job as a guide to morbid tourists who I conducted through the fuselage of a German Junkers 88 bomber which had earlier been shot down by our fighter boys. The venue was in the market square of Stamford, a village near Wittering. The charge was sixpence per head per tour, the money going to a Spitfire fund. I was most impressed with the layout, the engineering and the finish of the Ju88 and thought it to be superior to any of our equivalent bombers of that time, both in finish and engineering design.

In retrospect, the fighter pilots appeared to be an immature lot when compared with our chaps who had been quietly subdued by long, painstaking trips and continuous, steady casualties. On completion of operational bombing tours some of our pilots were given a rest and a change in fighters, but those that I knew to take this course were soon killed. Mike Homer was one to die like this.

While engaged on this searchlight co-operation work I worked closely with No. 29 Squadron, the Blenheim night fighters involved, and at the end of the exercise I was offered a job with them as a flight commander. One reason for this offer was that up to that time, Bomber Command crews had destroyed more enemy aircraft, at night, over England than the RAF night fighters and it had been suggested that a few experienced bomber pilots joining the night fighters might change this situation. I declined the offer as I did not wish to become part of No. 12 Group commanded by AVM Leigh-Mallory. The job was eventually taken by Guy Gibson when he was on rest after his first tour on Hampdens.

On 8 November, Dereck received a startling order.

While at Wittering I received a signal ordering me to report to Air Vice Marshal Harris, the AOC of No. 5 Group at Grantham. Harris later commanded Bomber Command. When I received this order I shuddered and wondered what misdemeanour I was being asked to explain. Until then, neither I nor any of my fellow pilots of similar humble rank had ever seen him. I flew to Grantham. I was ushered into his office, and without delay was questioned about a long-drawn-out affair which had taken place earlier in the war at Waddington, when the then station commander, G/Capt Anderson, had caused near mutiny among the operational aircrew by putting undue pressure on them.

On most operational bombing stations at that time there was an almost regular sequence of events leading up to the actual operation. Normally, crews were detailed for operations by at least midday and would have carried out any required flight tests by then. Later in the day they would attend briefing and wait around for take-off. Should the weather forecasts deteriorate greatly, all ops would be cancelled, 'scrubbed', and all crews would be stood down at once and go to fill in the night as they wished, be it at the pictures or pubs, or with their popsies, or whatever.

When G/Capt Anderson was in charge, if the weather deteriorated, he stood crews down, one by one, in order of their order of take-off, hoping that there might be an improvement in the weather. With this system some crews stood by anxiously most of the night. The crews hated the system, their morale suffered and their love lives were disorganised. Things became tense.

Another matter concerning morale which Harris discussed was the case of a friend of mine, F/Lt Smythe DFC, who was on rest from operations at Waddington during this period, carrying out the duties of station navigation officer. Although he was on rest from ops, he was approached by Anderson one day and urged to fly on a particular sortie for which he was promised he would receive a Bar to his DFC. He flew, and was killed.

F/Lt Thomas Laidlaw Smythe DFC of 44 Squadron failed to return on the night of 11/12 September 1940. His aircraft was Hampden P1338. This was a special mission to Bremerhaven to bomb the German ocean liners *Bremen* and *Europa* in order to prevent the Nazis from using them as troop transports during the anticipated invasion of England. Smythe and his crew, P/O Stanley Wise, Sgt William Jones and F/O Wilfred Coombes, are all buried in Becklingen War Cemetery at Soltau.

The affair would have been forgotten had Smythe's father not been among the top brass of the Army and kept asking questions. As nearly all the other pilots who had been around when this happened were either dead or were POWs in Germany, AVM Harris wanted my version of the affair. I told him the little I knew of it.

Harris then asked me what I was doing just then and what I would like to do. In reply I said that I had heard rumours of a squadron being formed with a new type of bomber aircraft and that I should like to be in it. He made no comment, but picked up his phone and spoke to someone or other saying, 'French will be joining 207 tomorrow.'

I flew back to Wittering, in a dream, calling at Waddington on the way (207 Squadron was being formed there) to arrange accommodation and other details concerning the posting.

Dereck was moving on again, but this time he was happy about going...

11

Manchesters – 207 Squadron

The first British aircraft to have the name 'Manchester' was the A. V. Roe and Co. Ltd (Avro) Type 533 in 1918. It was a twin-engined biplane bomber built at Avro's factory near Southampton. Two prototypes were produced but because of problems with the intended two ABC Dragonfly engines, the first machine, F3492, had to have a pair of 300hp (223kW) Siddeley Puma high-compression water-cooled engines. This first flew in December 1918 as the Avro 533A Manchester Mk II. It was not until late in 1919 that the troublesome Dragonfly engines were finally installed in the other prototype, numbered F3493, and it flew for the first time as the Manchester Mk I. It was too late. By the time the manufacturer's and service trials had been completed, the Air Ministry's interest in the Avro 533 Manchester had lapsed. By then the need for a new bomber had evaporated. The Great War was over. Only three were built.

Two decades later, the prototype of a new Manchester, the Avro Type 679 (aircraft L7246), flew for the first time on 25 July 1939. It took off from Ringway airfield in Cheshire, south of Manchester city.[1] The genesis of the new bomber can be traced back to reports in 1936 that Germany's newly revealed air force was being rapidly expanded into a potent war machine. As part of its response, Britain's Air Ministry issued Specification P.13/36 asking for the submission of designs for a twin-engine tactical medium bomber, an all-metal monoplane more powerful than the Armstrong Whitworth Whitley, Vickers Wellington and Handley Page Hampden about to enter RAF service.

History was about to repeat itself. The new aircraft that emerged was the combination of a completely new airframe with equally new, underdeveloped engines. Just as the first Manchester had been plagued with problems, so too would the new machine, particularly with engine problems...

My move to Waddington was like returning home as I had been stationed there most of the time since my first squadron posting in 1938. I knew most of the permanent RAF chaps there as well as the best 'watering holes' in and around Lincoln.

No. 207 Squadron was unique in that at its formation all the pilots, with the exception of Wing Commander 'Hetty' Hyde, the most senior test pilot in the RAF, had completed a tour of operations. Most of them had been decorated and were keen types looking forward to operating in a new type of aircraft, capable of carrying more than three times the bomb load of the Hampden, over the same distance, at a greater speed, with an equal ceiling, with more firepower in defence and very much improved aircrew comfort. At that time, morale in No. 207 Squadron was higher than in any other unit with which I served. There was a great rapport between the CO and the rest of us. He respected our operational experience and we envied and admired his great flying experience and skill.

Late in August, Noel 'Hetty' Hyde was already stationed at Waddington flying Hampdens on operations with 44 Squadron, when he had been sent for by AVM Harris at No. 5 Group Headquarters. The AOC informed Hyde that he had been chosen to reform No. 207 Squadron with the new Manchester. This former Fairey Battle squadron had remained in the UK when the other Battle squadrons had been deployed to France and been absorbed into No. 12 Operational Conversion Unit (OTU). To learn everything he could about the new bomber, Hyde promptly went on attachment to the Aeroplane & Armament Experimental Establishment (A&AEE) at Boscombe Down in Wiltshire. He began familiarisation flying the first production aircraft, L7276, on 1 September 1940.

To build his new command, Hyde was on the lookout for experienced aircraft captains capable of bringing the new machine up to operational status. He was fortunate that a number of pre-war pilots like Dereck were reaching the end of their first tours on Hampdens. His first enrolment was an Australian who had been in his flight in 44 Squadron, Johnnie Siebert, who had been recommended for a DFC. Early in September, he and Siebert and their crews began handling trials using the second Manchester prototype, L7247, assisted by Rolls-Royce engineers and flight personnel from the Avro Company.

No. 207 Squadron was officially reformed at Waddington on the first day of November, and on the 6th its first aircraft, Manchester L7279, was collected from No. 6 Maintenance Unit (MU) at Brize Norton and flown to Boscombe Down. On the 8th, Hetty Hyde, Charles Kydd and the engineering officer flew the aircraft to Waddington for the first time where they were joined by all the squadron's allocated personnel, around seventy-five airmen of all trades. Almost as if to greet the arrivals, a German intruder bombed Waddington that night but the Manchester was not damaged.

The nature of the air war was changing. In daylight, the *Luftwaffe* had been fought to a standstill by Fighter Command's Hurricanes and Spitfires in the Battle of Britain without achieving air supremacy before the onset of winter. The threat of a German invasion of southern England in 1940 had diminished. German bombers, like their RAF counterparts, now mainly operated after dark as the nights lengthened.

For the RAF, bombing of the invasion barges and ports across the Channel was less of a priority, particularly when photographic reconnaissance revealed the barges were dispersing. Bomber Command could extend its effort to targets in Germany again. As a countermeasure, the *Luftwaffe* set up a special unit, *I/NJG2*, with intruder aircraft instructed to lurk in the darkness over Lincolnshire and Yorkshire hoping to spot and bomb the RAF bases as the bombers returned and landed. However, Britain's night defences were improving too. On 8/9 November 1940, a German bomber, Dornier Do17Z Nr.2817/R4+HK of *2/NJG2*, was damaged over Lincolnshire by an RAF Beaufighter and returned to its base on one engine. Two of its crewmembers were injured. It is possible this may have been the aircraft that rained its bombs down on Waddington this night.

The squadron's second aircraft, Manchester L7278, was collected the same day that Dereck arrived. Dereck's diary entry for 10 November 1940 reads: 'To Waddington, Manchesters, F/Lt Siebert, S/Ldr Hyde, S/Ldr Kydd DSO DFC, F/Lt Burton-Gyles DFC.'

These diary entries indicate how quickly our lives changed. Our moves were activated long before any paperwork regarding postings was promulgated. Of those I met at 207 Squadron on 10/11/40, all had vanished from the scene within a few months. Siebert, I had been with at Point Cook in 1937. Others who turned up were F/O F. E. 'Frankie' Eustace DFC and F/O W. J. 'Mike' Lewis DFC plus more air and ground crews. Two days later, representatives from Rolls-Royce hurriedly arrived to carry out urgent modifications to the cooling systems of each Manchester. The company had discovered another problem.

The Manchester was, I believe, originally designed as a dive bomber by Roy Chadwick (later Sir Roy) of A. V. Roe, being powered by two Rolls-Royce 'Vulture' engines of 1,760 hp. The engines were unusual, each having twenty-four cylinders in the form of an 'X' – actually, it consisted of two V12 engines mounted one above the other, driving the one crankshaft.

It had very sturdy flaps, which when lowered before diving limited the maximum speed to about 250 mph, with great stability in the dive. One problem with it was that if the pilot reduced flap at any time the nose fell instead of rising as in most other aircraft. This characteristic could become an embarrassment if flap was reduced in a steep dive; when the dive became steeper.

The Manchester had not been completely tested by either A.V. Roe or the RAF test unit at Boscombe Downs so it was decided that the first twenty of them should be allotted to No. 207 Squadron for further testing and to be used by the aircrew to train flying experience on the type as they brought the squadron to operational readiness. The twenty aircraft mentioned had various deficiencies, such as no engine-driven air compressors (required to keep the air pressure in the braking system at the correct level) and no cabin heating. We overcame the first of these problems by topping up the air pressure in the brake air bottles after every two landings and the second by the use of electrically heated flying suits.

It was noted in the squadron's Operations Record Book on the 20th that little flying had been accomplished due to the need to carry out the engine modifications. That situation changed the very next day. To test the new modifications, orders were received for L7278 and L7279 to be flown intensively until 500 hours had been achieved by both aircraft.

Dereck took part in the programme, but his log book entry for 24 November shows that there were risks: 'Manchester L7279, F/O Siebert, two crew. Waddington – Trowbridge – Shrewsbury – Gainsborough – North Allerton – Waddington – Hit by A.A. 3 hours 10 mins.'

On this trip we descended through cloud and happened to be over Linton on Ouse RAF station, where an air raid was in progress. The Manchester was, at that time, still on the secret list and the local anti-aircraft boys had no knowledge of it. They saw us and turned all guns onto us, putting a hole through one of our wings. My second pilot, F/O Johnnie Siebert (ex-Point Cook, 1937), normally a very steady, slow-moving type, moved with the speed of light, grabbed a Verey pistol, loaded it with the recognition colour cartridge of the day and fired it. We headed for home.

Bob Kirby wrote about this incident in his outstanding book on the Avro Manchester:

Flying Officer Siebert, Flight Lieutenant French and crew were ... briefed to carry out an endurance test in L7279. The test required them to fly at ceiling height of approximately 17,000 feet (5,200 m) between turning points at Waddington, Trowbridge, Shrewsbury, Gainsborough and Northallerton in Yorkshire. The crew was supplemented by two army officers. After almost three hours of monotonous flying, with fuel running low at the end of the northern leg, French decided to terminate the test, break cloud and return to Waddington. Everything was calm on board, the wireless operator and one of the army officers were playing noughts and crosses, when they had the misfortune to emerge directly over Linton-on-Ouse airfield, where a German air raid was in progress. They immediately came under intense antiaircraft fire from the airfield defences and by a rare chance one of the first shells burst close-by, tearing off part of the wing tip.

Feverish activity ensued whilst evasive action was taken and Siebert fired off a volley of colours of the day, accompanied by unprintable remarks regarding the aircraft recognition capabilities of the anti-aircraft crews. Various suggestions were made including landing and taking issue with the belligerents, but good sense prevailed and the aircraft returned safely to Waddington.[2]

A correspondence file was opened to cover the incident and to establish whether the fault lay with the trigger-happy anti-aircraft gunners or ourselves. All was forgotten when the squadron became operational and more urgent affairs were to hand.

Dereck was involved in another potentially lethal incident on 19 December. His log book noted: 'Manchester L7280, F/O Burton-Gyles, 3 crew, Local, Port engine on fire, 10 mins.'

This was a short, unpleasant trip. When on take-off, the hydraulic pipe operating the engine radiator flaps burst, spurting oil over the exhaust pipe. The engine caught fire. The shortest possible circuit and landing was made and the fire was extinguished on the tarmac. Engines were liquid cooled. The extensive use of hydraulic power in the Manchester to operate flaps, bomb doors, radiator flaps, etc., proved to be a weakness.

To iron out some of the problems of the aircraft, particularly as regards the engines, we received instructions to fly them at take-off revs (3,000-plus rpm) from ground level to 15,000 feet (4,500 m) on a fixed course from Debden to Catterick until a weakness appeared. Sometimes pistons came through the cylinder walls, but the main trouble was with the bearings, which broke down. I was told that this problem was eventually corrected by fitting silver bearings!

Rolls-Royce investigations focused on two particular areas: the suitability of the metal alloy out of which the bearings were machined, and the oil system in the aircraft. With regard to the metal alloy, the original 1 per cent tin lead-bronze bearings tended to break up, a problem which was made worse by the other problems of low oil-pressure. These standard bearings were at first replaced by 0.5 per cent silver lead-bronze bearings, which did not prove much better. Rolls-Royce metallurgists instigated a research programme to find a better alternative. Eventually they developed an LA4 type material containing 4 per cent silver alloyed with lead-bronze. At the same time as using the new LA4 alloy, in order to increase oil pressure in the region the engine bearings were turned slightly undersize, reducing the gap between bearing and crankshaft.

Waddington was visited by numerous VIPs in January, including royalty.

On 27 January 1941, we were visited by the king and queen with their escorts. They arrived by road, had lunch and invested a number of our chaps with decorations. On this particular day the weather was terrible, cloud to ground level and no one flying. It appeared, however, that the German intelligence had some knowledge of the royal visit and sent a bomber to seek them out. This aircraft was located at Grantham where it was shot down by our fighters. How the RAF fighters managed to find it in such bad weather we could not imagine.

On 21 January 1941, the new AOC of 5 Group, Air Vice-Marshal Bottomley, had visited Waddington to discuss the likelihood of 207 Squadron undertaking restricted flying operations. New Manchesters were arriving regularly from various maintenance units during this period and six crews began to prepare. The AOC was informed that the squadron would try to have four aircraft and crews fit for operations on 14 February.

The Manchester with its size and roominess had the advantage over the Hampden, in that pilots could be given a simple form of dual instruction before going off as first pilot; all new pilots went through this form of introduction to the type.

One sergeant pilot (Sgt Frost) who had already completed a tour of operations was posted to us, but he had already made up his mind that he did not wish to do another tour. I demonstrated the aircraft to him, showed him the handling drill for take-off and landing and then stood beside him as he took the controls and took off for a circuit. He got off without incident and came around on the approach run to land but he came in too high and too fast, touching down much too far along the runway. I could do nothing but grin and pray as we used up what little was left of the runway. We hit the aerodrome boundary fence, went across a friendly paddock, through another fence and so on, heading for Lincoln, until some soft earth pulled us up. He proved his point and was I believe posted elsewhere.

The behaviour of this sergeant pilot and his attitude towards doing a second tour of operations is a classic case of an aircrew member who thought 'enough is enough'. During any operational tour many aircrew fell by the wayside as it progressed; some had nagging wives and families in the background, some remembered too clearly the loss of their friends, some had too great a fear of AA fire and operations in general and let their imagination take over and refused to fly further missions.

These were, I believe, fine chaps who had been tried beyond their capacity to face any more combat flying. They were, rightly so (judged by the war atmosphere of the time), treated harshly by the RAF authorities, who feared that LMF (Lack of Moral Fibre) would spread like wildfire through the aircrew ranks. They had the victims whisked away to join 2,000 other similarly diagnosed cases held in confinement at Sheffield.[3] I believe that individuals have varying but finite amounts of courage to see them through life and when their particular allotment of courage is expended they opt out of the stressful situation they might be in and so escape.

In our bomber group at the time we used the expression, 'The higher the fewer', referring to crews who bombed from the maximum height possible, usually above effective AA fire, ensuring a greater chance of their survival, but at the cost of reduced bombing accuracy.

Motivation of aircrew is a subject seldom discussed by writers of events in Bomber Command, leaving one to assume that the one word 'patriotism' covered it. *Odd* chaps joined aircrew for purely patriotic reasons (love of country – my people are being attacked so I shall defend them). They were very few. Most were victims of the notion: 'My neighbour is aircrew; I shall become aircrew.' I cannot recall any aircrew who had not volunteered for the post.

The colonials, all from the British dominions, were classified as such. They were different in that most of them, primarily, had a love of adventure and service life was a means of achieving this. They would seldom admit to this as being their reason for enlisting but would give the usual excuse: love of country; defence of the Empire; and defence of their homes. Many English people were of the opinion that colonials in the services were mercenaries!

As it turned out, the six Manchesters were not needed on 14 February so the crews carried out night cross-country training the next day. On the same day more experienced pilots arrived at Waddington posted in after a spell as instructors at No. 16 OTU at Upper Heyford. They were P/Os W. G. Gardiner DFC and W. S. Herring DFM (known universally as 'Kippers') and F/O G. R. Taylor DFC.

For Dereck personally it meant reunions with George Gardiner and Dick Taylor, who were both formerly in 50 Squadron. It was George Gardiner who back in April 1940 had hauled the critically injured Duncan Good from the pilot's seat of the badly damaged Hampden and flown it back home, and fellow Australian Dickie Taylor had finished his first tour the following September, just ahead of Dereck.

It was on the night of 24/25 February 1941 that 207 Squadron flew its first operation, and it turned out to be unforgettable. Bomber Command was briefed to attack a 'Hipper' class cruiser known to be tied up in the port of Brest. Some thirty Wellingtons from 3 Group, twenty-five Handley Page Hampdens, six Manchesters from 5 Group and some Coastal Command aircraft were involved. When the night arrived, excitement ran high. A number of high-ranking officers from 5 Group and distinguished guests from the Avro and Rolls-Royce companies were invited to witness the operational debut of their new type. The aircraft were mainly from the original batch delivered to the squadron and they lacked their mid-upper gun turrets. Bomb loads consisted of twelve 500-lb (227-kg) semi-armour-piercing bombs, except for one aircraft, Manchester L7300, which for some reason only carried eleven. It was a bad night with poor visibility, scattered storms and snow on the ground – and the snow was still falling. The aircraft took off at closely spaced intervals between 6.35 and 6.50 p.m. and set course individually for the target area.

Besides Dereck and his crew, the other crews that had been ready for the mission were those of S/Ldr Leader Charles Kydd, and F/Os Johnnie Siebert, Peter Burton-Gyles, Frankie Eustace and 'Mike' Lewis. However, W/Cdr 'Hetty' Hyde was determined not to miss this first operation but as he did not have a crew of his own he decided to 'poach' Dereck's crew for the occasion. He was leaving a dejected flight lieutenant behind. Adding to Dereck's chagrin, he was given another job to do. But it was important.

No. 207 Squadron eventually became operational and attacked the naval base at Brest on 24/2/41. I did not fly on this trip. Wing Commander Hyde borrowed my aircraft and crew for the night while I stayed behind to play host to Roy Chadwick (later Sir Roy Chadwick), the designer of the Anson, the Manchester and the Lancaster. The night was a bad one with poor visibility, storms, snow on the deck and still falling.

All of the aircraft returned on schedule and without any trouble except for one piloted by F/O Burton-Gyles which returned late with hydraulic trouble. He had been able to lower only one wheel and could not alter the situation. Eventually he spoke to Roy Chadwick by TR9 (voice radio). Roy told him 'do this and try that'. Burton-Gyles (BG) tried all of the recommended ideas but the wheels did not move.

He was then told to do a normal approach and land on one wheel. BG did as he was instructed and lowered the aircraft onto the snow-covered runway. It touched down and quietly came to rest facing across the runway. Damage was done to the bomb doors, a wing tip and a propeller tip but the plane was back on operational flying within six weeks – all thanks to the robust design and construction of the aircraft and the superb flying skill of Burton-Gyles. He was killed later...

Two nights later, Dereck at last began operating in Manchesters himself. His log book noted: 'Ops 1A, 26/2/41, Manchester L7300, F/O Morgan, P/O Reid DFC, Sgt Buck, Sgt Hedges, Sgt Budden, Bombing Cologne, 6,000 lbs, 11,000 feet, 4 hours 40 minutes.'

That night, 126 aircraft were sent to bomb industrial targets in Cologne. At this stage of the war, accurate navigation in the dark was still a major problem facing RAF bomber crews and only 106 aircraft crews reported finding the target, which they bombed, causing large fires. Apparently, according to German records, only ten high-explosive bombs and ninety incendiaries fell on the western edge of the city and others fell in three village areas to the west. Although Dereck wrote in his diary that he'd had a 'good night', two of the five Manchesters from 207 Squadron suffered equipment failure and returned early. One machine developed a serious hydraulic failure within an hour of take-off. After the bombs were jettisoned into the North Sea, it returned to Waddington where it carried out a safe landing at 9.10 p.m.

Close to the enemy coast, the other aircraft experienced a serious drop in oil pressure in the port engine. The unreliability of the Vulture engines was well known by now, and Manchesters had been proven unable to maintain height on one engine, even when lightly loaded. With good reason, the pilot diverted to Flushing and dropped his bombs there before returning safely to Waddington at 10.10 p.m.

Dereck had been the commander of 207 Squadron's 'B' Flight since January but on 27 February he lost his flight when it was officially transferred on paper to provide a nucleus of trained crews for the newly re-established No. 97 Squadron. In theory, the new unit had three Manchesters available for operations, three more in the maintenance hangar having their bomb compartments modified by Avro technicians, and two others dispersed awaiting modifications. In fact, all the aircraft lacked many of their essential refinements so the squadron would not be ready to operate for another month. Meanwhile, fresh crews that required training were coming to Waddington for the new squadron and for Dereck to form a new 'B' Flight.

March: Australians still featured among the aircrew. I wrote in a letter home dated 1 March 1941: 'The five first pilots in this flight comprise three Aussies, one Canadian and one Pommy. Rather good I think'; and four days later, 'This flight should make a good showing someday.' After a year of operations, I should have known better than to make forecasts of this nature as within a few weeks I was posted to 97 Squadron, the second Manchester squadron, and the others were reported 'missing' or 'killed'.

On the 2nd, Waddington had a visitor.

This was a visit to inspect No. 207 Squadron by the new AOC of No. 5 Group, AVM Bottomley who had succeeded AVM Harris on Harris's promotion to Deputy Head of Air Staff. Bottomley arrived shortly after I had become a flight commander with the squadron. During the inspection, as we trailed along behind him through one of our hangars, he asked me what a strange-looking piece of equipment – something like a stove – was used for. I admitted I did not have a clue and then he exploded saying I should not be a flight commander unless I knew the purpose of every piece of equipment in my charge. A few weeks later I was posted to join 97 Squadron at Coningsby. I have an idea that Bottomley had little empathy with Colonials…

Dereck's next trip was on the night of 3/4 March, another mission targeting Brest. It did not go very well and led to an angry clash with Waddington's station commander. Dereck and his crew (F/O Morgan, Sgt Brown DFM, Sgt Buck and Sgt Budden) were flying Manchester L7302/EM-R, and carrying a 6,000-lb (2,700-kg) bomb load.

The weather in the target area was particularly bad, a series of violent thunderstorms with much lightning. My Flying Log Book records that we flew for 3 hours on instruments during the 5 hours and 45 minutes and on one occasion were struck by lightning. The Manchester carried, mounted on the inside of the fuselage, a device called IFF (Identification Friend and Foe). This transmitted an identification signal which told our home defence units our friendly nature, and was still on the secret list. I do not know why it remained secret as the enemy had surely salvaged many of them during 1940. On one occasion, a Hampden from 50 Squadron, pilot P/O Wawn (Australian), got into trouble in bad weather over Germany, causing his Gyro compass to go out of control and spin. When he reset it he apparently did so to read a 180° in error, so that instead of heading for England as he intended, he was heading east, further into Germany. I think this type of error was very possible under the conditions at the time, particularly for a pilot reared in the southern hemisphere.

He finally landed at Würms (Germany) thinking he was somewhere in Scotland. We heard about it the following night when Lord Haw Haw broadcast the arrival of four more POWs and a complete Hampden with all its secrets including an IFF set. To ensure the security of the IFF set in the event of a forced landing in enemy territory, it was fitted with a small Thermite bomb which could be exploded by pressing the appropriate button. On this night over Brest lightning struck the aircraft's fuselage near our IFF set and exploded the bomb. This destroyed the set, leaving a jagged hole in the side of the plane and a small heap of molten metal on the floor.

The search for the target being fruitless, I decided we had a better chance of getting back to base without a bomb load so I dropped them and headed for Waddington. Next day I was carpeted by the station commander and abused for what he described as 'throwing away bombs to the value of my annual salary.' I said, 'Sorry, but I brought a most valuable aircraft home safely to base in terrible weather conditions.'

Only two Manchesters had taken off for the mission, the other being captained by Peter 'BG' Burton-Gyles, who in fact let his second pilot, Sgt Les Syrett, fly the entire sortie. Unable to find the target because of the poor weather, they had returned with their bombs. The station commander, who undoubtedly noted BG's return *with bombs* and had been frustrated so often recently over having good bombs 'wasted', completely overlooked the fact that, unlike BG's aircraft, Dereck's plane had also been damaged to an unknown degree when it was struck by lightning in the thunderstorm. Bob Kirby agreed with Dereck's assessment:

> By this time an experienced pilot with approaching 1,000 hours flying and a tour on Hampdens behind him, French was equipped to make the decision to jettison the bombs in the interests of saving the aircraft and its crew. He was accordingly outraged to be 'carpeted' next morning by an insensitive station commander ... French could hardly believe his ears. Incredulously, he tried to explain that in terrible weather, jettisoning the

bombs had possibly made the difference between saving and losing the aircraft. He rapidly recognised that reason and commonsense was not one of that officer's strong points.[4]

No. 207 Squadron bombed Hamburg with four aircraft on the night of 12/13 March and this time everything went without a hitch. It was Dereck's third Manchester mission. Ominously, German intruders were active over England throughout the night, two Blenheims and a Wellington being attacked and damaged but all landed safely. As the weather continued to be favourable, Bomber Command went back to Hamburg the very next night. No. 207 Squadron provided five Manchesters including three crews who operated again for the second night. These were Dereck, Charles Kydd and F/Sgt Frank Harwood. They were joined by Hetty Hyde (with 'borrowed' crew) and F/O Hugh Matthews and his crew.

Four aircraft took off safely, but the fifth, Manchester L7313/EM-C, with Hugh Matthews at the controls, burst the tyre of its tail wheel while taxying. It was decided to replace the tail wheel out on the aerodrome, a task which took about 30 minutes. Matthews then restarted the engines and taxied to the take-off point where he received a 'green to go' from the control truck's Aldis lamp.

Unknown to those on the ground, the activity on the flare-path had been detected by a lurking German intruder, a Junkers Ju88 patrolling over the Lincolnshire airfields.[5] There is little doubt that this was Junkers Ju88A 'R4+NL' of *I/NJG2* from Gilze-Rijen in Holland, crewed by *Feldwebel* Hans Hahn (pilot), *Unteroffizier* Ernst Meissler (wireless operator) and *Unteroffizier* Helmut Scheidt (engineer). An experienced intruder pilot, Hahn had claimed a Blenheim shot down near Leeming the previous night for his third victory. He was about to try for his fourth. Undetected, the Ju88 pilot timed his attack to coincide with the moment the bomber became airborne and was most vulnerable. Manchester L7313 was riddled with cannon and machine gun fire just after crossing the airfield boundary. The crew never had a chance. The crippled Manchester crashed at Whisby some 5 miles (8 km) west of Waddington and as flames consumed it on the ground, some of the bombs detonated. F/Sgts Joe Marsden and Bill Cox, the wireless operator, were thrown clear, but suffered multiple injuries. They were taken to Lincoln hospital but Marsden later died. Bill Cox survived with the loss of a leg. The rest of the crew perished outright. Hans Hahn would claim a total of 12 victories at night over England. His last occurred on 11 October 1941 when his aircraft collided in the dark with an Airspeed Oxford (AB767) over Grantham, Lincolnshire. All on board both aircraft were killed.

Meanwhile, as part of a force of 139 bombers, Dereck French and the other three Manchester crews attacked the Blohm und Voss shipyards at Hamburg in fine weather. The entire raid caused 119 fires, including one in a timber yard. Fifty-one people were killed and 139 injured, the heaviest casualty list for the city in one raid so far. The four Manchesters returned safely to Waddington but during that night Bomber Command also lost six other aircraft: two Wellingtons, two Whitleys, one Blenheim and a Hampden.

On 20 March 1941, 207 Squadron suffered its second Manchester loss, again on operations. The squadron provided three aircraft to join twenty-one Whitleys of No. 4 Group targeting the Lorient submarine base in France. The aircraft were Manchester L7278/EM-A flown by Frank Harwood and crew, L7302/EM-R flown by Dereck French and crew, and L7313/EM-C flown by Charles Kydd and crew.

A closely guarded secret at the time was that the squadron took two American observers on the operation. The US Navy servicemen attended the briefing and Commander McDonnell accompanied Charles Kydd whilst Lieutenant Commander Wannamaker flew in L7302 with Dereck. The reason for US Navy, rather than US Army Air Force personnel being involved may have been to do with the target. Both of the Americans flew in full US naval uniform.

This was an attack on the German submarine pens at Lorient (France) and was different to our usual operations in that, just prior to take off, I was asked by the new station commanding officer, Group Captain John Boothman (he had been one of the team of RAF pilots engaged in the Schneider Cup tests for the world speed record in the air in 1929), if I would mind taking along a passenger as an observer. I agreed and was surprised to find that my passenger was a Lieut. Commander Wannamaker of the United States forces.

He wore his American uniform, and I still wonder what might have happened had we been forced down in enemy-occupied territory as at that time the US was many months away from being officially involved in the war. His presence aboard an armed RAF bomber would have required a clever explanation. The trip was easy – just another operation. Wannamaker was good company and seemed to enjoy himself.

It was a dark and moonless night. Two aircraft dropped their bomb loads at the estimated time of arrival (ETA) over the target, unloading in two separate sticks through cloud from only 10,000 feet (3,000 m). On the second run over the target, Sgt Wells, the navigator in Dereck's aircraft, accidentally knocked off the fusing switches at the last moment before the second stick was released with the result that the remaining three bombs fell away safe.

Bob Kirby noted that 'since all the aircrew positions were occupied, Wannamaker, the US Navy observer in French's aircraft, had to stand for the whole flight other than on take-off and landing. Near the target he had tapped Wells on the shoulder and asked what the fireworks were. "Flak," came the reply. Following their safe return the American had remarked, "Good show", whether in relief at getting his feet safely back on the ground or in praise of the operation is uncertain.'[6]

Charlie Kydd brought his American back safely too but he and Dereck were shocked to learn that Frank Harwood had crashed. His Manchester had come down on fire in a heavily wooded area in Leicestershire, 5 miles north-west of Cottesmore. There were two survivors, the observer F/Sgt Roy Holland and the rear gunner Sgt Hallam, who returned to Waddington the next day.

The take-off of a heavily loaded Manchester was always a very tense affair. Harwood's machine had been painfully slow in gaining height. After only 30 minutes in flight there was a major drop in oil pressure on the port engine. Half a minute later the rough-running engine caught fire and failed. The aircraft began to rapidly lose height. Harwood ordered the crew to bail out as he struggled to hold the machine steady. Four had jumped but two, Sgts Norman Birch and Bill Aitken, had not been able to open their parachutes in time before being killed hitting the ground. Both Frank Harwood and the wireless operator, Sgt Ben Hogg, who had remained behind to try and help Harwood carry out a forced landing, died in the crash.

Examination of the crash site revealed that the port engine had been flung clear on impact. It had two holes in the crankcase where broken con-rods had punched through. Subsequent investigation showed that this engine's failure had been cause by the break-up of the 0.5 per cent silver lead-bronze main engine bearing.

No. 207 lost its third Manchester on operations during the night of 27/28 March, and a day later Dereck had to write in his diary: '29/3/41. Waddo – Johnnie Siebert missing.' The squadron had been called upon to provide four aircraft in a force of thirty-nine aircraft to bomb Dusseldorf. Dereck did not fly on this mission. The four crews were those of S/Ldr Charles Kydd in Manchester L7311/EM-F; F/O Dave Romans in L7302/EM-R; F/Lt John Siebert in L7303/EM-P; and F/O 'Pappy' Paape in L7318/EM-K.

Soon after take-off 'Pappy' Paape experienced a major drop in oil pressure in one engine and, conscious of what had happened to Frank Harwood and his crew, turned back. He landed back at Waddington before the engine failed. Charlie Kydd and Dave Romans found and bombed Dusseldorf without difficulty. Johnnie Siebert bombed the target at around 10.30 p.m. but encountered concentrated flak. The concussion from one shell burst jolted the Manchester's starboard wing upwards. After the shock everything seemed normal, but as they approached the searchlight belt over the Dutch border the starboard engine began to smoke and lose power. The Australian promptly feathered the propeller and the engine stopped. Within a few seconds the port engine started to lose power too.

Siebert called out that he could not hold the aircraft up any longer and the Manchester fell into a nose-down sideslip to port. At the same time it was attacked by an Me110 night fighter. There is little doubt that the Me110 was from *III/NJG1* stationed at Eindhoven, Holland, and piloted by *Oberfeldwebel* Herzog, who had earlier shot down a Whitley of 78 Squadron. In his combat report he mistakenly identified both the Whitley and the Manchester as Wellingtons. There is uncertainty as to whether or not his firing actually hit Siebert's aircraft, which was doomed anyway.

The Manchester crew bailed out and all of them but one survived, captured by the Germans. Johnnie Siebert was the last man to jump. His body was found the next day. It was in a depression which indicated a heavy impact with the ground. His parachute was unopened. It is possible that he was too low and did not have time pull the ripcord or he may have been hit by the viciously sideslipping bomber.

Dereck knew nothing of Siebert's fate until years later when Bob Kirby contacted him while researching for the book he was writing about the Manchester. Kirby wrote:

> I have, of course, got the full story of how Johnnie Siebert lost his life, from his W/Op Jim Taylor. Johnnie was apparently the first Allied airman to lose his life in that part of Holland and the locals used his grave to demonstrate their defiance of the Germans in a small way by keeping fresh flowers on it during the war. After the war the tradition has been maintained and although there are many graves at the cemetery at Eindhoven, Johnnie's is the one they salute on what must be their equivalent of Remembrance Day, apparently during March or April.[7]

After carrying out night-flying tests on the afternoon of 30 March, No. 207 Squadron had four aircraft ready for another attack on the *Scharnhorst* and *Gneisenau* at Brest, a five-hour trip there and back. All the aircraft located the target, where two sticks each of six 500 lb (227 kg) SAP bombs were dropped from heights ranging from 15,000 to 9,500 feet (4,570–2,900 m). The four crews chosen were those of F/Lt Dereck French in Manchester L7302/EM-R; F/O Dave Romans in L7319/EM-X; F/O 'Pappy' Paape in L7309/EM-J; and P/O George Gardiner in L7311/EM-F.

For once everything went without difficulty. Dereck, Dave Romans and George Gardiner claimed that their bombs hit the dock while 'Pappy' Paape and his crew were unable to observe the results of their attack. All returned safely, although Paape's aircraft was nearly attacked by a British night fighter over Lincolnshire. Paape and his crew were completely unaware of the threat and it was only at the last moment that the Beaufighter pilot recognised the Manchester and turned away.

This was Dereck's last operation with 207 Squadron. He was posted to join 97 Squadron, the newly formed second Manchester squadron that had transferred across to Coningsby a couple of weeks earlier...

12

Manchesters – 97 Squadron

No. 97 Squadron had been a bomber squadron during the First World War. It was formed at Waddington as an RFC training unit on 1 December 1917 before moving to Netheravon to become an operational squadron at the end of March 1918. On 1 April, the RFC and RNAS were combined to form the RAF and in July the squadron received Handley Page 0/400 bombers prior to moving to France. There it joined the Independent Force which was employed in the strategic bombing of targets in Germany, a role it retained until the November Armistice. It returned to Britain in March 1919 and re-equipped with D.H.10s before leaving for India in July. There, on 1 April the following year, it was renumbered to become 60 Squadron.

No. 97 reformed at Catfoss on 16 September 1935 as a night bomber squadron equipped with Handley Page Heyfords. On 7 June 1938 it became a training squadron. It converted to Whitleys in February 1939, but on the outbreak of hostilities in September it moved to Abingdon, still as a training squadron. Redesignated to become No. 10 OTU on 6 April 1940, it began to reform again at the beginning of May, but three weeks later it was disbanded again before receiving any aircraft.

On 25 February 1941, a new No. 97 Squadron began to reform at Waddington from a nucleus of personnel and Manchesters drafted from 207 Squadron. It transferred from Waddington east-southeast towards Boston to Coningsby on 15 March. Coningsby, located at the edge of the Lincolnshire Fens, was a brand-new airfield. Its construction had started late in 1937 as part of the RAF's urgent pre-war expansion programme, but it took four years to complete because of frequent drainage problems. The very first unit to take up residence was 106 Squadron with Hampdens which arrived on 23 February 1941. It began operations from there on the night of 1/2 March when five of its aircraft took part in a raid on Hamburg without loss.

A fortnight later, 97 Squadron arrived with its Manchesters. After settling in, 97's crews flew their first Manchester operation from Coningsby on 8/9 April. Dereck French was flying the seventh operation of his second tour, but that very same evening his former crew, who had remained in 207 Squadron at Waddington, failed to return. The target was Kiel, which was being attacked for the second night in a row.

The previous night, 229 aircraft had staged the largest raid on a single target in the war to date. It was a bright moonlit evening and widespread damage was caused to naval installations, factories and civilian homes. Two eastern dockyard areas responsible for manufacturing U-boats were heavily damaged. Both yards were temporarily put out of action and a fire in a naval armaments depot lasted for two days. Eighty-eight people were reported killed and 184 injured. Two Wellingtons and two Whitleys were lost.

The following 8/9 April attack on Kiel was by 160 aircraft which included twelve Manchesters from 207 and 97 Squadrons. Four aircraft were lost – two Wellingtons, one Hampden, and one Manchester – but nine other aircraft crashed in England. This raid inflicted more damage on the town than the docks. Buildings struck included a bank, a museum, an engineering college and the gasworks. Gas and electricity were cut off and the water supply in some areas failed. Casualties were believed to be the heaviest of the war so far in a German city, with 125 people killed and 300 injured. About 8,000 civilians and 300 naval personnel were bombed out and large numbers of civilians resolved it was better to leave the city by any means possible, including on foot. These two consecutive raids on Kiel were probably the most successful of the war on any target to date.

Dereck did not comment on his own experiences during this raid, just noting it in his log book as flying Manchester L7308 with as crew Sgts Hudson, Currie, Pendrill, Williams and Stanley, but he did record later: 'This was the same raid on which my old crew from No. 207 with W/Cdr Hyde were shot down.'

Hetty Hyde had with him F/O H. T. Morgan (second pilot), and Sgt John Wells DFM (observer), Sgt W. Buck (wireless operator), Sgt D. Budden (second wireless operator/air gunner), and Sgt L. 'Lofty' Hedges (rear gunner). Manchester L7302/EM-R had no mid-positioned turret so Sgt Budden occupied the front turret. As they began their bombing run over Kiel, they were suddenly illuminated by a cone of searchlights and pounded by flak. Hyde took desperate evasive action but, blinded by the searchlights and unable to identify the target, he called for the bomb aimer to jettison the bombs. That done, he pushed the Manchester's nose down and dived out of range of the lights into the protective darkness. They were on the way home halfway across the narrow neck of Schleswig south of Flensburg when they realised the starboard engine was glowing red hot. It burst into flames and the fire was soon streaming back fifty yards behind the wing's trailing edge and spreading out of control towards the starboard wing tank. Hyde had no choice but to order the crew to bail out.

They were shot down and became prisoners of war. Hyde, being Hyde, did the right thing and escaped three or four times before finally making a successful attempt, via Sweden, to Britain. Hugh Morgan had been my second pilot on Manchesters while I was with No. 207 Squadron, and a very good one. Pre-war he had been an undergraduate at Cambridge. He too became a POW, completing his university studies after the war and becoming a British Consul with the Foreign Office. He was a super type.

Two nights later, on 10/11 April, the primary target for thirty-six Wellingtons, twelve Blenheims and five Manchesters was Brest. The five Manchesters were all from 97 Squadron. Dereck was at the controls of aircraft L7992 and this was the squadron's second Manchester operation. All five aircraft reached the target but Dereck wrote in his diary when he returned after his flight of 6 hours and 10 minutes that it was a 'filthy trip – w/t u/s'. Nevertheless, good bombing results were widely reported and it was established later that four bombs actually hit the *Gneisenau*, which had also been damaged a short time before by a torpedo bomber from Coastal Command. There were 140 German casualties during the raid, fifty killed and ninety injured. One Wellington was lost.

There was nearly a Manchester casualty as well. Shortly after 0200 hours as F/Lt J. Sherwood approached to land back at Coningsby his aircraft was attacked by a German intruder. The initial attack was wide of the target and, reacting quickly, Sherwood raised his flaps and undercarriage and took evasive action. He was diverted to orbit a nearby beacon until the danger had passed when he returned to land undamaged. It had been a close escape. Next day, machine gun and cannon shell cases were picked up all over the airfield. Dereck recalled the incident and how close it was.

Confusion often arose as to the identity of aircraft circuiting a drome at night. On one night at Coningsby, a German intruder followed one of our 97 Squadron Manchesters home to base and entered the aerodrome circuit and began firing at the Manchester it was following; putting some 113 holes in it; the empty 20 mm shells fell from the German aircraft landing on the aerodrome. Our Manchester landed safely; amazingly none of the crew were hit while the intruder escaped unscathed.

Soon after this incident, again at Coningsby, we were in the mess late one afternoon, having high tea when an air raid alert sounded. We ignored it until we heard the explosion of the first of a stick of bombs as they headed towards us from across the aerodrome. By the time the last bomb had fallen no one was to be seen; all having dived under tables or out of the windows. This sneak raid was carried out in full daylight; no damage was done to RAF personnel or aircraft but one of the first bombs to fall hit a farmhouse beyond the aerodrome boundary.

It was 207 Squadron's turn to operate on 12/13 April and this time it could only muster six aircraft for another attack on the German capital ships at Brest. Sixty-six aircraft were involved altogether: thirty-five Wellingtons, thirteen Whitleys, twelve Hampdens and 207 Squadron's six Manchesters. Because of poor weather conditions, only thirty-seven aircraft bombed Brest, the majority of the others choosing to bomb Lorient, the alternative target. The only compensation was there no RAF losses.

The Manchesters performed poorly because of a series of incidents. One returned to Waddington after only 30 minutes because of a hydraulic leak. Dense cloud cover over the Continent made locating the target difficult. Another crew gave up any hope of finding the target and returned to Waddington with the bomb load intact. As Dick Taylor made his bomb run over what was believed to be the general target area, a hydraulic failure caused the bombs to prematurely jettison on the approach. Two other crews dropped their bombs through the cloud cover and were unable to observe any result. Only one crew claimed to have carried out two visual attacks, their first bombs estimated to have straddled the *Gneisenau* and the others to have fallen 'somewhere' in the target area.

During the following day, the Air Ministry announced that forthwith all Manchesters would be grounded 'in view of the failure to resolve the extreme difficulties being experienced with the Rolls-Royce Vulture engines'.

The unusually high losses in the Manchester squadrons had been causing concern in the upper echelons of Bomber Command and the decision was made to ground them while attempts were made to solve the problems. This grounding really meant that we were off operations but carried out extensive test flights, height tests and high-level bombing practice. Some engines failed, the faults were corrected, yet on test the engines failed again and once more we were grounded. A diary entry sums it up: '18/5/41. "97th Foot" again.'

During this period I returned to Waddington to undergo a third Blind Approach Training Course, using Anson and Blenheim aircraft. The visit was a happy one in that I was returning to familiar faces and scenes, although while

I was there the aerodrome was bombed by an intruding German aircraft. The air raid sirens went and everyone took shelter in the slit trenches but F/Lt Petchel Burt (Waddington accounts officer) and I watched the show.

The German plane came in low over the drome, dropping a few bombs and then a land mine, all of which seemed to be aimed at the hangars. The bombs fell first, one of them falling directly on to a slit trench where a number of NAAFI girls were sheltering. Some of these were killed and were dug out the next day. The land mine drifted down on a parachute, missed the aerodrome and by chance struck the spire of the church in the nearby Waddington Village when it exploded, blasting the roofs off most of the nearby buildings and flattening some of the tombstones in the Church graveyard. The bomber had no opposition during his attack, the station defence personnel being either asleep or in their shelters.

A few minutes after the bombing another aircraft appeared following the same course and at the same height as the first; this second plane received full treatment from the AA and small arms fire on the aerodrome without being hit. This was fortunate as it turned out to be one of our own RAF fighters from Digby, which was being vectored along the track of the intruder.

Flying Log Book, 26/5/41. Manchester L7382. Sgts Pendrill, Currie, Ashmore, Williams, Wood. Test – 22,000 feet. No load. 2 hours 10 mins.

Flying Log Book, 28/5/41. Manchester. L7382. Sgts Pendrill, Ashmore, Currie, Wood, Williams and Mr. Chishoim. Test – 18,000 feet. 1 hour 35 mins.

These flights are revealing in that they form part of the extensive tests the Manchester was to undergo, and in this case show that the ceiling attained was a few thousand feet greater than we could achieve in a Hampden aircraft under similar conditions. The ceiling a loaded bomber could reach was at that time most important, as very often the top of the cloud layer over Germany was in the 15,000 to 16,000 feet range which was about the ceiling of the average laden Hampden, with the consequence that on the way to a target one could either stay low, below the cloud layer, and suffer anti-aircraft fire and searchlights or fly at the aircraft ceiling level and suffer icing conditions, tiresome instrument flying and sluggish controls. An aircraft that could carry a 7,000 lb bomb load above the critical 15,000 to 16,000 feet level was, in my opinion, a great improvement on the Hampden. The Manchester's weakness was its power units – the Rolls-Royce Vulture engines – which weakness was solved by the change to the power of four Merlin engines and the creation of the Lancaster.

Few who later flew the Lancaster failed to appreciate the effort that had gone into the testing of its prototypes and give due credit to the many crews of the Manchesters who died so that the Lancaster could become an operational reality. This train of thought can be extended to embrace operations in general, and is well expressed in *The Royal Air Force and Two World Wars* by Sir Maurice Dean, who states: 'Without the harsh lessons learned between 1939 and 1942 the final triumphs of Bomber Command could never have been achieved.'¹ [The first Lancasters arrived at Waddington on Christmas Eve.]

Among the Manchester pilots at Coningsby was an unforgettable character, Paddy Ayton, an Irishman with a great love of fun and adventure. I was with him one day visiting our local watering hole at Boston (on the Wash) when he got the idea that it would be more convenient if he owned a car. We found a used car yard and Faddy bought his car; this was all very well except for the fact that Paddy was unlicensed and had never driven a car; he promptly dismissed these shortcomings – 'If I can fly a bleeding Manchester I can certainly drive a car' and set about proving it. The road from Boston to Coningsby was narrow, and bordered for much of the way by canals; it was, fortunately, nearly free of traffic, otherwise we should never have survived the journey. That drive was worse than any operational sortie I had done.

Paddy did not remain at Coningsby long enough to enjoy his new toy to the full; on 10/11 May he failed to return from a raid and was presumed dead.

The main effort that night was a successful raid by 119 aircraft on Hamburg, which was carried out in perfect visibility. At the same time a minor attack was made on Berlin by twenty-three aircraft, of which only twelve reportedly bombed the city. Two Stirlings as well as P/O R. S. 'Paddy' Ayton's Manchester, L7323/OF-A, failed to return. He ditched in the North Sea while returning and his was the first bomber lost by 97 Squadron since it had reformed on 25 February.

Paddy Ayton wasn't dead. Later news filtered through to us that he had ditched in the North Sea, had got his crew into their dinghy and by using their parachutes as a sail had after several days landed on the coast, in enemy-occupied territory. He survived the war as a POW and took up flying again as his postwar career.

F/O Jimmy Whitecross (Canadian) went missing in a Hampden from Waddington, and no further news was received of him until he arrived back at base, having walked across France, into Spain and so back to England.

Jimmy Whitecross was a member of 50 Squadron when on 28/29 April his Hampden, AD834, was last heard from on w/t at 2359 hours. The message revealed that his mines had been planted, but the port engine was failing. Not long afterwards the bomber crashed near Loudeac. Two crewmembers were killed and the other became a POW. Whitecross managed to evade capture and he eventually made the difficult journey over the Pyrenees to Spain accompanied by two other officers of the RASC.[2]

No. 50 Squadron lost two Hampdens on 'Gardening' trips that night. The other was aircraft AD728, which was presumed lost in the target area. Three of the crew were buried at various locations along the French coast but the pilot, S/Ldr Duncan Good DFC, was not found and his name can be found on the Runnymede Memorial. So can the name of Jimmy Whitecross and those of his crew.

As Jimmy Whitecross was nearly at the end of his first operational tour, it was agreed that he be repatriated to Canada, but shortly before this was to take place he volunteered to fly in the search of one of one our Hampdens which had ditched in the North Sea. He was not seen again. [A signal was received from his aircraft that the engines were failing.]

We, the aircrew, were briefed from time to time on what action we should take in the event of going down in enemy territory. We carried various escape aids: tiny magnetic compasses hidden in our uniforms, usually under our wings, silk maps of parts of Europe and a wallet of French and Belgian bank notes. In India/Burma, this last item was replaced with a very heavy money belt of silver rupees, which in the event of a crash at take-off were quickly scavenged by the chaps cleaning up the runway.

Despite the troubles with the Manchester, life at Coningsby was good. We flew when our aircraft were not grounded, fished a lot in the streams running into the Wash, had our usual series of off-duty parties and drinking sessions and, during spare daylight hours worked at our vegetable garden in front of our Flight office, on the aerodrome. We grew potatoes, onions, radishes and lettuce. During the planting of the potatoes, a dispute arose between a New Zealander and a Canadian as to the best planting method. One adopted the method of planting the tuber in a furrow and 'hilling' up the plants as they grew; while the other insisted on planting his seed potatoes in the top of a ridge. Both systems soon produced plants, but before they came to maturity both pilots had failed to return from raids.

The commanding officer of No. 97 Squadron was Wing Commander Denys Balsdon, a steady, oldish, regular RAF type, who on joining us asked me to instruct him in the flying drill of the Manchester, it being a plane with which he was not familiar. This was usual and I told him what I knew of its tricks. One day in the period when we were once again non-operational, he asked me to prepare a Manchester and crew for a day trip. I did this and we flew to West Freugh, near the Scottish border, where we were picked up by a blonde girl in a sports car and taken to a country estate, on which was a beautiful tree-lined lake with a rowing boat and fishing gear. Balsdon and I spent the day rowing and spinning, catching one small trout. (My catch.) Next morning, while eating it for breakfast I mentioned the 1,000-pound trout I was enjoying; £1,000 being the cost of flying a Manchester for three hours at £350 per hour.

During briefing W/Cdr Balsdon had the nervous habit of tossing and catching a quite heavy silver 'Mary Theresa' dollar which he always carried with him as a talisman. I wondered what happened to it later, when his luck ran out and it ceased to help him. This was when he was returning in a badly damaged Manchester from a daylight raid on Brest, and as he lowered his flaps to make his landing approach, the aircraft spun in, crashing on the drome. All were killed.

That happened on 18 December, the force from 97 Squadron consisting of eleven Manchesters led by W/Cdr Balsdon, one of which was acting as a spare in case any aircraft had to abort on the flight across from England. Balsdon had decided to take the crew of F/Sgt George Pendrill. Other crewmembers on board L7490/OF-U were Sgt Gibson, the squadron navigation leader, and F/Lt Wright, the squadron bombing leader. The Manchester was hit by flak over the target area which inflicted damage and wounded the tail gunner. When the aircraft managed to reach Coningsby again, it is not known if Denys Balsdon or George Pendrill was at the controls.

Several Manchesters had already landed before L7490 made its approach. The aircraft made a normal circuit but it was noticed to be slightly above the glide path as it came over the boundary fence while letting down. Then the engines were heard to open up to full power Apparently the pilot had decided to overshoot and go around again for another approach, but instead of increasing speed and climbing, for some unknown reason the bomber stalled and plunged into the ground. It burst into a ball of flames, an inferno from which there could be no survivors.

One other Manchester failed to return, Manchester R5795/OF-W. Flying the aircraft was P/O Neville Stokes, an Australian serving with the RAF. He and his crew were on their first operation. Over Brest, a few seconds before bomb release, a flak burst on the port side of the aircraft damaged the port wing and caused the aircraft to yaw to the left, lose speed and fall behind the formation. They were on the way home but straggling when the Me109s pounced. The rear gunner and the mid-upper yelled for Stokes to take evasive action but he did not reply. Perhaps he could not. Perhaps he was badly wounded or fully occupied concentrating on keeping the damaged Manchester in the air. Deadly cannon fire riddled the rear fuselage. Three of the crew managed to bail out. Neville Stokes remained at the controls as the Manchester continued to lose height on an even keel before finally plunging into the sea.

The Manchester was a comparatively spacious aircraft and the aircrews tended to forget that there was a limit to the load it could carry at take-off. On normal bombing trips we usually carried up to 7,500 lb of bombs together with a load of propaganda leaflets for the Germans and boxes of small cloth bags of tea to be thrown out over Holland; this tea came from the Dutch colonies (Indonesia) and was sent as a goodwill gesture. Naturally, we were never short of a cup of tea in our flight offices. Besides these usual items to be dropped, we discovered that the crews had carried aboard odd loads of 'specials' such as house bricks, which had the reputation of causing much damage when dropped into a built-up area, and empty beer bottles, which were said to scream like sirens as they dropped. These little extras gave the crews a certain satisfaction and a personal interest but had to be restricted in the interests of safety on our take-off.

Diary: 26/6/41. 'We lost Frankie Eustace. Bloody Manchesters.'

On the night of 26/27 June, 207 and 97 Squadrons, along with 61 Squadron, the third Manchester unit, which was on its third operation, were off again to Kiel, at the same time as fifty-one bombers went to Cologne and forty-four to Dusseldorf. Eighteen Manchesters were involved. One aircraft from 207 Squadron burst a tail wheel tyre while taxying for take-off and consequently was left behind. The remaining machines were off between 2310 and 2325 hours. Dereck and his crew were flying Manchester L7424.

Around an hour after taking off, a desperate message was received by Coningsby from the wireless operator of F/O Frankie Eustace's aircraft, Manchester L7374. The rear gunner, Sgt McLaren, had been killed apparently by a night fighter attack. No more transmissions came in. German night fighters were becoming increasingly active.

Anxiously, those at Coningsby counted their Manchesters as they returned one by one. Frankie Eustace, a New Zealander, was a great character widely known and popular with everybody. The story was often told of how one night his windscreen shattered because of a bird strike while he was returning across the North Sea from an 'op'. Without goggles, he made the rest of the flight home with the wind blasting straight into his face. His eyes looked like two raw hamburgers when he landed and for a week afterwards. This night sadly he and his crew did not return. Later it was learned that they had crashed on the coast of one of the German Frisian Isles with the loss of all the seven-man crew.

Frankie was engaged to be married. His beautiful golden cocker spaniel, Jill, was given to his grieving fiancée.

No. 61 Squadron also suffered its first operational casualty that night when Manchester L7304, piloted by F/O Ken Webb, crashed near the

North Sea coast at Brunsbüttel in Germany. This aircraft was possibly another victim of the rising menace of the German night fighters. All of the crew perished and were buried in the Kiel War Cemetery.

This simple diary entry [about Frankie Eustace] indicates how our attitude to the Manchesters had changed during just over six months of familiarising tests and trials and disappointing operational work when we had unnecessarily lost many of our most skilled crews. We were fed up with the inefficiency of the Manchester, so that a few days later I was delighted to receive promotion to squadron leader and a posting to the newly formed Australian No. 455 (RAAF) Squadron, which was being assembled at Swinderby on the Roman 'Fossway' near Lincoln.

This unit – the first Australian bomber squadron to operate against Germany – was to be equipped with Hampden aircraft and basically staffed with RAAF, ground and air personnel who were already on their way via Canada. These were to be bolstered by a nucleus of experienced RAF types to show them the ropes.

When Dereck arrived at Swinderby there was a surprise. He found that the station, although nominally under the operational control of No. 5 Group, was equipped with Wellington bombers, not Hampdens!

13

455 (Raaf) Squadron – Arrival

No. 455 Squadron was the first Australian bomber squadron to operate against Nazi Germany. It was formed under Article XV of the Empire Air Training Scheme (EATS), but its beginning was confusing. The agreement that brought the EATS into existence was signed at Ottawa in Canada by British and Commonwealth representatives on 17 December 1939. According to the terms of this agreement, Britain would supply nearly all the aircraft and a nucleus of skilled personnel, and the Dominions would fulfil the other requirements. The Australian government committed to the creation of nine Elementary Flying Training Schools, seven Service Flying Training Schools, four Air Observer Schools and four Bombing and Gunnery Schools within Australia.

The Australian government also gave its approval to a plan for the progressive formation of RAAF squadrons under Article XV of the EATS Agreement. Two were to be formed by March 1941; six by July 1941; nine by September 1941; twelve by December 1941; fifteen by March 1942; and eighteen by May 1942. Canada and New Zealand were similarly committed. RAAF, RCAF and RNZAF units created under this system were to be under the command of the RAF and would be allotted RAF squadron numbers ranging from 400 to 499. The Australian numbers were to start at 450.

First to form, Nos 450 and 451 Squadrons, were committed to the fighting in the Middle East; 452 Squadron was the first RAAF Spitfire Squadron formed in Britain, and 453 Squadron was formed for the defence of Singapore and equipped with American-built Brewster Buffaloes. No. 454 Squadron had a false start. When formed in Australia in May 1941, it existed for two months until it was then disbanded the following July. It was later reformed as a light bomber squadron in Palestine at the end of September 1942.

No. 455 Squadron's confusing start was because it actually had two separate beginnings, half a world apart. The first was in Australia at RAAF Williamtown, NSW, in May 1941 when F/O John Lawson reported for duty. Lawson found that he was the adjutant, temporary commander, and only member of the squadron! Over the next weeks, the new unit slowly expanded in numerical strength as personnel were posted in and preparations started for movement to the UK.

Meanwhile, another 455 (RAAF) Squadron was officially formed in England. It was established at Swinderby in Lincolnshire on 6 June 1941 under the command of W/Cdr J. E. C. G. F. Gyll-Murray RAF. Designated to be a medium-bomber squadron within RAF Bomber Command's No. 5 Group, it was to be made up of three flights of Handley Page Hampdens, but at this stage it had no crews and over a month would pass before it received its first aircraft.

Liaison between the UK and Australia was muddled; the ground staff assembling in New South Wales was for a squadron comprised of two flights crewed to fly Vickers Wellingtons! There were actually Wellington bombers around at Swinderby, as Dereck found out when he reported in.

When I arrived at Swinderby I found that the station, although nominally under the operational control of No. 5 Group, was equipped with Wellington aircraft flown by Polish crews of Nos 300 and 301 Squadrons. These Polish squadrons operating with the RAF were comprised of Poles who had fought and escaped from Poland, some coming across Europe, some via Egypt. They had a great hatred of the Germans and were fiercely aggressive fighters. At take-off for operations, they always tested all guns on the runway before take-off, and again, over Lincoln, once they were airborne and headed for Germany. They were commanded by a group captain who flew as often as any of his crews until he failed to return from a raid.

Their operational casualties were high. They played hard and worked hard, they had rip-roaring parties, drinking mainly spirits and eating yards of Polish sausage. During my stay with them, they were visited by their leader, General Sikorsky (on 16 July 1941), and a lot of the RAF top brass, including Air Chief Marshal Portal.

General Vladislav Sikorski was head of the Polish government-in-exile in London and C-in-C of the Free Polish Forces. On 4 July 1943, he was killed when his aircraft crashed as it was taking off from Gibraltar.

First Viscount Portal of Hungerford (1893–1971), Air-Marshal Sir Charles Portal was Britain's chief of the air staff and chief of the war staff for most of WW2 and therefore responsible for British air policy.

During April–October 1940, he was head of Bomber Command and afterwards was made chief of the air staff. Later in the war American commanders respected his grasp of strategy and detailed knowledge of the RAF, which made him a key figure in the Casablanca, Washington, and Quebec conferences of 1943 that determined Allied strategy.

The station virtually came to a halt for a few days prior to and during the visit, which involved speeches, parties and buffet-style feeding. During the parties, which included both Polish females and males, a climax was usually reached when a victim of either sex would be seized by the arms and legs by four or more of their comrades and swung and thrown up to the ceiling. The throwers at this stage performed a turn of 360°, catching, or attempting to catch their victim on the way down. Occasionally they missed their catch and their colleague was carried out on a stretcher.

They were a super, aggressive bunch of chaps, who delighted in buying black market pigs from the local farmers, slaughtering them in their quarters and disposing of the gut and rubbish down the station's sewage system, usually causing a blockage. The ways of these magnificent fighters seemed strange to us, as I observed while I was inspecting a manor house they used as a billet with the idea of taking it over for the incoming RAAF. I discovered that they appeared not to bathe as we did but kept themselves very clean by a dry cleaning system of frequent use of Nivea cream. Later, while with them, I woke one morning after one of their wild parties to find myself the owner of a car I had bought from one of them. It was a Singer with a fluid fly-wheel, clutch-less gear change, a neat enough little car to go to Lincoln or Nottingham on nights off duty. Price £35.

One night while returning in it from Nottingham with S/Ldr Reg 'Runt' Reynolds, Runt decided to change gear from top gear to reverse while we were travelling at about 45 mph (70 km/hr). This would have been possible under normal circumstances, the car would have slowed to a stop and then gone into reverse. On this occasion, however, there was a horrible crunch and we came to a halt. Later we found that the original owner of the car, to overcome an oil leak from the clutch unit, had bolted the discs of the clutch together to make it into a solid drive. The result was that thirteen teeth were torn from the crown wheel of the differential. A search of the car wreckers' yards yielded a suitable crown wheel and pinion and we were once again mobile. S/Ldr Reynolds later achieved fame and a DSO when he became the first to carry out a daylight raid on Berlin in a Mosquito. I think he survived the war.

On 30 January 1942, three de Havilland Mosquitoes of 105 Squadron led by S/Ldr 'Reggie' W. Reynolds DFC – known to Dereck as 'Runt'

Reynolds – carried out the famous daylight raid on Berlin which disrupted speeches in the city's main broadcasting station to celebrate the tenth anniversary of Adolf Hitler's seizure of power. Listeners heard a few muffled words just as *Reichsmarschall* Hermann Göring was due to speak followed by a confusion of voices, then a shout or bang. After that the microphone was switched off and martial music played. Afterwards, Sir Arthur Harris conveyed to the crews his 'warmest congratulations on the magnificent daylight attack [which] cannot have failed to cause consternation in Germany and encouragement to the oppressed peoples of Europe'.

Cars featured to a great extent in our lives as they gave us a chance to get off the station and relax whenever we were off duty or on leave. Petrol, although severely rationed, was sufficient with care and a bit of scrounging to go to our usual haunts in the nearby villages and towns. While at Coningsby I wrote in a letter home on 3 April 1941: 'I sold my Ford 10 yesterday for £40 which was not bad really as I had owned it for over two years and had only paid £57/10/- for it originally. I have spent £10 already today in buying a remarkably good 1930 Bugatti racer. It is very old but should give me a lot of fun, if I can get it insured and put on the road. Most insurance companies will not touch RAF personnel with old racing jobs.'

In another letter home on 27/4/41, I wrote: 'At present I have no car. I sold my old Ford then purchased a Bugatti for £10 and sold it within ten days for £30 and am now without transport.' The Bugatti was a beautiful piece of engineering, having a long sleek body with an engine which looked like an oblong block of aluminium. The piston stroke was very long. When I first bought it, it was unserviceable with a seized front wheel bearing, which no one had been able to replace as the wheel hub was seized. When I acquired it, I contacted the Bugatti agents in London and had them send me a new bearing and, on loan, a special hub extractor. With this and the help of a few RAF ground staff and as many blow lamps as we could borrow, we heated and pulled off the hub with little trouble, fitted the new bearing and were soon mobile again.

Petrol was a problem but we overcame this by running the car on pure alcohol which we borrowed from the RAF (permanently). This alcohol came in four-gallon (15-litre) tins for use as an additive to the petrol of our Hampden aircraft to prevent the fuel freezing in the carburettors at height. The Bugatti performed perfectly with this and showed its potential when we tested it on the aerodrome roads and on the main runway. Later I was to re-buy the Bugatti for £20. I have no record of reselling but presumably did so. Of interest, the value of this car in 1985 would be in the range of $80,000 to $100,000; in 1991, $1,500,000!'

The Singer I sold when I left England to go overseas to Bob Holmes, an Australian from Perth. The sale price was decided by spinning a coin, £30 or £50. Naturally enough it sold for £50. Soon after this, basic petrol rationing was abolished and car values slumped further.

RAF Swinderby was located almost on the Lincolnshire/Nottinghamshire county boundary. It was one of the airfields planned during the expansion programmes of the 1930s, but construction had still not commenced when war broke out. It eventually started in the first weeks of 1940 and by the early summer part of the airfield was ready to hand over to the RAF. It had been built as a bomber airfield allocated to No. 1 Group, which was in the process of reforming the remnants of the Advanced Air Striking Force that had been massacred in the Battle of France. When it finally opened in August 1940, its first occupants were elements of the Polish Air Force that had escaped from both German and Russian invaders and reached Britain. No. 300 (Masovian) Squadron had been formed at Bramcote in Nottinghamshire the previous month and temporarily equipped with Fairey Battle light bombers. The move to Swinderby had not been to their liking. The CO, W/Cdr Waclaw Makowski, a highly experienced flier who had been general manager of LOT, Poland's state-run airline, complained the RAF station was not yet finished as it had no chairs, no beds, no bar and no vodka! By the time the second Polish unit, No. 301 (Pomeranian) Squadron, arrived, Swinderby's station commander had done his best to make life easier. Most importantly, there was now a makeshift bar – with vodka. Waclaw Makowski and his 301 Squadron counterpart, Roman Rudkowski, declared their units were now ready to go to war!

They did so for the first time on the night of 14/15 September 1940, three aircraft from each squadron bombing invasion barges in the harbour at Boulogne. The invasion ports of Boulogne, Calais, Dunkirk and Ostend became regular targets in the coming weeks, but the first twin-engined Wellingtons also began arriving in mid-September. Over the next two months both squadrons were converted.

Swinderby had been constructed without hardened runways and to operate with fully laden Wellingtons from the marshy grass surface became increasingly difficult. However, with the opening of Winthorpe outside Newark, which had concrete runways, the Poles were able to operate from there when conditions at Swinderby deteriorated.

John Lawson, who arrived in the UK at the head of the personnel from Australia, later wrote an outstanding history, *The Story of 455 (RAAF) Squadron*. It was published in 1951 by Wilke & Co. Ltd of Melbourne. Dereck's personality and forthright opinions left a deep impression on him, and he noted Dereck's impact on the squadron:

On June 30, 1941, Squadron Leader D. J. French, DFC, and Squadron Leader Sherwood reported for duty at RAF Station, Swinderby, Lincolnshire, on posting to 455 Squadron for duties as Flight Commanders... French was a picturesque and turbulent character... He had had considerable operational experience as a member of 50 Squadron (also then stationed at Swinderby) and was the first Australian airman decorated in the War. He had a good knowledge of RAF customs and procedure, and an unequalled knowledge of ways of diversion and entertainment available in Lincolnshire. In spite of his years of experience in the United Kingdom he remained aggressively Australian. His keenness for all things which he considered to be getting on with the War was unequalled, but he always remained his own judge of what things amounted to getting on with the War, and what things were merely incidental, and the freely expressed exercise of this judgment did not always make for popularity with station administrative officers and their kind – nor was he invariably tactful in his dealings with squadrons or flights other than his own. French remained with the squadron as commander of 'A' Flight until March 1942, earning a Bar to his DFC for his operational work with the squadron. He was a god to 'A' Flight and remains to all who knew him a legendary and stormy figure. After leaving 455, French, who by then had almost completed his second operational tour in United Kingdom-based bombers, completed a third tour with a Wellington squadron in the Middle East and a fourth tour as commander of a squadron operating in the Burma theatre. No pilot who relied on luck rather than ability completed one operational tour, let alone four tours. French was a magnificent pilot.

When he did report in, Dereck reported out again almost immediately. He wrote in his diary: 'For years the RAF has been thinking of forming a unit composed of Australians! Well it looks as if it is at last about to eventuate. I am in it and am at present the only Aussie. When I first arrived here on 1/7 things were very slack so I took seven days leave and went down south.' His personal comments about the early days of the squadron were written years later.

The formation of No. 455 Squadron RAAF was interesting. This unit, the first Australian bomber squadron to operate against Germany, was to be equipped with Hampden aircraft and basically staffed with RAAF ground and air personnel who were already on their way via Canada. These were to be bolstered by a nucleus of experienced RAF types to show them the ropes.

The personnel slowly assembled, first a temporary adjutant, F/Lt Hennah, an old Australian long domiciled in England, and an engineer officer, F/O Bennett, an Australian Rhodes scholar, the brother of Air Vice Marshal D. C. T. Bennett of Pathfinder fame.[2] Hennah was soon replaced by the arrival of several hundred RAAF chaps from Australia via Canada under the control of F/Lt John H. Lawson of Castlemaine, Victoria, as permanent adjutant, and F/Lt Bilton as medical officer. John Lawson was a solicitor by training and although he did a good job as squadron adjutant he could have developed a better empathy with the aircrew had he forgotten he was a non-combatant and taken part in the odd operational flight with them. A fellow solicitor, Lt Col Birch AIF of John's vintage, refused to be a non-combatant and led his own infantry battalion. Our intelligence officers in the Middle East sometimes flew on operations, while an RAF doctor (Wilson) is said to have flown on ninety-two operations. The accountant officer at Waddington, S/Ldr Burt, sometimes flew on operations; eventually he abandoned his rank of squadron leader in the regular RAF, reverted to the rank of pilot officer (flying) and was killed over Berlin.

A combatant/non-combatant gap existed in the RAF which extended to the attitude between flying personnel in training groups and operational units. There was, no doubt, a percentage of chaps who hung on to jobs in Training Command as long as they could so as to avoid operations. This attitude was a barrier to many tour-expired aircrews happily accepting postings to training units for fear that they, too, should be regarded as keeping out of the firing line. From the written records of Guy Gibson, Leonard Cheshire, Mick Martin and others it is clear that they were prepared to fly tour after tour of operational work in preference to being posted to Training Command.

Early in the war, at Waddington, a F/Lt Wines was posted to a unit as adjutant where he made full use of his non-combatant status. Following the earlier operations, as our casualties mounted the numbers of cars of deceased and missing aircrews grew. These cars were stored in a spare hangar until instructions were received from next of kin for their disposal. After some time it was found that many were being sold to a used car dealer, who happened to be Wines' brother, in a semi-legitimate manner. The aircrew felt that they could do little about this through the normal channels but waited until the customary 'rough and tumble' following the next mess dinner when they played rougher than usual and F/Lt Wines was found to have several broken ribs. There was an inconclusive official enquiry into the incident. F/Lt Wines got the message.

When I returned to Australia some years later quite a few people went to great pains to explain to me how they had been either too old or unfit to take part in the war as a combatant. They were reluctant to believe the tales

I told them of selfless people who had every excuse to be non-combatant but remained in the firing line. One such was F/O Guy Treasure DFC, a regular officer pilot of 50 Squadron who, on most occasions before take-off for operations, stood beside his plane, vomited and then went off to do the job in hand. Guy was a super-sensitive Yorkshire man with a rare musical talent. He had never received music lessons but could get a tune from a line of wine glasses or bottles or, as I saw him do once, get a melody from the organ in the Lincoln picture theatre. Someone helped him on this occasion with the stops.

Another selfless character I should record I met on the night of 7 May 1940 on the midnight train from London to Grantham. I was asked by the guard to provide some company on the journey to another RAF type. This turned out to be an old pilot officer air gunner with three rows of ribbons below his A/G badge. He told me that he had been commissioned since 1902, had a son of my age and was on operations. Later, by reading his biography, *Late Victorian* by John Marlowe, I found him to be P/O Sir Arnold Talbot Wilson, KCIE CSI CMG DSO MP No. 75884 RAF of 37 Squadron (Wellingtons) who was that night returning to his unit for the last time after attending a session of Parliament.

While researching the story of Sir Arnold Wilson, I was surprised to find that he was the author of quite a few books, some on the Middle East and India, with one on gallantry and another on worker's compensation, which indicated the wide range of his interests and causes. Naturally enough he was a radical, with a certain sympathy with the Nazi doctrine of National Socialism, yet as he was resolved to prove that patriotism was greater than politics he arranged his enlistment in the RAF as a pilot officer air gunner.

People such as these make the excuses of the non-combatants sound hollow and pathetic. Wilson was killed in action aged fifty-six on 31 May 1940 over France, just a few weeks after we met.

Sir Arnold Wilson was probably the oldest and most decorated airman to be killed on bomber operations. He was a holder of the King's Medal and Sword of Honour at Sandhurst, was formerly a Lt Col in the 32nd Sikh Pioneers, and between 1933 and 1940 he represented the Hitchin (Herts) Division in the House of Westminster. He was a member of 37 Squadron RAF and perished when Wellington L7791 crashed south of Dunkirk on 31 May 1940.

No. 455 Squadron grew to operational strength but was without aircraft because of an interruption to the scheduled supply of bombers when the Manchesters were considered to be a failure and the aircraft production line was adjusted to produce the Lancaster. During this time, Dereck learned that Dicky Taylor, who was still in 207 Squadron flying Manchesters, had failed to return. It happened on the night of 12/13 August. The target was Berlin.

There were three targets for Bomber Command that night. Besides Berlin, Hannover was attacked by sixty-five Wellingtons and thirteen Hampdens for the loss of four Wellingtons. Thirty-six other Hampdens raided Magdeburg without loss.

Seventy aircraft – forty Wellingtons, twelve Halifaxes, nine Stirlings, and nine Manchesters – took off for Berlin but only thirty-two of them reached the target and bombed in the area. Three Wellingtons, two Halifaxes, one Stirling and three Manchesters failed to return. After only a brief encounter with searchlights and flak in the defensive belt at the Dutch coast, Dick Taylor and his crew approached the target area at around 12,000 feet (3,650 m). The searchlights seemed more numerous and more dangerous than before. They seemed to be working in groups and co-ordinating with the heavy anti-aircraft batteries. Box barrages of flak were exploding at the apex of the searchlights that caught and held any unfortunate bomber.

On the bomb run Taylor held the aircraft, Manchester L7377, straight and level as the bomb aimer located their designated aiming point, the German Air Ministry building on Alexanderplatz. The crew felt their single huge 4,000 lb HC 'Cookie' drop onto the modified bomb doors, pushing them open, followed by a vibrating noise as the doors sprang shut again. 'Bomb gone!'

Suddenly they were coned by mercilessly bright searchlight beams. Within seconds a co-ordinated, intense flak barrage opened up. At first the shells exploded well ahead and above the aircraft, but it was not long before they were hit. Splintered shards of debris from the Perspex canopy shattered by flak showered into the cockpit. Shrapnel struck Dick Taylor in the wrist and severed an artery. The next group of shells detonated underneath with ear-splitting explosions, and concussion shook the aircraft again. Armour-plated doors behind the radio operator's seat that provided access aft burst open. Horrified, the radio operator F/Sgt Bill Wetherill saw that the inside of the fuselage behind his position had been transformed into a raging inferno. The aircraft was doomed!

Only two out of the crew of six, Bill Wetherill and gunner Sgt Donald McPhail, survived the crash but both suffered severe burns and were treated by German doctors. Don McPhail succumbed to his injuries two days later while still undergoing treatment. He was buried in the War Cemetery at Berlin along with the other crewmembers who had perished outright.

Bill Wetherill needed constant hospital treatment and his injuries were such that in 1943 he went before a neutral Red Cross medical

Above left: W/Cdr Dereck Jack French DFC & Bar. (Dereck French)

Above middle: Leo French, Dereck's father. (Dereck French)

Above right: Nell French, Dereck's mother. (Dereck French)

Below: Course A, RAAF Point Cook, January 1937. Cadet Dereck French is seated in the front row, second from the right. (RAAF Museum Point Cook)

"A" COURSE JAN.1937 ENTRY

Cdts.WHYTE.PARKER.TAYLOR.GALVIN.MILLETT.LAC.ALLEN.CPL.1 INKLATER.Cdts.BOYLAN.PODGER.McINNES.DOLPHIN.PRICE.WIBER.

Cdts.ROWAN.SCOTT.SAVAGE.RIDING.DOUGLAS.DAVISON.LAC.POMERY.Cdts.FITZGERALD.GIBSON.CROSS.OAKLEY.CREMIN.

Cdts.POLKINGHORNE.ROLLEMAN.Cdts Sgts.SUTHERLAND.HAMPSHIRE.U/O.GARRISSON.P/O's.ADLER.BLACK.U/O.WOODMAN.Cdt Sgt.BIRCH.
Cdt Sgt.GREEN Cdts.TOWNSEND.FRENCH.LEER.

Above left: In the cockpit of a Westland Wapiti at Point Cook. (Grant Lindeman)

Above right: Former RAAF cadet, the eccentric Francis James after his 'departure' from Point Cook as he appeared when Dereck met him again in England early in 1941. (Dereck French)

Below: Prototype Handley Page Hampden. At the time of its debut in June 1936, the Hampden was one of the world's most advanced warplanes. (MAP)

Dereck French's RAF 'office', the narrow cockpit of a Hampden. It offered the pilot an excellent fighter-like field of vision. (Dereck French)

The bomb aimer's view looking out through the nose of a Hampden. (Dereck French)

The Hampden's distinctive appearance inspired an assortment of nicknames ranging from 'The Frying Pan' to 'The Flying Tadpole'. (MAP)

The Hampden's slim boom carrying the tailplane is obvious and gave the aircraft its distinctive appearance. (MAP)

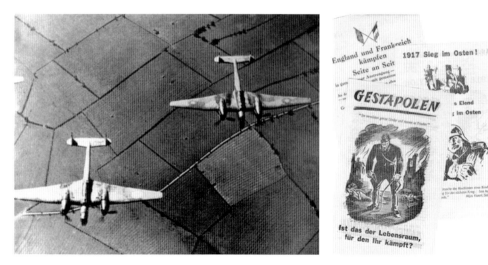

Above left: Hampdens flying in formation at low level over the countryside. (MAP)

Above right: Typical propaganda leaflets which were dropped on Germany instead of bombs during the early war period. (Alex Gould)

Below: Dereck French with his regular 50 Squadron crew. L to R, Sgt Alan Horsfall, Dereck (front), Cpl Alexander Barrass (back), P/O William Arthur Coote Mulloy of South Africa, usually referred to as Bill or 'Slug' Mulloy. (Dereck French)

Above: Dereck and his crew back from Bergen after successfully bombing the German cruiser *Königsberg*. (Dereck French)

Right: Dereck in RAF dress uniform to receive the DFC from HRH King George VI. (Dereck French)

Below: The DFC entry in Dereck's log book. He was the first Australian to be decorated in the Second World War. (Dereck French via RAAF Museum Point Cook)

Stavanger airfield, April 1940. (Alex Gould)

Hampdens under attack, in this case during a training exercise with Hurricanes. The Hampdens were found vulnerable to beam attacks because their front and rear guns could not be brought to bear. (Alex Gould)

Above left: Preparing to load a mine. (Alex Gould)

Above right: Merv Thomas of 50 Squadron. (Dereck French)

Dick Taylor and crew of
50 Squadron. (Dereck French)

Bob Wawn of 50 Squadron.
(Dereck French)

Above: Bob Cosgrove (left), son of the
Premier of Tasmania, and Desmond Sheen
in the pool on their ship during the journey
to England to join the RAF. (Pat Hughes)

Right: Alan Mulligan of 83 Squadron.
(Dereck French)

AIRMEN and sailors who have been decorated for gallantry in the present war

FLIGHT-LIEUT. C. G. OLIVE, D.F.C. of Queensland, led his flight and sometimes his squadron over France and later throughout operations fighting in defence of the British Isles

CAPTAIN H. M. L. WALLER, D.S.O. captain of H.M.A.S. Stuart, and officer in charge of the Australian destroyer fleet in the Mediterranean, has served with the R.A.N. since 1913

FLYING-OFFICER L. R. CLISBY D.F.C., who shot down eight German planes in May, in six combats. He was reported missing on the Western Front on May 14

SQUADRON-LEADER W. H. GARING, D.F.C. of the Australian No 10 Squadron of the Coastal Command, fought off three enemy attacks on H.M.S. Mackton

FLYING-OFFICER D. J. FRENCH, D.F.C. of Brighton, IV., gained his award for courage in the Norwegian campaign

COMMANDER M. J. BUCHANAN, D.S.O. of Melbourne, commanded the British destroyer Valentine which was damaged and beached off the Dutch coast. He was one of the last men to leave Dunkirk

FLYING-OFFICER S. F. B. SHEEN D.F.C. of Sydney won his DFC for gallantry in air operations on the Western Front

FLYING-OFFICER G. R. TAYLOR, D.F.C. of Brighton, IV., gained his award after 12 operational flights over enemy territory as captain of aircraft

News of Australians serving in the RAF was difficult to find for the people back home in the early war years. In this photo spread in *The Australian*, the picture of Dick Taylor is correct but the picture meant to be Dereck French is not of him. It is a shot of the South African Bill 'Slug' Mulloy, a member of Dereck's crew. (From *The Australian* via Beryl Olive)

Introducing the Avro Manchester, 207 Squadron. Rushed into service, Manchesters were plagued by problems, particularly with their Rolls-Royce Vulture engines. (Robert Kirby via Mike Taylor)

Avro Manchester, forerunner to the immortal Lancaster. (Robert Kirby via Mike Taylor)

BOMBS GONE!

FAR BELOW a speeding Manchester, smoke and flames belch up from the Nazi naval base at Brest. Drawing shows...

Above: A press article about the Manchester that Dereck pasted into his log book. (Dereck French)

Right: W/Cdr Denys Balsdon, CO of 97 Squadron. (Robert Kirby via Mike Taylor)

Below: The first Lancaster was actually a Manchester fuselage married to new wings housing four Rolls-Royce Merlin engines. (Tom Scott)

Loading bombs on a 455 Squadron Hampden, January 1942. (Jack Lawson via Dereck French)

Hampdens of 455 squadron attacking shipping, this time a training exercise captured on film by RAAF photographer Tom Scott. (Tom Scott)

Preparing to take off. (Tom Scott)

Leaders of 455 (RAAF) Squadron, August 1942, L to R: F/Lt J. N. Davernport; S/ Ldr J. Catanach, who was captured and later murdered by the *Gestapo* after the 'Great Escape' from *Stalag Luft III*; W/Cdr G. M. Lindeman, the CO; F/Lt L. P. Oliver; and S/Ldr R. Holmes. (Grant Lindeman)

Right: Loading a torpedo into a Hampden. (Jack Lawson via Dereck French)

Below left: Donald Bennett of Pathfinder fame. (Tom Scott)

Below right: Australia House, RAAF Overseas Headquarters, London. (Tom Scott)

Convoy to Africa at a time when the U-boat menace was at its height. (Dereck French)

Above left: Intelligence Officer of 108 Squadron, F/Lt A. B. Read. (Roy Chappell)

Above right: W/Cdr Don Saville, CO of 104 Squadron. (Roy Chappell)

Preparing to ferry a flight of Hurricanes; the Blenheim IV will be the navigating aircraft. (MAP)

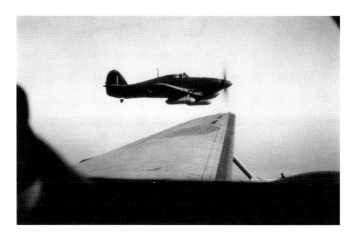

Ferrying flight. Guiding a Hurricane. Note the long-range fuel tanks. (Dereck French)

Ferrying flight. Escorting a Bristol Beaufort over the pyramids. (Dereck French)

Above left: Training paratroopers; 'a good drop'. Chaklala, November-December 1942. (Dereck French)

Above right: Dereck (in background) and S/Ldr Bill 'Housie' Houston of 215 Squadron, December 1942–June 1943. (Dereck French)

Below: Wellington ICs coming into formation for a paratrooper drop. (Dereck French)

Above left: Barbara Rigg was the very first full-time female bank teller in the National Bank. Dereck recalled that when the two met at a 'welcome home to Australia' party for Dereck, 'there was definitely chemistry at work'. (Barbara French)

Above right: Greg Graham advised Dereck to rejoin the RAAF as he had done when they met up again in the Middle East. He was best man at Barbara and Dereck's wedding. (Greg Graham)

Below: Press clipping of the marriage of Barbara and Dereck French shortly after his return to Australia. (Barbara French)

FIRST AUSTRALIAN to win D.F.C. with R.A.F. Wing-Commander Dereck French, D.F.C. and Bar (right), and his bride, formerly Barbara Rigg, with best man Squadron-Leader G. F. Graham, and matron of honor Mrs. June Bentley. Ceremony at St Stephen's, Caulfield.

NAME   FRENCH, Dereck J

Award BAR TO DFC. Reg. No. 36129   Rank W/CDR.   Service ROYAL AIR FORCE

Recommended by Governor-General on   O - R

Promulgated in *London Gazette* on   26/6/42.   G. H. File   -

Promulgated in *Commonwealth of Australia Gazette* on   -

Citation (G. H. File   )   NCA

Insignia received from London 12/7/45. PN LONDON. 20/9/45.   G. H. File   L/53.

Insignia presented by   The Governor of Victoria,

At Government House, Melbourne, On   7/9/45.   G. H. File MELBOURNE/6.

Address of recipient on presentation date   15 Denman Avenue,

                  EAST ST. KILDA.   VICTORIA.

Remarks

Other Awards   D. F. C. ,

                                                      2276.

Invitation to Government House Melbourne

The Bar to Dereck's DFC was finally presented to him by the Governor of Victoria at Government House, Melbourne, on 7 September 1945, although it had been promulgated in the *London Gazette* on 26 June 1942, over three years earlier. (Barbara French)

The Royal Air Force Memorial at Plymouth. (Dennis Newton)

board for assessment. On the panel were a Red Cross doctor, a German military doctor and a British POW doctor. The board recommended his repatriation. In October 1943, he was removed to Sweden where he was placed aboard a hospital ship and then returned to England. No. 207 Squadron had lost its very capable commander of 'A' Flight. Acting Squadron Leader George Richard Taylor DFC was almost at the end of his second tour of operations. He had been flying his forty-seventh mission.

Meanwhile, Swinderby had passed into the control of No. 5 Group in July so both of the Polish squadrons departed for Hemswell to remain with No. 1 Group. The nucleus of 455 Squadron was joined in the middle of July by Dereck's old unit, 50 Squadron, which transferred across after operating for a year from Lindholme in Yorkshire. It was still flying Handley Page Hampdens. For 50 Squadron it meant a return to Lincolnshire where it had been one of the original No. 5 Group squadrons. It and the new Australian squadron would develop a close working relationship in the coming months. Unfortunately, the changeover was marred by an accident on 19 July at Lindholme when one of 50 Squadron's Hampdens crashed upside-down soon after take-off, killing all four men on board.

After some time, the Australian squadron began taking possession of its first bombers. Dereck's log book shows that in mid-July he began working up on three separate aircraft, Hampdens AE198, AE242 and AE243. Hampdens AE198 and AE243 appear to have been delivered directly to the squadron, but AE242 had previously belonged to 44 Squadron at Waddington.

From mid-August, Dereck listed two additional Hampdens in his log book, AE264 and AE296. Both had previously belonged to 207 Squadron before it converted completely to the troublesome Manchesters. All of the incoming machines had been part of the fourth batch of 300 Hampdens produced by English Electric Co. at Preston from October 1940 onwards. On arrival at Swinderby they all had to undergo inspections, have equipment checks, be flight tested and brought up to operational standard before they could be sent out on raids.

Dereck flew a couple of other types during August too, even having a half-hour spell in a fighter, Hawker Hurricane Z3345! Very unusual. Being a bomber boy, he naturally had the opinion that all fighter pilots were immature show-offs.[3]

It was on the night of 25/26 August that individual members of 455 Squadron flew on operations for the first time. P/O Symons and Sgts Pratt, Redwood, Rawlings and Hobbs, all RAF members of the squadron, integrated as crew members aboard 50 Squadron's Hampdens in a raid on the German city of Mannheim. The 50 Squadron aircraft were included in a force of thirty-eight Hampdens and seven Manchesters, which claimed moderate bombing results. Three Hampdens were lost, including one aircraft from 50 Squadron, but all the personnel from 455 Squadron returned safely.

This system of integration with 50 Squadron for experience was used again two nights later, on 27/28 August. Once again the target was Mannheim. This time ninety-one aircraft were involved: thirty-five Hampdens, forty-one Wellingtons and fifteen Whitleys. No aircraft were lost but seven Wellingtons and one Whitley crashed in England. The bombing results seem to have been better too, as many fires were seen through the ground haze. P/O Symons and Sgts Pratt, Redwood, Rawlings and Hobbs flew their second missions and Sgt McLean his first. Wireless operator F/Sgt Maidment DFM made the first flight of his second tour.

There was the usual two-day break before, on the night of 29/30 August 1941, one of 455 Squadron's own aircraft was used on a mission for the very first time. It was Hampden AE296/F for Freddie. Its pilot was S/Ldr Dereck French DFC and his crew consisted of Sgt Pratt (navigator), F/Sgt Maidment DFM (wireless operator) and Sgt Bernard (gunner). In a reversal of the usual arrangement, Bernard was actually a member of 50 Squadron flying with 455 Squadron for experience. At the same time, Sgts Redwood, Rickard, W. J. Smith and Urpeth (all RAF) of 455 Squadron flew with 50 Squadron for experience.

The target was Frankfurt, with its railways and harbours to be used as aiming points. This was the first 100-plus-aircraft attack on the city, the raiding force of 143 aircraft being made up of seventy-three Hampdens, sixty-two Whitleys, three Manchesters and five of the newer four-engined Halifax heavies.

Poor weather did not permit accurate bombing, and returning crews reported that the attack became general in the target area. Dereck simply noted in his log book that it was the twelfth sortie of his current tour and that the whole operation took 6 hours and 40 minutes. Squadron adjutant John Lawson wrote: 'French's operational report was typical: "Operation carried out without incident until arrival at base, when approximately 40 circuits were made before permission granted to land. Duty successful."… A typical French operation and a typical French comment.'

A Hampden from 61 Squadron disappeared without trace, and 50 Squadron lost two Hampdens during the night. One of these crashed while returning, possibly low on fuel, 8 miles (13 km) from Lincoln.

Two of the crew were injured. The other was Hampden AD839, which crashed in the vicinity of Abbeville on the Somme in France. All were killed, including 455's Sgt Robert Urpeth, who had only been with the squadron for a few days. He is actually listed sometimes as belonging to 50 Squadron, and along with the other crewmembers of Hampden AD839 he was buried in the extension to Abbeville's Communal Cemetery.

No. 455 Squadron was the first Australian bomber squadron to operate against Nazi Germany, and its war was just beginning...

14

455 Raaf Squadron – Operations

The war situation had dramatically changed again in the early hours of 22 June 1941 when the Germans began their massive invasion of the Soviet Union. At four o'clock in the morning local time, the Soviet ambassador in Berlin was called to the *Wilhelmstrasse* and told that Germany had entered Russian territory in response to 'border violations'. Hitler was repeating the same lie he had used to justify his invasion of Poland back in September 1939.

In fact, Operation *Barbarossa* was the culmination of months of planning by the German general staff in response to Hitler's orders. It was launched along a 1,800-mile (2,880-km) front from the Baltic to the Black Sea. Just over 3 million troops in 151 divisions were thrown into the offensive. They were supported by an armoured punch of tanks, guns and aircraft employing their usual overwhelming *blitzkrieg* tactics. The plan was to destroy the Soviet Union and Bolshevism once and for all – and do it quickly.

From the outset the Germans achieved crushing successes on the ground and in the air, due to the technical superiority of their equipment and their extensive combat experience. By nightfall, the panzers had penetrated deep into Russian territory inflicting heavy losses, and the Soviet Air force had lost 1,811 aircraft, 1,489 of them on the ground. The *Luftwaffe*'s losses amounted to just thirty-five aircraft.

The British government's first official reaction came that night in a speech broadcast from London by Prime Minister Winston Churchill. In it, he promised Russia 'any technical or economic assistance in our power'. On 12 July, Britain and Russia signed an agreement forbidding either to make a separate peace with Nazi Germany. It paved the way for increased mutual assistance. That very night bombs fell on Moscow for the first time. On the 21st, the Soviet capital suffered its first full-scale air raid by 127 *Luftwaffe* aircraft. Exactly a month later, German troops cut the rail link between Leningrad and Moscow, but it was on this day too that the first British convoy set out from Iceland bound for Archangel in northern Russia. This was the beginning of what would become the dramatic and costly Arctic convoys.

In practice, only limited support could come from England because of the serious setbacks British forces had suffered in the Mediterranean and North Africa. The RAF was the only weapon of attack in Britain's arsenal that could strike directly at the Third Reich from the west, and Bomber Command was its spearhead. Now its offensive missions had to escalate and intensify. It had to become more active and aggressive – and more accurate.

By the end of 1941, the Germans had developed very effective defensive countermeasures against the RAF's night bombing attacks. A huge unbroken belt of searchlights extended from north of Hamburg down into France. In places it was more than 100 miles (160 km) deep and it bristled with an extensive band of anti-aircraft batteries. To be caught in a concentrated cone of searchlights and anti-aircraft fire was dangerous in the extreme.

Added to this, from January 1941 to February 1942 the *Luftwaffe*'s defensive force of night fighters grew from four *Gruppen* and one *Staffel* to seven *Gruppen* and one *Staffel*: from 195 to 367 aircraft. The dangers for the lone raider flying in the dark were multiplying. Bomber Command's tactics now involved careful planning of the routes to and from the target, and accurate timing to confuse the defences. The essentials were careful routing, good navigation and good timing.

The question of operational height in late 1941 and early 1942 was still largely a matter for each squadron to decide. Acting on the advice of its veteran flight commanders, Dereck French and Runt Reynolds, 455 Squadron adopted the principle of bombing from as low an altitude as was practical considering the ferocity of the enemy's defences. Their methods proved very effective and the squadron built up a good record of successful target location and bombing. Jack Lawson wrote: 'Tactics were then still largely a matter of individual development by crews under the advice of their squadron veterans. 455 was fortunate that it had veterans of the calibre of French, Reynolds and Banker.'

At the beginning of September, the squadron still only had two aircraft. Dereck recalled: 'As more aircraft arrived we made full use of them, carrying out mining and bombing operations which included a raid by S/Ldr (Runt) Reynolds DFC on Berlin, a long trip for a Hampden.'

The raid Dereck alluded to took place on 2 September 1941. Reynolds bombed successfully but out of a force of forty-nine aircraft, five failed to return, including two Hampdens. As it turned out, this operation was one of the last occasions on which Hampdens were ordered to attack the German capital as this target was close to the limit of the type's range. Two other 455 Squadron crews carried out mine laying near the Friesian Islands on the same night. One of them was most probably flying an aircraft borrowed from 50 Squadron, as 455 still only had the two Hampden aircraft on strength. The squadron carried out mine-laying missions around the Frisians again on the nights of 7/8 September, 11/12 September and 12/13 September.

Dereck's second operation for 455 Squadron also took place on 12/13 September. Frankfurt was the target and altogether the RAF bomber force consisted of seventy-one Vickers Wellingtons, thirty-one Handley Page Hampdens, eighteen Armstrong Whitworth Whitleys and nine of the big four-engine Short Stirlings – nearly 130 aircraft. As was common in these earlier bombing raids, finding the target continued to present major difficulties. Thick cloud prevented accurate bombing but those crews who did release over the target claimed that large fires were started.

According to surviving records, Frankfurt reported that seventy-five high-explosive bombs and 650 incendiaries were dropped on the city and on the nearby town of Offenbach. Thirty-eight fires were started. Nearly all of the damage was to civilian housing, although two explosions did destroy a workshop at a rubber factory in Offenbach. Eight people were killed, seventeen injured and an estimated 200 were bombed out. The town of Mainz, almost 20 miles (32 km) from Frankfurt, reported numerous bombs falling and nineteen people were killed.

Two Wellingtons were lost that night, and there was almost a third casualty – Hampden AS296 from 455 Squadron flown by S/Ldr French and his crew. Dereck wrote afterwards in his diary, 'Shaky do, holed tanks.'

This was an interesting trip on which I had been instructed to carry out various fuel consumption tests. It was proposed that I should fly to the target area at as low a speed as possible, returning at normal cruising speed after the bomb load had been dropped. I carried out the exercise as instructed, closely watching the fuel gauges and became convinced that the fuel economy plan was completely wrong as the gauges indicated a greater fuel consumption than I had ever experienced in a Hampden. We landed at Swinderby with near-empty tanks.

We then discovered that fuel was still trickling from a jagged hole in one of the wings. What had happened was that as we crossed the enemy coast on our way to the target we had passed through the anti-aircraft belt as usual and had been given the usual welcome, a part of which had gone through one of the wings puncturing the self-sealing tanks and allowing a steady loss of petrol. We had been lucky.

Danger was ever-present and tragedy could strike anyone, anywhere, anytime. Dereck used up more of his quota of good luck a few days later, but this time he was not flying a mission.

Soon after 455 at Swinderby became nearly fully operational, I was on duty as the officer in charge of night flying when an English RAF sergeant pilot named Taylor, who was detailed to operate that night, attempted to take off but aborted the attempt and returned to the tarmac, reporting that he could not get the plane airborne. I realised that he probably did not want to go on that particular mission, that he could be LMF (Lacking Moral Fibre), and told him to park the aircraft so that it could be tested in daylight.

Next morning I took it off, still with the bomb load of the previous night on it, carried out the usual night flying test and landed, having found everything as it should be. After landing I taxied to the tarmac for servicing for the next operation and to give the armourers easy access to the bombs, I selected 'Bomb Doors Open'; a procedure carried out with engine power in lieu of an arduous hand-pumping job. As soon as the bomb door opening procedure was complete, there was a horrible upward jolt as the aircraft lifted, released from the 2,000 lbs (900 kg) of bombs which had fallen some 6 feet (1.8 m) to the tarmac. I sat petrified for a second waiting for the blast – but nothing happened!

It appeared that the aircrew on the previous night had accidentally switched the 'Bomb Drop' switch to the 'On' position, completing half of the electric circuit required for bomb release. The remainder of the circuit was completed when the bomb doors became fully open. These particular bombs had an additional safety device in the form of a small metal propeller on the nose and theoretically remained safe until this was removed, being screwed off by the air as it fell to earth.

Fortunately on this occasion theory worked in practice. The small metal propeller remained in place, but Fate was being tempted again and again, and Dereck was edging ever closer to using up all of his nine lives. In his log book for the 12/13 September mission to Frankfurt, he noted: '12/9/41, Hampden AS296, Self, F/Sgt Maidment DFM, Sgts Rawlings and Smith. Ops. – Frankfurt – a/c. holed. One 1,000 lb bomb and two 500 lb bombs, time 7 hours 15 minutes.'

Flight Sergeant Maidment DFM, mentioned in Dereck's log book, was a youngster from Birmingham on his second tour of operations. He had joined the RAF as an apprentice pre-war and afterwards received aircrew training to become a wireless operator. Although he had been decorated for gallantry on his first operational tour, he refused many times to accept a commission because he could send more money home to his parents as a senior NCO than as a junior officer. He deservedly received great respect, and was 'of the highest value to the squadron' – in fact, at first he had been the only operationally experienced wireless operator in it. 'F/Sgt Maidment DFM was a survivor, being one of the original wireless operators of pre-war No. 5 Group having been with us in 50 Squadron where he had fifty or more operations before he joined 455 Squadron.'

Normally, when each new crew arrived from the Operational Training Units one of its untested wireless operators had to be replaced by an experienced man for at least two missions. F/Sgt Maidment volunteered to do this willingly and flew with almost every new pilot while the new wireless operators gained necessary experience in the rear gunner's position. Of him, Jack Lawson wrote:

> Always cheerful, he was a mimic and comedian of no mean order. He had great muscular strength and used often to hang by one arm from the roof of the van taking crews to their aircraft before take-off; in that position he performed gymnastics, cracked jokes and gave monkey imitations. He dispelled an incalculable amount of pre-take-off nervousness.[1]

The young man from Birmingham was posted from 455 Squadron back to 50 Squadron when his second operational tour was about half finished. He completed it with his old unit successfully and unscathed.

When a third Hampden finally arrived it was quickly put to work. On the night of 15/16 September all three of the squadron's aircraft took part in an attack on Hamburg but it was during this operation that the squadron lost its first crew when Hampden AE249 failed to return. P/O Officer A. J. Hibell, Sgt W. N. Pratt, Sgt H. Hobbs and Sgt P. H. Claydon were posted missing and later reported as killed. This was the first loss on bomber operations by an RAAF bomber squadron in the Second World War, but the crew was all RAF, not RAAF.

P/O Hibell, who was one of the squadron's first pilots, was flying his third operation and making his first attack on a so-called 'experienced' target. In 1941, crews were classified according to the experience of their pilots. A pilot new from an OTU was called a 'freshman' and each freshman crew was required to operate successfully on at least two occasions against supposed easy targets. The English Channel ports, mine-laying expeditions and for some unaccountable reason, Emden, were all classed as 'freshman targets' and, unless there was a particular reason, these targets were not allocated to experienced crews. After two such missions, a pilot and his crew were classified as 'experienced' and could then be assigned to bomb any objective.

Hampden AE249 had been shot down by a Messerschmitt Me110 night-fighter from *I/NJG1* flown by *Oblt* Walter Barte and it crashed near Winkeldorf, Germany. Two of the crew, P/O Hibell and Sgt Clayden were taken prisoner but Sgt William Norman Pratt and Sgt Hubert Hobbs were never found. Their names have been included on the Memorial at Runnymede for those airmen who have no known grave.

To lessen the damage that could result from the loss of senior officers, RAF policy dictated that squadron commanders were not to go on operations more than once a month, except in exceptional circumstances, and flight commanders were not to operate more than once in every ten days. As these personnel had their normal duties of command plus rostered duties as the officer-in-charge of night flying, they were fully occupied despite the restrictions, but members of their crews usually found themselves at a loose end. This was how F/Sgt Maidment had the time to volunteer to fly with the new 'freshmen' crews.

Flying his usual aircraft, Hampden AE296, with his usual crew, Dereck set out on a sortie to Berlin on 20/21 September but after only half an hour in the air there was a recall signal to return to base. In all, seventy-four aircraft had set out and they were all recalled because of deteriorating weather conditions over the German capital. None flew on to Berlin but according to RAF records, ten aircraft did bomb alternative targets, their crews claiming they did not receive the signal. Whether or not Dereck received the signal is open to conjecture, but he was one of those who decided to bomb an alternative target anyway. He dropped his load – one 1,900 lb (862 kg) bomb and two 250 lb (113 kg) bombs – on Bremen. Out of the Berlin force, three Wellingtons and a Whitley failed to return and twelve more aircraft crashed on returning to England. Dereck and his crew returned safely but had to land at Linton-Upon-Ouse in Yorkshire and fly back to Swinderby the following day.

Thirty-four aircraft were also dispatched to Frankfurt that same night but they were recalled too. Some flew on regardless and bombed the target. No aircraft were lost but three aircraft crashed in England.

Although twenty-eight 'freshmen' crews from various squadrons had also been dispatched to bomb Ostend (and they did all return) the night of 20/21 September had proved costly for Bomber Command for few tangible results. It had to do better. Dereck outlined some of the main difficulties that the bomber crews faced and needed to overcome:

Another deficiency [in the earlier Hampdens] was that we had no automatic pilot (George), which meant that we had to sit strapped into the cockpit and concentrate on flying for up to eight hours or more. Gradually 'George' became available and was fitted, and our job became easier. These early auto-pilots were not exactly first class, some had a frightening habit of exaggerating a minor correction such as lifting a wing and then over correcting until the aircraft was weaving about almost out of control. This was a frightening thing to have happen to one when one was relaxed and half asleep heading for base after an operation.

Another hazard we had to beware of were the barrage balloons both over Britain and Occupied Europe. These were grouped about important targets such as ports, large towns, factories and shipping conveys and were flown at heights of 5,000 to 7,000 feet (1,500–2,100 m) with the idea of keeping raiding aircraft above this height and so reduce the accuracy of their attack. Britain had its groups of balloons strategically sited, in the main, around ports along the east coast with clear flight path lanes between the groups so that our bombers could fly along these lanes to and from their missions.

Much research had been done pre-war on these balloons, some of which I had seen at Mildenhall, when a Fairey Battle with an armoured steel cage around the cockpit deliberately dived into the balloon cable at a fair height. The plane appeared to stop in mid-air, swerve a little and then fly on to land unharmed. Later the Hampdens were fitted with a series of projecting knobs, about as large as a fist, on a thin strip of armour plate along the leading edge. Each of these contained a slot within which was a trigger device that fired a shotgun cartridge propelling what was a simple cold chisel, this cut the balloon cable against the anvil-like forward part of the device.

These balloons had the disadvantage that they tended to break away from their winching gear during severe storms and gave our fighter boys any amount of excitement before they shot them down, preventing any further damage to power lines as they drifted free over Britain with their cables trailing.

The balloons carried a transmitter which sent out a continuous series of beeps which could be received on our aircraft intercom. Returning from Germany one night, I had been flying in cloud for an hour or so and was approaching the UK at about 5,000 feet (2,100 m) when I decided to turn up the anti-balloon receiver gear.

The balloon beep signal came blasting through, indicating that I was in the middle of a barrage, simultaneously a round white mass appeared in the cloud directly ahead. This seemed to grow at an alarming rate and I felt sure I was about to fly into a balloon. Instinctively I yanked at the controls to make an almost vertical climb to escape and soon found that I had broken through the upper layer of cloud and was flying directly into a full moon; a nasty frightening experience but also lucky as many of our chaps did come to grief in the balloon barrages. After about a year of war a summary was made which showed that our British-based balloons had claimed more RAF victims than intruding German planes. Other victims of the balloons, indirectly, were our maintenance fitters who, while working on the aircraft engines, occasionally triggered off the balloon cable cutting device and usually lost a finger or two.

If we accept the idea that our politicians were the primary cause of our unpreparedness, we must then conclude that the senior service officers of that period should also accept blame, as they had weakly agreed to the parsimony of the government. They, were also to blame, with few exceptions, in that their thoughts on warfare, strategically and tactically, were akin to the thoughts and ideas they had had during WWI.

Among the exceptions to this was Air Marshal Harris who stated that commanders of his bomber squadrons should be pilots who had been over Berlin, not last war, not last week, but last night. In other words pilots who were really up to date with the operational hazards and requirements of the hour. Another was Air Marshal Basil Embry, who always insisted that he be fully operational in any command he was given, a wonderful example to the aircrews serving in his command and at the same time ensuring that he knew exactly the hazards and difficulties his crews had to face.

...Another difficulty we had to face was weather. Western Europe was an area of unpredictable meteorological conditions and it required great knowledge and skill to make anything like a reasonable forecast. This was primarily due to the movement of the Gulf Stream around the UK. This forecasting was done in No. 5 Group generally by a civilian meteorologist, a Mr Matthews, who briefed us with confidence on the weather we could expect. In general he was unbelievably accurate, but when he was wrong in forecasting we lost heavily.

One night while we were away over Germany a dense fog suddenly swept over England making most of our aerodromes useless for landing purposes; next morning I counted nine Hampdens crashed at Waddington, all having crashed while making desperate attempts to land before they ran out of petrol. Strangely enough, only a few aircrews were killed. This weather menace was always with us in the European theatre of war, being responsible for many of our early losses.

The last enemy, and perhaps the least fearsome we had at that time, were the German defences. A series of belts of searchlights crossed our main flight paths into Germany as well as being grouped about the major towns and targets. These seemed to operate with a master beam which caught a victim in its light when other lesser beams coned in on it. This was a hazard, in those days at heights only up to about 10,000 feet (3,000 m).

To be coned by searchlights war a horrible experience as the coned zone usually attracted a mass attack of heavy anti-aircraft fire which filled a box about the cone. This heavy AA fire was dangerous enough but it left large whitish smoke shapes floating about like balloons. These, although harmless, appeared as another frightening menace.

At that time, apart from the bomb load, the target and the time of take-off which one learned at briefing, each pilot was free to choose his own route to his target and his height and method of attack; this resulted in individuals developing particular methods of carrying out an operation. We also used individual methods of taking avoiding action, such as de-synchronizing our engines to confuse the searchlight and AA location devices. We thought at the time that their location devices were sound operated and considered Radar unknown to them. We developed the habit of 'weaving' – a change of direction yet still maintaining a general course – and used this when over enemy territory except when on the final bombing run when we flew at a set speed and height and direction as asked for by the bomb-aimer.

German night fighters were used to deter us but at the time they were neither numerous nor efficient and did not bother us much although we kept a careful watch out for them. Our rear gunners often reported 'fighter to the rear' or 'fighter to the beam' and usually fired a burst at whatever it was they felt they had seen, but without any follow up. I think that any person on lookout at night, concentrating on shades and shadows must eventually succumb to their imagination and see strange images.

Our rear gunners often reported lights following us and after a while would give the light a burst or two of fire. These lights usually turned out to be the Pole Star, which we never managed to shoot down.

To carry out our operational work in Bomber Command we were, for security reasons, given barely sufficient information at briefing to carry out the particular task in hand, and it was only much later – post-war – that one was able to read the true reasons for the various actions for which we had been briefed and to form an assessment of the results of these actions.

In this post-war appraisal of our efforts it appears that in general our bombing operations at that time, carried out at great cost, were effective only in that they were just about the sole means of taking the initiative. The British Army was under reformation after the loss of much of its hardware at Dunkirk, while the Royal Navy was busy in the role of keeping the marine supply lines to the UK open, while at the same time doing its best to create a shipping blockade against Germany. Our RAF bombing offensive was a constant reminder to the Germans at home that Britain was yet to be dealt with. This said, it is true that these raids forced the employment of more than 1,000,000 Germans in home defence, such as anti-aircraft, searchlight, fighter and air raid precaution units as well as in repairing the damage caused by the raids. These 1,000,000 souls were employed at direct cost to the other German fighting forces, particularly to those on the Eastern Front.

No. 455 Squadron again operated with its limited strength on the nights of 29/30 September and 30 September/1 October, but things were changing. Late in September and early October more 'freshmen' crews arrived but their numbers did not keep pace with the arrival of new aircraft. For a short time there were not enough crews to fly all the available machines. Among the newcomers were P/O Tony Gordon and Sgt John Shannon, who were the first junior RAAF pilots. Another RAAF pilot to arrive was P/O Jim Catanach who had already flown several operations with 144 Squadron.

The sortie rate the squadron was flying began to increase steadily and the ground staff, who had once complained of the lack of work, now found plenty to do preparing the new aircraft for operations. No. 455's ground staff was still a mixture of RAF and RAAF airmen but they 'got on well together'. Around this time, the first promotions of Australian personnel came through to take up NCO vacancies.

Dereck's next mission was an attack on the shipyards at Kiel on 23/24 October. There were 114 aircraft dispatched – forty-three Wellingtons, thirty-eight Hampdens, twenty-seven Whitleys and six Manchesters – but only sixty-nine reached the target area. Surviving German records from Kiel described the bombing as taking place in two widely separated waves. Most of the damage was caused during the second attack with hits being scored on the naval base, the *Deutsche Werke* U-boat yard, a dance-hall, a bakery and a number of houses. Four people were killed and five injured. At one stage the local defences caught three of the bombers in their searchlight beams at the same time and one was shot down while trying to dive out of the light. This was the only aircraft lost and it happened to be a Hampden from Swinderby, this time from 50 Squadron.

There were also some minor operations. Thirteen aircraft were despatched to raid Le Havre; nine Stirlings were sent to Brest; and four aircraft to Cherbourg. One Hampden failed to return from attacking Le Havre, an aircraft from 44 Squadron at Waddington which was lost without trace.

On 29/30 October, Dereck and his crew took part in a raid by forty Hampdens and five Manchesters on Schiphol Airfield in the Netherlands. When they arrived they found the area was covered by cloud making the airfield impossible to find. One Hampden, an aircraft of 106 Squadron from Coningsby, failed to return. It crashed into the sea off Lincolnshire. The body of the pilot was recovered but the other members of his crew were never found. Meanwhile, sixteen Wellingtons were sent to attack the three German capital ships at Brest but they too could not find their targets. All returned safely.

For 455 Squadron, the month of November began fairly quietly with the usual mine-laying operations and successful attacks on Cherbourg and Terschelling, all without loss. That all changed on the night of 7/8 November, which brought tragic losses not only to the squadron but to Bomber Command itself.

At Bomber Command HQ High Wycombe, the C-in-C Sir Richard Peirse, undoubtedly frustrated by the latest protracted stretch of bad weather and recent poor bombing results, decided to mount a major effort. A total of 392 bombers were detailed to raid mainland Germany, with Berlin as the main target for over 200 aircraft, the channel ports of Ostend and Boulogne plus a mine-laying operation in Norwegian waters near Oslo. This was the largest force committed so far; the numbers involved exceeding by nineteen the record set less than four weeks earlier.

Weather predictions for the night were far from favourable. Strong winds were forecast for the parts of northern Europe through which the bombers would have to pass. Despite a late forecast showing there would be storms, thick cloud, icing and hail over the North Sea along the routes the bombers would need to fly to Berlin and back, Peirse persisted with his decision. AVM Slessor of 5 Group objected, pointing out that Berlin was always a high-risk target for his Hampden squadrons, which would be operating at close to their maximum range, even if the weather was good. Committing these aircraft to attack the German capital under the circumstances would be suicidal. Sir Richard was adamant that the operation would continue but after some 'discussion' Slessor was allowed to withdraw his part of the Berlin force and send it to Cologne instead.

Of the Berlin force which was reduced now to 169 aircraft, only seventy-three managed to reach the general area of Berlin. Although there were claims of fires started on the outskirts of the city, other results were 'unobserved'. Berlin records relating to the night reported scattered bombing in numerous areas. Twenty-one aircraft – ten Wellingtons; nine Whitleys; and two Stirlings – failed to return, representing 12.4 per cent losses from those dispatched. The total effort for the night reached 392 sorties but thirty-seven aircraft (9.4 per cent) were lost. This was more than double the previous highest number of losses for night operations. Many of the casualties most likely crashed in the North Sea after experiencing icing up or running out of fuel in the appalling weather conditions.

Out of the sixty-one Hampdens and fourteen Manchesters of 5 Group sent to Cologne, plus thirty Halifaxes, Hampdens, Wellingtons and Whitleys sent on 'rover patrols' into other areas, six aircraft – two Hampdens, two Wellingtons, one Halifax, and one Whitley – failed to return. The two missing Hampdens were from 455 Squadron out of seven that took part. Both crews were by current squadron standards regarded as 'experienced' so their loss was sorely felt. Hampden AE243/UB-B had taken off from Swinderby at 6.30 pm on the 7th to fly a 'Rover Patrol' towards Cologne and did not return. The crew were all RAF and all sergeants. Maurice Jenkins, Keith Morris, Donald Rawlings, and George McGarvey were all buried in Heverlee War Cemetery, Belgium. P/O Tony Gordon and his crew in Hampden P1201/UB-P took off ten minutes afterwards and disappeared. It was reported much later that they were all POWs. Tony Gordon is believed to have been the first Australian in the RAAF to be taken prisoner while serving in an RAAF bomber squadron in WW2. His English air gunner Sgt E. Holt (RAF) subsequently died as a result of injuries.

Although the Cologne attack was initially considered successful by some at the time with crews reporting many fires, that was not the case. The city records noted only two houses destroyed and fourteen damaged with five people killed and five injured. There was no damage to industrial targets. Meanwhile, where the bombs that were dropped by forty-three crews meant to target Mannheim actually fell remains unknown, despite a large fire reported. It was probably a decoy.

In his preliminary report to the Air Staff following the costly events of 7/8 November, Sir Richard placed much of the blame on the poor weather. While this was accepted at first, there is no doubt that the events of the night combined with the results of the enquiry that followed, were instrumental in causing his departure as C-in-C on 8 January 1942. Sir Richard was summoned to a meeting with Prime Minister Churchill at Chequers the evening after the heavy losses suffered on the Berlin raid. The whole future of Bomber Command had been under review since the middle of the year based upon a survey of all the recent photographs of bombed targets. The study was carried out by Mr D. M. Butt, a civil servant in the War Cabinet.

The Butt Report was completed by 18 August and its conclusions were damning. It was found that only one in four of the crews who claimed to have bombed a target in Germany were within 5 miles (8 km) of the nominated target. In the full-moon period, the proportion increased to two in five on all targets and about one in three on German targets: but in the no-moon periods only one in fifteen crews on average bombed within the five-mile zone on all targets and about one in twenty on German targets. These disappointing figures were made worse by the fact that one-third of all crews dispatched did not even claim to have reached the target area at all! Casualties on the scale that were being suffered since mid-July could only be justified if they were commensurate with successful bombing results, but this was obviously not happening.

During the weeks after the report being issued, there is evidence suggesting that Sir Richard's operations were no longer concentrating on priority targets which could sever the transportation links from the Ruhr war industries. The bombers were being sent instead to places of lesser importance, targets that were less well protected by flak, searchlights and ground haze. By achieving successes against these, it may have been hoped that the adverse comments of the extremely critical Butt Report could be countered. Be that as it may, the principal factor that determined Sir Richard's fate was the long run of heavy losses that were dramatically compounded on 7/8 November.

On 13 November, the Air Ministry informed Peirse that only limited operations were to be carried out in the coming months while the whole future of Bomber Command was deliberated. A new policy had to be formulated, new techniques adopted and a new leader found. The bomber offensive against Germany in its present form was to be virtually halted for the midwinter months.

There were new ideas on the table already, some of them put forward by the renowned pre-war Australian pilot/navigator, Donald Bennett. He had pointed out to the RAF Directorate of Bomber Operations that such poor results were not surprising in view of the lack of navigational aids and the elementary training the crews were receiving. He suggested creating a special pathfinder force with expert navigators utilising the most up-to-date navigational equipment to lead the main-force crews to the target and use flares to pinpoint the objective.

For 455 Squadron, the sorties of 7/8 November were quickly followed by attacks on the docks at Dunkirk by freshman crews, and an abortive strike by some of the experienced crews on Essen. After these came a period of operational inactivity. This was attributed to the fickle Lincolnshire weather, low-lying cloud and fog which prevented operations until the last night of November.

On 30 November/1 December, five of the squadron's Hampdens took part in an attack by 181 aircraft on the Blohm und Voss shipyards at Hamburg, even though by now Hamburg was one of the best defended targets in Europe. Moonlight illuminated the harbour and the crews of 122 aircraft claimed good bombing results. Thirty-five aircraft from this force bombed alternative targets. Hamburg's records listed twenty-two fires, two of them large, and casualties of sixty-five people killed and 176 injured, with over 2,500 persons bombed out. The cost to Bomber Command was thirteen aircraft: six Wellingtons, four Whitleys, two Hampdens and one Halifax failing to return. Kiel and Emden were also raided, and there were other minor operations. For a total effort of 246 sorties, fifteen aircraft were lost – a marginally better result.

The two Hampdens lost on the Hamburg raid were again from 455 Squadron, the crews of which were all reported later as 'presumed killed in action'. The aircraft were Hampden AE430/UB-M flown by an all-sergeant RAF crew of Charles Blunt, Les Manning, Arthur Gee and Ernest Waller, all buried in Kiel War Cemetery; and Hampden P1272/UB-R flown by Sgt John Shannon RAAF, P/O Alan Sands RAAF, Sgt Alex Shorey RAF and Sgt Vic Towers RAF who were all buried in Hamburg Cemetery.

Dereck's good luck had continued in November as he had not been rostered to fly a mission. His log book shows that he did not fly at all between the 11th and 25th, which suggests he probably had a period of leave.

Early December saw many changes in the squadron. It was a period of continuous build-up. Aircraft strength attained the establishment figure of twenty-seven and the number of full crews reached the twenty mark for the first time. Runt Reynolds left the squadron and his place as OC of 'B' Flight was taken by SLdr Dicky Banker DSO DFC, who had almost completed his second tour of operations. S/Ldr Jim Clift OBE, an Australian serving with the RAF, was posted in and made the commander of 'C' Flight, which was organised on a skeleton basis. Dereck knew him from before the war.

Until late 1941 Squadrons of No. 5 Group each had two Flights, 'A' Flight and 'B' Flight. At this time with the idea of developing a greater striking force an extra Flight, 'C' Flight was formed at each Squadron. 'C' Flight of 455 Squadron was commanded by S/Ldr Jimmie Clift OBE, an Australian who had been in Training Command. While with this command he had pirated an idea we had developed in 50 Squadron to give aircrew simulated flight crew training on the ground using a Link Trainer. The pilot operated the Link Trainer while the crew were in phone connection (TR9) with him and simulated operational flights were carried out. Clift saw this arrangement in use at Waddington, took the idea back to HQ, incorporated a fuselage of an aircraft wreck for the crew accommodation and received an 'OBE' for his effort. From this primitive aircrew training device was developed the present day flight simulator, commonly used by civil aviation.

The squadron also gained a new commanding officer. W/Cdr Grant Lindeman, an Australian with six years of RAF service who arrived to take over from W/Cdr Gyll-Murray. Jack Lawson described him:

> The new commander made an immediate and favourable impression on all. He was Australian and (for purposes of morale at least) ostentatiously proud of it – young, keen and with an obviously alert observation and retentive memory in all Squadron matters. His first days with the squadron were memorable – correspondence and organisational arrears were tackled, all squadron men were interviewed and all property inspected. In three days it was obvious that he knew everybody, that all squadron information was firmly planted in his mind, that he knew what he wanted of the squadron and that he was determined to get what he wanted. At the end of those three days he proposed a party, and with his flight commanders and others made a highly successful attack on the Horse and Jockey Inn at Waddington. Initial target location was a difficulty, but once in the target area the attackers raided very successfully. The new 'Wingco' was put down as one who played as hard as he worked. Next day those who had attended thought it prudent to be on hand early in the morning. It was well that they did so, because the wing commander was also early, carrying on his work as though he had a good night's rest. The party was not mentioned by the 'Wingco' until after stand-down that day. The squadron knew where it stood. Work was work and play was decidedly play, but, after play, work went on again as if nothing had happened to interrupt it.[2]

Weather conditions in Lincolnshire, and reportedly over Germany, were appalling from the beginning of December until after Christmas. No attacks were made on major targets during this time, although a considerable number of mine-laying sorties were flown and attacks on Channel port targets were carried out without loss. Around this time Dereck had an intriguing visitor

I was visited by Sir Keith Murdoch of the Australian Press, seeking information as to the fate of one of my friends, S/Ldr R. Taylor DFC, who had failed to return from a raid during August. Dick Taylor had trained with me at Point Cook, had come to England with me, had served in 50 Squadron with me where we had each completed an operational tour on Hampdens, and later had followed me to 207 Squadron where he was killed on Manchesters.

Dick's father was the sports editor of one of Sir Keith's papers and had asked him to find out any further news regarding his son. I called to see Mr Taylor when I arrived in Melbourne several years later and found him to be still badly distressed at the loss of his son.

I told Sir Keith what little I knew, when he invited me bring some 455 chaps to a dinner and show in London to meet some of the newly formed No. 452 Squadron (RAAF) fighter chaps including Bob Bungey, Paddy Finucane, Bluey Truscott, Bardie Wawn and others. Wing Commander Bob Bungey DFC commanded 452 at the time, having served in the Battle of Britain with distinction. He was later posted back to Australia with the rank of acting wing commander, which he had earned and carried for a long time, to find that the RAAF personnel staff demoted him to his substantive rank of flying officer. Bob took his service pistol and went to the seashore near Adelaide where he blew his brains out. So much for RAAF recognition or appreciation of war service outside of Victoria Barracks. This ruling was later changed to allow personnel returning to Australia with acting ranks to retain those ranks.[3]

Sir Keith Murdoch's party in London was scheduled for 20 December, but before that the war situation changed suddenly and dramatically yet again, this time on the other side of the world. Using carrier-based aircraft, and without declaring war, the Japanese launched a surprise attack on United States military bases at Pearl Harbor in Hawaii on 7 December causing heavy casualties and extensive damage to the American Pacific Fleet and shore installations. Other Japanese attacks including landings that had already taken place simultaneously at Kota Bharu in Northern Malaya, and in Thailand at Singora and Patani near the Malayan border.

Then, in quick succession, the Royal Navy lost two of its most powerful capital ships, the *Prince of Wales* and the *Repulse*, off Malaya on 10 December, bringing Britain's great fortress at Singapore under serious threat. A grim new war was flaring up, spreading rapidly across the Pacific and into South-East Asia.

It was now that Hitler again demonstrated his flawed judgement, although few realised it at the time. In accordance with the Tripartite Pact signed by Germany, Italy and Japan in Berlin back on 27 September 1940, the *Führer* declared war on the US three days after the Japanese launched their attacks. Despite being already locked in battle with the Russians and having failed to knock Britain out of the war while she had no allies other than the Empire nations, his actions brought the two most powerful nations in the world, Soviet Russia and the US, into the war on Britain's side.

Meanwhile back in England, the RAF base at Swinderby became non-operational while it was being converted from a grass airfield to an aerodrome with sealed runways. This was to prepare for the heavier aircraft coming into service. No. 455 Squadron used Skellingthorpe for operations which they shared with 50 Squadron. Skellingthorpe airfield had been newly built among gravel pits and birch trees 3 miles (5 km) west of the centre of the city of Lincoln itself, and it took its name from the nearby village. It was actually 50 Squadron's new home having moved in there during late November. This meant that while 455 Squadron's personnel stayed in their comfortable pre-war quarters at Swinderby, they 'commuted' to Skellingthorpe for operations, a procedure that would continue for the next three months.

It was while he was at Skellingthorpe on 17 December that Dereck was issued with top secret orders to lead a special force of six Hampdens on a highly dangerous low level mission. They were instructed to attack the three huge German capital ships, battlecruisers *Scharnhorst* and *Gneisenau* and cruiser *Prinz Eugen*, sheltering in the harbour at Brest – in daylight. The chances of surviving such a raid were far from good. Perhaps this was it. Perhaps Dereck's flow of good luck was finally running out.

15

The Big Ships

They were massive; and they were dangerous – very dangerous. Since March and June 1941, three of Germany's major capital ships had been sheltering in the occupied French port of Brest. Two of them were huge battlecruisers, the *Scharnhorst* and the *Gneisenau*, each of 26,000 tons and armed with nine 28 cm, and twelve 15 cm guns. The third was the cruiser *Prinz Eugen* of 10,000 tons, armed with eight guns of 20.3 cm and twelve guns of 10.5 cm calibre.

Operating with escorts or as lone raiders, these vessels had sunk more than 100,000 tons of shipping since the beginning of the war. Off Norway in June 1940, the *Scharnhorst* and *Gneisenau* had sunk the RN aircraft-carrier HMS *Glorious* and two escorting destroyers. On 24 May 1941, the *Bismarck* and the *Prinz Eugen* had sunk the battleship HMS *Hood* with just three of her crew surviving. *Bismarck* was hit during the engagement and, because she was losing fuel, her captain decided to head for Brest. She became the quarry of an extensive hunt by British ships and aircraft. Three days later, *Bismarck* was found, crippled by naval gunfire and finished off with torpedoes, but the *Prinz Eugen* reached the safety of the heavily defended French port.

Although holed up in Brest for maintenance and repair, these warships were still a serious potential threat. Even without venturing out on the open sea, they tied down a large portion of the British fleet. The Royal Navy not only had to keep considerable forces on the alert in order to be sure convoys in the English Channel were protected, but also had to suspend the use of resources intended to operate in the Mediterranean against Axis shipping that was supplying Rommel in North Africa. British capital ships, including battleships and aircraft carriers, had to kept at Gibraltar in case of emergency.

The German ships were within range of the RAF. Brest was easy enough to find but it was heavily defended and ship targets required a high degree of accuracy to bomb. All told, the RAF would make 299 attacks on the warships sheltering in the harbour and lose 43 aircraft and 247 airmen in the process. As well as that, much of Bomber Command's attacking strength was being diverted from the more difficult-to-locate targets in Germany. Aerial reconnaissance needed to constantly monitor what was going on in the port.

On the other side, with the increasing intensity of the RAF's air attacks, the Germans had to anticipate that one day their warships could be put out of action completely. In which case all the positive effects of their threatening 'fleet in being' would end and so would any hope of the *Kriegsmarine*'s surface fleet resuming operations in the Atlantic. In fact, the *Gneisenau* would be hit twice by bombs and the *Scharnhorst* once, very heavily.

In December the British judged that the warships were close to becoming seaworthy again. On the 13th, Hampdens from Nos 44 and 144 Squadrons were detailed to lay mines in the mouth of Brest Harbour. It had to be done in broad daylight and without fighter escort. Of three Hampdens involved from 44 Squadron, the pilot of the first, S/Ldr Burton-Gyles DSO DFC (the same man who had landed his Manchester on only one wheel in February when returning from the first Manchester bombing raid) brought his aircraft back safely after laying his mines precisely in the right place, but when he landed he found his plane had suffered substantial damage. A wingtip had gone, an aileron was almost gone, the mainplane was full of holes, an engine fairing had gone, one of the airscrews had been hit, one rudder had been shot away and one of the wheels of the undercarriage had been punctured. Sgt Hackney, the pilot of the second aircraft tried to lay his mine next but found it impossible to place it down in the allotted position. The third aircraft, Hampden AE196, piloted by W/Cdr Sidney Misselbrook DSO was missing, lost without trace.

No. 144 Squadron at North Luffenham was also involved in laying mines off Brest that day and the Hampden (AD921) flown by P/O David McLaren and his crew was lost without trace too. The members of both crews are all commemorated on the RAF Memorial at Runnymede for those who have no known grave.

Meanwhile, Swinderby became non-operational for a lengthy period while it was being upgraded from a grass airfield to an aerodrome with sealed runways ready for the bigger, heavier bombers of the future. For operations, 455 Squadron used Skellingthorpe which they shared with 56 Squadron until Wigsley, a satellite aerodrome of Swinderby, was ready. It was at this time that Bomber Command chose Dereck for a 'top secret' operation.

While at Skellingthorpe on 17 December 1941, I received from No. 5 Group a Secret operation order instructing me to take control of six Hampdens, three from Swinderby and three from Luffenham, each armed with one 1900 lb GP (General Purpose) bomb fused with 11 seconds delay, and from Chivenor in North Devon carry out a low level attack on the German battle cruisers *Scharnhorst* and *Gneisenau* and perhaps the cruiser *Prince Eugen*, which were said to be in Brest harbour – weather conditions permitting.

CVR

IMMEDIATE

17 DEC 1941

CVR
GPS   NR 118   IMMEDIATE SECRET
PASS TO   CHIVENOR

ADDSD TO   SWINDERBY = LUFFENHAM = S/LD FRENCH (455 SQUADRON) AT
            CHIVENOR = REPEATED = ALL OTHER 5 GROUP STATIONS FOR
            INFORMATION .
FROM   NO 5 GROUP

A. FORM ''B''.638
B. 17 DECEMBER 1941
C. AS ALREADY ISSUED
D. TO CAUSE MAXIMUM DAMAGE TO ENEMY CRUISERS
E. 17 DECEMBER AND 18 DECEMBER
F. SWINDERBY 3 HAMPDENS
    LUFFENHAM 3 HAMPDENS
    ALL TO OPERATE FROM CHIVENOR UNDER COMMAND OF S/L FRENCH 455 SQDN

G. TOADS.
    =====
    THE PRIMARY TARGET IS THE GERMAN BATTLECRUISERS SCHARNHORST AND
    GNEISENAU BUT THE CRUISER PRINZ EUGEN MAY BE BOMBED AS AN
    ALTERNATIVE . NO OTHER VESSELS ARE TO BE ATTACKED.
H. NONE ISSUED .
J. NIL
K. AND L. AT DISCRETION OF S/L FRENCH.
M. AT DISCRETION OF S/L FRENCH BUT NO BOMBS ARE TO BE DROPPED
    AFTER 11.45 ON 18 DECEMBER ..
N. (1) THIS OPERATION IS TO BE CARRIED OUT BY SINGLE AIRCRAFT
         TAKING ADVANTAGE OF ADEQUATE CLOUD COVER.
    (2) IT IS NOT TO BE UNDERTAKEN IF THE CLOUD BASE IS HIGHER THAN
         (1500 FEET WITH 10/10 CLOUD 2000 FEET THICK) AND IMMEDIATELY
         THESE CONDITIONS CEASE TO PREVAIL THE OPERATION IS TO BE
         ABANDONED .
    (3) ALL AIRCRAFT ARE TO CARRY ONE 1900 LB GP BOMB FUSED 11
         SECONDS DELAY .
    (4) INTERCOM IN ACCORDANCE WITH 5 GROUP SIGNAL INSTRUCTIONS NO 1.
O. ACKNOWLEDGE BY TELEPRINTER.
P. 1415 +

Q F C + .
CC IN E. = DECEMBER +
A.MASON BB +
GPS   R....1828 FOOTE BBIMM+
  KKK

The 1,900 lb (862 kg) GP bomb was unknown to me and was apparently the largest general purpose bomb then available. Our job was to drop these between the cruisers and the dry docks in which they were standing, and by blasting out the supports cause the ships to topple over.

I arrived at Chivenor to arrange things for the rest of the team and to see them arrive individually. One came in too high, made a terrible approach and landing, dropping heavily, causing a tyre to blow out and catch fire. I waited for the fire to spread and the Hampden with its 1900 lb (862 kg) bomb go up, but luck was with us again and all we needed was a new wheel.

The operation order as regards weather was very limiting and I spent all day and all night in the operations room studying the weather reports as they came in from Hudsons of a 'stopper' patrol, one being flown by an Australian, F/Lt Terry, who kept a watch on activities on the approaches to Brest. By this time in my operational life I knew that my chance of returning from a raid of this nature was rather slight, especially as I had heard rumours of another Hampden raid which had gone badly a week or so earlier.

The Hampden raid Dereck had heard rumours about was the costly operation carried out by Burton-Gyles and the others on the 13th. On that occasion the task had been placing mines at the mouth of Brest Harbour. Dereck's mission was to go into the harbour itself at low level in a hunt for the capital ships. Audacious! There was little doubt about how the formidable German defences would react. The exploit could very well result in him receiving a Victoria Cross – most likely posthumously. Up to now Dereck had led a charmed life, but this was suicidal. Once again Dereck's good luck held.

The required weather conditions did not occur – much to my relief! The operation was cancelled and we returned to our respective bases. That same night 100 of our bombers attacked the ships, and more carried out a daylight raid the following day with the loss of two Manchesters.

In fact, the losses were far heavier. The overnight raid on Brest on 17/18 December involved 121 aircraft – seventy-two Wellingtons, twenty-five Hampdens and twenty-four Whitleys. Of these, eighty claimed to have bombed the approximate position of the German warships. One Hampden from 44 Squadron failed to return.

The follow-up daylight attack was carried out by eighteen Halifaxes, eighteen Stirlings and eleven Manchesters. Accurate bombing was claimed and black smoke was reported rising from the *Gneisenau* but the German defences were effective. The big Stirlings in particular were treated harshly by Messerschmitt 109s and four were lost. A fifth Stirling managed to return its crew back to base safely but it had been so badly damaged by flak and fighters that it had to be declared beyond repair. One Halifax had to ditch about 60 miles off the English coast, but fortunately only one crew member was injured. The two Manchesters that did not return were from Dereck's former unit, 97 Squadron.

Dereck had been visited by Sir Keith Murdoch prior to his proposed special Brest raid and had been invited to bring a couple of friends to a dinner and show in London. With the mission cancelled, he was free now to take up the invitation.

I arranged accommodation in London at my usual haunt, the Green Park Hotel, for Bob Anderson, Gordon Lind, Len Jeffries and myself while we were to attend Keith Murdoch's entertainment but found on arrival that there had been a mix up in the dates and they accommodated us in what they called their annexe. This annexe turned out to be a brothel and I had a difficult time explaining that I had no prior knowledge of the place.

Dereck, of course, neglected to mention the nature of the annexe in a letter home to his parents.

20/12/4. Al party given by Sir Keith Murdoch in London. Well, I went to London with three Aussie boys from our squadron. We were met at Kings Cross station, whisked away in a taxi and taken to a theatre where we met Sir Keith, A/Cdr McNamara and F/Lt Finucane, the Irish-Australian fighter ace. They were with some 40-odd Aussies from the Australian Fighter Squadron over here.

The show was the latest in London, a thing called *Get a Load of This* and was very good. We had cigarettes and programmes issued to us and after the show were escorted into a big double-decker bus which took us to the Cafe Royal where a slap-up dinner was prepared for about 50 of us. Sir Keith certainly did us well and we appreciated it very much. 452 Squadron (Fighters) at the close of the dinner presented him with a beautiful silver model Spitfire. He is a rather remarkable man and seemed to accomplish a hell of a lot in the short time he has been in England.

It was becoming usual for various representatives from the Australian press to visit 455 Squadron from time to time. When that happened, everyone went out of their way to stress to the visitors that because the squadron was so far away from home, it was actually a neglected and forgotten arm of Australia's military services. Dereck's conclusion was that this approach paid off, as in the same letter he wrote:

Australia House has just come good and sent us packets and packets of comforts for the troops including 350 Christmas hampers – 600 flannel undershirts and 250 pairs of sox as well as a cheque for £50.

It was a good Christmas, the first for 455 Squadron. The Handley Page Company, manufacturers of the Hampden bombers, generously donated cheques to those squadrons operating the type. Part of 455's donation was put into the Christmas Eve party in the airmen's mess. Gp/Capt H. V. Satterley DFC, the Station Commander, was an invited guest, and there was a large band of gate-crashers. One man who attended was LAC Lagettie wearing as a decoration an imposing head bandage. He was extremely fortunate to be there as he had just recently walked through the spinning propeller of a Hampden by accident and miraculously survived!

In the usual air force tradition, Christmas Day was celebrated by officers and sergeants acting as waiters in the airmen's mess and later by evening dinners in the officers' and sergeants' messes. Few personnel from 50 Squadron, with whom 455 had close links, were present. The squadron itself had gone north on temporary detachment to provide air cover for a secret commando raid on Namsos.

'Atrocious' weather conditions prevailed over Lincolnshire and Germany from the beginning of December until after Christmas and no attacks were made on major targets in that period. The squadron continued with mine-laying nevertheless, and there were a few attacks on the Channel ports, all without loss.

A week later it was back to business as usual. The year 1941 ended with a few days of fine weather and Bomber Command launched major attacks on three separate targets the night of 28/29 December: Wilhelmshaven, Huls and Emden. Eighty-one aircraft from No. 5 Group went for Huls, among them Dereck in Hampden AT114 with F/Sgt Maidment DFM, P/O Jeffries and Sgt Smith. Huls was a favorite strategic target for No. 5 Group, being a manufacturing centre for synthetic rubber. It was well inland and was usually difficult to pinpoint, but on this occasion with the countryside covered in snow the target was easily identified and attacked in the full moonlight. On his return, Dereck noted in his log book, 'Ops. Huls 9,000 feet. Very successful op. Full moon. 5 hrs. 20 mins.'

Although bombing results were deemed to be good, the raid was also costly with four Hampdens failing to return. All of the crews perished.

455 Squadron emerged unscathed this time. One Wellington was lost on the Wilhelmshaven raid and a Whitley did not come back from Emden. The attack on Huls was Dereck's last mission for the year.

To maintain the pressure on the German capital ships, Bomber Command sent sixteen four-engined Halifax bombers to attack them in Brest harbour on the 30th. Fourteen aircraft bombed in the right area but three were lost and all of those that returned were damaged by flak.

The New Year brought comparatively good flying weather and January became reasonably busy with operations. Although the weather was described as 'comparatively good', Lincolnshire was actually in the grip of the coldest winter for years and Skellingthorpe airfield was windswept, cold and without shelter. The runways were constantly covered with sheet ice and snow, and clearing them was an onerous, never-ending job.

The first operation of the year for 455 Squadron was a mine-laying mission to La Rochelle on the night of 2/3 January. Four aircraft took part and all reported laying their mines successfully, but Hampden P5328 flown by P/O Charles Ludwig crashed near Oxford on the way home. The aircraft burst into flames on impact and its wreckage was so scattered that the cause of the crash was impossible to establish. Ludwig was a quiet and efficient Scotsman and a graduate of Aberdeen University. He had been with the squadron for several weeks. He and his crew – P/O John Willox; Sgt Jim Stansfield, a New Zealander in the RAF; and P/O Alec Christie – were all killed. Alec Christie had been the squadron's first RAAF wireless operator to be commissioned.

As well as the regular mine-laying missions, raids on other targets were carried out in quick succession: three successful attacks on Emden; two on Hamburg; two on Munster; and one each on Cherbourg, Wilhelmshaven, Hanover, St Nazaire and Brest without loss.

Dereck's first mission in the New Year was on 6/7 January when Bomber Command sent nineteen Hampdens on roving patrols over Northern Germany. He labelled it as a 'nuisance raid' over Emden and the Ruhr in his log book and delivered his load accordingly. That night, thirty-one Wellingtons of No. 1 Group again attacked the German warships at Brest. One aircraft was lost. Although no extraordinary bombing results were claimed, not realised by the RAF at the time one bomb fell alongside the *Gneisenau* holing her hull and causing flooding in two compartments. The German command clearly realised that if the ships stayed in port, and the RAF kept up its assaults, they were vulnerable. The odds against them not receiving crippling damage increased day by day.

The RAF did not let up, continuing its pressure almost nightly. The previous evening, 5/6 January, 154 bombers had also raided Brest. Eighty-seven aircraft had been ordered to target the *Scharnhorst* and *Gneisenau*, while the remainder were to bomb the naval docks. A smoke-screen prevented accurate bombing but large fires were claimed to have been started. On this occasion no aircraft were lost. On 8/9 January, Brest was the target for 151 aircraft, one Manchester failed to return. The next night, 82 aircraft attacked Brest again, this time without loss. While the raid was in progress, five Hampdens were laying mines outside the harbour. On 11/12 January, 23 Wellingtons and three of the big four-engined Stirlings raided Brest again without suffering losses. And so it continued. Meanwhile, Dereck had other concerns: 'During December 1941 and January and February 1942, I became very much aware of events in the Pacific and I formed the idea that I should attempt to return towards Australia where I hoped I could put to use the experience I had gained in Europe.'

In a letter home dated 17/ January 1942, he said, 'Since I wrote last the Pacific question has become rather grim and we can only hope that the war will not extend to Australia.' He applied for a posting to a theatre of war closer to home.

The situations in the Far East and Pacific had indeed deteriorated with the start of the New Year, going quickly from bad to worse for the Allies. On 3 January, Japanese bombers raided Kuala Lumpur rendering it unusable. General Archibald Wavell, the former British commander in North Africa, was appointed to the newly established ABDA (American-British-Dutch-Australian) Command with instructions to hold the 'Malay Barrier' (a line from Malaya through the Dutch East Indies to Borneo) but rapid Japanese expansion was well on the way to making ABDA Command's existence very short-lived.

Next day saw the first Japanese air raids on Rabaul in New Britain. The first was carried out by twenty-two twin-engine Mitsubishi G3M Type 96 'Nells' bombing the airfield near the village from 12,000 feet. Over fifty high-fragmentation bombs were dropped. Late in the afternoon, eleven Kawanishi H6K Type 97 'Mavis' flying boats made two bomb runs over Vanu Kanau airfield. The RAAF air defence force, which had arrived the previous month with only four Lockheed Hudsons and ten hastily armed Wirraway 'fighters' (actually trainers based on the North American T-6), was totally outclassed and ineffective.

Three days later, on the 7th, seven Japanese 'Mavis' flying boats bombed Ambon in bright moonlight. It was Laha's first air raid. Buildings and workshops were damaged but there were no RAAF casualties. The Japanese were back bombing Laha again on 11 January, this time badly damaging the runway and igniting a fuel dump.

At Singapore on 17 January, Sembawang aerodrome was heavily bombed resulting in widespread damage including three Lockheed Hudsons and three Brewster Buffalo fighters destroyed. Sembawang was also heavily bombed on the 20th and again on the 22nd.

On 20 January, aircraft from a Japanese four aircraft carriers force attacked Rabaul. The RAAF officer in charge, W/Cdr John Lerew, had already pleaded in vain with RAAF Headquarters in Melbourne for modern fighters but there were none available. Two of his patrolling Wirraways were shot down by Mitsubishi Zeros. His six remaining Wirraways scrambled. One crashed just after takeoff, two were shot down over the sea, two force-landed damaged and one survived intact. According to myth, each lost Wirraway accounted for a Japanese aircraft, but that was only the face-saving propaganda of the time. The Japanese suffered no losses.

On 23 January, there were Japanese landings on Rabaul, Balikpapan in Borneo, near Kavieng on New Ireland and on Bougainville in the Solomons. At Rabaul, the isolated garrison defended fiercely before moving inland. Out of 200 who surrendered, 150 would be killed in cold blood the following March. Most of the remainder eluded the enemy and were taken off the island in a series of rescue missions over the next four months. Rabaul would soon be transformed into a major Japanese naval base. Two days later in Malaya, Batu Yahat, the last defensive position near the Muar River, was abandoned. From 29 January, RAF and RAAF units began evacuating from Singapore to Sumatra. Meanwhile, the remaining RAAF Hudsons at Ambon had to be withdrawn because of mounting enemy air raids. On 31 January, the causeway linking the Malay Peninsula to Singapore Island was demolished. Because of confused Allied leadership a determined and well-trained Japanese army of 35,000 had succeeded in ejecting General Arthur Percival's 60,000 British, Indian and Australian troops from Malaya.

The situation was deteriorating in North Africa too. British forces there had been weakened. Vitally needed reinforcements had to be diverted to the Far East instead and two Australian divisions were being withdrawn to defend Australia. At the same time, even as they were retreating, the Germans had been receiving new supplies of tanks and equipment and the Africa Corps' General Erwin Rommel, was planning a surprise counter offensive. By the end of January he had launched his counterattack and retaken Benghazi.

Meanwhile, for 455 Squadron back in England, bombing raids and mine-laying operations continued without casualties until the night of 21/22 January. That night the squadron lost two freshmen crews. Three aircraft had taken off bound for Emden captained by S/Ldr J. Clift OBE; Sgt G. Poulton and Sgt E. Thompson. S/Ldr Clift, another Australian serving with the RAF, had been made the commander of 'C' Flight and was well-known in air force circles because of his 'Clift Trainer'.

Until late 1941 Squadrons of No. 5 Group each had two Flights, 'A' Flight and 'B' Flight. At this time, with the idea of developing a greater striking force, an extra flight, 'C' Flight was formed at each squadron. 'C' Flight of 455 Squadron was commanded by S/Ldr Jimmie Clift OBE, an Australian who had been in Training Command. While with this command he had pirated an idea we had developed in 50 Squadron to give aircrew simulated flight crew training on the ground using a link trainer. The pilot operated the link trainer while the crew were in phone connection (TR9) with him and simulated operational flights were carried out. Clift saw this arrangement in use at Waddington, took the idea back to HQ, incorporated a fuselage of an aircraft wreck for the crew accommodation and received an OBE for his effort. From this primitive aircrew training device was developed the present-day flight simulator, commonly used by civil aviation.

There were two main targets that night, Bremen (54 aircraft) and Emden (38 aircraft including the three Hampdens from 455 Squadron). Two Hampdens and a Wellington failed to return from Bremen; three Hampdens and a Whitley did not come back from Emden. Clift returned after an unsuccessful search for the target in appalling weather conditions including unpredicted fog and severe icing. The other two 455 crews were later presumed killed. The lost aircraft and crews were Hampden AE352 which disappeared without trace with Sgt Evan Thompson (RAAF), P/O James Stanfield (RAAF) from New Ireland, Sgt Wilfred Giles (RAF) and Sgt William Mabbet (RAF); and Hampden AT119 shot down over Holland by a night-fighter with Sgt G. Poulton (RAAF), Sergeant Ian Ince (RAAF), Sgt Sam Williams (RAF) and Sgt George Wilkinson (RAF). Poulton, who became a POW, was the only survivor.

At the beginning of February Dereck wrote home.

1/2/42. The last three weeks have been a jolly hectic period for Australia now that the Japs are on the warpath. Over here in England we (Aussies in an Aussie Squadron) naturally feel a bit anxious and want to get back to a theatre of war nearer home. With this in mind I put in an application to be posted nearer home and only yesterday heard that it had gone as far as Bomber Command. This means that I stand a good chance of posting but as I have been here for a long time now and am rather 'long in the tooth' as regards night operations my old Group are reluctant to play ball. They cannot gain much by keeping me as within the next six months I should have finished ops here and have been sent on a long (so-called) rest to a training unit.

The squadron was also in a state of flux at this time because of the logistics of switching from Swinderby and its satellite Skellingthorpe, from where operational flying was carried out, to its new satellite airfield, Wigsley.

The 5th of February was a day of thick, low-lying fog causing extremely limited visibility – even 'the very birds were walking'. Operations were out of the question and flying training impossible, but the people at Group Headquarters seemed restless. They sent repeated requests for details of whatever training programme was being arranged. The questions came to Dereck who was in temporary command while Grant Lindeman was on leave. Irritated, he attributed Group's seemingly overzealous attention to boredom on a dull and foggy day.

Tongue- in-cheek, Dereck facetiously advised that he had organised a special 'star recognition class' for navigators. He and several others then proceeded to a cinema in Lincoln. On the way there, he noticed the sky was miraculously clearing! Soon every star in the sky was shining clearly on a still and moonlit countryside. He realised that his tongue-in-cheek 'star recognition class' was really possible. In the cinema after the film had started, a message appeared on the screen, 'Squadron Leader French to return to base at once.' In a letter home later he wrote: 'I sneaked out to a quiet flic the other night (Lincoln) and was hauled out of it after an hour when they flashed a notice on the screen to the effect that I was wanted.'

Dereck returned to base contemplating what trouble might be ahead. On arrival, he was ordered to have all available aircraft and crews on hand for a briefing half an hour before dawn ready for a possible dawn take-off. A busy night of preparation followed. There was no indication of the target so the armourers had also to be prepared to bomb-up at short notice with loads which were not yet determined.

The rostered crews were taken from Swinderby to Skellingthorpe for their pre-dawn briefing. There, instructions were then given to stand by for further orders! These did not come until much later in the morning. Eight aircraft were to be loaded with sea-mines to be 'planted' in areas off the Friesian Islands in the afternoon. The mission needed cloud cover for success and three of the eight aircraft, finding no cover, returned home according to orders. Four aircraft did find enough cloud cover and planted their mines but one aircraft, Hampden AE308/UB-L, with a very young, all-RAF, all-sergeant, crew failed to return. They were Bernard Brown (pilot), Robert Billington (navigator), David Pickersgill (wireless operator) and Eric Bland (air gunner). Their aircraft, Hampden AE308/UB-L was, in fact, shot down into the sea by a Messerschmitt 110 of *II/NJG1* flown by the German ace *Hptm* Helmut Lent. In all, thirty-three Hampdens and thirteen Manchesters were involved in the mining operation and Brown's aircraft was the only machine lost.

For those crews who did not go mine-laying, the standby at Skellingthorpe continued. Orders were again received for all crews to be ready for a dawn take-off the next morning. The dawn take-off was again postponed on 7 February, and that afternoon six 455 Squadron aircraft were detailed for more mine-laying off the Friesians. This time the German fighters were more active and out of a total of thirty-two Hampdens carrying out mining, three were shot down. Fortunately, all of 455 Squadron's crews completed their tasks and returned safely without incident except for one brief sighting of another Messerschmitt. This was 455 Squadron's last operation from Skellingthorpe. From now on the squadron would fly from Wigsley.

Grant Lindeman returned from leave on 8 February and resumed command. Wigsley airfield was about 7 miles west of Swinderby and under the operational and administrative control of Swinderby's Station Commander. Over the 8th, 9th and 10th, the transfer of 455's men, aircraft and equipment from Swinderby and Skellingthorpe was achieved smoothly despite the complications of still maintaining standby during the move. For the first time almost all of the squadron now lived and worked at one place, although the engineer officer and a party of men of the maintenance flight remained at Swinderby. The only others present not belonging to 445 were staff personnel for flight control, intelligence and messing duties.

Wigsley itself was new with a series of long concrete runways bordered by a perimeter road about 5 miles (8 km) long surrounded by dispersal sites for aircraft. There were no hangars. It was designed for the big new four-engined heavy bomber so taking off and landing in the comparatively small twin-engined Hampden was easy. On the other hand, there were comparatively long distances to cover between facilities. For example, the messes for officers, sergeants and airmen, plus very limited bathing facilities, were in a dispersed area around two-thirds of a mile from the squadron and flight offices and control tower. Further away still were the sleeping quarters in three separate dispersed camps. A fourth dispersed camp was said to be for WAAFs, but there were none there during the squadron's occupation.

Back in September and October 1939 this area had been the rural country on which Dereck and his companions in 50 Squadron and 44 Squadron had been permitted to shoot wild game once or twice a week. That was before the Air Ministry's bulldozers moved in. It had been first-class for bagging rabbits, hares, quail, pheasants, partridges and sometimes the odd woodcock. How things had changed. Now, over and over, the pilots were more stressfully and frustratingly employed on dawn readiness and daily standby. Discontent was growing. What was going on?

On 8 February a meeting was held at the Headquarters of RAF Coastal Command to consider the status of the big German ships taking refuge in Brest Harbour. Tides and predicted weather conditions were considered as well as the three big ships risky circumstances in the French port. Reconnaissance reported that, 'During the past three days, all three big ships have been exercising and should be ready for sea. There are four large destroyers and a number of small torpedo boats and minesweepers in Brest.' It seemed likely they might be planning to move – but if so, which way would they go, and when?

It was possible they could break out and make for the Mediterranean or perhaps the Atlantic. While feasible, it seemed more likely they would seek a safer haven rather than risk facing a superior British force of capital ships on the open sea. Another option was that they might break out and try to head up through the English Channel to Germany. This passage would have to be carried out under a protective air umbrella by the *Luftwaffe*'s land-based fighters, with the support of shore batteries along the coast and be escorted by strong flotillas of smaller naval vessels assembled in the various Channel ports. The weather and hour of sailing could be chosen to cause the British the greatest difficulty in intercepting the force. In fact, the British Home Fleet in its current position and deployment had no significant naval force which could seriously threaten such a passage.

The likelihood of a Channel dash had been thought of before. In April 1941, Bomber Command examined the possible routes that the German naval units might take if they left Brest. Its Operational Order of 1 May 1941 dealt with the possibility of the ships attempting to pass through the Strait of Dover in daylight. Plans to respond to such a breakout were drawn up under the code name of Operation *Fuller*. On 19 December 1941, Coastal Command Chiefs of Staff opposed the transfer of torpedo-bombers to the Middle East giving as their reason that 'in the event of a breakout of the German heavy ships from Brest, Coastal Command would need a greater force of torpedo-bombers than are at present available.'

Taking everything into account, the Commander-in-Chief of Coastal Command, Sir Philip Joubert de la Ferte, concluded 'The plan to break through the Channel will be put into execution at any time after Tuesday, 10 February 1942'. His words were prophetic.

And so at Wigsley, and indeed on many Bomber Command airfields, the frustrating routine of standby and cancelled orders persisted until the night of 11/12 February, although the cause of the standby fuss was still not known at squadron level. That night, Bomber Command issued orders for normal bombing attacks on two main targets, Mannheim and Le Havre. Three aircraft from 455 Squadron took part in the raid on Mannheim. All bombed successfully and returned safely. This was actually the first operation carried out from 455's new aerodrome.

None of the forty-nine aircraft sent to bomb Mannheim were lost due to enemy action, but in separate incidents a Wellington and Hampden crashed with engine trouble. One man was injured. From a force of thirty-one bombers dispatched to Le Havre, one Wellington disappeared without trace. Eighteen other Wellingtons raided Brest in worsening weather and one failed to return.

Next morning, 12 February, 155 Squadron's standby was abandoned. Wigsley received completely different orders that required all officers who had not previously attended at least two courts martial to attend a court martial at Swinderby as 'officers under instruction'. This meant that every junior officer, at least one member from all the available crews, was involved. The disgruntled men were assembled in a large bus and sent off to the court martial. According to stories told later, instead of going to Swinderby the bus driver went to Skellingthorpe by mistake. When the officers found there was no court martial at Skellingthorpe, they persuaded the driver to proceed on to Lincoln where, on arrival, they rapidly dispersed. They were not in the mood to waste their time chasing down an elusive court martial after six frustrating days of standbys.

Much later in the morning, Wigsley received an angry enquiry from Swinderby wanting to know the whereabouts of the 'officers under instruction' – but at almost the same time, a more serious event pushed this problem into the background.

Shortly before midday a message came through that a German naval force including the battlecruisers *Scharnhorst* and *Gneisenau* and the cruiser *Prinz Eugen* was proceeding up the English Channel at high speed, probably heading for Emden or Kiel. The Germans had chosen a good day for leaving Brest. Low cloud and poor weather concealed their movements. They were not reported until late in the morning after a Spitfire pilot spotted them off Le Touquet. The warning came at a time when most of Bomber Command had been stood down for the day. Only No. 5 Group was at four hours' notice. A desperate attempt had to be mounted to stop them. As far as it was able to be implemented, Operation *Fuller* was put into effect. All the available RN and RAF units were ordered to attack the German ships before they could escape into the night.

For months we had been bombing Brest in the hope of destroying or damaging the battle cruisers *Scharnhorst*, *Gneisenau* and *Prince Eugen* with a great cost of lives and aircraft and with little success. They broke out on the night of 11 February 1942 and were not sighted until late on the morning, of the 12th steaming north in formation with a large escort, well up the English Channel. It was this that had caused the interruption of my picture show. At Wigsley, the panic was on…

The immediate difficulty for 455 Squadron was that every crew had at least one member missing somewhere in Lincoln. A van was sent to find them. In the long run it managed to collect all the escapees. However, they arrived at haphazard intervals. Realising that normal crewing up was impossible the CO Grant Lindeman allocated aircraft to any pilot, any navigator and any two wireless operator/gunners that could be combined to form a complete crew as they became available, regardless of the usual crew arrangements.

'Scratch' crews were formed as chaps arrived; aircraft were bombed-up and were sent off individually to see what could be done to stop the ships. Our aircraft were loaded with GP (General Purpose) bombs which were virtually useless against targets of this nature.

The original plan [Operation *Fuller*] for attack by Bomber Command on these vessels should they make an escape dash from Brest had been to drop semi-armour piercing (SAP) bombs of up to 500 lb for the job. These SAP bombs were not really effective if dropped below about 7,000 feet and as the cloud base on 12/2 in the Channel area varied between 700 feet and 2,000 feet most of us carried the comparatively ineffective GP bombs.

Cloud cover over the German ships was reported to be at about 1,000 feet. Bombs which would explode when dropped from that height would not penetrate the deck armour of the bigger ships. Bombs which would penetrate armour before exploding had to be dropped from a much greater height to be effective. Besides that, the dropping of bombs through cloud on comparatively small, mobile targets and hitting them was virtually impossible. After contradictory orders and much loading and unloading of aircraft, this problem was tackled by loading some machines with bombs for low level use and others with armour-piercing bombs, and hoping somewhat optimistically that one or the other might work.

Dereck's log book shows that he was allocated Hampden P5325 for the mission and he was crewed with P/O Daly, Sgt Roberts and Sgt Marshall. His bomb load consisted of four 500 lb bombs and two 250 lb bombs.

While all this was happening, part of the Fleet Air Arm's meagre force of available torpedo-bombers, six slow Fairey Swordfish biplanes, was being shot out of the sky by *Luftwaffe* fighters and anti-aircraft fire from the ships. None survived. The leader of the formation, Lt Cdr Eugene Esmonde, was later awarded a posthumous Victoria Cross.

The first aircraft from Bomber Command were airborne at 1.30 p.m. and by the time darkness fell 242 sorties had been flown. Almost every type the command had flew, but not as part of a cohesive force. They could only mount piecemeal attacks, *if* they could find the enemy. Altogether, Bomber Command put into the air ninety-two Wellingtons, sixty-four Hampdens, thirty-seven Blenheims, fifteen Manchesters, thirteen Halifaxes, eleven Stirlings and ten new US-built Douglas Bostons, which officially were not yet operational. It was the largest Bomber Command daylight effort of the war so far, but it was wasted. In the poor weather conditions, most of them were not able to find the fast-moving German ships. Those that did had to run the gauntlet of either heavy anti-aircraft fire, or fighters, or both.

According to subsequent reports only thirty-nine aircraft – less than one in six – located the targets, attacked them and returned. Nine Hampdens of 455 Squadron took off individually to attack the warships. Of these, five of them, more than half, attacked and returned. A sixth aircraft was never seen again but it was thought certain to have attacked.

Jack Lawson interviewed his former CO, Grant Lindeman, after the war for his book *The Story of 455 (RAAF) Squadron*. He recorded that 'The comments of Lindeman – a great lover of the sea and student of ships – on his reactions were entertaining…"What beautiful ships. Why should anyone want to bomb them?"; then, "Thank God I'm in a Hampden and not a Whitley"; and finally, "What a fool I am to be here at all."'

Lindeman 'bombed a ship from 800 feet and climbed into cloud before seeing his bombs burst.' Clift reported the anti-aircraft fire from the ships as so intense that he was frightened to put his hand out of the cockpit. Sgt Wincott, who bombed at 5.06 p.m., had his aircraft hit by flak while making his attack and did not see the results. Dereck wrote:

Targets of the nature of this convoy, could, at that time, have been damaged only by torpedoes or a dense mine field... Cloud in the target area was about 9/10 with its base at about 1,000 feet and visibility below the cloud was good although it was rather frightening as all types of RAF bombers appeared fleetingly in the lower cloud layers as they searched. Eventually we found the enormous convoy – and it *was* enormous as by this time it consisted of the three major cruisers supported by six large destroyers with 50 odd E-boats and mine sweepers steaming at full speed in a formation resembling a walking stick and leaving a very visible wake. We bombed one of the major vessels but did not seem to do any harm. The anti-aircraft fire was rather savage, but we received little damage.

In fact, Dereck's aircraft *was* damaged but not critically and he simply noted laconically in his log book, 'A/C Holed'. For him and his scratch crew this nightmarish sortie lasted three hours and five minutes before they landed more or less unscathed back on the ground at Wigsley. In another letter home shortly after, he wrote:

Since we came in here the two German battleships *Gneisenau* and *Scharnhorst* broke out of Brest and gave us a lot of excitement as they made north towards the Helgoland Bight. We took part in this, together with many other craft. I lost my deputy flight commander, a chap named F/Lt Perrin who was about 33 and had been at Point Cook in 1930. Wally Perrin was a Mining Engineer whose life should not have been wasted in such a way.

The loss of Walter 'Wally' Perrin was a sad one for Dereck and the squadron. He was well over the normal aircrew age and had trained at Point Cook as a pilot in about 1930 and had completed his Air Force service and been placed on the reserve. At the outbreak of war he sought flying duties with the RAAF but was told that he was too old and most likely to be called up for administrative duties. To avoid this possibility, he left Australia and worked as an engineer in Johannesburg. In May 1940 he worked his passage to England and the RAF did accept him for aircrew duties. Unfortunately, he could not produce his flying log book so he was obliged to complete and pass his training course like any other recruit. When his pilot training was completed he was assigned to duties in Training Command, where he attained the acting rank of flight lieutenant, but that was not what Perrin wanted. By foregoing his acting rank and making persistent requests, he obtained a posting to an operational training unit and finally a posting to 455 Squadron for operational flying. With the squadron he quickly made his mark and again received promotion to the acting rank of flight lieutenant. On his last flight he was accompanied in Hampden P1156/UB-F by P/O Alex Abbott (RNZAF) as navigator; F/O Ed Symons (a Canadian in the RAF), wireless operator; and Sgt Ralph Tomlinson (RAF), air gunner. They disappeared without trace, probably shot down into the sea. Their names are commemorated on the Runnymede Memorial.

None of the bombing attacks caused any serious damage to the German warships but during the night the two largest, the *Scharnhorst* and the *Gneisenau*, were damaged by mines in the vicinity of the Frisian Islands. *Scharnhorst* struck mines twice and *Gneisenau* once. This was where the Hampdens and Manchesters of No. 5 Group had been active during the preceding week. A total of ninety-five mines had been laid in the area, fifty-one by Hampdens and forty-four by Manchesters, at a cost of four Hampdens lost. The capital ships and their escorts were forced to slow down, but all of the enemy ships eventually managed to reach the relative safety of ports in Germany before daybreak. The only damage to the German battlecruisers was caused by mines – perhaps they were placed there by 455 Squadron...

The cost to Bomber Command of the 12 February action was fifteen aircraft missing and two crashed on return. Coastal Command's No. 16 Group lost three Beauforts in torpedo attacks and two Hudsons in bombing sorties. Fighter Command lost six Hurricanes, six Spitfires and four Whirlwinds, mainly off the Belgian and Dutch coasts, and the six Swordfish of the Fleet Air Arm's 825 Squadron were wiped out.

It had been a disastrous day for the Royal Navy and the RAF, but for Dereck and 455 Squadron it was not yet over. That night four freshman crews were sent to lay mines in the Emden area but the crew of Hampden AD783/UB-U reported engine trouble and turned back. The aircraft was seen to crash in the village of Eagle within sight of the airfield. Dereck attended the scene.

One of our mining Hampdens in trouble with engines, turned for base soon after take-off but crashed in flames into the little village of Eagle in Lincolnshire. I went to the crash scene, saw the mine in the fire and had just had the village cleared of people when it blew up and took most of the roofs from the houses. The only casualties were our 455 Squadron crew who were all killed.

Those who perished were Sgt John Kennedy (RNZAF), Sgt Verner Hopwood (a Rhodesian in the RAF), Sgt William Kelly (RAF) and Sgt George Metcalfe (RAF). Dereck's sortie against the big ships was his second last with 455 Squadron.

16

The End of England – Reflections

The escape of the big ships from Brest to ports in Germany did not mean the campaign against them would be abandoned. In the ensuing days, the cruiser *Prinz Eugen* was damaged by a torpedo from the submarine HMS *Trident* and she took shelter in a Norwegian fjord near Trondheim. The Fleet Air Arm went after her but an air attack on 21/22 February was unsuccessful because of poor weather. Meanwhile, the RAF raided Wilhelmshaven and Kiel and continued with mine-laying operations outside various ports and Heligoland. During the escape, the *Gneisenau* had struck a mine and been lightly damaged but *Scharnhorst* had hit two and suffered damage described as 'serious'. The following night, Bomber Command raided the floating dock at Wilhelmshaven which was capable of being used to repair any of the big ships. During a raid on Kiel harbour by sixty-one bombers on 25/26 February, the *Monte Sarmiento* was destroyed with the loss of up to 130 lives.

Next night, forty-nine aircraft raided Kiel again. A direct hit on the bow of the *Gneisenau* by a high-explosive bomb caused severe damage and killed 116 of her crew. This effectively marked the end of this huge battlecruiser as a fighting unit as she was never repaired. Her guns were later removed and positioned for coastal defence.

In the meantime, No. 5 Group's Hampden bombers continued with their widespread mine-laying operations – their 'gardening'. A representative of the Australian press, Justin Arthur, visited 455 Squadron and afterwards described the typical activities of those aircrew who were involved each night. His report was dated 26 February 1942:

OUR AIRCRAFT LAID MINES IN ENEMY WATERS.
ALL RETURNED SAFELY.

by Justin Arthur

I have just returned from the station where from these Australians manned bombers – big twin-engined Hampdens with distinctive twin-tailed slim fuselage – fly and can testify that all returned safely, although one bore marks of three direct shell hits received at very close range. Although the procedure of pilots before they take off on night raids is now thoroughly known to all men on the station, there is, nevertheless, an air of suppressed excitement as night draws on. Sitting in the mess you'll see pilots who are picked for that particular job, sitting apart from others, perhaps trying to snatch a little sleep in easy chairs near the stove. Later in the night they went to the briefing room where they received instructions before the raid, and were told their primary and secondary targets – if due to weather or other reasons it is impossible to reach the main objective, pilots are always given alternative or secondary targets, where they can unload bombs and mines, because it is dangerous to return and land in the darkness with a load of high explosives. A meteorological officer (a civilian) attends the briefing, and tells pilots of the kind of weather they can expect en route and over the target. If he decides that weather conditions are going to be too bad, then operations are 'scrubbed', i.e., abandoned, for that night.

Bomber Command does not risk valuable crews and machines if the weather is impossible, although these Hampdens do take off during quite difficult conditions. For instance, the night I was there, there were flurries of snow and an overcast sky – in pilots' language 10/10 cloud.

After briefing some pilots and crews went to bed for a few hours sleep; others came in to the mess and joined in a game of poker; others read or dozed. I played poker with the squadron doctor – Flight Lieutenant John Milton, ex-Sydney gunnery officer, Flying Officer Bennett, from Brisbane, and Squadron Leader Derek [sic] French, from Melbourne, who is one of the most experienced pilots in the squadron, and has done a lot of flying in Whitley and Manchester bombers in addition to Hampdens.

The Squadron Adjutant, Flight Lieutenant Jack Lawson, of Castlemaine Victoria, played a race game with some pilots, and the squadron's mascot, a small black kitten, played with a piece of paper on the floor. The squadron is a bit worried about the kitten, as it doesn't seem to grow very much, but it is very playful. Somebody told me that lack of growth must have been the result of dropping it to see if it could land on its feet. It always did, but apparently it didn't help it grow. As the time for the raid drew closer, pilots, observers, gunners, radio-operators, got up and put on flying suits, and 'Mae-Wests', while ground crews ran up motors and prepared rubber dinghies in case of emergency. Each crew member gets a little parcel to carry with him, containing chocolate, peppermints, and other sweets 'something to chew on the way'. Each Hampden carries four men – pilot, navigator, radio-operator-gunner and rear-gunner. The space inside is restricted owing to the narrow fuselage, but is warm compared with some bombers, so that the crew are fairly comfortable. Hampdens are not the fastest bombers in the service, but eminently manoeuvrable, and pilots like them very well.

Squadron Leader French was the officer-in-charge of operations that night. He took me to the control tower, from which I could see long rows of lights, showing paths for the aircraft taxying and taking off. It was snowing slightly, and the sky was completely over-clouded as the first bomber taxied to the take-off position. The captain's voice came over the radio saying he was ready, and the control officer gave him the word to go ahead. There was the roar of motors amid the general rumbling noise, as other bombers taxied along the flare paths, and I dimly saw a big black shape in the runway lights, as the pilot got the machine's tail up, and soared into the darkness. 'Well, that's one away,' French said. 'It's always a ticklish business getting them off with heavy loads of mines and bombs. There's no time to make mistakes in this business, and if they crash, well it is too bad.'

All this time planes were moving along the taxying paths into position, and one after another they sped along the runway, and lifted easily. One or two showed white lights as they took off, but French said they needn't have done that, it was only necessary to show the red and green navigation lights.

The noise of the engines gradually died away, and we settled down to await their return. It was to be a relatively short job, and the first bomber was expected back at just about daylight. By now, the board in the control room showed all bombers to be airborne, except one, whose magnetos failed at the critical moment. This fault was detected while the pilot was running up the motors, and there was never any danger that the machine would have taken off in such a condition.

Two WAAF watchkeepers sat by the radio receivers ready to pick up the first news of the returning bombers, and the Control Officer and Intelligence Officer sat in easy chairs in front of the stove, while French and I went for a walk round the station. He showed me the dinghy crew standing by their machine. This crew goes into action if a machine is reported to be forced down, and when the position is located, they fly out and drop special large rubber dinghies fitted with all kinds of equipment such as books, brandy and rations, wherein the crew of the bomber can make themselves more comfortable than in the small dinghy carried aboard their own plane.

Streaks of dawn were showing in the sky as the radio receivers in the control tower crackled into life, and the Hampden bomber 'J for Johnny' announced he was approaching the field. The WAAF gave him the necessary weather data, and told him to land at such and such a runway, and received an acknowledgement.

Long rows of yellow lights outlining the runway sprang up, and as the darkness turned to daylight, the big bomber circled the field, approaching with the rumble of engines, and touched down lightly and came to a halt with squealing brakes. The pilot's voice came over the radio and announced that 'J for Johnny' had landed and taxied off the runway. It was the end of the night's work for him.

'That was a good landing,' French explained, 'He did a good wheel landing, i.e., he touched down on the main wheels instead of the conventional three-pointer and let the tail gradually sink down as the plane ran along. This makes a gentle shockless landing, which is very necessary if the plane is bringing back mines, which are the touchiest things, and are liable to go off if they're not watched.'

As we watched plane after plane coming in, after getting instructions from the control tower, they landed, taxied off the runway, and the crews went in for interrogation.

'We ran into plenty of flak, but dropped our mines OK,' Pilot Officer Jim Catanach of Melbourne, told the Intelligence Officer. 'We felt and heard plenty of bumps and bangs, but she kept flying alright. We came in low, and dropped delayed action bombs among the crews of a big anti-aircraft battery on the island at the mouth of the Elbe River. There were some pretty big explosions.'

When Catanach's plane was examined, it was seen that there were pretty good reasons for the crew feeling bumps. The port rudder and fin were almost completely shot away; there was a shell hole in the fuselage about six feet from the tail, and another hole just behind the port motor. These weren't just holes from shell splinters, but direct hits from small calibre – possibly two inch high explosive projectiles, but despite all this Cattenach had landed, as though nothing at all was wrong. It was a tribute both to his piloting ability and to the staunch all metal machine.

It was getting late, and all the machines were in except one with an all-Australian crew – Captain Pilot Officer Bert Martin of Sydney; Pilot Officer Navigator John Leggo of Newcastle; Wireless Operator-Air Gunner, T. Foxlee of Brisbane; Air Gunner Sgt T. Simpson of Hobart. Minutes went by with no sign of Martin's machine. Everyone was still hoping but inclined to think he must have 'bought it' somewhere over enemy waters, when there was the roar of a machine, which skimmed down over the field, circled around and landed. It was the missing

Martin, without a scratch on his plane. He had apparently stooged around after laying his mine and dropping his bombs, and had done some machine gunning around the Heligoland Light.

Now they had all come home safely, and the weary crews turned in to get some sleep.

Not one of our aircraft is missing.

Dereck remembered the correspondent, 'Justin did a lot of good work for the Australians working with the RAF. He was a young keen type who, I believe, later trained as aircrew and was killed in action.'

It was with one of these mine-laying missions that Dereck brought his operational flying with 455 Squadron to a close. His log book shows it took place on the night of 7/8 March. He flew Hampden AT189 crewed with P/O Jeffries, F/Sgt Maidment DFM and Sgt Smith.

My next and last trip with 455 was just another mine laying trip to Lorient, a submarine base south east of Brest. The crew included Sgt Smith who had flown with me many times as an air gunner, but who at times I wished would find another crew. He was a nice enough little married English RAF chap – the only married type I can remember being crewed with. He was a good rear gunner but it seemed that whenever I went for a drink at any of the watering holes of Lincoln, his wife would appear magically and give me a verbal bashing as to why he should not continue to fly on operations. It was, perhaps, really to escape Mrs Smith that I applied for a posting. I do not know the ultimate fate of her husband.

Len Jeffries, a Queenslander, was a good friend and navigator of my basic crew while I was with 455 Squadron. He remained with the squadron when I went to the Middle East, when he reached the rank of flight lieutenant and was awarded the DFC and a MID for his efforts.

One Hampden out of seventeen which the RAF dispatched that night failed to return, an aircraft from Dereck's old unit, No. 50 Squadron. Quoting from Jack Lawson's book, Dereck commented later:

455 Squadron achieved much during its short life with Bomber Command; it quickly became operationally efficient, so that within five months of commencement of operations, 'the Squadron learned with great interest and satisfaction that the official summary of operations showed that 455 had achieved the best percentage record in No. 5 Group for primary targets located and attacked during January – a very good record indeed for a squadron composed almost entirely of inexperienced crews.'

The squadron unconsciously performed the role of an operational training unit for many who were to go on to greater bombing feats. Foremost among these was H. B. 'Mick' Martin who was to become the most highly decorated Australian pilot of WW2. He flew as deputy leader to Guy Gibson on the Dam Buster raid and was later knighted becoming AVM Sir H. B. Martin with two DSOs, three DFCs and an AFC – a truly super Australian.

Mick was in my 'A' Flight of 455 Squadron at Wigsley and had been ordered to carry out with others NFTs (night flying tests) on their Hampdens. I chanced to look out of the flight office window and saw three Hampdens doing a close formation take-off. Mick Martin was leading it. Mick's navigator was another Australian to achieve fame with the Dam Busters. He was Jack Leggo DFC and Bar. He was later knighted.

During April 1942, Nos 455 and 144 Squadrons left Bomber Command and became part of Coastal Command assuming a torpedo dropping role with that command. During September 1942 a detachment of these torpedo Hampdens [455 led by Grant Lindeman] flew to Russia and operated for about six weeks before being returned to the UK by sea on a naval vessel.

The Hampdens were handed over to the Russians, as it seemed doubtful if they could safely make the return flight against the prevailing westerly winds, using low octane Russian fuel from a base so close to the front that the German Air Force was constantly aware of their activities.

On the way to Russia, two of the sixteen Hampdens failed to make it. One crashed in Sweden and all in the crew were killed, the other flown by S/Ldr Jimmy Catanach forced landed in Norway where the crew became German prisoners. Catanach took part in the 'Great Escape' after which he was, with fifty others, recaptured and murdered by the Germans.

The 'Great Escape' took place on the night of 24/25 March 1944 when seventy-six Allied prisoners escaped via a tunnel from the German POW camp *Stalag Luft III* (Sagan). Just three men managed to make a successful 'home run'. The rest were recaptured. On Hitler's orders, fifty of these men were singled out by the *Gestapo* and murdered. The incident has been the subject of numerous books and articles, most notably *The Great Escape* by Paul Brickhill, and a major film of the same name (albeit with a fictitious element added to it for American audiences).

For his work with 455 Squadron, Dereck was awarded a Bar to his DFC but with the Squadron's April transfer out of Bomber Command to Coastal Command and the worsening situation on the other side of the world, coupled with his desire to be closer to home, it was time to move on.

Although my application to be posted to a theatre of war closer to Australia had been eventually approved and I had been granted 'embarkation leave', owing to shipping shortages the leave was extended for week after week, during which time I grew tired of recurring farewell parties. During this period, I spent a considerable amount of time at the Ludgate Club in Fleet Street, London, a hangout of the Australian press representatives.

Also on embarkation leave with me was S/Ldr Bluey Truscott, who was returning to Australia. He was accompanied by a girlfriend, Margot. We gave him a rip-roaring send-off party one night only to have him return the next night for a second one – his embarkation leave having been extended further. He was later killed in Australia.

Probably the most publicised and best known of all of the Australian aces, red-haired Keith 'Bluey' Truscott was born in Prahan, Victoria, on 17 May 1916. He served in the first RAAF fighter squadron in Europe, 452 Squadron, scoring many successes, and in January 1942 he was promoted to command. On his return to Australia he received a hero's welcome. When RAAF authorities attempted to reduce him to his substantive rank of flight lieutenant because there were no squadron commander vacancies available, there was such a public outcry that he was allowed to retain his rank and was posted to New Guinea as a supernumerary squadron leader in 76 Squadron RAAF. Flying P-40 Kittyhawks in the Battle of Milne Bay in August/September 1942, he became the squadron's CO when S/Ldr Peter Turnbull was killed and led the unit back to Australia at the end of the year. During the night of 20/21 January 1943, he shot down a Japanese bomber over Darwin to bring his score to 15 plus 3 probables and 3 damaged. He was killed in a flying accident on 28 March 1943.[1]

Another farewell worthy of record was to the Australian war correspondent Reg Leonard (later knighted) who had been a true and helpful friend to all in 455 Squadron, in fact to all Australians in the UK. He presented any grievances our Australian chaps might have had to those at home by means of his articles with the Australian Associated Press. His flat in London was an open house to any Australian aircrew without a bed. Reg Leonard was really responsible for the formation of the Codgers Club nearly opposite the Ludgate Club in Fleet Street.

Reg Leonard's farewell dinner was held at the Waldorf. It was a posh affair attended by about a dozen chaps from the press and air force, all of whom made speeches. 'Codgers' was a corner of the bar of Ye Olde Codgers Inne, where Eve, the daughter of the proprietor, kept a book called *Bastards I've known from Down Under*, which contained more than 7,000 names of Australian chaps who had visited the place. Codgers was a popular watering hole for visiting Australians who seemed to gravitate to 'Kangaroo Corner'. I was a very early entry in the list of members.

Among those present at Reg Leonard's farewell were AVM McNamara VC RAAF,[2] who was in charge of RAAF affairs at Australia House in London, and

S/Ldr Hughie Birch DFC[3] of 10 Squadron RAAF, who had trained with me at Point Cook in 1937. It was a good show.

I had been with the RAF by now for more than four years and had seen a fair amount of service life both in peace and war. I was grateful for the opportunity I had to see so much of the UK, and to have been on hand to take part in so many interesting and exciting flights. Even so, I realised I had been more than lucky to have survived almost unscathed.

What I did not know then was that from mid-1942 on, Bomber Command operations would become more massive and professional and the bomber casualty figures would grow as the German defences escalated, so that aircrew were very lucky indeed to survive a single operational tour.

The new AOC of Bomber Command was Air Chief Marshal Sir Arthur Harris, formerly Dereck's AOC in No. 5 Group and soon to become known as 'Bomber' Harris. Under his auspices Bomber Command was expanding and changing. It was recovering from its heavy losses of 1939–40, re-equipping its squadrons with new aircraft, and receiving an increasing influx of new crews under the Empire Air Training Scheme. It was also re-assessing its training and tactics. Many outdated and seriously flawed bombing ideas from WW1 and the years of peace were discarded. Bomber crews had not been achieving good results because of their frequent inability to even find their targets in the dark and, if they did, to bomb accurately. There had been a lack of navigational aids and the elementary training the crews were receiving had been rushed and inadequate.

Probably the most significant change was the creation of a special pathfinder force with expert navigators utilising the most up-to-date navigational equipment, to lead the main-force crews to the target. This was the brainchild of another Australian, former Queenslander Donald Bennett. Although Harris did not initially favour the idea, the search began for the best navigators, pilots and aircrew for specialised training in locating and accurately marking targets at night.

Bennett also wanted the best aircraft (his decision to request de Havilland Mosquitoes was inspired), and the finest radar equipment for navigation. An apparatus called *Gee* had just been introduced and two new devices, *H2S* and *Oboe*, were in the pipeline. *Gee* received radio pulses from England which could enable an aircraft's navigator to follow a set course and determine their position on the track to a target. Bennett worked closely with the scientists to perfect the *H2S* and *Oboe* systems. They would all profoundly affect the accuracy and efficiency of the night bombing campaign.

H2S was a ground-scanning radar set in the aircraft which allowed bomb aimers to detect a target through cloud cover, and *Oboe* was a system that guided aircraft to a specific location with ground-based radar from England; unlike *Gee*, which only received, the transmitted pulses were echoed back from the aircraft to the source of origin in England.

For bombing accuracy, Bennett and the Pathfinders developed and used three main pyrotechnic methods of illuminating targets. They were code-named *Newhaven*, *Parramatta* and *Wanganui*. *Newhaven* was visual ground marking. Aiming points were first identified with hooded flares that shone downwards to allow more accurate marking by a second wave of aircraft dropping Target Indicator (TI) flares. *Parramatta* was blind ground marking. Aircraft using *H2S* dropped target indicators to illuminate the general attack area. Backup aircraft then dropped more TIs in a contrasting colour more precisely on the target. *Wanganui* was sky marking, an involved technique used when targets were obscured by cloud. Hanging flares were dropped using radar navigation. Main-Force bombers, flying on fixed courses, released their bombs when the flares appeared in their sights.

The latter part of 1942 saw these new methods tried, tested and constantly improved. From 1943 onwards, the Third Reich began to suffer the consequences of the lethal whirlwind it had unleashed in September 1939.

On 8 January 1943, the Pathfinder Force achieved group status, becoming Bomber Command's No. 8 Group. Harris retained Don Bennett in command, and before 1943 closed he was a thirty-three-year-old air vice-marshal, the youngest in the RAF, having risen from wing commander within a year! During the course of the war, the Pathfinder Force grew from five squadrons of assorted aircraft to eighteen squadrons of Lancasters and Mosquitoes. It flew almost 55,000 sorties and marked over 3,000 targets. The new technology and proficiency it developed contributed significantly to Bomber Command becoming one of the most potent juggernauts in the air war. German scientists never managed to completely jam the new radar devices, nor duplicate the flares for setting decoys.

Despite No. 8 Group's acknowledged accomplishments, Donald Bennett was the only group commander in Bomber Command not awarded a knighthood at the end of the war. His autobiography, *Pathfinder*, was first published by Frederick Muller Ltd in 1958. Books by others and many articles have followed. Bennett died on 15 September 1986 aged seventy-six. His widow, Ly, took over as patron of the Pathfinder Association.

The cost in lives lost for those serving in Bomber Command was huge. Figures vary slightly according to parameters but Martin Middlebrook and Chris Everitt in their *Bomber Command War Diaries* assessed Bomber

Command's RAF casualties at 38,462 aircrew killed (which would include many from the Commonwealth dominions who, like Dereck, were serving in the RAF); RCAF killed 9,919; RAAF killed 4,050; RNZAF killed 1,679; Polish Air Force killed 929; other Allied air forces killed 473; SAAF killed 34; and other dominions 27 – a massive total of 55,573. That was only part of it. On top of that there were those with lingering wounds, physical and mental, and injuries that were permanent.[4]

The next three years of Bomber Command's war belong to another story. Dereck was not to be part of the RAF's war over German-occupied Europe for much longer. It was time for him to take on another role. His fate lay elsewhere.

I had found squadron life to be very satisfying with the great variety of personnel and action one encountered, not to forget the fairly active social life one had when off duty. Nevertheless, it was frustrating as few flying friends were around for any length of time, having either been killed, posted or listed missing. The turnover of aircrews was rather grim.

It was fairly common and easy in those days to arrange aircrew postings so that fellow colonials could serve together. On one occasion while on leave in London I met a RAAF aircrew, F/O Seth Manners, and wangled a posting for him to join 455 Squadron. I found that he had joined the squadron and been killed over Essen before I had completed my leave.[5]

I met Sgt W. H. Pearson in London and arranged for him to join 455. His posting was confirmed and he continued with the squadron when it went into Coastal Command on 19 April becoming F/Lt Pearson DFC. He survived the war.

An indication of the turnover of the RAAF aircrew that were being posted to 455 Squadron was given in a letter home:

'1/4/42. Just recently a lad P/O Harland came to our squadron and he told me he had been at your home in Brisbane just prior to embarkation from Australia. He seems to be a nice chap and should do well over here.[6]

Another new member is a P/O Keck. He is a nice chap and is the nephew of old Keck who had the orchard next door to our place at Beakie (Beaconsfield, Vic.).'[7]

These unfortunates were killed on operations within ten days! Memories that remain of the early war years are mainly of different people who unconsciously played an important part in our lives at the time.

One who deserves mention was a lady, Doris, the barmaid at the Waddington Horse and Jockey Inn who for years mothered the colonials at the local RAF station. On one occasion she laboriously knitted a woollen waistcoat in RAF grey for me. This must have been an ordeal for her as she had earlier told us that she detested knitting. Later in the war, November '41, she invited F/Lt Geo Weston,[8] a NZ pilot with the RAF, and myself to attend a party with her one Sunday evening at a pub in a village to the east of Lincoln. We arrived to find the pub closed to the general public and the guest of honour absent.

Eventually we learned that the guest of honour was Doris's illegitimate son who had just turned twenty-one. He was serving on the HMS *Ark Royal* at the time and survived its sinking a few weeks later.[9] He had been conceived in Australia when Doris had been working as a governess on a station in outback NSW, which probably accounted for her affection for us colonials.

Another memorable character whom Dereck met was American war correspondent Therese Bonney, who turned up at 455 Squadron early in December 1941. He wrote about her in a letter to his father:

4/12/41. About three nights ago we were visited by a most unusual journalist, a Miss Therese Bonney of the USA. She was, I should say 45, wore blue ski trousers, red shirt, red turban and a black leather driving coat which had a row of decorations along the pocket. Incidentally, she kept this on the whole time – meals and all. Other equipment consisted of a bag of cameras slung around her neck, with a flash torch in her hand. She had been in Finland, France, Belgium and Holland and was a most interesting lady. Her ideas of life and the war were very clear and heartened us considerably.

Yet another character was G/Capt Sir Thomas White KBE DFC:

Early in 1942, No. 455 Squadron was visited by the CO of RAF Station Bournemouth, Tom White, later Group Captain Sir Thomas White KBE DFC. Most of our RAAF personnel passed through his depot en route to squadron work and his visit was by way of 'showing the flag' and probably had a political motive, he being of the establishment with political inclinations.

He asked that he be allowed to fly with us on an operation, which was really out of the question in a crowded Hampden, where one already had barely room to scratch oneself. The decision as to whether he could fly or not was tossed about until it settled with me; and I chose the negative.

The idea of senior officers taking part in operations is, I think, a very important one and White is to be congratulated for presenting the annoying idea. Too few senior airmen flew operationally and so really knew little of the problems their aircrews faced. Similarly, senior army and naval types lacked battle experience because they kept out of the battle. In WWI, neither General Haig nor any of his staff ever once visited the front line.

White became the Minister of Air in Australia. Earlier, he wrote the story of his time as a POW of the Turks and his escape during WWI.[10] He is mentioned in the autobiography of Air Marshal George Jones RAAF[11] when he was said to have approached Jones (who was then Chief of Air Staff) and asked that he be recommended for a CBS – not a backward type! Later in the war he gave me 'Letters of Introduction' to various Australian politicians, which I destroyed.

One memory of 455 days was related to articles supplied to us by the Australian Comforts Fund. John Lawson and I cornered an Australian press representative and persuaded him to publish an article in the Australian papers telling of a forgotten, neglected RAAF squadron in the slush of a Lincolnshire winter. Almost instantly we were inundated with goodies from down under, including some very useful sheepskin waistcoats. Everything was distributed among the troops liberally and everyone appeared to be happy until we learned that a steady business had been established at the local pub where the current price of sheepskin waistcoats was thirty shillings. After this the distribution system became more circumspect and a register was kept of the recipients of saleable commodities.

Another incident occurred when I was with 455 at Wigsley. An irate local farmer appeared and complained that his henhouse had been raided and some of his hens were missing. The only piece of evidence he had was an RAAF Forage Cap which he found at the scene of the crime. Eventually an Australian suspect was found and paraded before the adjutant, John Lawson, on a 'chook' stealing charge. The case proceeded and eventually the accused was discharged on the grounds of insufficient evidence of identification. This was all in order, but Lawson was really put on the spot when as the discharged accused was being marched from the office (court) he turned around and said, 'May I have my cap back now?'

We had a few villains among the 455 chaps! They had, on enlisting in the RAAF in general, been really keen to be involved in the active flying of the air force and were, it appears, conned into signing on with the promise that they would fly. Naturally enough they were soon frustrated when they found that the promise to fly was not to be kept and they were ground crew. Two of them, resenting this, took things into their own hands and stole, or borrowed, the station's Tiger Moth. Each station usually had one for communication purposes. They managed to get airborne and by some miracle or other flew around until they saw Waddington where, by another miracle, they landed it in one piece – a truly remarkable feat! I cannot remember what became of the culprits, but with initiative of this nature they should have become aircrew.

During the early operations of the war the Hampdens of No. 5 Group always carried a wicker basket containing carrier pigeons which we were supposed to release with messages on their legs should we get into difficulties and force land either on land or at sea. A special drill was used to release the bird while in flight, in that it had to be put out of the aircraft facing into wind, otherwise it would have its feathers plucked out by the slipstream.

They were a cursed nuisance, requiring special care and feeding if one was diverted to a strange aerodrome on return from an operation. The only time I knew of one being used was when one of our Hampdens went down into the sea off the east coast of England. The crew got safely into their dinghy and carried out the drill of releasing their pigeon. It made a few circuits and then landed on the fuselage of the still floating aircraft. It was still there when they were picked up by a rescue launch and finally arrived back at Waddington some hours after them. I believe the owners of these birds were paid a fixed amount for each operation their birds flew.

Another custom of early operations was that we were supplied with Benzedrine tablets, small white pills, which we were instructed to take one an hour before reaching our target and again one hour before arriving back at base, the idea being to make us more alert on each occasion. This was all very well in theory but we found that if we followed the instructions we lost the ability to achieve a normal sleep pattern. To correct this we were then given a different pill (this was I think Nembutal), which we were instructed not to take until we were actually in bed. The after effect of this one was to sleep walk for days. There was a bonus to all this however as we round that if one took one of the Benzedrine tablets with alcohol at a party one was soon the life and soul of it, but felt like death the next day. We survived.

During our early flying training days with the RAF, we had been a mixed bunch, colonials with English, Scottish and Welsh. On completion of our training we were selected, seemingly in a haphazard fashion, to be posted either to fighter or bomber squadrons. Many on the course were to become a part of Fighter Command where they encountered death or glory, or both.

Alan Deere, a New Zealander, was one who achieved renown during the Battle of Britain and survived the war.[12] Another was an Englishman, Dave Mawhood, who was to lose his sight in battle.[13] Doug Paton, another Englishman, was killed.[14] A good friend was Brian Carbury, also from New Zealand, who earned a DFC & Bar. I met Brian a few months after this at Stratford-on-Avon where he was staying at the same pub with his new wife, the widow of his late flight commander. When next I heard of him a few months later, he had been cashiered and kicked out of the service for signing cheques beyond the capacity of his bank balance – not the action of an officer and a gentleman.[15] Many of those who became fighter pilots were killed but their casualty figures were small compared with those of Bomber Command.

Charles Kydd was my flight commander when I first joined 207 Squadron. When I left 207 the CO, 'Hetty' Hyde and Charles Kydd took me out to dinner and presented me with a bottle of Emu brand Australian dry-red to be opened after the war. Charles was soon killed and Hetty became a POW (with my old crew) and some pommy b......d unsealed the Emu grog and left me with a bottle of red vinegar!

Babe Learoyd was one of our Hampden friends from Scampton. After he received his Victoria Cross, he was something like a yo-yo, being promoted and posted and then demoted and reposted – a nice chap. He had two Australians with him when he earned the VC, Ellis Ross and Allen Mulligan (Mull), who both went down on the raid.

This happened on 12/13 August 1940. F/Lt Roderick 'Babe' Learoyd, an Englishman from Kent, led five Hampdens in a daring low-level precision night attack that successfully breached the vital Dortmund/Ems Canal. Flak claimed two Hampdens which, as Dereck remarked, were both flown by Australians, and all the others were heavily damaged. F/O Ellis 'Rossy' Ross DFC in Hampden P4410/OL-H was killed and F/Lt Allen 'Mull' Mulligan flying P4340, was shot down and captured. While a prisoner in *Stalag Luft III*, Allen Mulligan described what happened to another Australian POW, Alex Gould, also a former Hampden pilot, who was in the habit of writing everything down in a note book which he ingeniously kept hidden from the Germans:

> Low level attack on Dortmund-Ems Canal. Went in No. 2 at 50 feet. Light flak and MGs set starboard engine on fire – climbed to about 400 feet. Port engine vibrating badly and aileron control U/S. Managed to stop a flat spin and then crash landed in a field. Burning starboard engine torn out of mainplane. Navigator & W/Op killed. Airscrew from port engine came through side of cockpit pinning me in. Port engine caught fire – flames increased for a short time, then went out. Goons arrived but I could not be cleared until airscrew was removed which took 4½ hours – but there was no hurry, they could have taken 4 years![16]

Both Allen Mulligan and Alex Gould survived the war, as did Babe Learoyd, who was one of only seven RAF Victoria Cross winners to do so.

Dereck realised that his requested posting away from the UK would signify the close of a chapter in his life. In a letter home dated 5 March 1942, he wrote: 'I feel glad of the promised change. My main hope it (the posting) will be to Australia or at any rate will be near enough to enable me to get home occasionally.' A month passed.

Finally, a signal arrived for me to report to an embarkation unit near Liverpool. I had suffered a series of prolonged and wearing farewell parties, and had disposed of any surplus kit I could not take with me – I was more than ready to be gone. At the embarkation unit I met other would-be travellers awaiting calls to their various boats. We formed a group and checked out the pubs and clubs of the seedy coastal town. While there I received orders to put up another stripe and to report to the embarkation unit at Bristol as a wing commander.

I arrived at Bristol in company with an old friend, W/Cdr Bradley, who had been a fellow patient at Rauceby Hospital in 1940. He had been flying Fairey Battles during the Battle of France, and, like most of his fellow pilots, been shot down and had twisted his spine in the crash. At Rauceby the medical staff attempted to correct this by putting him under an anaesthetic and then all the staff available twisted and pulled his body until they considered the spine was in its true position. The treatment worked, partially.[17]

On arrival at Bristol, we were treated almost like secret service agents. We were whisked away by car to a secluded old manor house in the countryside where, after much careful scrutiny and identification, we were escorted to a room where we received our orders as OC, RAF troops at sea. I was to command the RAF personnel on the *Highland Princess* and Bradley was to command those on the *Highland Chieftain*. Next day, 12/4/42, I boarded to leave England for, as yet, an unknown destination.

Letter Home 10/5/42. "There is one thing which I must say now and that is that having got out of England after four and a half years I have no intention, desire or reason to return to it...'

He never did.

17

Convoy

The war had spread to the Pacific. The Japanese had raided Pearl Harbor, advanced through Indo-China into Malaya, taken Singapore, and seemed likely to continue on to occupy Australia. The war in the Middle East was very active; the Allied and Axis forces fought, pushing one another back and forth along the North African coastal strip, without being involved in any decisive battle.

The war in Europe was fairly static, the only form of Allied attack on the Axis forces being the strategic bomber offensive by the RAF. A steady flow of new, heavier bombers – Manchesters, Stirlings, Halifaxes and Lancasters – were appearing. Some of these were very successful aircraft, others little better than stopgaps, while the bomber aircraft supply, both in the UK and in North America, began to flow at a rate well in excess of our losses.

At this time the main element in our favour was the active entry of the US into the war, with the promise of full military support, personnel and supplies. This positive image of the progress of the war and the fact that I had almost completed my second tour of operational bombing influenced me in applying for transfer to a theatre of war closer to Australia. The application was successful and I received orders to report to RAF Embarkation Unit, Padgate. Promoted from squadron leader to acting wing commander, after a few days waiting around Liverpool and finally Bristol, I embarked as OC RAF Personnel on the *Highland Princess* on 12 April. Next day we took on our RAF personnel, 709 of them, and were ready to sail. The *Highland Princess* was in peacetime a refrigerator ship of about 10,000 tons and had been used in the frozen meat trade between England and South America.

For security reasons, once one was aboard no further shore contact was permitted. The embarking troops were checked in and dispersed to their rather primitive accommodation by the usual efficient RAF establishment, adjutant etc., who made my task as CO a comparatively smooth-running duty.

During the checking of the troops on arrival, one was found to be missing: a very small Englishman, ACI Fisher, who arrived later with a large escort of military police. It appeared that he had received notice of his overseas posting, but had decided against such a move and had not reported as ordered. He had been picked up by the RAF police, had been charged with being AWOL and was under sentence to serve twenty-eight days' detention when he arrived aboard. Cell confinement at sea in war time was dangerously unreasonable, so I deferred his sentence until we were on land again, wherever that might be. At this stage of our journey none of us had any idea as to our destination. As to ACI Fisher, I doubt that he ever served his time as I later met him in Durban, a free man. On his arrival he had explained to me that while he had been in custody he had received no pay and asked me to lend him a few shillings so that he might buy cleaning equipment to polish his kit. I lent him a small sum and was pleasantly surprised months later when he approached me in Durban and repaid me in full.

Accommodation aboard was fair to bad. Some officers shared cabins while the other ranks slept in hammocks slung from meat-hooks in the holds, which situation created problems as we entered the tropics and it became necessary to cool the holds by refrigeration.

Before we left Bristol a party of merchant seamen came aboard. They were on their way to man a damaged vessel that had been repaired in southern waters. When they found that they were to be accommodated in three-tier bunks and not in two-tier bunks as they had been promised, they went on strike and walked off the ship. So much for a concerted war effort!

We put to sea on 14/4/42 and steamed north into the Irish Sea, joining the remainder of our convoy (about 22 vessels) off the mouth of the River Clyde. Included in the convoy were the *Rangatira*, the *Empress of Japan*, the *Empress of Canada*, the *Highland Princess*, the *Highland Chieftain*, the *New Zealand*, the *Hecla*, the *Aorangi*, the *Sudan* and naval escorts. As we steamed north through the Irish Sea we saw a few free-floating mines, which drifted through the convoy until they were sunk by gun and rifle fire from the vessels. We were lucky to pass them in daylight hours.

For the first few days at sea, most aboard were sea-sick and meals were retained for as long as it took to move from the table to the side of the ship where special vomiting bins were positioned. We settled down to sea-board life. In a convoy, the speed was that of the slowest vessel, probably 7 to 10 knots. For the first fortnight we trudged along, seeing nothing much to excite us but a few flying-fish as we zig-zagged around the Atlantic.

Among the air force chaps aboard were a number of RAAF aircrew personnel on their way to the Middle East who on Anzac Day got together and had a riotous party, which caused a stir.[1] There was some very good

Chilean and South African wine to be had – officers only – but this soon ran out. Another serious shortage aboard was drinking water, which for a time was rationed.

For security reasons our position at sea was very much a secret, yet each day I had the satisfaction of being able to tell the ship's captain our (nearly exact) position which had been worked out by our aircrew navigators, using their sextants and the necessary knowhow.

During the voyage the convoy was subject to very rigid black-out regulations at night. Smoking on deck was strictly prohibited, as it was said that the light from a match was visible for miles at sea. One of our aircrew, a sergeant pilot, broke this ban and was found smoking on deck during the blackout period. He was nabbed by military police and charged.

The offense was a serious one and warranted trial and punishment; so the senior conducting officer aboard, an old lieutenant colonel, ordered that he be immediately court-martialled and punished. What the old chap did not realise was the short life expectancy our RAF aircrew had at that time, and that to court-martial a trained member of an aircrew would break up that crew, and so in a small way disrupt the war effort. As I did not wish this to happen, I argued for hours with the old colonel to this effect. Eventually we came to an agreement. A summary of evidence was taken and it was agreed that the culprit should undergo a court martial at the first port of call. On 29 April 1942 we sighted land for the first time since leaving Britain and came to anchor well out to sea off Freetown, West Africa.

The Portuguese had been the first Europeans to explore this western area of the African continent and they had named it Sierra Leone, meaning 'lion mountains'. Here, mangrove swamps stretched along the coastal strip in front of wooded hills that led up to a plateau in the interior with the eastern region becoming mountainous. Freetown, situated on the coast, was ceded to English settlers in 1787.

In 1808 the coastal area became a British colony, and in 1896 the hinterland was proclaimed a British protectorate. Freetown acted as the capital of British West Africa from 1808 to 1874. It also served as the base for the Royal Navy's West Africa Squadron, which had the duty of enforcing Britain's ban on the slave trade. When the squadron liberated slaves on trading ships, they mostly brought them to Sierra Leone and to Freetown in particular, where they settled. The freed slaves were joined by West Indian and African soldiers who had fought for Britain in the Napoleonic Wars. The town expanded rapidly, its population integrating the descendants of many different peoples from all over the west coast of Africa.

During the Second World War, Britain continued to maintain her naval base at Freetown. This was a major staging port for Allied shipping traffic in the South Atlantic and the assembly point for convoys to and from Britain. Nearby Lungi Airfield was a base for the RAF.

West Africa was a vital link in the supply chain to the Middle East, particularly for the RAF. In the early days of the war, when airfields in Europe were still available, the way to send fighter and shorter-range bomber aircraft to the Middle East had been to fly them from England across France, and then via Tunis and Malta to Mersa Matruh, much as Dereck and his companions had done when delivering the three Blenheim Is in August 1939, just before war was declared. Fully loaded with fuel, fighters could just manage the longest hops while the bombers could make the journey with fewer stops. Prior to France's collapse, three Blenheims and six Hawker Hurricanes had in fact reached Egypt in this way. After France surrendered, the route was closed but long-range bombers could still fly direct from Britain to the Middle East by refuelling at Malta. Fighters or shorter-range bombers could not. A new way needed to be found.

Fortunately, the British Overseas Airways Corporation (BOAC) had already established a flying route from West Africa across the jungles and desert to the Sudan and then on to Egypt. The RAF adopted it and adapted it for sending its reinforcements. Takoradi, a small town which had a good harbour on the equatorial coast of West Africa in Ghana, was chosen as the first terminus. The airfield there was enlarged with workshops for assembling crated aircraft that arrived by sea from Britain. Additional sites across Africa to Egypt were then chosen, considering the shorter range of the fighters. Landing grounds were cleared at the necessary intervals. RAF ground parties with fuel and supplies were set up at these places. When the first shipload of Hurricanes arrived in West Africa, they were assembled at the workshops, tested, and flown off to the east in a small formation led by a Blenheim which navigated the route. They arrived in Egypt in time for the first desert campaign.

With the war escalating and expanding, the route was urgently streamlined and extended. Reinforcements, supplies, equipment and aircraft reaching West Africa had to be shifted quickly. More airfields were cleared with workshops built to assemble the aircraft. The supply route had to succeed – and it did.

Meanwhile, in accordance with the Rome-Berlin-Tokyo Axis Agreement, Hitler had declared war on the US on 11 December 1941, just days after Japan's attack on Pearl Harbor. President Roosevelt responded with his country's own declaration of war against Germany and Italy. This was followed by the US Congress empowering its armed forces to operate anywhere in the world.

With the US fully committed to the war, it was obvious there would be a mounting flow of military supplies, personnel and support coming from the New World. In an offensive designed to cut off Allied ships attempting to cross the Atlantic to Britain and her armed forces in North Africa, Germany deployed the bulk of its submarine fleet off the eastern coast of the North American continent, including the West Indies and Caribbean. This led to a slaughter of Allied shipping during March/April 1942, which the U-boat commanders came to know as the 'Happy Time', but it also meant that the German submarine fleet was thinly spread elsewhere.

Before early March, four months had passed since there had been any U-boat activity in the waters off Freetown, but that suddenly changed. In the first eight days of the month four ships, three British freighters and the 7,600-ton Norwegian tanker *Sydhav* were sunk, all of them ships sailing alone. The crew of another vessel spotted the tracks of two torpedoes, obviously fired from a submarine, as they missed their intended target. A pair of U-boats, the *U-68* captained by Karl-Friedrich Merten and *U-505* commanded by Axel-Olaf Leowe, had announced their arrival. Their orders were to operate independently, and both had torpedoes and mines.

These sudden losses in the Freetown area jolted British naval authorities into rapid countermeasures. Ships already in port were prevented from sailing independently. They were reorganised into convoys and provided with naval escorts. As this was happening over the following days, the U-boats encountered no more shipping so their captains requested permission to cross the Atlantic to Brazil. The *U-68* was instead sent southward to Lagos, Nigeria, while the *U-505* was ordered to remain off Freetown.

Travelling southbound to Nigeria, *U-68* met a number of single ships off Cape Oalmas, Liberia, and in the twenty-four-hour period over 16/17 March sank four more British freighters with torpedoes and gunfire. It then proceeded on towards Lagos as ordered. On 25 March, an aircraft patrolling over an escorted five-ship convoy spotted the submarine as it was about to launch an attack and scared it off. Rounding Cape Palmas on 30 March, another five-ship convoy was encountered and this time *U-68* managed to torpedo and sink a 5,900-ton British freighter.

On receiving reports of the 'heavy shipping off Cape Palmas' from the *U-68*'s captain, the *U-505* set course for that area. By the time it arrived, conditions had changed. The traffic off Cape Palmas was being closely escorted and the U-boat itself came under attack. After being bombed by a patrolling aircraft, and hunted and depth-charged by an escort vessel, the submarine escaped to the south into the open sea. Finally, on 3 April, twenty-nine days since its previous success, the *U-505* did find ships. In two surface attacks at night over twenty-four hours, it sank two freighters, one American and one Dutch. Satisfied, the captain then gave orders to cruise back to Sierra Leone to hunt ships in the vicinity of Freetown.

When Dereck's convoy anchored off Freetown on 29 April, more than three weeks had gone by since the last reported sinking. Although there was RAF air cover from Lungi Airfield, the ships did seem to be a long way out from shore.

Our distance from the shore was to ensure that we anchored beyond the range of the local mosquitoes, which were reputed to be carriers of yellow fever, a killer to those not immunised. No passengers were allowed ashore here but myself and about 200 officers and men who disembarked to fly across the Congo to Egypt. Ashore in Freetown, I became the guest of the RAF Senior Medical Officer of the area, an Australian, Wing Commander 'Kiwi' Corbett, an old friend from the UK, who showed me the sights and the nightlife of the town – such as they were. My most abiding memories of the lush, green, steamy, tropical town of Freetown with its teeming inhabitants were of a by a large sign hung over the main street from roof-top to roof-top advertising 'Joe Abrahams – Sympathetic Undertaker' and the monster cockroaches one encountered in the toilets below the weather-board houses, raised for coolness. This was where the offending sergeant pilot who broke the black-out ban by smoking on deck was put ashore with his crew and the relevant charge sheets. With the others he flew across Africa to fight in Libya. I do not know whether he survived the war or if he was ever court-martialled. The offence was certainly a serious one, yet I think that this manner of handling the case was well suited to the exigencies of war at that time.

On 5 May 1942 we left Freetown and headed in a general southerly direction, seeing the odd Swordfish and Albatross aircraft as well as plenty of flying fish and marine bird life. We did our best to keep all on board as busy as possible, some troops acted as look-outs, some manned small gun-emplacements, educational classes were held in many subjects, including Swahili. There was constant letter writing, all letters being censored by the officers. Some of the mail censoring was rather revealing when it was found that some chaps were sending identically worded intimate letters to different girls. Perhaps they had all employed a master scribe?

I had a schedule of orders for use as the voyage progressed, amongst which was the instruction that before disembarkation at Durban I was to estimate and make application for the quantity of condoms the troops considered they required to pass uncontaminated through Durban to Bulawayo, where they were to train as aircrew. At that time the incidence of venereal disease was high, and someone had thought of supplying condoms as a means of getting the amorous aviators past the dangers of Durban unscathed. When the estimates of the number required came to hand, we were staggered to find that we would need to order thousands! We finally solved the problem by putting the amorous types onto a train on the wharf at Durban and sending them direct to Bulawayo.

My duties as OC RAF Troops were many and varied, apart from the usual activity of administration and discipline and the daily tour of inspection of the ship with the Captain and his entourage. Once I was called upon to present prizes at a boxing tournament when the victor had lost both of his front teeth during the fight, an unwanted and unnecessary injury to receive at this period of his war. Another odd duty was when I was requested to sign an authority to allow an underage airman to undergo an operation in the ships sick bay for the removal of his appendix. The operation was a success. Most of the RAF personnel aboard were very young English would-be aircrew going to Rhodesia for training under the Empire Air Training Scheme.

Dereck's charges had already completed their initial training in the UK ready for their flying training in Southern Rhodesia to graduate as pilots, observers or air gunners. With its small white population, Southern Rhodesia was not able to contribute much manpower to the Empire Air Training Scheme but the country's wide-open spaces and normally good weather made it an ideal area for flying. As its contribution, Southern Rhodesia established aerodromes and built accommodation for flying schools so quickly that within four months of the commencement of the scheme, the first trainees were able to start their course.

Every flying school was situated near one of the three main towns, the only significant centres of population in the country. These were Salisbury, the capital, Bulawayo, the second city and the entry point for travellers from South Africa, and Gwelo situated in the Midlands. All three towns housed only a small white population and each had a large number of black people both in the town and in compounds outside town limits.

As well as the many thousands of RAF trainees sent to Southern Rhodesia, 674 RAAF trainees were also sent direct from Australia. Prior to Japan's entry into the war, ten drafts were despatched over fifteen months, the first draft in August 1940 and the last in November 1941. At that point, it was mutually agreed that the danger of sea transport across the Indian Ocean and the need for aircrew at home necessitated ending the arrangement. Most RAAF volunteers under the Empire Air Training Scheme were trained in Canada during the war. Dereck had some misgivings about his charges.

They were very young and irresponsible, and did not have the high standard of the recruits who had joined up earlier in the war. They came aboard kitted out with the normal RAF issue gear; but as we had few or no replacement stores with us, as soon as one item of kit became lost overboard or stolen, a chain reaction of stealing swept through the ship. There was a shortage of uniform caps and headgear among the troops, probably lost overboard, and these were stolen every night, usually as a person left the well-lit saloon of the ship and went on to the blacked-out deck; his eyes took time to adjust to the dark conditions and during that moment their headgear disappeared.

We had great difficulty while in the tropics keeping the troops healthy as there was insufficient ventilation in the holds and conditions became very unpleasant. To combat this we used the refrigeration plant, which gave a little relief but created a great temperature gap between above and below decks, which in turn caused severe respiratory troubles among the men.

Ten days out from Freetown there was trouble.

During the morning of 15 May 1942 one of our escort vessels, thought to be a submarine servicing vessel, either struck a mine or was torpedoed and was last seen steaming out of control in wide circles. The convoy continued on its way, although some of the escort ships went to the aid of the disabled one, while aboard the *Highland Princess* we stood by, as ready as we could be, for further trouble.

During this standby, I thought of the £4,000 to £5,000 I had in my charge. It was in small denomination English currency notes and was to be used to pay our troops on disembarkation. Up to then I had kept it in the safe of the ship's purser so I decided that should I have to go over the side, the money would go with me. I withdrew it from safe-keeping and had it by my side in a parachute bag for the remainder of voyage, just in case.

Later that day another vessel in the convoy – a merchantman – either the *Hecla* or the *Sudan* experienced a similar hit and went to the bottom. We heard later that this ship had on board the tanks of the Tank Regiment, which was on the *Highland Princess* on the way to fight in Madagascar.

Just over a week earlier, on 4 May 1942, British and South African troops had invaded the large island of Madagascar, a French colony situated off the south-east coast of Africa. This was to prevent its possible seizure by the Japanese. The attack was staged from South Africa and it was in order to wrest control of the island from the pro-Nazi Vichy French administration.

It should be remembered that the Vichy government had already allowed Japanese forces to occupy French Indo-China giving them bases from which they could attack southern China and more recently Thailand, Malaya and Borneo. Geographically, Madagascar was well placed to provide a base from which an enemy could strike at the main Allied shipping routes around the Cape of Good Hope into the Indian Ocean to India and Ceylon, and the Red Sea route to the Middle East. The immediate worry was that the French might allow the Japanese to set up facilities there for servicing their own, or even German or Italian submarines. The island would not be finally secured until early November.

The day following the convoy's losses, aircraft from South Africa, Avro Ansons, began patrolling over the ships. In his 1942 Diary, Dereck wrote: '14/5: Off Capetown. 15/5: 2 mines −1600 hrs − *Hecla*, *Sudan* Bags of flap. 16/5: Off SA − Ansons.'

A few days after losing the *Hecla* and the *Sudan*, the *Highland Princess* berthed safely at Durban on 18 May and Dereck's duties as OC RAF Troops were over, for a time. Dereck's convoy had run the gauntlet not knowing that both enemy submarines which had been in the vicinity had actually already left for their home base. According to German records, after the *U-505* cruised back to the Freetown area, it spent two more weeks hunting without sighting so much as a fishing boat. It returned to Lorient on 7 May, having been out for eighty-six days, during which it sank four ships, 25,000 tons. Altogether, *U-68* and *U-505* had bagged eleven Allied ships sinking about 65,000 tons using torpedoes. They succeeded as well in disrupting the movements of Allied merchant shipping in the South Atlantic and most likely kept naval escort vessels *in situ* that might otherwise have been shifted over to the Americas. If the Germans had had more submarines at their disposal, they would have sent at least some of them to Africa's west coast, but their U-boat fleet was almost fully committed to the campaign in American waters. Because of this, Freetown would be left in peace again for several months.

With the Mediterranean route no longer practical for merchant shipping apart from the desperate attempts to keep Malta supplied with food and military equipment, Durban at this time was the most important staging post for transporting British personnel to the Middle East and Far East.

At Durban, most personnel in transit were accommodated at the Clarewood Transit Camp a few miles out of the city. The officers mess there catered for more than 1,000 officers of the three services; a wonderful piece of organisation to supply accommodation, tented ablutions and food for so many. The district was most hospitable to the thousands of British, yet below the surface there was a strong anti-British element among the Boers.

Most of the troops had never before been outside the UK and the experience of being in a great city, in a perfect climate (something similar to Sydney) with beautiful sandy beaches and shops full of food and goods such as they had not seen before was enough to cause many of them make plans to migrate after the war, which many did. To thinking people there was a drawback to this beautiful place. This was the shocking colour bar, whereby people of non-European extract were restricted in the use of public facilities such as transport, seats, toilets and the beaches.

South Africa's declaration of war on Germany had only gained a slim majority of support in parliament and was far from universally popular, particularly amongst the Afrikaners. Members of the pro-Nazi *Ossewabrandwag* movement strongly objected to the country's participation and actively carried out sabotage against Prime Minister Jan Smuts' government. Smuts took severe action against the movement by jailing its leaders for the duration of hostilities. Because of the strategic importance of controlling the long sea route around the Cape of Good Hope, he immediately set about fortifying South Africa against the possibility of a German sea invasion.

One problem South Africa faced continually during the war was the shortage of men. Due to its racial policies, it would only consider arming those of European descent limiting the available pool of eligible men aged twenty to forty to about 320,000. Nevertheless, the South African Army and Air Force (SAAF) played a major role in defeating the Italians during the 1940/1941 East African Campaign. Converted SAAF Junkers Ju86s carried out the first bombing raid of the campaign on 11 June 1940, just hours after Italy's declaration of war. The SAAF also made a significant contribution to the air war over North Africa, Sicily, Italy, and the Balkans. As well, many South African airmen volunteered to serve in the RAF, most doing so with distinction.

On 28 May 1941, General Smuts was appointed a Field Marshal of the British Army, becoming the first South African to achieve the rank. Ultimately, however, he would pay a dear political price for his pro-British regime, eventually leading to his downfall. Meanwhile, Dereck was in Durban.

The hospitality was very well organised, so that all visitors were given the chance to visit any of the local show places, and have access to most of the clubs. Concessions and sometimes free transport was available to uniformed personnel. The people who appeared to gain most from this hospitality were the Jewish troops who were taken into the care of the local Jews and wanted for nothing. We resolved that in future wars we would be classified as Jews.

I was fortunate to have travelled from England with an oldish ex-pilot, then senior RAF Accounts Officer, Wing Commander Chadwell, who kept a fatherly eye on me. He decided that we should investigate what allowances were available to chaps in our situation and soon we were living almost free of charge at the Mayfair Hotel in Durban. This luxury palled after a time and we went back to our tents at Clarewood Transit Camp, from where we continued to see the sights, to go swimming and fishing and generally enjoy ourselves.

On one excursion I chanced on a nice little village on the coast – Isipingo – a good beach, a good river and a good pub, where I stayed for a while leaving most of my luggage in my tent at the Transit Camp. The luggage included a leather suitcase of clothes which I left on the earthen floor of the tent. During about a week of my absence, white ants drilled holes through the leather and up through the layers of clothing. I wrote to my parents:

I am at present in Durban where I arrived about a fortnight ago after a five weeks sea voyage. Reason for being here so long awaiting shipping is, I think, due to the British occupation of Madagascar and the increased demand for sea transport for that job. Life is very pleasant here, the people are most hospitable which is a welcome change after four years with the insular English. Since arrival here I have been staying at a very nice pub in the town, where for 12/- a day we live like Lords. It is grand to wander around the town at night, to look at the streets lit up, the shop windows crammed with food, clothes and luxuries, all unrationed and all so much in contrast to England of today.

This place is an eye-opener to the thousands of pommies who pass through here. They land expecting to find mud huts and natives, instead they discover that they are in a city better in all ways than any they have been in before.

Durban assumes a festive rig-out for 'Convoy Week', as it is called. Dances and other shows are arranged and the troops have a grand time. Bus, tram and trolley rides are free; cinema prices are halved and all manner of concessions are granted to HM Troops. We went to visit a place called Umhlanga Rocks, where I saw some good fish in rock pools and thousands of oysters growing wild. I like this life far better, as each morning I catch a train from camp to a very nice little river mouth called Isipingo, where there is good surfing and fishing.

In a jocular letter written months later on 29 September to his brother Neil, Dereck added cheerily, 'Left England in April, as Wing Cdr. I/C RAF on a Trooper. Wandered for weeks over bloody seas ... put into Durban where I spent six rather glorious weeks easing the repressions of grass widows and widows.'

After sight-seeing in and about Durban from 18 May 1942 until 27 June, I embarked with about 7,000 other HM troops on the 40,000-ton *New Amsterdam*, a ship which had been built for the pre-war North Atlantic passenger trade, being lavishly fitted. She was very fast and did not have to travel in a convoy, steaming flat out for Aden.

Once we had passed Aden we continued to the north in the Red Sea at normal speed until we berthed at Port Taufiq at the southern end of the Suez Canal. I had gone aboard this ship as just another passenger, but after a few days a lieutenant colonel in charge of one of the decks (1,000 chaps on each deck) was found to have an illegal wireless set in his possession and was arrested, and I was appointed to take over his duties and once again became OC Troops. We arrived at Port Taufiq on 9/7/42 and disembarked VQVQ (our transport movement code) and entrained to a holding camp at Kasfaret, which I noted in my diary as being 'not bad for desert'.

Next day, Dereck went to RAF Headquarters in Cairo and applied for a flying job.

18

The Desert Air Force

When war broke out with Germany in September 1939, there were nineteen RAF squadrons stationed in the Middle East and Mediterranean. Fourteen were located in Egypt and the Sudan, one in Palestine, one in Iraq, three in Aden and one in Malta. They were under the command of ACM Sir William Mitchell, who handed over to ACM Sir Arthur Longmore in May 1940, just prior to Italy declaring war on 10 June. Their equipment consisted of an extraordinary assortment of some 300 aircraft including Bristol Blenheims, Westland Lysanders, Gloster Gladiators, Fairey Battles, Vickers Wellesleys, and obsolete bombers, transports and biplane fighters. In opposition to these were about 500 Italian aircraft in Libya, East Africa and the Dodecanese. They were similar in performance to the RAF aircraft, but their already large numbers could be easily boosted further from Italy, where the *Regia Aeronautica* had around 1,200 more machines.

The RAF began offensive operations over Libya from the outset but its resources were too limited for large-scale attacks, and obtaining reinforcement was difficult. Long-range aircraft could fly from Cornwall to Gibraltar and then via Malta to Egypt. Fighters were usually crated and sent by sea, but the route through the Mediterranean came under increasing attack by the *Regia Aeronautica*. To counter this, Britain developed the air route from the West African Gold Coast port of Takoradi. The crated aircraft from England were assembled there, fitted with long-range fuel tanks and then flown to Nigeria and across French Chad to the Sudan by RAF pilots.

Being between Italy and North Africa gave Malta a vital strategic position in the Mediterranean war. When Italy began hostilities the only operational aircraft on the island were four FAA Gladiators and five target-towing Fairey Swordfish. One Gladiator was damaged and the remaining three, famously christened Faith, Hope and Charity, formed the island's only air defence until a few Swordfish and Hurricanes arrived at the end of June. More Hurricanes followed in August and November. Three Martin Marylands arrived in September, and a squadron of Wellingtons came in November. It was with this *ad hoc* force that the RAF went onto the offensive from Malta.

In North Africa during November, two Wellington squadrons arrived in Egypt from the UK, plus a squadron of Hurricanes via Takoradi. Another Hurricane squadron and three Blenheim squadrons were deployed west from the defence of Egypt and Canal Zone to the front. Britain's armed forces enjoyed considerable success at first in the Western Desert, as Libya's vast expanse was called. Spearheaded by the 6th Division AIF, an offensive began on 9 November. By early February1941 the Italian positions all the way past Benghazi to El Agheila on the Gulf of Sirte had been overrun, and 130,000 prisoners had been taken. Unfortunately at this juncture, British strength on the ground and in the air was diluted when several units were diverted to defend Greece.

Benito Mussolini's invasion of Greece on 28 October 1940 had resulted in the Greek government requesting help from Britain, particularly to support the Royal Hellenic Air Force (RHAF), which only had seventy-five aircraft. Three Gladiator squadrons and three Blenheim squadrons were dispatched to hastily prepared bases near Athens. Meanwhile, on the ground, the Greek army managed to inflict such humiliating reverses on the invading Italian forces that eventually Hitler had to intervene.

Elsewhere, strong concentrations of Italian forces in Abyssinia, Eritrea and Italian Somaliland overran part of British Somaliland, but their early successes were short-lived. British ground forces were supported by RAF squadrons based in the Sudan, Aden and Kenya, and the Italians were subjected to effective bombing attacks. Thanks to the Royal Navy's domination of the seas, British reinforcements arrived in January 1941 and commenced a three-pronged invasion from the Sudan, British Somaliland and Kenya. In the south, the invading forces were supported by the South African Air Force (SAAF). On 6 April, the British entered Addis Ababa and began to mop up. This took some time and the last Italian troops did not capitulate until the following November.

Germany's *Afrika Korps* arrived in the Western Desert in February 1941. It was under the command of the dynamic General Erwin Rommel, who would quickly gain renown as 'The Desert Fox'. His ability to co-ordinate his panzers, artillery, infantry and aircraft sent the British Eighth Army reeling back across the desert. By April 1941, the British were back behind the Egyptian border, leaving only some well-defended positions around the port of Tobruk held by a mixed force of British and Australian troops.

On 6 April 1941, the *Wehrmacht* invaded Yugoslavia and Greece. By then, four Commonwealth divisions had reached the Greek mainland, and two more Blenheim squadrons were on their way, together with three squadrons of Gladiators, Hurricanes and Lysanders. Two temporary detachments of Wellingtons followed, but none of the reinforcements were enough to stop the overwhelming German juggernaut twenty-seven divisions and 1,200 aircraft. Allied opposition was crushed. After nine days of fighting only forty-six RAF aircraft remained serviceable and Yugoslav's air force and the RHAF were all but wiped out. On 20 April, the surviving RAF aircraft had to be withdrawn to Crete. The remaining British and Commonwealth troops were evacuated to Crete too.

Worse was to follow when German airborne troops invaded Crete on 20 May. The *Luftwaffe* mustered about 650 aircraft plus over 700 air transports and gliders to carry the invading force of 15,000 men. Although the defenders outnumbered the enemy, most of their equipment had been left behind in Greece. The only air cover available was twenty-four RAF and FAA aircraft consisting of Hurricanes, and outclassed Gloster Gladiators and Fairey Fulmars. The island was beyond the range of fighters based in Egypt. The outcome of the battle was uncertain for several days but then, at the expense of enormous casualties, the Germans finally triumphed. The Royal Navy managed to evacuate half the survivors but lost three cruisers and six destroyers in the process.

These setbacks threatened to undermine the situation in two key areas: Iraq, where Britain was responsible for internal security; and Syria, where there was a possibility the Vichy French Government might make access to its airfields available to the *Luftwaffe*. A German presence in these countries would threaten Britain's Middle East oil supplies.

Iraq's pro-British government was ousted at the beginning of April 1941 by Rashid Ali, who supported the Axis. About 9,000 Iraqi troops besieged the RAF air base at Habbaniya near Baghdad from the beginning of May, subjecting it to artillery fire, but RAF personnel and local levies put up an epic defence. Wellington bombers from Shaibah on the Persian Gulf bombed the Iraqi positions, while Gladiators and Hawker Audaxes from the Habbiniya Flying School made strafing counterattacks. After several days the Iraqis retired to Baghdad, where they were overcome by a British column at the end of May. The previous pro-British Iraqi government was restored.

British ground forces invaded Syria in June 1941, advancing steadily supported by approximately sixty RAF and FAA aircraft including No. 3 Squadron RAAF, which was newly equipped with Curtiss P-40 Tomahawks. Vichy French troops resisted tenaciously supported by about a hundred aircraft, but were finally forced to capitulate on 14 July.

All of this made the situation in the Mediterranean clearer. Britain's Eighth Army faced the Axis forces in the Western Desert where Rommel posed a threat to Egypt, the Suez Canal and, if successful, India. Meanwhile, Malta was the vital base from which the RAF and FAA could attack the enemy's supply lines and positions. On 1 June 1941, AM Sir Arthur Tedder took over the RAF's Middle East Command.

One of Hitler's primary aims had always been to invade Soviet Russia, despite the Russo-German Non-Aggression Pact of August 1939. His inability to subdue Britain in 1940 and secure his western front had been his first major setback, delaying his intended course of action. Early in June 1941, the German armed forces, including the *Luftwaffe*, began to redeploy most of their strength to Germany's border with the Soviet Union, but Hitler's plans needed to be delayed for vital weeks because Germany found it necessary to divert forces to the Mediterranean to bolster its Italian ally. The invasion, Operation *Barbarossa*, finally began on 22 June. German troops, tanks and aircraft quickly plunged deep into Russian territory. Although highly successful at first, by engaging in war on all fronts the Third Reich was actually planting the seeds of its own eventual destruction.

By the following November, RAF aircraft strength in the Western Desert numbered about 660 machines, plus another 120 based on Malta. These included Blenheims, Wellingtons, Marylands, Hurricanes, Tomahawks, Swordfish, Albacores, Beauforts and Beaufighters. Britain's Desert Air Force (DAF) had evolved into a remarkably resilient organisation thanks to its serviceability and its capacity to move from base to base quickly.

Not including home-based aircraft in Italy and Sicily that were maintaining pressure on Malta, the German war machine could muster 180 aircraft in Greece, and in Libya Rommel could call on 240 *Luftwaffe* aircraft plus some 300 aircraft of the *Regia Aeronautica*.

On 18 November, following a fierce aerial bombardment by the DAF on the enemy's airfields and land transport, the Eighth Army opened its Operation *Crusader* offensive. Assaults included low-level attacks by cannon-firing Beaufighters, and the targeting of the enemy's sea supplies from the air and by RN submarines.

Unknown to Rommel, the British also held a trump card, a top-secret advantage. Thanks to the capture of an 'Enigma' coding machine, they were able to decrypt the messages the Germans were passing to their forces in North Africa and elsewhere. The state of the *Afrika Korps* was known, as were the sailing dates of almost all Axis convoys and their cargoes. Reconnaissance aircraft from Malta knew where to hunt for the convoys and the RAF was able to concentrate its few anti-shipping aircraft at critical times. Resources had to be stretched to the limit to exploit the

'Enigma' advantage, and used in such a way that would not reveal to the Germans that their codes had been broken. In November, fourteen of twenty-two Axis supply ships sent from Italy to North Africa were sunk.

Starved of supplies, the Germans and Italians fell back to Agedabia and the Eighth Army relieved Tobruk. Australian troops had already been rotated out earlier thanks to the RN's destroyers of the remarkable 'Scrap Iron Flotilla', but this time the garrison's relief was short-lived. In December the situation suddenly changed again. Two large convoys, heavily escorted by units of the Italian Fleet, did succeed in reaching North Africa. Rommel was able to go over to the offensive again. By 6 February the Eighth Army had retreated as far as Gazala.

Meanwhile, in January 1942, around 400 German aircraft arrived in Sicily, under the command of *Generalfeldmarschall* Albert Kesselring. Malta underwent an intense campaign of aerial bombardment. Despite the arrival of a handful of Spitfires, only six serviceable fighters and a few bombers remained by the end of March. Forty-seven Spitfires were flown to the island from USS *Wasp* on 20 April but air attacks destroyed most of these on the ground the following day. Malta's defences were weakened and the Axis commanders considered plans to invade.

Replenished, Rommel struck again on 26 May 1942 and achieved success immediately. On 20 June, he besieged Tobruk once more. Kesselring brought every available bomber in the Mediterranean to give support. This time the garrison surrendered the following day. A huge haul of more than 30,000 prisoners was taken, plus vast stores of ammunition and stashes of rations – German soldiers were even able to send home food parcels of Australian bully beef! Of greatest value was the capture of 1,500,000 gallons of precious fuel.

Rommel wanted next to drive on to Egypt, but Kesselring preferred to remove the thorn in their side by carrying out Operation *Herkules*, the invasion of Malta. Rommel's plan found favour with Hitler and the Desert Fox was promoted to field marshal. The *Führer*'s decision was also influenced by the pressure of reversals in Russia and the need to defend Germany itself from increasingly heavy attacks by RAF Bomber Command. Operation *Herkules* was abandoned.

From England on the night of 25/26 June, RAF Bomber Command sent its third '1,000-bomber' raid to Bremen. Known as the 'Thousand Plan', the first 1,000-bomber raid had taken place on the night of 30/31 May 1942 with a devastating attack on Cologne. It was the beginning of a series of spectacular raids. The second occurred on 1/2 June 1942 attacking Essen. However, after this third raid to Bremen, assessment of the overall bombing results and the high loss of aircrew showed they were too costly for what they achieved and Bomber Command discontinued such large-scale operations. The Bremen raid was also the last time that Manchester bombers were flown on operations.

On 24 June, General Claude Auchinleck took command of the Eighth Army in North Africa. Despite the loss of some 60,000 men, the British began forming a line of defence at El Alamein, just 70 miles from Alexandria, the narrowest point between the North African coast and the impassable Qattara Depression. The DAF had fallen back in good order to prepared airfields. Rommel's armoured columns crossed into Egypt but they were running out of momentum. Their attacks were being broken up again and again, day and night, by the DAF fighter-bombers and bombers. During a typical night mission on 25/26 June, fourteen DAF Wellingtons successfully bombed and strafed an enemy column advancing between Sidi Barrani and Mersa Matruh.

By 30 June, the British were waiting at El Alamein for the next thrust from the *Afrika Korps*. It came the following day, 1 July, but the Germans and Italians found themselves being bombarded and battered by severe artillery fire. Rommel himself was pinned down by a bombing raid as he endeavoured to go forward to direct his harassed troops. That night, and throughout the next day, the pounding from British artillery continued, leading Rommel to recognise that he could not break through.

On the 21st, partly because of the pressure from Prime Minister Churchill and partly to prevent Rommel from consolidating his defensive positions, Auchinleck tried to launch a counteroffensive but the attack failed with heavy losses. A follow-up attack on 26 July was similarly frustrated and Auchinleck called it off the next day. He began to plan a new offensive for the middle of September.

Although there was now a stalemate on the ground, the momentum of the fighting was changing yet again. While the Eighth Army with its shortened lines of supply built up its strength behind its defence positions at El Alamein, the DAF shot up Axis road convoys and bombed airfields and ports. German and Italian transport aircraft flying reinforcements between Crete and Libya were intercepted and decimated. Further Allied reinforcements in the form of USAAF bomber and fighter squadrons were beginning to arrive in Egypt and preparing to go into action alongside the RAF.

Such was the situation in July 1942 when Dereck French reported to RAF Headquarters in Cairo looking for a flying job. At this time there were nearly 200 RAAF aircrew scattered throughout the Wellington squadrons in the Middle East.

I found that wing commanders (flying) were two for a penny in this theatre of war, but by reverting to the rank of squadron leader I was able to join a Wellington bomber squadron, No. 108 Squadron in No. 205 Group as an extra flight commander.

Before joining the squadron I went in search of a cabin-trunk of my possessions which had travelled independently from Durban. I eventually found it in a kit-holding depot out of Cairo, with the gear of thousands of other servicemen, many of whom had come to grief at sea while in transit. I was most annoyed to find that the trunk had been thoroughly pilfered. As the unit was operated by RAF ground personnel, I could only think of them as being a bunch of bastards for making such a profitable business out of the war. Most of our ground staff were magnificent chaps but these types of opportunists were too common.

Wing Commander J. Lawson of the Air Ministry Personnel Department is quoted in John Terraine's *The Right of the Line*, as saying '...there was evidence that a number of young men enlisted voluntarily or opted for ground duties with the RAF with the knowledge that such employment was the least dangerous in any of the services.' When ground crew recruiting closed, 'a proportion volunteered for aircrew duties. Not having the slightest intention of going on. They intended to fail in the initial stages and thus be transferred to ground duties.'[1]

I encountered a further example of the activities of these undesirable RAF ground chaps later, when I was ferrying an aircraft from Egypt to India. On this occasion, on checking the aircraft emergency gear I discovered that the water supply (canned water similar to beer) had been consumed and the empty cans replaced. I hate to imagine what our fate would have been had we force-landed in the desert.

No. 108 Squadron already had three squadron leaders, including S/Ldr Don Jacklin DFC and Bar, an old friend from pre-war days in the RAF, with whom I had flown many hours. I knew him in 1938 at Flying Training School at Ternhill and later with the Hampden squadrons of No. 5 Group. He survived the war. The squadron was stationed at Kabrit on the southern end of the Bitter Lakes where we were accommodated in tents and hutments around the aerodrome and the lake edge, a good, cool place to sleep in the Egyptian heat. Many of our tents were dug half their height into the sand around the lake, an idea which gave us coolness as well as protection from bomb blast in attacks by marauding aircraft.

Sharing Kabrit with Dereck's new squadron were 104 Squadron and 148 Squadron. All were equipped with Wellington bombers, but unlike 108 and 148 Squadrons, which were both equipped with Wellington ICs, 104 Squadron had Wellington IIs.

The commander of 108 Squadron was Wing Commander Roger Maw DFC (Wizo), an unusual, lovable character much prone to playing jokes. Roger, or 'Wizo' as we knew him, was much older and more sedate in some ways than nearly all of his aircrew. He was greatly respected and ran a very good squadron, seemingly with little effort.

On one occasion, he left me as his deputy while he took our squadron's Miles Magister on leave to Palestine. On his return I asked him if the aircraft had been satisfactory. He told me that he had trouble with one of the wheels. Investigation showed that the tail wheel had been punctured. Roger had simply stuffed it with grass and returned to our base with his load of Palestinian liquor.

On another occasion he had taken some aircrew for a day out in Cairo. On the way home they had stopped for refreshments at a military canteen where Wizo decided to make a souvenir of a kitchen chair or two. They were soon heading for home with the loot, being pursued by military police that were held up at our guard house. The booty was retained. These chairs became useful mess equipment, having potty holes cut in the centre of each seat, each hole being the centre of a bright RAF roundel.

Despite his larrikin characteristics, Maw was a clued-up bomber captain. He thought up a scheme known as the 'Maw Plan'. The plan was used on targets such as Tobruk where it was the practice for each crew to bomb individually when they arrived at the target area. Using the 'Maw Plan' the watches of all crews were synchronised before take-off and the bombs were released at fixed times, say, every ten minutes. This system prevented the anti-aircraft gunners from concentrating on any particular plane. The idea worked well, saved lives and we had to thank Roger Maw for it.

Our squadron was equipped with Wellington IC aircraft which were fitted with Bristol Pegasus engines, similar to those in the Hampdens. The second Wellington squadron at Kabrit was 104 Squadron, which was equipped with Wellington Mk IIs powered by Merlin engines, liquid-cooled, that tended to overheat in the desert.

No. 104 was commanded by an impressive Australian, Wing Commander Don Saville. He was quite old by our standards, 39, and was said to have about 10,000 flying hours to his credit, before flying operationally. He had graduated from RAAF Point Cook in 1927 and flown with the RAF until 1936, after which he had flown as a civil pilot, both as a flying instructor and with airlines. He was a magnificent pilot with tickets entitling him to service and to fly most aircraft.

I witnessed this ability while I was with 108 Squadron at Landing Ground 237, Kilo 40. He had been briefed for a long-distance raid which required that he land at Kilo 40 to refuel before setting off across the Mediterranean. He arrived late for refuelling, when he explained that on the way he had experienced engine trouble, which had caused him to force-land in the desert. He had, himself, repaired the engine and had then taken off to come on to Kilo 40 – and he'd done it with a 4,000-lb bomb aboard! When

I first met him at Kabrit in July '42, he presented me with an Australian Digger hat from a large stack he had scrounged in some way or other. This I wore for the remainder of my time in the Middle East and in India-Burma.

Don Saville completed a tour of bombing operations, 35 raids, as CO of 104 Squadron in the Middle East, for which he was awarded the DFC. He then went to the UK where his next command was 218 Squadron – Stirlings. He was killed with this squadron in July 1943 while carrying out a raid on Hamburg and was awarded a DSO for his work with them.

On Don's last raid it appears that with his aircraft badly damaged, he remained with it until all his crew had parachuted, he being killed in the crash. The crew apparently landed in the township of Hamburg where all but one were hanged or killed by the local populace; the survivor chanced to land in the grounds of a military unit and became a POW. A biography of Don Saville has been written by Roy F. Chappell of Hobart, who was an intelligence officer with 205 Group RAF in the Middle East.[2]

On first arrival at 108 Squadron, I was wearing an 'Australia' shoulder flash (denoting country of origin) on my uniform and was soon told to remove it before flying on operations, as the Italians had at that time got into the habit of killing anyone wearing the 'Australia' insignia who chanced to fall into their hands. I wondered about this at the time and concluded that it was a form of pay-back for similar treatment given earlier to Italian troops captured by the AIF. I had received similar orders to remove the 'Australia' flashes from my uniform before proceeding into Durban, where a short time before a large contingent of AIFs returning to Australia had left a legacy of hate after rioting through the city.

I joined the squadron on 15/7/42 and on the following night flew a Wellington for the first time when I went to raid Tobruk.

Dereck's aircraft that night was Wellington IC, HF834, and his log book shows that the members of his crew were P/O Beckworth and Sgts Champion, Cowan, and Biggar. The load carried consisted of seven 250-lb bombs and three canisters of incendiaries, which were dropped from 9,000 feet. He found that Tobruk and back was an eight-hour trip.

This first taste of operations in the Middle East was very different to what I had met with in Europe. The weather was wonderful, while the opposition, by way of anti-aircraft, searchlights and night-fighters was negligible.

The bomb load carried by the Wellington IC at that time was up to 4,500 lbs, depending on the distance to the target. The bombs commonly used were GP (General Purpose) 250 lb and 500 lb as well as the 40-lb anti-personnel ones. We also carried containers of 4-lb incendiary bombs and really nasty 250-lb rod bombs. These 250 pounders were used mainly against desert targets, such as tanks and transports. They were basically ordinary 250-lb GP bombs with a steel rod attached to the nose-cone so that on impact the blast centre was about a foot above the ground and caused great damage. Its disadvantage was that it remained live once it was fitted to an aircraft, and in the event of a bomb hang-up (when a bomb failed to release) it usually fell off as the plane touched down, destroying the plane and its crew. If there was any chance of having a bomb hung-up after a bombing run we usually carried out violent manoeuvres to dislodge it before landing. On one occasion when this precautionary measure was successful, the bomb happened to fall into one of our army camps, which did not make us too popular.

On some short-distance sorties we carried eighteen of these horrors. These short raids were to the battle area, less than 100 miles from our base, and needed to be carried out with great accuracy as the front lines were very close together and our own troops stood a fair chance of being hit. To my knowledge, this happened on at least one occasion when one of our ground units had enthusiastically advanced beyond its ordered destination and lost a hundred men to our bombs.

The accuracy of our bombing was achieved by flying from pre-determined marker beacons in the desert and circling the target area at 3,000 to 4,000 feet, until light from flares dropped by Albacore aircraft illuminated suitable targets. This bombing, being done from about 3,000 feet, was most effective, but although we had little to fear from anti-aircraft fire or fighter attack it was hazardous in the extreme, as a number of Wellingtons converged on every flare dropped as they looked for suitable targets, all the while being buffeted by the slipstreams of other planes. There was always a possibility of a mid-air collision. It was scary. We photographed the results of our bombing, and one night produced a photograph showing thirteen tanks or trucks burning.

Navigation on these trips was rather simple. We had few landmarks in the desert and there was a certain amount of black-out over the Nile delta, but as the distances to the target areas were short we had very little trouble finding the required beacon for the night. Returning to base was easy, as we homed in on a brilliantly illuminated camp that housed 100,000 Italian POWs not far from our aerodrome. For this we were grateful.

At that time 108 Squadron operated only by night and aircrew usually took a midday siesta. On 24 June 1942, I was enjoying my after lunch rest when I was awakened by explosions coming from the direction of the runways. On investigation I found that an armourer bombing-up an aircraft for operations that night had dropped a 40-lb anti-personnel bomb (nasty things which were always alive), which had exploded, killing five men and burning three Wellingtons. We taxied the surviving aircraft to safety but found when we air tested them that some had been warped by the blast of the exploding bombs, so much so that two pilots were required to hold the controls when landing.

If our aircraft happened to force-land in the desert areas of the Middle East, Persia (Iran) or India as the result of enemy action or mechanical failure the aircrew were likely to be found by local tribesmen. These people, in some parts were pro-British and in others strongly anti-British. To induce these people to give help to our crews each crew member carried what was known as a 'Goolie Chit'. This took the form of either a card or a letter, written in Arabic, addressed to the Arab people from the British government explaining who they were and promising a liberal reward if the aircrew were helped and returned unharmed to the nearest British base. The name 'Goolie Chit' was derived from the Arabic word 'goolie' meaning testicle. In some parts, both pre-war and during the war, some crews who had been captured by tribesmen had been handed to the women folk to play with, after which they were castrated and returned to the British. We were always very careful to carry our 'Goolie Chit' at all times.

A memorable character from my days at Kabrit was an Englishman, S/Ldr Jimmy Sergeant, a flight commander of 104 Squadron with whom I shared a tent dug into the shore of the Bitter Lakes. This sharing was a good arrangement as being on duty at least every second night we seldom slept in the tent on the same night. He had lived an interesting and adventurous life, had been married and looked forward to life after the war. His main idea was that post-war we should start a school for would-be brides based on the advertisement, 'Brides: Why go to your wedding bed unprepared? Come to the school of French and Sergeant for training in the arts.' When he flew on operations he always took with him a very large jungle knife, which went with him when he failed to return from a raid on 7 August 1942.

During the time 108 Squadron was stationed at Kabrit, the US Army Air Force entered the war in the Middle East using B-25 Mitchell Bombers. They had been trained to operate by day but soon after their arrival in the desert decided to follow the RAF example and bomb by night. With this in mind they sent a squadron off on a night cross-country exercise around Egypt – not over the battle area – which soon taught them that they had much to learn. Only one B-25 made it back to base. The following day they went to 205 Group authorities and asked for help and advice. Their weakness lay with poorly trained navigators. The aircrew training in the USAAF tended to emphasise pilot training. Their pilots were magnificent.

Bombing operations in the Middle East differed from those in the UK in that we had little or no social activities to distract us from the job on hand; we lived under more or less primitive tented conditions and apart from the odd 'booze-up' in Cairo, Tel Aviv, or towns along the canal, we simply got stuck into our work, bombing the enemy as our contribution to the successful prosecution of the war. This attitude also applied to the ground staff who did a magnificent job keeping our aircraft serviceable under very poor working conditions. Aircraft serviceability percentage figures were much higher than those in the UK and many times higher than those in India-Burma, where we were constantly hindered by shortages of important spare parts.

Another factor which was of great benefit to our war effort was the good Mediterranean weather, which was near perfect for our purpose. Apart from the frequent afternoon dust storms, we could always expect and found good flying conditions for our night operations: little or no cloud, no ice, snow or fog, and superb visibility. With the idea of saving aircraft flying hours, daylight air tests and non-essential flying were avoided.

Many crews came to us with their aircraft from the UK and completed an operational tour (thirty to thirty-five sorties) within eight or nine weeks and were sent on rest. Morale was high, although decorations in this theatre of war appeared not to be handed out as generously as in the UK. One aircrew member who flew with me at this time was Harry Godfrey. Harry was a capable, colourful product of the Empire Training Scheme. He had originally flown to the Middle East from the UK as a member of No. 458 RAAF Squadron, a Wellington bomber squadron commanded by Wing Commander N. G. Mulholland DFC. Mulholland, whose crew was made up of most of the squadron's key officers, was shot down off Malta leaving 458 without leaders.

Mulholland's aircraft, Wellington AD539, was intercepted on 16 February 1942 by a Junkers Ju88C night fighter flown by Oblt Rolf Jung of 4/NJG 2 and shot down into the sea 30 miles from Malta. 458 Squadron's gunnery officer, F/O Willis-Richards, was rescued by an Italian destroyer but the rest of the crew perished. W/Cdr Mulholland was from Brisbane.

The squadron was disbanded for the time being and Harry G. was posted into No. 108. No. 458 was later reformed as a Wellington torpedo-dropping squadron. During Harry's service in the Middle East and in Italy he took part in sixty-five bombing raids, for which he received no thanks or recognition of any kind, not even MiD (Mentioned in Dispatches).

Our main target at the time was Tobruk where our task was to destroy shipping and shipping facilities to prevent supplies getting to Rommel who was nearly to the Nile delta. We noticed that opposition to our attacks on Tobruk varied from night to night and our intelligence section decided that the difference was due to the fact that on some nights the Tobruk guns were manned by Italian crews when we had little or no opposition, while on the remaining nights German gunners were in control and we really had to be wary. From this idea was developed the existence of a mythical German gunner who became known as 'Eric the Twerp of Tobruk'. The theme was taken up by our squadron intelligence officer and artist, A. B. Read, who incorporated Eric in remarkable paintings he produced on our mess black-out screens.

Like other Middle East units, 108 Squadron had its lighter moments when during the evening those off duty got together in the messes over a few cans of American beer and chanted the usual RAF songs. The one most favoured and perhaps most pertinent to the area was sung to the tune of *Clementine*.

Down the flights each bloody morning,
Waiting for a clue,
Same old notice on the flight board,
Same old Target – Guess where to?
One O Eight – One O Eight,
Though we say it with a sigh,
We must do this bloody mail run
Every night until we die.

At this time in the Middle East a certain antipathy developed between the army and the RAF. The army considered that the air force received too much praise and publicity and led an easier life than theirs; while the air force thought that the army could, and should, be more aggressive. This attitude was acknowledged to be widespread when a paragraph appeared in our DROs (Daily Routine Orders) to the effect that, in future, army officers were not to be referred to as 'Daffodils'. It was said that the terminology was based on the idea that daffodils were droopy, only came out in the spring-time, and were rather yellow.

In fact, Prime Minister Winston Churchill in London had actually become exasperated with the defensive posture being adopted in the Middle East. He arrived in Cairo on 3 August with a contingent of his military advisers, among them General Alan Brooke, General Archibald Wavell, Field Marshal Jan Smuts and Air Chief Marshal Arthur Tedder. During his tour of the army positions, he pressed over and over for offensive action. Auchinleck resisted, not wanting to be pushed into attacking before he was fully equipped and ready. On the 6th, Churchill sent a message back to the War Cabinet in England proposing a complete revision of the Middle East command structure. Auchinleck would be moved out to a new command covering Persia and Iraq. In reality, it meant demotion.

It was on the next night that Jimmy Sergeant's aircraft failed to return. S/Ldr Jimmy Sergeant (spelled 'Sargeaunt' in other records) and his crew took off from Kabrit at 2240 hours on the night of 7/8 August in Wellington II, Z8436, to raid Tobruk. They crash-landed with engine failure 25 miles north-west of the target. Setting out across the desert, he and his crew walked for 16 miles before they were captured. His crew was one of those that had been detached from 458 RAAF Squadron.

On 13 August, General Harold Alexander replaced General Auchinleck as C-in-C Middle East and General Bernard Montgomery assumed command of the Eighth Army. From this point on Montgomery's name would become synonymous with that of the British Eighth Army. Alexander and Montgomery had the sense to continue resisting Churchill's persistent pressure to attack. As Auchinleck had planned, they would not do so until they were absolutely ready. The build-up continued. Six days later, Dereck's squadron was moved from Kabrit to Kilo 40 – Landing Ground 237 along the Alexandria–Cairo road.

19

El Alamein

During the stalemate in North Africa in the second half of August 1942, the Desert Fox made preparations to launch a final offensive with the object of breaking through to Cairo. At the same time on the Allied side, General Montgomery used the time to strengthen the Eighth Army's positions at El Alamein and to build up powerful reserves backed up substantially by armour. Amid this build-up, beginning on the 19th the Wellingtons of 236 Wing with Wizo Maw's 108 Squadron and 148 Squadron transferred from Kabrit to Landing Ground 237 – Kilo 40 along the Alexandria–Cairo road. Just before this took place, Dereck French and his tent mate, S/Ldr Donald Jacklin, set about acquiring some extra creature comforts.

Before this move Don Jacklin and myself decided that we should be comfortable at our new base. Having seen a number of seemingly unoccupied tents erected in a line in a nearby army camp, we made plans to rescue two of them. It was so easy. We took one of our 30-cwt flight-commanders trucks and during siesta time one day drove into the camp, were saluted by the camp guard, selected two empty tents, pulled them down, put them onto our truck and drove back to Kabrit. We were very comfortable in the new desert aerodrome, our tents serving both as our flight offices and our sleeping quarters.

On one occasion while he was with 108 Squadron Don became excited about a forthcoming leave to be spent in Tel Aviv, where he had been promised a night of passion by a young Jewess. We watched his eager departure and were puzzled by his despondent return, and then we heard the sad news. When he met his lady friend she had given him a good inspection and had then decided that she would not sleep with him – his fingernails were not clean enough.

The station commander of Kilo 40 at the time was Gp/Capt J. H. T. Simpson DFC, a wonderful chap who had been stooging about the desert for a long time, having completed a tour of duty as CO of a bomber squadron. One night, due to a change in the bombing programme, he was required to remain on the station and so miss out on a social engagement he had arranged in Cairo. He explained the situation to F/Lt Jumper and myself and asked us to deputise for him, to seek out his lady friend at the National Hotel and convey his apologies to her. We found the lady who readily accepted our story and then proceeded to ply us with drink, finally putting us both to bed.

Our bomber aircrews operated approximately every second night and we were permitted to go to Cairo to relax between raids. Some had the habit of getting roaring drunk and so into trouble. After a time a procedure developed between the military police in Cairo and our unit whereby the police would call us to say that they had so and so and his crew in the lock-up and ask for instructions. We then consulted the operational programme for the night and instructed that the offenders be released at a certain time, which would just allow them to get back to Kilo 40 in time for briefing and take-off.

Operational briefing at the time in this area was extremely simple for experienced crews. The usual procedure was roll call; the target for the night (usually Tobruk); the weather (usually perfect); the bomb load; and time of take-off. A briefing was sometimes completed in minutes.

Memories of Kilo 40 include the unit medical officer's keen regard for our health and his fight against fly-borne illnesses. One aspect of his campaign was his effort to prevent the flies feeding and breeding. All waste food was carefully disposed of and the latrines carefully constructed. They were very simple: a deep trench about 30 feet long was dug and the capped by a long fly-proof box-like seat with up to a dozen lavatory holes cut at intervals along the top, these being fitted with fly-proof hinged flaps. It was an all-ranks arrangement and one of the sights of the camp was to see a line-up of chaps, seated on the job, out in the desert – all very hygienic.

Not so hygienic was one potential hazard created by the work of our intelligence officer/resident artist and inventor of 'Eric the Twerp of Tobruk', the mythical German anti-aircraft gunner. Read used empty beer cans when mixing his paint and cleaning his brushes. We usually drank our beer direct from the can once the entire top had been removed. One had to take particular care during our beer drinking to avoid cans containing paint or turpentine.

Almost daily we experienced severe sandstorms, which raged for about two hours during our afternoon siesta period. After these storms everybody and everything was covered with a layer of fine sand. It found its way into our food and our bedding and when the storms continued for longer than usual they covered our bomb dumps scattered about the landing ground. The carpet of fresh sand enabled us to see the footprints of visitors who had sneaked into our tents such as desert foxes and small birds.

At the breeze-way entrance to my tent, I hung a porous earthenware chatty (pot), which held about a gallon of drinking water. As it cooled the water the chatty very slowly dripped water on to the desert sand below where I had planted a few seeds of cantaloupes purchased in Cairo. These seeds quickly germinated and were well on to becoming strong plants when I moved on, indicating the fertility of the desert sand.

One day at this landing ground an army unit arrived. It proved to be a party of Royal Engineers who announced that they had been sent to investigate the possibility of finding a supply of underground water. To perform this duty they had come complete with their own water diviner. Later talk disclosed that along most of the North African coastal strip underground water could be found almost anywhere, provided one bored deep enough.

... Morale was very high, aircraft operated nearly every night, sometimes carrying out two raids a night when the targets were close to hand, such as in the Alamein battle area. We carried out raids on the usual targets such as the port of Tobruk and tanks and transports in the battle area. Our chaps raided aerodromes on Crete and on odd occasions dropped agents into the Balkans. These agents appeared to be nondescript characters who appeared, said little, lived with us for a day or two until the weather and other conditions became suitable, and then took off for their work areas. We never saw them again.

Another chap at Kilo 40 at this time was there with us unofficially because of unusual circumstances. One night back during my stay in Durban, I saw what I took to be an RAF squadron leader pilot wearing various decorations including the British DFC, which was placed after what appeared to be a lesser British medal. This type of error in dress could pinpoint phoney types who hang about the drinking haunts in almost all theatres of war; either acting as spies or being unbalanced chaps who dressed in officer's uniforms for kicks or to obtain some benefit by wearing the regalia. I duly tackled this squadron leader and learned that he was S/Ldr George Mareou of the Hellenic Air Force (which uniform was identical with that of the RAF but for a small square on the upper ring of rank) and that he was correctly uniformed. What I had assumed to be a lesser British medal was in fact the Greek DFC. Years before, George had been trained to fly by the RAF, spoke perfect English and was engaged to an Englishwoman in Rhodesia. Months later I met him again in Cairo, when he told me that he had just been released after a month or so in prison, having been confined by his own Greek Air Force group.

Greece, like other occupied countries became divided into parties: those who were prepared to accept the German occupation of their country and those who preferred to continue to fight. George was of the latter group and had been punished for his attitude. We solved his problem temporally and unofficially by having George join us in the desert where he flew with us on operations in our Wellingtons, again unofficially. I do not know if he survived the war. He was an interesting and unusual type.

Rommel launched his final offensive on 31 August 1942, but he ran into trouble. His plan had an air of familiarity about it; two feint attacks near the coast followed by the main thrust to the south with the intention of turning the Eighth Army's left flank. It had been anticipated. Montgomery's defensive dispositions meant that the bulk of the British armour was ready and waiting on the Alam el Haifa Ridge, where the offensive was halted.

Allied air supremacy made heavy air attacks possible to support the tanks and guns. The role of the bombers was two-fold. During the series of summer battles, the night bombers often made two sorties a night over the battlefield searching for 'targets of opportunity' which were usually illuminated by Albacores of the Fleet Air Arm. During lulls in fighting the Wellington squadrons, which were actually reduced to six in number with the conversion of 38 Squadron into a torpedo-bomber unit, attacked ports and airfields. What had been the 'milk run' to Benghazi in 1941, was now the 'milk run' to Tobruk. They were boosted during this time of heavy fighting by a Wellington flight from 162 Squadron.

Under constant, relentless bombardment, the Axis forces were obliged to withdraw with substantial losses, retreating more to less back to where they had started by 7 September. Rommel had suffered a major setback. He was in desperate need of more reinforcements, new equipment and fresh supplies – and especially more fuel.

The Middle East High Command arranged a special combined forces operation to be carried out on 13 September 1942. The plan was that we should heavily bomb the ports of Tobruk, Benghazi and Barce, while simultaneously the Royal Navy would carry out a bombardment from the sea. These actions were to be quickly followed by marine intruder forces which were to meet up with sections of our Long Range Desert Group (LRDG), destroy any shipping and shipping facilities they could find and then retire.

The whole operation was code-named Operation *Agreement*. Its objective was to destroy harbour installations and deny Rommel ports for receiving reinforcements and supplies. It was an ambitious plan requiring a complex series of co-ordinated tasks.

The DAF Wellingtons, including 108 and 148 Squadrons from Kilo 40, were to concentrate on Tobruk. Prior to the mission, aircraft from 104 Squadron flew forward from Kabrit and landed at Kilo 40 to top up their fuel before they too set out for Tobruk. Leading them in was Wellington 'X for X-Ray' flown by the highly experienced W/Cdr Don Saville, the squadron's CO, who had presented Dereck with an Australian slouch hat 'obtained from somewhere', which became his favourite.

During 1945, while the war was still in progress, this raid was mentioned in a propaganda booklet produced by His Majesty's Stationary Office titled, *RAF Middle East – The Official Story of Air Operations in the Middle East, from February 1942 to January 1943.* Obviously meant for public consumption, it stated:

> The night bombers returned relentlessly to the target of Tobruk. The greatest attack was on the night of September 13th/14th, when a combined operation was carried out against the town. While naval and military units were making a landing, the bombers, in greater strength than ever before, plastered the town with bombs up to a weight of 4,000 lb. each throughout the night. Fires that sprang up around the docks and the fuel storage tanks spread into conflagrations. The pilot of a heavy bomber returning from a simultaneous raid on Benghazi reported that when he passed Tobruk there was one fuel tank 'glowing and pulsating like a big red orchid.' At the start of the raid and for the first hour, the whole Tobruk AA barrage was firing furiously. When the last bomber turned east there were only three guns still firing, wildly and intermittently.

Dramatic stuff, but this was, of course, only part of the story. As Dereck French often liked to quote, 'Truth is the first casualty of war.' The assaults attempted on the night of 13/14 September 1942 achieved little; some were disastrous. At Tobruk harbour there were heavy naval losses consisting of two destroyers, a light cruiser (HMS *Coventry*) and some small craft. The landing parties met heavy opposition and failed to take their objectives while suffering considerable losses, although one land raiding party temporarily captured the inlet of Mersa Sciause and destroyed coastal guns. It was subsequently learned that the unusually heavy air attacks designed to occupy the enemy's attention had actually aroused the suspicions of the German leaders, who astutely placed Tobruk and the other ports on alert.

In all, 101 aircraft from 205 Group attacked Tobruk that night and four Wellingtons were lost, three from 70 Squadron and one from 108

Squadron. One of the aircraft from 70 Squadron was Wellington IC, BB462/G, piloted by P/O M.V. Hodge. He had on board as second pilot G/Capt Captain R. Kellett, 205 Group's Senior Air Staff Officer, who had planned the air part of the operation. This aircraft suffered engine failure over the target and was forced down in the desert behind enemy lines. Kellett, Hodge and the others evaded capture for a week before they were all finally taken prisoner on 20 September.

The 108 Squadron aircraft lost was Wellington IC, HF864/S flown by P/O E. R. Wardley with Sgt L. S. Cowell, P/O F. P. N. Dyer, W/O C. T. Ord, Sgt F. Buckley and Sgt H. Hellewell. A message was received from the aircraft stating that it was returning with engine trouble, but it did not make it. The crew apparently had to force-land and was captured. W/O Ord was killed when the Italian ship *Scillin* was torpedoed by a British submarine on 14 November.[1]

Also shot down over Tobruk were three USAAF B-25 Mitchells of the 81st Bomber Squadron. The Americans had been briefed to raid Sidi Haneish and a fourth B-25, from the 82nd Bomber Squadron, was shot down over that target during its bombing run. One senior American officer, Colonel C. G. Goodrich of the 81st, had protested over the use of the B-25s at night because of the obvious flames given off by their exhausts but his objection had been overruled. He and three of his crew were captured. After these losses a ban was imposed and the B-25s reverted to day bombing.

The raid on Benghazi failed too. There the new Special Air Service (SAS) led by Major David Stirling found the enemy ready and waiting. Under heavy enemy fire they had to withdraw but lost eighteen jeeps and twenty-five other vehicles in the process. The one bright spot was the Long Range Desert Group (LRDG) attack on Barce. Twenty-four Italian aircraft were blown up and other damage was inflicted.

The LRDG drove up to 1,600 miles behind the enemy lines to achieve this aim, so the problems were immense. Apart from this, too many people were involved in the planning and security was breached – the enemy were prepared with the result that the operation was, in the main, a failure.

The LRDG was an amazing commando-style unit which operated for weeks behind the enemy lines, where, using Jeeps, they carried out lightning raids against enemy aerodromes and units. They destroyed hundreds of aircraft and other equipment using 'sticky' bombs (explosives which could adhere readily to any target) and at one time submitted a recommendation that their leader, Major Stirling, be awarded a DFC on the grounds that he and his men had destroyed more than 250 enemy planes – a tally greater than any RAF fighter squadron could claim. The claim was refused.

Earlier the LRDG had been responsible for the return of the aircrew of a Wellington of No. 104 Squadron who had failed to return from an attack on Tobruk on the night of 25 July 1942. They had been forced to land in the desert, had captured a German car, had been themselves captured, escaped and finally met a party of LRDG chaps who had arranged for them to be flown back to Kabrit from a secret desert aerodrome. The crew comprised the pilot, Sgt Wills and P/O John King, an Australian.

The USAAF's B-25 day bomber units were placed under RAF command and from mid-September on operated alongside the RAF and SAAF bomber squadrons. The South Africans had given up their worn-out Martin Marylands and were now operating with Baltimores and Bostons along with two squadrons of Blenheim Vs.

At this time a long-range bomber force came into existence equipped with the Handley Page Halifaxes from Nos 10 and 76 Squadrons detached from Bomber Command in the UK. These were the first four-engined heavy bombers to arrive in the Middle East having landed in Palestine in mid-July. Early in September they were reformed into a new 462 RAAF Squadron. At this time, 462 RAAF Squadron was unique in that it contained English and Dominion air and ground crews but not one of them was an Australian! Although nominally and officially a unit of the RAAF serving in the RAF, it was Australian on paper only and remained so until early 1943 when the supply of personnel from Australia at last began to catch up with demand.

Meanwhile, the Liberators of 159 and 160 Squadrons which had been allocated to the Far East were stopped from continuing their journey until September so they could reinforce operations in North Africa. These long-range bombers, supported by B-24s and a handful of Boeing B-17 Flying Fortresses of the USAAF's 'Halpro' Detachment operating under RAF control, carried out a series of daylight formation raids on airfields and ports on Crete, as well as on Benghazi.

The tide of war was turning inexorably in favour of the Allies. Both sides realised that the next major assault would come from the British, and it would come soon. Large numbers of ships were unloading reinforcements and huge quantities of supplies in the Suez and Bitter Lakes areas – new divisions for the Eighth Army and vast amounts of new equipment that included American Sherman tanks which were reputed to be as good as anything possessed by the Germans. When the time came, the DAF would have the task of opening the battle and weakening the enemy at his every point of resistance.

One night, at the beginning of the final battle of El Alamein when our crews were carrying out two raids a night our magnificent CO, Roger 'Wizo' Maw, showed the 'larrikin' side of his character again as he helped the armourers re-arm the aircraft for the second trip.

All was well until he started to juggle a 40-lb anti-personnel bomb, much to the horror of the ground-staff who realised the danger. The armourers thought him quite mad, and went on strike. We managed to lure Wizo away, and the war went on.

It was not long after this on the night of 19/20 September that W/Cdr Roger Maw DFC failed to return from another raid on Tobruk. His aircraft was Wellington IC DV872/W, one of two aircraft missing from 236 Wing believed to have been shot down over the target. An SOS that was apparently transmitted from 'W for William' was picked up by another aircraft. Wizo Maw and his crew were all captured, news heard with pleasure by many.

Maw died in 1992 aged eighty-six. After his death it became known that as a POW in *Stalag Luft III* he had been the carpenter who had actually constructed the Wooden Horse used as an escape aid and immortalised in Eric William's classic book.[2]

Following Rommel's loss at Alam el Haifa, it was apparent to the Desert Fox that a drive to the Suez Canal was no longer viable. With his overstretched supply lines and his increasing weakness in men, equipment and resources, the best he could hope for was to stay put where he was. He therefore strengthened his defences by completing the laying of a massive minefield that stretched from the coast to the Qattara Depression, and positioned his forces in such a way as to ensure that any attempted attack would meet an integrated defence with infantry, artillery and tanks working in close coordination. Unfortunately for him, by now Allied air superiority was so dominant that no reliable, adequate picture of Allied movements was possible.

On the other hand, thanks to aerial reconnaissance Montgomery was kept fully informed of the disposition of the enemy forces facing him. He planned an offensive on lines different from any hitherto undertaken by either side in the Desert War so far. An armoured force sweeping around the flanks was not practical given Rommel's defences. The general plan of the coming battle was to first involve infantry forcing two corridors through the Axis minefields. Armoured units would then pass through the enemy front lines to hold off their tank units while the infantry eliminated the enemy infantry holding the forward positions. The main thrust was to be in the north, where two corridors were to be cleared through the minefields. Further south, a third corridor was to be created, but there the attack would be limited; the 7th Armoured Division, which was to hold off the panzer units, being required to be ready for the final breakthrough.

While General Montgomery had ample evidence of what was happening on the Axis side, General Georg Stumme, who had taken command of the Axis forces on 23 September, had little to go on. Rommel, who was ill and suffering from jaundice, had returned to Germany to recover, When the Eighth Army did attack on the night of 23/24 October, the Axis high command had no clear idea of from where the main thrust would come.

The offensive began with a massive artillery barrage by 800-1,000 guns, an awe-inspiring experience for anyone who heard and saw it, including the bomber crews flying overhead at the time. Meanwhile behind this barrage, intensified by air bombardment, 10th Corps in the north was painstakingly forcing two corridors through the enemy minefields, and to the south 13th Corps, forcing a single corridor, was achieving what Montgomery wanted, holding a German panzer division in place until the night of the 26th.

The progress of the battle was slow but sure. On the 24th, General Stumme died of a heart attack as the result of a mine explosion. Rommel, who was already returning upon news of the attack, resumed command the following day. Gradually the British salients, such as that of the Australian 9th Division in the north, were enlarged and in the early hours of 2 November the final phase of the battle, Operation *Supercharge*, began. In the face of fierce resistance and strong anti-tank screens, progress was still slow, but then gradually Rommel's strength began to crumble, and on the 3rd there was evidence that his forces were preparing to withdraw. Early the next morning (4 November), the 5th Indian Brigade broke through, and the Axis army began a wholesale retreat. The battle of El Alamein was won, and with it, in the long run, the war in North Africa would be won too.

The cost of the battle was heavy on both sides, as Montgomery had warned that it would be. Total Axis losses during the battle were estimated at some 59,000 killed, wounded and captured. The Eighth Army lost about 13,500 men – but the Axis resistance in the Western Desert was broken. The Eighth Army's advance would eventually take it to Tunisia, where, with the Anglo-American and Free French armies driving through from Algeria, it would finally crush the *Afrika Korps* and Italy's North African armies at long last.

The success at El Alamein and the following pursuit of the Germans and Italians was the last major victory achieved by the British and Commonwealth armed forces alone. From now on all the fighting in North Africa and into Europe would be alongside their allies in the US armed services. Prime Minister Winston Churchill would declare the victory in North Africa to be 'the end of the beginning' of the Second World War.

During September '42, I formed the impression that the tempo of the war in Europe was changing in our favour, while that in the Pacific remained critical as the Japanese advanced on Australia. It was at this time that I came across a signal in the Squadron Adjutant's Office asking for a crew to deliver a Wellington to India Command. With the idea of moving a step closer to home, I applied for and got the delivery job.

Dereck's next confrontation would be in the Far East, against a completely different foe.

20

India and Ferry Command

September 1942 I gathered a crew and flew via Palestine–Iraq (Habbaniya) down the Persian Gulf to Sharjah and on to Karachi, (India). Sharjah, on the southern end of the Persian Gulf was an RAF station and staging post for ferrying aircraft. It consisted of bare landing ground and a large fort, like something from a *Beau Geste* movie. This was used as station headquarters as well as for accommodation.

Sharjah is the capital city of the emirate of Sharjah. In 1932, Imperial Airways established a regular air service through Sharjah by making it an overnight stop on the Eastern British Empire route. Al Mahatta Fort was built to house the airline's guests.

Sharjah had the reputation as being the end of the line for any RAF types who may have blackened their records in other parts. There I met W/Cdr Gyll-Murray DSO who had been with us in 455 (RAAF) Squadron. I had not taken to him then and had considered him to be a privileged, ineffectual member of the British establishment, but I soon learned that I had badly misjudged him. During his trip to the East, the vessel in which he travelled was sunk. The O/C Troops panicked. Gyll-Murray took charge and by good leadership saved most of the troops aboard.

Sharjah was a torrid place – bare, sandy and as hot as hell, although the fort was fairly comfortable. I disliked the aerodrome there as our usual take off run was to the south where there was a range of rocky hills which seemed to get dangerously higher as we took off heavily laden in the hot rarefied air. It made climbing a slow process. And so on to Karachi.

Karachi airport was the terminal point of arrival from the west for aircraft both civil and military. On arrival there we were ordered to remain aboard while the plane was generously sprayed internally to kill any insects – particularly yellow fever-carrying mosquitoes.

No RAF authorities at the base seemed to know where the Wellington was to be delivered and suggested that I take it to St Thomas Mount at Madras where 215 Squadron was stationed. I did this and became an unofficial member of the squadron, which at the time was non-operational.

St Thomas Mount (known in Tamil as Parangimalai) is a small hill located very close to what is now Chennai International Airport. The ancient Syrian Christian community of India traces the origin of its church to St Thomas the Apostle, who is believed to have been martyred in St Thomas Mount. From the 17th century, this part of Chennai was populated predominantly by Anglo-Indians.

At the beginning of the Second World War, No. 215 Squadron RAF had been a Wellington bomber training unit based at Bramcote near Coventry, and then at various bases until the beginning of December 1941 when it was earmarked for overseas service in the Far East. Its personnel sailed for India in February 1942 and its air echelon flew out at the end of March. After reassembling at Pandaveswar in India, it was engaged in supply-dropping flights during the aftermath of the British retreat from Burma and then from August 1942 started patrols along the east coast of India, operating from St Thomas Mount.

On 23 December 1941, less than three weeks after the bombing of Pearl Harbor, during the invasion of Malaya Japanese bombers had targeted Burma's major port of Rangoon, some 4,000 miles from Japan itself. They caused an estimated 4,000 casualties among the half-million civilian population that day.

A wall of mountains isolate north Burma from the world with mountain ranges running from north to south down the length of the country. Rivers and roads follow the valleys between the mountains and do not meet until they reach the plain in the south and the coast. Rangoon was really the only entrance from the south to most of Burma itself and it was also the start of the Burma Road supply line to China. By the end of 1941, Rangoon was the only port left in Asia through which the Allies could supply the Chinese who were fighting the Japanese in their country. By first bombing the port and then taking it, the Japanese High Command aimed to plug that last pipeline into China and so isolate and starve it of supplies. There were also other prizes – the oil and rice of the Irrawaddy plains and the possibility of advancing to invade India itself. The bombers and their escorting fighters returned two days later on Christmas Day. This time there were 5,000 casualties. Then the Japanese came, sweeping in from the southeast through Siam (Thailand) and French Indo-China. In just a few weeks they would occupy almost the whole of the country.

The official history recorded that it is not known how many of the Burmese, Indians and Chinese who comprised the half-million population of Rangoon fled in horror or how many of those died on the way of cholera, malaria, the jungle and hunger. About 400,000 reached India at the end of a march of nearly 1,000 miles, but for a long while after they had stopped walking the survivors continued to die of the effects of their ghastly journey. They swarmed aboard trains and trucks or became a stream of refugees taking flight on foot. Some escaped to India by sampan or other vessels but those on land at first ran north to Mandalay and then north again following the jungle-thick valleys between the mountains towards the isolating wall of rugged, jagged peaks of the rising Himalayan Mountain Chain. The British were driven northwest into India, the Chinese ever northwards into Yunan Province in southwest China.[1]

The Himalayas run from India's northwest adjoining Afghanistan generally east-south-east and then east until reaching northwest India. From there they bend southeast, then south, gradually losing height until petering out in southern Burma and adjacent countries. Various ranges have local names but they belong to the one great chain.

There was no road into India. The charts of 1941 were inaccurate because so little of the country had been surveyed. Retreating British troops and fleeing Burmese civilians had to hack through the jungle and climb finding their own way through the mountains. It had been vital for the Allies to hold northern Burma in order to use Myitkyina north of Mandalay as a terminal for sending supplies by barge downriver to Bhamo and transfer onto the Burma Road. When the Japanese seized Myitkyina on 8 May, Allied access to the Burma Road was effectively cut.

In March every year, a gentle wind rises south of the Equator and blows north towards the tropical heat of Asia. By the time it enters the Bay of Bengal around mid-May its power is strengthened enough to lift clouds of moisture from the sea. The Himalayas deflect this east and west and so the monsoon storms break on Burma and Bengal about the last day of May. The monsoon renders life almost unbearable and stifles every movement.

Between June and October the Japanese had to stop their offensive even though they were replenished by the supplies that reached them via newly occupied Rangoon. The British and Burmese fleeing north and northwest, and the Chinese and Americans fleeing north and then northeast just had to keep going regardless until they reached safety.

In India, the 1942 monsoon came as a grey-blue horizon stretching across the Ganges plain. The sky changed to grey-black and with each passing moment it grew darker until the wind built up into a gale. June to October became a time of prolonged misery and extremes of discomfort. These conditions had to be endured for months on end and when the storms did abate there was still the stifling heat.

Meanwhile, the 'Europe first' strategy adopted by the Allies meant that supplies allocated to India for the future campaigns in Burma were only a trickle compared with those flowing into the other theatres. A balloon barrage was raised for the first time in Calcutta in June, and a few more squadrons of fighters and bombers gradually filtered into Bengal Command. There was a slow build-up of strength to face what inevitably lay ahead.

After months, as the monsoon blew itself out, the RAF squadrons began moving forward to airstrips across the Bay of Bengal in the Chittagong area. It was at this point that Dereck French arrived at St Thomas Mount and from October, 215 Squadron RAF became involved in the training of airborne forces.

The general atmosphere of the station at St Thomas Mount was unreal and inefficient compared with the operational urgency of England and the Middle East. After a week there I was sent with a Wellington to find a suitable flight route to move the squadron to the North West Frontier area, Chaklala, where it was to be employed training parachutists for the army.

This flight was an eye-opener to me and enabled me to form an idea of the capability and attitude of the RAF in India at the time. The aircraft I used for the trip was a well-worn Wellington Mk IC with engines so tired that I was required to carry a spare drum of engine oil in the fuselage to top up the engines at each landing. The route took me to Delhi where I went to the RAF HQ and asked for maps to guide me on to Chaklala. I was told that these were not available so I went to a Delhi book shop where I bought a school atlas, which served the purpose.

At an RAF aerodrome (Ambala) at which I landed I noticed that the old Wellington was the centre of attraction and did not understand why until I learned that it was the first plane with a retractable undercarriage to land there.

Our arrival at Chaklala chanced to occur on a Saturday afternoon, which was it seemed a bother to the station staff, for when I asked for fuel and oil I was told that everything was locked up for the weekend and that I should have to wait until Monday morning. The station was still working to a peacetime tempo. I also found that the RAF in this area was subservient to the Indian Army, which was responsible for our rations as well as aerodrome construction and maintenance. I was asked by the army commander how many rounds of .303 ammunition there was aboard a Wellington (about. 8,000) and was then instructed to have it all removed to the garrison armoury for security each night. This order was both stupid and unreasonable, so naturally we did not obey it.

The Indian Army at that time really had no idea that a major war had been in progress in other parts of the world for the past two-and-a-half years and thought only of their frontier skirmishes with the local tribesmen, which flared up from time to time. These tribesmen were strongly anti-British and were in the habit of using their rifles to fire at any of our aircraft which chanced to come within range. We were not aware that we were being used for target practice although occasionally evidence in the form of the odd bullet hole would be found during maintenance inspection.

Having checked out the route for 215 Squadron to fly north, I returned to the unit at St Thomas Mount aerodrome at Madras. The place had little attraction for we did little flying and apart from collecting the magnificent tropical butterflies which were abundant in the area (these were killed with chloroform from the RAF sick quarters) there was little to do but have drinking parties and get into mischief. I did not realise at the time how disastrous this lack of useful activity would prove to be for the squadron. When I later took command of 215 Squadron at Jessore in Bengal, I found it difficult to roster complete flying crews for operations as 10 per cent of the chaps were away undergoing 'map-reading' courses. Map-reading was our slang for hospitalisation for treatment of VD.

We flew to Chaklala and were again immersed in the tangled inefficiency of India Command. Our Commanding Officer, W/Cdr Warrington (later to be drowned with his wife sailing in the Irish Sea), found on arrival in the north that he had been superseded by a new CO, W/Cdr Charles Webster, who was awaiting our arrival to take command. The trouble was that the signal authorising the change of command had not been received and we had the unhappy situation of two COs trying to run the squadron. Eventually, the necessary signal did arrive and W/Cdr Warrington left the scene.

Our work was to drop parachutists, officers and ORs – British, Indian (mainly Mahrattas), and Ghurkhas – in batches of eight with full equipment from a round hole cut in the mid-floor of the Wellingtons. Their drops were made at 300 feet, the chutes being opened by a static line which remained fastened to the plane. They were commanded by Brigadier Hope-Thompson, a dynamic 32-year-old (very young for such a rank in the army) who, with a group of high-calibre subordinate British officers, worked closely and enthusiastically with us to carry out the training programmes. They were all volunteers, and were required to do five drops each, after which they received their parachutist's wings and were returned to their respective units to await the call for special duty. The few who fell by the wayside and could not continue to jump to complete the course were quietly returned to their units to resume their previous duties without criticism.

The dropping took place at a special area where a medical officer stood by to attend to any casualties. This proved to be a necessary precaution as owing to poor quality Indian-made parachutes, which were perhaps poorly packed (each parachutist packed his own chute), we found that we were killing six of every 1,000 who jumped: far in excess of the normal casualty rate of one in every 6,000. One medical officer could not take the strain of waiting for the parachutes to open as anticipated and became a nervous wreck. He was sent home to the UK as a psychiatric case. I felt that I should experience the other side of the jumping operation and do a drop myself. With this in mind, I obtained permission from the authorities to do so, but when the high casualty figures came to hand, and after I had sat-in on many courts of inquiry after each accident, I changed my mind. The jumping was a nerve-straining ordeal but I cannot remember any Ghurkhas failing in this way. They were an admirable, cheerful bunch of troops who after generations as mercenaries with the British seemed fatalistic and fearless.

After each troop of them completed the course and qualified as parachutists they usually held a party for the aircrews involved in their training jumps. This was an open air concert where they entertained us and kept us plied with grog. In this case the grog was white rum. It was lethal and as it looked like water it proved to be a trap for the unsuspecting guest. At the conclusion of these parties they had a guest hold a goat by the horns while one of the Ghurkhas sliced off its head with one stroke of a kukri. The kukri with its scabbard was then presented to the guest as a mark of honour or as compensation for the generous sprinkling of goat's blood he had received.

Chaklala aerodrome was a few miles from the large town of Rawalpindi, the civilian and military hub of the area. It had little to attract us in our leisure time, yet we found a good supply of idle saddle horses belonging to army officers absent on duty elsewhere. They were made readily available for us to use and exercise.

During these rides we located suitable shooting and fishing spots for further investigation. On one such ride with Lt/Col Abbott of the parachutists we came across a clear, fast-flowing stream among the foothills of the Himalayas that seemed to be teeming with fish. Abbot was most impressed and said that we would return later in the day with bait and get a feed of fish. We did this. Abbott picked me up in an army transport and we returned to the fishing hole. I was curious as to what type of fishing gear he had brought along, but wondered no more when he produced a box of hand-grenades, which he used to great effect. After each explosion numbers of disorientated fish appeared in the pool which we, having no net, gathered by stripping and swimming in the icy water. We collected a large number and full of hope took them back to our camp. They looked good but when cooked, we found to our disappointment that they were almost inedible being full of small 'Y' shaped bones similar to those found in the European carp family. So much for our fishing. The shooting proved to be more productive as we usually returned to camp with hill partridges and hares.

We, the RAF, tended to pooh-pooh the security sensitivity of the Indian Army chaps with regard to the local tribespeople until one day we found that one of the locals had slithered into our camp at night, avoiding the guards, had slit a hole in the side of a tent and removed a box of tools the size of a coffin by sliding it downhill. We were in serious trouble over this as this particular box contained all of the special tools required by our armourers to bomb-up our Wellingtons. By following the skid marks on the ground, we found the box in a gully below the aerodrome. It had been forced but to our delight we learned that nothing had been stolen, except all the engineer's files. In fact some of the local tribesmen were quite capable of copying almost any metal artefact, even the Lee-Enfield .303 rifle, from scrap metal.

While at Chaklala I took the opportunity to take leave with two of my crew, F/O Norman Ruck (English) and P/O (Junior) Beca RNZAF in the beautiful valley of Srinagar (Kashmir). The visit was made by car on a two-day drive through the steep gorges of the Jhelum River, staying overnight at an isolated dak bungalow along the way.[2] The scenery was magnificent – snow-capped peaks towered above the frightening, winding road cut from the steep slopes, below which every square inch seemed to be terraced down to the edge of the Jhelum River, and green with crops, mainly rice. The road was very narrow and a nightmare for even the best of drivers. On one corner a local saint or holy man had died. His followers apparently followed their usual custom and buried him on the spot – in this case in the middle of the road. Traffic passed each side of the tomb.

Our accommodation in Srinagar was in a rather luxurious house boat moored on the lake adjoining the town and included a cook and cleaner who looked after us very well. Hawkers in small flat-bottomed punts called regularly selling all manner of goods, food, fruit, nuts, silks, furs and local artefacts such as carved woodwork and jewellery, so life was easy for us.

The town of Srinagar was fascinating being packed with industrious locals as well as many Tibetans selling produce from the fertile, warm valley hemmed in by snow-capped mountains. It had been for generations the regular holiday resort, the 'Hill Station' for the British service people who took leave and spent the summer there, so avoiding the unpleasant heat of the lowland country. Many army wives were in residence there while their husbands were away on war duty elsewhere. These women would meet at the Srinagar Club each midday to grog-on and listen to the wireless broadcasts of news on the progress of the war.

On return to Chaklala from Kashmir we decided to make a second visit, this time by air, and on 12 November 1942 took a Wellington and followed the Jhelum River through the steep valleys into the snow-ringed basin and Srinagar. We timed our trip so that we should arrive over the town at noon when the European folk would be gathered at the Club to hear the news. We did this and showed 'the colours' in RAF style. Flying through the valleys was rather scary.

Apart from routine dropping, we were once called upon to show the flag by laying on a flying display over the town of Rawalpindi. This was a great success, which frightened some of us as much as the inhabitants of the town. Another task we were given was to do a squadron drop before an audience of senior army officers at Risalpur, towards the Khyber Pass. I was on the ground with the army during the exercise, which became a major cock-up due to the leading aircraft making a navigational error. The formation missed the main target area and dropped everything over the audience. A few heavy arms containers dropped without their parachutes opening and fell among the parked cars, then the main body of the parachutists descended among the army. They were not impressed.

Early in December 1942, I received notice of promotion to acting wing commander again and a posting as Senior Staff Officer of Ferry Wing (India) with its headquarters at Karachi. The Wing was part of No. 226 Group, which was essentially a technical and maintenance group. It had not been influenced greatly by the war, and the attitude of most of its officers was what I imagine was that of the non-flying base wallahs in Singapore before its collapse.

The Ferry Wing itself was an active unit comprising the CO, G/Capt P. Wright DFC, and officers from almost every part of the Empire as well as a team of ferry pilots. It was responsible for the delivery of aircraft from Egypt to India and Burma, as well as ferrying time-expired ones back from the Burma front for rebuild at Karachi. It was housed in what were really mini-palaces previously occupied by the local upper crust. Our own accommodation was on a similar scale. My function was to ensure co-ordination between the administrative and the ferrying sections of the wing. This was easy enough and gave me opportunity to be airborne, rather than chairborne, and to visit many unusual places.

We had as a 'hack' a Mk I Blenheim which had earlier crashed in West Africa and was eventually repaired and ferried on to India. By then Blenheim Is were no longer used operationally so it was acquired by the Ferry Wing. We stripped it of all unnecessary weight – guns, armour plate, etc. – and had a useful, fast and comfortable air-taxi.

The immediate staff of Ferry Wing comprised about twenty officers from most parts of the Empire, who ran their particular departments such as Navigation, Medical, Signals or Spiritual, and so on. The leader of the Medical Section was W/Cdr Ritchie, an oldish doctor who seemed to practise no medicine but was part of a fishing threesome we formed to fish (when possible) every Thursday, from a local dhow in Karachi Harbour.[3] The third member was S/Ldr Poole ('Padre Poole the Pissy Priest'), our group spiritual adviser, who was more addicted to spirits alcoholic than to spirits theological. We used prawns as bait and always returned with a good bag of fish, mainly a type of catfish which we had prepared in our mess.

Padre Poole had served in WWI after which he had become a 'bush-brother' in the Australian outback, followed by a stint as an RAF padre – and a very good one at that. He concentrated on the social problems of his flock in a most worldly way and did much good.

A supernumerary in the wing, Capt Percy Bodley of the South African Air Force, attached himself to me and became my navigator in the Blenheim. We carried no other crew, but took along any passengers who wished to go in our direction.

Perc Bodley SAAF was a Blenheim pilot who had lost his hearing during the fall of Singapore and had been grounded from operational flying. Early in 1942, he had been a second lieutenant in 113 (Blenheim) Squadron RAF. This squadron had served previously in Libya and Greece where it lost all of its aircraft during the German invasion and its personnel were evacuated to Crete and then Egypt. Re-equipped, it resumed bombing operations in June 1941 but with the outbreak of war in the Far East it was transferred to Burma where it arrived at Mingaladon on 7 January 1942. That evening, without having proper inspections, the crews successfully attacked Japanese shipping and the docks at Bangkok. It bombed the advancing Japanese until its surviving crews and aircraft were withdrawn to Calcutta in March 1942.

Perc was a flamboyant type who kept a log book of his romantic conquests. At one stage in his career with us he could not pay his mess bill, so G/Capt Wright had him promoted to major and posted to an obscure outpost – Jiwani – along the west coast towards Persia (Iran). The only access to the place was either by plane, boat or camel, so Perc was more or less marooned until his bank balance came good and he could return to Karachi and pay his debts.

I spent a leave with Perc at Jiwani where one day we took a jeep and explored the hills to the north-west, probably crossing the border into Persia. The arid area was almost deserted, although in one steep valley we found a party of Indians destroying grasshoppers. They did this by digging trenches across the floor of the valley and destroying the hoppers (of which there were millions) using a flame thrower. This district was one of the main breeding grounds for the grasshoppers, which caused so much havoc in this part of the world. Some months earlier, a group of Russian biplanes had operated from Jiwani spraying the hoppers before they reached the flying stage.

Another holiday activity of the area was fishing and swimming along the coast. Both activities were dangerous; the fishing because it was common to catch lethal sea snakes (we cut the line) and swimming because of the presence of stinging jelly fish. Historically, this part of the Baluchistan coast was of great interest to us as some two thousand years earlier Alexander the Great had passed through the district with a part of his army when returning from India. They are said to have roughly followed the coast, obtaining water from wells they dug on the shore. This information came to us via our historian, Padre Poole, a keen student of Alexander.

After a few weeks at Karachi, G/Capt Wright decided that we should do the right thing and leave our cards at Government House. We did this and soon received invitations to attend a sherry party at 1800 hours one evening. We attended and had barely downed our first sherry when the hostess, Lady Hope I think, confronted us and said, 'Time to go,' so we went – so much for vice-regal hospitality.

While with Ferry Wing it was decided that I should fly to Egypt to investigate and find a new route for ferrying aircraft from Egypt to India. We normally flew from the Nile Delta to Palestine along the oil pipe line to Habbaniya in Iraq, down the Persian Gulf to Sharjah and along the coast to Karachi. It was feared that the Japanese might break through from Burma into India and eventually cut our air route through Iraq.

In March 1943, I flew by Empire Flying Boat to Egypt via Iraq. We encountered terrible snow storms over Iraq and Jordan and were compelled to fly on to Cairo, it being too rough for us to land on the Dead Sea. On this ghastly trip, nearly all the passengers were flat-out with air sickness; the exceptions were myself, a British rear-admiral (with a bag of sweets) and a soldier with a tumour on the brain.

The pilot of the flying boat was Captain Dudley Travers DFC, a WWI pilot who had continued flying as a commercial pilot between wars. He was one of the finest pilots I flew with. After being forced to fly on to Cairo, he made his landing on the Nile between bridges and boats seem to be child's play.

The new route I was to investigate was up the Nile to Khartoum, then to Asmara in Ethiopia, east to Aden and along the southern Arabian coast via Masirah Island, where the RAF had a very primitive ferry staging post, to Karachi. It was a feasible route although Asmara aerodrome was more than 7,000 feet above sea level and presented problems.

The programme on the trip to Egypt included a look at ferrying facilities west from Cairo towards the battle area. The officer in charge of the Ferrying Group of the Middle East was F/Lt/ Acting Mr/ Commodore Whitney-Straight who provided me with a Mk IV Blenheim and told me that I could fly anywhere I wished, provided I took along any freight or passengers going in my direction. The first passenger turned out to be a nursing sister heading for Benina (near Benghazi). She travelled in the cockpit and cluttered up that limited area, particularly so when we lost our way in a sandstorm and landed at Solluch to find our whereabouts. We eventually reached Castel Benito, the airport for Tripoli, where we stayed the night. Tripoli had been recaptured from the Axis troops the previous day and was in a mess. As the Italians retreated, they had destroyed what they could, including the sewerage system, which polluted the water supply. They had not, however, touched the wine supplies, which became our main thirst quencher at all times.

On the return trip to Cairo I spent one night at El Adem, the completely wrecked airport of Tobruk. It had been flattened during the fighting, but for one corner of one of the hangars that remained unscathed, which was called the 'Viper's Nest', being set aside as accommodation for VIPs (Very Important Persons such as myself). It was luxurious.

That day, while landing at Marble Arch one of our tyres blew out, punctured by a piece of the shrapnel littering the runway. This was no problem as a new wheel was soon taken from one of the dozens of available wrecks and fitted to our plane. The trip to Tripoli took us over many of the places where heavy fighting had taken place during the final push west. The main road was a narrow bitumen strip about 1,500 miles long strewn with thousands of wrecked transports and tanks, while every few miles there were landing grounds ringed with wrecked aircraft crashed, destroyed or abandoned during the advance.

Before leaving India on the flight to Egypt I had been asked by an Indian friend, Lt Col Hanut Singh, to buy for him while in Cairo a number of gold trinkets such as Indian women wore hung on a chain around the wrist, as well as cosmetics (Elizabeth Arden face cream and lipstick), these goods being in short supply in India. I shopped around Cairo, buying the trinkets and cosmetics for Hanut, and a parcel of Palestinian liquors and wines for myself. As well I bought a length of RAAF blue uniform cloth which I intended having made up in India. While in Cairo I signed an application to transfer back to the RAAF at the conclusion of my contract with the RAF.

The idea of transferring to the RAAF came to me from S/Ldr Greg Graham, who had been with me at Point Cook and who had already arranged his own transfer. He later acted as best man at my wedding and then amassed great wealth as a tourist property developer on the Gold Coast, becoming a millionaire.

After Greg 'Shorty' Graham had taken up his short service commission in the RAF, he joined 80 Squadron in March 1938 and moved with it to Egypt in May. From 10 June to 18 November 1940 the squadron operated in the Western Desert against the Italians and during this period F/O Graham was credited with destroying a CR42 and a SM79 probable. His promotion to flight lieutenant came through on 3 September.

On 18 November he moved with the squadron to Greece. The campaign in Greece continued against the Italians with 80's Gladiators operating from Yannina and Paramythia. On 19 November while flying Gladiator N5814 he claimed a G.50 and a CR42 over the Koritza area and two more of the same on 4 December. 80 Squadron was re-equipped with Hurricanes on 15 February 1941 and on in Hurricane V7852 he shot down a Ju88, which crashed north of Politika. With the Allied forces overwhelmed by the Germans during the last days of April, Graham stayed on with about twenty others burning and demolishing anything of value at Elevsis before being evacuated to Crete, thence to Alexandria.

After more than three years with 80 Squadron, on 27 May he became Chief Flying Instructor at 71 OTU, Ismailia, and was promoted to squadron leader. In April 1943, he transferred to the RAAF and after various appointments left the service in November 1944. He was credited with seven (six plus one shared) destroyed and shared one probable.

Greg and I met one night at Shepherd's Hotel in Cairo. It became an unforgettable evening when a Lt. Col., very drunk and wearing parachute wings on his chest, had brought service to a halt in the hotel by threatening to throw glasses of grog at all and sundry, regardless of rank. I tackled him about wearing his parachute wings on his chest, when they would normally be on his upper arm and was politely told that if I had done as many drops as he had done I could wear them up my arse. He turned out to be the remarkable Paddy Mayne of the SAS and LRDG.[4] I believe that he was eventually awarded the DSO and three bars.

Lt Col Hanut Singh was a Rao Rajah of Jodhpur (illegitimate brother of the Rajah). He had been educated in England and was a graduate of Sandhurst. He flew with us from time to time and invited some of us to be guests at the wedding of his kinsman Maharaj Kumar Shri Hanwant Singh, at the New Palace, Jodhpur. It was an unbelievable event attended by only the male members of the Singh family and their guests, the females watching proceedings from behind screens on the mezzanine. The table settings were extravagant, some of the bowls and dishes being made of gold. We were accommodated in large comfortable tents, each of which had its own toilet facilities; all in marked contrast to the millions of the homeless poor of India, of whom in 1943 between 1,000,000 and 3,000,000 died of starvation in Bengal alone.

Hanut owned a large stud which was managed by an able Eurasian lady, who was also his mistress. When he had originally asked me to shop for him in Cairo, no mention was made of money and I was a bit uncertain whether I should ever be reimbursed for my trouble, however, on my return I received full payment for everything.

After completing my work in the Middle East I picked up a Blenheim V (Bisley) at Heliopolis for delivery to India, having as crew a navigator and a wireless operator. The W/Op was an Australian (RAAF), F/Sgt Jameson. I did not hear from him again until 1991 when he wrote to me regarding the names of Australian airmen killed in WW2 whose names were still not on the Honour Roll at the War Memorial, Canberra.

We had been airborne for a couple of hours on the first leg of our flight, heading for Khartoum, when the reduction gear on the propeller of one engine disintegrated causing the complete loss of power in the engine. Luck was with us as we were within gliding distance of Luxor aerodrome, the only landing ground for many miles. We landed safely and found that the aircraft was completely unserviceable, requiring a new reduction gear.

We made ourselves at home, had lunch and went on a tour of the antiquities of the Valley of the Kings (Luxor). Next day we got a lift back to Cairo in a Beaufort, then another lift by Hudson to Khartoum where we were able to pick up another Blenheim V. The stay at Luxor was highlighted by everybody leaving the dining room during lunch and going outdoors. We thought this strange until we were told that they had gone out to look at the rain, Luxor being a part of the world where little or no rain falls. We stayed overnight at Khartoum, a peacetime RAF base where the station mascot was a small lion cub which had got into trouble rolling in wet tar!

Next day we flew to Asmara, 7,200 feet, where the take-off was scary, using the full runway to become airborne after which one fell away into the valley of the Red Sea and then to Aden. On this leg of the journey we received a wireless message instructing us to call at a landing ground, Riyan, and pick up a parcel for an air vice marshal at Karachi. This message came in Morse code and was apparently received incorrectly. The landing ground for the pickup of the parcel should have read 'Aden' and not 'Riyan'. Further along the coast of Yemen we eventually found Riyan, where we landed and found that they had no parcel for us and they had never heard of the AVM from Karachi. When we finally reached India I was abused by the AVM for not collecting his parcel – a case of whiskey – at Aden. He even insinuated that I had taken delivery of it and consumed it along the way!

The flight along the southern Arabian coast showed us remarkable examples of soil erosion, where miles of the country took the form of islands of land, about the size of a house block, divided by deep gorges. The land levelled out as we proceeded further east, becoming more like a sandy desert, which type continued until we reached Masirah Island, the RAF's very primitive ferry staging post. The petrol supply to the island was off-loaded into the sea in four-gallon tins from dhows and allowed to float ashore, where it was gathered and poured into the aircraft by hand – a very dicey method of refuelling. The empty tins were used as building blocks after they were filled with sand. Our final leg to Karachi was uneventful. I completed the report on the new ferry route, which I doubt was ever used as the Japs failed to advance into India.

I found, in general, that working with Ferry Wing (India) was interesting and rewarding, although it had drawbacks, mainly due to the peacetime attitude of many of the chaps who were not exactly interested in the successful prosecution of the war. I was generally free to enjoy plenty of flying in all types of aircraft and to see more of India than most other visitors. I had been issued with an AI Travel Pass which allowed me the highest movement priority by any means of transport available and which made travel easy.

One of my duties while with the wing was to site flying control towers at a number of landing grounds under construction by the Indian Army Works Department, which built our aerodromes. These aerodromes were built along an arc to the north and north-west of India and were to be used as air force bases should the Japs advance into India. They were well constructed, even having underground operation rooms.

One day while with Ferry Wing I received orders to take command of ARC, the Karachi airport, which was the first aerodrome at which aircraft from the Middle East and Europe landed on reaching India. I took over, but only for one day, when I was replaced by one of the RAF India establishment, a wing commander who had used his influence to get this nice posting away from operations.

This type of activity did not make me very happy so I began to agitate for a posting back to operations. My agitation was put into action through the recommendation of my fishing friend W/Cdr Richie (Doc). He did his work well and I soon received orders to proceed to Jessore (Bengal) and take command of 215 Squadron RAF.

21

215 Squadron Raf

Dereck French's new orders were to proceed to Jessore (Bengal) and take command of 215 Squadron RAF, which was still equipped with Vickers Wellington Mk IC aircraft but now employed on bombing targets in Burma.

By the middle of 1943 the RAF had 52 squadrons, including transport units, in the Burma-India theatre. Of these, eighteen were fighter squadrons and eleven were light bombers. The fighter squadrons were equipped with Hawker Hurricanes and Curtiss P-36 Mohawks; the heavy bombers with B-24 Liberators; the medium bombers with Wellingtons, and the light bombers with Bristol Blenheims and Bisleys and Vultee Vengeance dive-bombers. From June to November, aircraft strength grew from 2,453 to 3,699. At the same time, the USAAF strength increased from 185 aircraft to 265, out of which 210 were combat ready.

At Jessore and around Calcutta there were five fighter squadrons mainly for the defence of Calcutta, one photo reconnaissance squadron, one transport squadron and three bomber squadrons, two of them, No. 99 and No. 215, flying Wellingtons. Three Vengeance dive-bomber squadrons were undergoing training.

There were four RAF groups operating in India and Burma: Nos 221, 222, 224 and 225. Located at Colombo and Bangalore respectively, Nos 222 and 225 Groups were under Air Headquarters, India Command. Nos 221 at Calcutta and 224 at Chittagong were under Air Headquarters, Bengal. The majority of Australian aircrew in the India–Burma theatre were serving in Nos 221 and 224 Groups, whose squadrons were mainly on the forward airfields and around Calcutta. There had been rapid development of airfields in the theatre. In March 1942, there had been four airfields with all-weather runways. By the end of the 1943 monsoon season there were 285 airfields completed and more were under construction.

This 215 Squadron came into being at Newmarket Heath, Cambridgeshire, on 9 December 1941, earmarked for overseas service. In February 1942 its personnel embarked for India by ship where they arrived in April. The squadron's air echelon was formed at Waterbeach, Cambridgeshire, on 21 February and after training with Wellingtons flew out to India at the end of March. At first it was engaged in supply-dropping flights during the aftermath of the British retreat from Burma but in August coastal patrols began along the east coast of India. In October, airborne forces training began and it was March 1943 before the squadron was ready to undertake bombing missions over Burma.

There had been other 215 Squadrons before this one. The first 215 Squadron, a night bomber unit in the Great War, was disbanded in 1919. It was reformed as a bomber squadron again in 1935 but in September 1939 it was designated a training unit and became part of No. 11 OTU in April 1940. A new 215 Squadron began to form at Honington but this was again absorbed by No. 11 OTU the following May.

Dereck was ordered to go to Jessore by air and to take with him only 1 cwt of baggage, including camping gear and bedding.

Shortly before leaving Karachi I was detailed to act as one of the Wing Commander Escorts to an Australian, W/Cdr Dennis, who was under arrest pending his trial by court-martial for homosexuality. Our duty was to escort the prisoner for time spans of 24 hours, not letting him out of our sight during this time. One Sunday, during my spell of duty, he expressed a desire to attend Holy Communion, so I had to escort him to church and go through the actions of being a Christian and receive the consecrated bread and wine. Another experience!

I flew to Bengal in a Dragon Rapide of a civil airline. The pilot of this plane was 'Aga', an old Indian friend of Waddington days (UK). He was a lousy pilot who, while with the RAF, had earned the reputation of becoming lost while flying almost daily. He finally gravitated to the lowest of flying duties, towing a drogue (target wind sock) behind a very safe aircraft for student pilots to practise their air-gunnery upon. Our flight necessitated staying overnight at Delhi. Here Aga took me to a posh Indian club, The Chelmsford. Next day we flew on to Dum Dum, Calcutta, where I was to be screened by the AOC of 221 Group, A/Cdr H. V. Rowley, an ex-fighter pilot with little or no knowledge of bombers and their uses. I entered his large office and could at first see nobody, then I spotted a chap on the floor under the table feeding a cat with a saucer of milk. This was A/Cdr Rowley.[1]

We chatted for a time, when he said, 'See you at 1830 hours at Group Captain Wilson's room. Dress: a towel!'

I turned up at 1830 in my towel, where the screening began with loads of grog, mainly Indian rum, after which we dined, dressed and were taken on a tour of the brothels of Calcutta by the strange AOC, this being his idea of screening his new squadron commanders. I apparently passed his screening for next day I went to Jessore and took over 215 Squadron. Jessore was a large rambling town of thousands of Indians, with no Europeans apart from one elderly French priest. It was situated about 100 miles north-east of Calcutta, to which it was connected by road and rail. It lay in the centre of the vast delta of the Ganges and its tributaries.

The aerodrome was an engineering masterpiece, being constructed among the paddy fields and waterways with nothing in the way of stone or hard filling being available. The average water table was about 18 inches below the earth surface, which gave us many problems, particularly with the disposal of our dead and of our sewerage. The graves were dug into the mud below the water line and grass was sprinkled on to the water to make it all look better. We found that about 100 years earlier there had been a large British population at Jessore engaged in the indigo and jute industries, and that they had solved the problem of the high water table when they buried their dead (often young children), when they erected large blockhouses on each grave site, the bodies being sealed up in these, above water level. The blockhouses were made of mud brick and masonry. To overcome the sewage disposal problem we dug holes deep into the mud with a post hole digger and mounted concrete seats over them, when they became full, they were sealed with cement and another hole dug nearby.

No. 215 Squadron RAF was equipped with very old Wellington IC aircraft which had seen much service both in the UK and the Middle East before being retired to the India–Burma theatre of war. The squadron was one of two Wellington units at Jessore, the other one being 99 Squadron, commanded by an old friend W/Cdr Maddox. 215 had been commanded by W/Cdr Charles Webster, another old friend, who for some reason or other had ceased to function as a commanding officer. He had neglected the unit and was living in Calcutta with a lady friend. Charges against offending personnel had not been processed for about three months, so there was plenty of administrative work to do. The two flight commanders, S/Ldrs Cross and Chisholm happened to be very senior to me in the Air Force List and resented my posting, which had been made because of my operational experience. They had apparently been in a backwater of the RAF until then.

Operationally, the squadron was just ticking over, partly because Jessore was still under the influence of the southwest monsoon. It rained daily and aircraft servicing was very difficult because of it, as well as the shortage of aircraft parts in this theatre. We operated occasionally. No. 221 Group in Calcutta rang us on a scrambled telephone and asked for our serviceability for that day. We usually had only four or five aircraft fit to fly. They then gave us our operational instructions for that night and we would do the necessary servicing, test flights, bombing-up and briefing.

Our targets were usually obscure aerodromes which were very difficult to locate in a country that had few landmarks. These objectives were not clear and understandable by Middle East and UK standards and because of this vagueness one never felt that one had done a good job.

We encountered little opposition from anti-aircraft fire or fighters, our main dangers being the poor quality aircraft we flew, the mountains between our base and Burma, and the atrocious weather. The area had a poor reputation for flying conditions; Sir Charles Kingsford-Smith disappeared in this area in the *Lady Southern Cross* in November 1935. We encountered clouds shaped like a blacksmith's anvil which we had been ordered never to fly into. They were capable of upturning an aircraft or tearing its wings off. If one flew in the rain below one of these clouds in a Wellington, the aircraft would be forced to lose height. One night one of our Wellingtons tried to fly through one of these and was thrown upside-down.

Sometimes we were sent in daylight to photograph sections of the Arakan coast where it was proposed to create a landing and a new front to push back the Japanese. This front did not eventuate, the war being fortunately brought to a swift conclusion by the use of the atomic bomb.

One of our aircraft failed to return from one of these 'daylights' down the Arakan coast and after about five days I sent the usual condolence letters to the next of kin of the missing airmen. Several days later we received a signal from Chittagong that the crew was safe there, having drifted about in a dinghy in the Bay of Bengal for nearly a week. It had rained each day and they had survived on rainwater and the emergency rations in the dinghy. They eventually returned to Jessore, but as they were badly shaken by the experience we had them posted back to the UK. During my stay with 215 Squadron this crew was the only one of those reported missing from whom we received any news as to their fate. Any aircraft reported missing usually remained 'missing'. To give crews a chance if they came down in the jungle, we evolved a package of 'jungle escape gear' based on our experience especially for use in Burma or the Pacific islands.

Shortly before I took over command of 215, a crew which included Ross Gregory of Melbourne, a noted cricketer of the day, failed to return from a sortie. Later, when I returned to Australia I carried with me Ross's diary, which I gave to his father. Some years later I saw the diary again at Murchison, Victoria, in a military museum owned by Keith Gregory, Ross's cousin. A small world.

A strange operational duty allotted to us was to drop, by night, thousands of prickly steel objects, about the size of an orange, along the mountain-pass roads that connected the Arakan coast to the Irrawaddy River Valley. These roads were used by Japanese transport vehicles to carry supplies from the coast to their fighting forces over the ranges. The idea was to hold up the transport convoys on the narrow roads by puncturing their tyres and so make them choice targets for our fighter-bombers to attack later.

There was an amount of healthy operational competition between 99 and 215 Squadrons which came to the fore one night. No.99 had the only Wellington in 221 Group capable of fitting a 4,000-pound bomb and orders were received to attack a target in Mandalay with one of them. Sometime later, we in 215 were delighted to hear that the massive bomb shipped carefully from the UK and then railed to Jessore to be dropped on Mandalay had actually only killed one deer!

By August/September 1943 the war in Europe and the Middle East had begun to swing in our favour and there was a move to build up forces in the Far East to combat the Japanese. Part of this move was the appointment of Lord Louis Mountbatten as 'Supremo India' in charge of all British and American forces.

Lord Louis Mountbatten rose from the rank of captain in command of a destroyer at the beginning of the war to Supreme Allied Commander South-East Asia at its end. Having been born into an aristocratic family, he was related to most of the royal households of Europe. His father, Prince Louis of Battenberg, had served throughout his life in Britain's Royal Navy and at the outbreak of the Great War he was First Sea Lord. Unfortunately, as a wave of anti-German sentiment spread throughout Britain, Prince Louis was hounded out of office because of his ancestry.

Young Louis Mountbatten, then a Royal Navy sea cadet, was determined to succeed in the face of this slur on his family. As a young sailor he astutely specialised in signals, recognising that the navy's future success would depend largely on the quality of its communications. Just before WW2, Mountbatten was appointed to command the 5th Destroyer Flotilla. In December 1939 his ship struck a mine but he and his crew were able to bring her back to port. During another action in the North Sea, his ship was torpedoed and had to limp back towards Scapa Flow in serious danger of sinking. Despite a night of increasingly rough seas, Mountbatten refused to evacuate and scuttle the vessel and eventually made port. The builders were astonished that she had survived. Commanding from other ships in the flotilla, he built on his reputation for skilled seamanship and daring. In May 1941 in the Mediterranean, his flotilla supported the Allied forces in Crete, but his destroyer was attacked by Stuka dive-bombers and sunk. Mountbatten narrowly escaped drowning.

He was next appointed to command the aircraft carrier HMS *Illustrious*, but before sailing he was recalled personally by Prime Minister Churchill to take up the post of 'adviser on combined operations'. His involvement in planning a programme of raids such as the commando expedition to Norway on 26 December 1941, Bruneval in February 1942, and St Nazaire the following March led to his appointment as Chief of Combined Operations with the acting rank of vice-admiral in the Royal Navy, lieutenant-general in the army and air marshal in the RAF, and then becoming a full member of the Chiefs of Staff Committee.

Although the Dieppe raid in August 1942 was a conspicuous failure, there is universal agreement that it provided invaluable experience for the planning of the D-Day assaults on Normandy in 1944. A year before this event, however, Mountbatten was appointed Supreme Commander South-east Asia. He arrived in India on 7 October 1943 and found himself at the centre of a complicated military command structure which included Field Marshal Archibald Wavell as Viceroy of India, General Claude Auchinleck as Commander-in-Chief India, and the US General 'Vinegar Joe' Stilwell as Deputy Supreme Commander. There was also Generalissimo Chiang Kai-shek, the Chinese leader whom Mountbatten described as 'the worst headache I had to cope with'. He clearly had a formidable task before him. Dereck found Mountbatten's presence imposing:

On arrival he visited all of the units under his command, including Jessore. He arrived by air one day, when all personnel were paraded before him. He asked for a box, mounted it and ordered all to break ranks and gather around. He then addressed them saying, 'I have come along to have a look at you chaps and also to let you have a look at me,' which was a good start and went down very well. Later we entertained him to refreshments, which we had gone to much trouble to arrange, even to the extent of sending to Calcutta for pastry treats. He looked around, bypassed all of the treats and hopped into a bowl of local bananas, to him a luxury having just arrived from the UK.

The visit was like a fresh breeze. He re-organised the old Indian Establishment and brought the British and the American forces together by appointing joint commands in which a USAAF officer and a British officer of equal rank worked together. Under this system, my immediate operational boss was a USAAF General. He was a delightful old farmer who one day attended a briefing for a night raid into Burma. He sat through the briefing, chewing and spitting on the floor, and then said, 'Say Commander, I'd like to fly with one of your boys tonight.'

I showed him the crew listed for the night and told him to take his pick. He chose a very junior sergeant pilot and flew on the trip with him. This type of action is what is really required of a senior officer from time to time, primarily to find out what happens on an operational raid and secondly to raise the morale of the unit by showing that he is prepared to take the same risks as his crews. We used tractors to move our Wellingtons around on the ground and the old farmer-General spent much time with me explaining the exact level of water required in a tractor tyre to ensure the maximum traction.

We had a navigational problem when we flew by night in Bengal, the lack of landmarks and beacons by which we might fix our position. In an attempt to solve this problem we had for months asked 221 Group RAF to place marker beacons in the Sunderbans (river delta country) between our base and Burma, and had been told that to do so was impossible as there were no suitable beacons available. The Sunderbans was an immense area of the Ganges delta, barely above sea level, consisting of waterways and islands covered with fairly dense jungle and mangrove scrub. I asked the USAAF General if he could help and the beacons were in place and working within three weeks!

The RAF had a few observer posts, usually a corporal and a few men, scattered along the waterways, whose duty was to watch for Japanese aircraft and report their activities to Group headquarters in Calcutta. Theirs was a terrible job, being completely isolated on small clearings cut out of the jungle and being supplied about once a week by a small river steamer, the SS *Vanu*. The Station padre, S/Ldr (Rev) Hutton at Jessore decided that he should accompany the *Vanu* on one of the supply trips and attend to the spiritual needs of the isolated airmen by holding a church service at each observer post, and invited me to keep him company. I gladly accepted as the area was a shooter's and naturalist's dream, being the home of thousands of Chital deer (spotted), wild pigs, monkeys, estuary crocodiles, leopards and Bengal tigers and many species of unusual birds.

We boarded the SS *Vanu* at Kulna and spent about a week steaming from outpost to outpost, shooting as we went. I had borrowed a .303 inch rifle and ammunition and had on hand hundreds of rounds of 12-gauge cartridges for my shotgun, so we were well equipped. One day we pulled alongside a native fishing boat which was slowly towing a bamboo basket, nearly as large as the boat itself. The basket was a holding net for fish caught along the way by otters, which the fishermen kept tethered to the boat. The tethered otters shepherded the fish into scoop nets from which the fish were transferred without damage to the very large bamboo holding basket which was towed for weeks behind the boat until a town was reached. I believe the Chinese use cormorants in a similar manner.

Our main quarry was Chital deer, one of which we usually managed to bag each day, This regular shooting was necessary as in the humid climate meat could not be kept fresh for more than a day so that we lived on very fresh venison which had not been hung in any way and was as tough as old boots.

We also shot wild pigs from the boat as they swam from island to island. I had been told that if pigs swam they cut their throats with their trotters; another myth, they swam as naturally as any other animal. One day we shot a very large boar which did not give up until it had been hit by at least a dozen .303 bullets. It finally died on one of the islands which happened to be densely covered with prickly holly bushes, with leaves similar to Christmas holly. Some islands grew nothing but a species of tall mangrove which the Chital deer ate and trimmed completely bare from ground level to about six feet, above which, and out of reach was a dense canopy of leaves.

The targets we preferred most were the estuary crocodile which we found often sunning themselves on the mud banks. I managed to shoot several of these, one of which was more than twelve feet long. We had them dragged aboard and skinned, salting the skins and leaving the carcases for the crew. They ate some of the flesh, which looked like that of a big fish.

The boat crew were a mixed lot of Indians, the majority of whom appeared to be Muslims. These brought the boat to a stop quite a few times a day, got out their prayer mats and faced Mecca asking for Allah's blessing. We could not find out how they established in which direction they looked to Mecca.

Jessore aerodrome was situated a few miles out of town and consisted of a main runway and a few small squadron and flight offices. The land had originally been used for rice growing, general agriculture and grazing. The area was inadequately fenced and quite often during night operations we had near misses as stock wandered over the take-off strip. The drome was in very flat terrain, being generally clear of trees except for one very tall one near our flight offices. This had a series of steps and ladders leading to a look-out tower which was supposed to be manned by troops on the look-out for infiltrating Japanese.

One day while the maintenance crews were preparing the aircraft for operations, we were alerted by a sound resembling an air-raid siren, and on investigating we saw the maintenance crews leaping down from one of the aircraft and running away. As the sound continued we watched the bombs fall from the belly of the plane onto the tarmac. This continued until no more bombs remained and the sound faded away. It turned out that one of the maintenance chaps had by mistake pulled a lever which had caused an enormous rubber capsule in the bomb bay to inflate and this had forced the bombs from their fasteners. Fortunately, none exploded as they fell. The inflation device was a recent installation for use in the event of the aircraft being forced to put down in the sea, when it would help to keep the plane afloat a bit longer and give the crew more time to escape.

We had at the aerodrome, a large fuel depot with petrol stored in 44 gallon drums. One night in the town of Jessore we heard explosions and saw the glow of fires coming from the direction of the drome, so raced to investigate. We found that a local Indian had been stealing petrol from the dump using a kerosene lantern to find his way. The open flame from his lamp ignited the petrol and the whole dump was destroyed. The culprit escaped but an RAF guard who tried to put the fire out died of burns. We lost thousands of gallons of fuel and I was kept busy answering the enquiries of the dead RAF chap's next of kin for details of his end – a sad business.

Jessore was a wonderful place for shooting. It was flat, swampy and consisted predominantly of lakes and waterways. The area was the destination of many types of duck, snipe and water birds which each year migrated across the Himalayas from Russia and China. Bird life at Jessore was prolific. Of particular interest were the snipe, which when they first arrived were in very poor condition after their long flight and put-to-flight they simply took off and flew in a straight line and were easy targets to hit. After a few weeks of rest and good feeding they quickly fattened and when roused took off in the typical zig-zag snipe manner and were most difficult to bring down.

One day while shooting these birds, I swung around to take a second shot at a wounded bird as it made another attempt to escape. I followed it in flight and fired only to find that I had hit the bird and also a young beater who was bent over picking up another bird. He remained bent until I went to him and found that a few No. 6 shot had lodged under his scalp. We took him to the nearest Indian village where we found a chap who claimed to be a doctor and who said that he would remove the pellets and look after the victim for the night. He suggested that the charge for this service would be the equivalent of 7/6d and a further 7/6d for the victim, which sounded very reasonable. Everything went well for during the following week the same beater once again volunteered to pick up for us – no doubt anticipating a further 7/6d.

Ammunition for these shooting excursions was readily available thanks to a pilot of 215 Squadron, F/Lt James. James had escaped from Singapore – how, I do not know – and eventually joined 215 Squadron. He was not a particularly keen type and soon after my arrival at Jessore he came to see me before he returned to the UK. During this meeting, he explained that he was a Freemason –why, I don't know – and then said that he was leaving a box in his quarters which I could have. After his departure I found the box contained thousands of rounds of .45 inch ammunition, suited for use in both .45 calibre pistols or in Thompson sub-machine guns. I could only assume that the bullets had come from Singapore.

At that time .45 inch ammunition of this type was in very short supply in our unit so I approached our Armament officer with the offer of a swap – a round of .45 for a round of No. 6 shot 12 Gauge ammunition; and so came into the possession of thousands of 12 gauge cartridges which lasted me until I had settled down in Australia. These 12 gauge cartridges were issued to bomber units for use by their aircrew in clay pigeon shooting.

Our living quarters and messes were in the town of Jessore in buildings we had taken over from the locals. My own quarters were in what had been a girls' school. This was three storeys high, being made of pise (packed mud), the walls at ground level being nearly three feet thick. It was a nice cool building to live in.

The construction of this type of structure, common in Bengal, was quite simple. The mud was dug by hand from a site adjacent to the building and then packed between boards and bamboo frames which were raised as the structure grew. There was a slight taper in the walls, so that they became thinner towards the top. The roof was constructed with very wide eaves to keep the monsoon rains from damaging the mud walls. A great amount of mud was used leaving a large tank (a dam in Australia) at the side of the building which was used as a water supply as well as a place to grow fish, these being netted once a year. They looked like European carp.

Our flying life at Jessore was neither exciting nor rewarding, mainly due to poor aircraft serviceability. This meant that the aircrew had more leisure than they would have had in Europe or in the Middle East, to indulge in outside interests, in my case shooting and bird-watching. Bengal was a bird-watcher's paradise.

No. 215 Squadron had the usual RAF chain of command: Adjutant, F/Lt Hinman, Medical Officer, F/Lt Hill, Signals officer, etc., which made my work as the CO not too exacting. F/Lt Hinman had been a pilot, who some reason or other had been grounded and with his background of flying had become a super-efficient adjutant. In civil life he had been in the hospitality industry, hotel management, and knew every PR trick in the book. He understood our difficulties – poor aircraft, poor targets, poor weather conditions, poor accommodation – and did his best to help us overcome them.

He had a weakness which came to light when he formed a friendship with a local Indian girl, Dhabu, for whom he bought saris and on one occasion introduced her to our mess. Soon after this he went on leave and on his return while bringing him up to date with squadron matters I mentioned that there had been two more cases of VD in the squadron, both of which had been traced back to his friend Dhabu. He saw the light. VD was rife in India at that time.

Our ration issue at Jessore came from the Indian Army – sides of beef weighed barely a quarter the weight of a side of Australian beef and all other food items were proportionally low in weight. To overcome this in the Officer's Mess, I bought suckling pigs from the locals, reared them on mess swill, shot them myself with a service pistol and had them prepared for the table. They were a good food supplement.

In Bengal, pigs were considered to be unclean and were not permitted to be kept in villages and towns. They were usually shepherded in mobs along the roads between towns, grazing as they went. On one occasion, while out shooting I bagged a large boar which we ate in our mess. It was later claimed that the boar was a domestic one and we received the bill for it.

Our medico, Doc Hill, was a magnificent, efficient, conscientious chap who looked after our medical health as best he could in a lousy climate where about 80 per cent of the personnel developed malaria as well as the many skin infections of this part of the tropics.

Another interesting and invaluable character in 215 Squadron at that time was Corporal Murray. He had great linguistic ability, being fluent in Bengali and Urdu and was our only means of communicating with the local people. He was a well-qualified graduate from an English University. Every three months, I recommended that he be commissioned and each time the recommendation was rejected. I could not understand this, although I suspected that he was not politically acceptable to the RAF hierarchy.

During one quiet period at Jessore, I was ordered to Bangalore, Mysore, to act as an air umpire of the air component of a large military field exercise comprising thousands of military types. My senior and fellow umpire was Group Captain the Earl of Bandon (known to us as the 'Abandoned Earl'), a remarkable character. We lived in tents during the exercise, shared a batman and generally looked after ourselves, while army types with equivalent rank had about three hangers-on to care for them. After about four days the show finished with an appraisal held in a large theatre in Bangalore. There the Earl gave his version of the use of the air force components by the army and told the many generals that they had no idea of the potential of an air force, or how it should be used. He was not very popular.

While at Jessore I once took leave with S/Ldr Tony Ennis DSO DFC of 99 Squadron (the other Wellington unit at Jessore) at Puri, a beach resort south-west of Calcutta. Tony was, I believe, one of three RAF brothers all with the DSO. He came to grief later at Imphal when he took off to fight attacking Japanese planes and was shot down and killed.[2] We travelled by train and at each stop were circled by hordes of starving children begging for food or money. It was a shocking experience. This was 1943, the time of a terrible famine in Bengal in which between 1–3 million people died of starvation. Each morning while we were at Puri we saw many dead in the streets, mainly children. I could not help but think that there was plenty of food on hand but it had been gathered into the hands of merchants who priced it beyond the buying capacity of the peasant people. Another factor creating the famine was the system of land ownership, which allowed absentee landlords to overcharge their tenants.

Accommodation at Puri was in a luxurious railway hotel on the beach. Everything was in full supply except for alcohol, but we overcame this shortage when some army officers (ex-Burma) arrived with cases of Indian rum – rather lethal, but very good when consumed half and half with coconut juice.

On 17 June 1944, during the closing stages of the battle of Imphal, S/Ldr Tony Ennis had the misfortune to run into a patrol of Nakajima Ki43 Oscars of either the 50th *Sentai* or the 204th *Sentai*. He was instructed to fly his Wellington on a series of daylight bomb delivery sorties from Kumbhirgram by following a designated air corridor. After landing, turnaround had to be as quick as possible. The bombs, not having detonators at this stage, would be simply released from the bomb bays by spilling them out.

He took off at 0710 hours to fly to Kangla but was diverted to Palel where sixteen 250-pound bombs were offloaded. He then returned to Kumbhirgram and later flew in two more loads, the last delivery being made at noon. Despite an alert of the enemy fighters in the valley, he left again almost immediately but failed to reach Kumbhirgram. Later a report came in from the army that a Wellington had been seen going down in flames at 1215 hours. It fell into enemy territory a few miles from Churachandpur to the south-west outside the valley. S/Ldr Anthony Ennis DSO DFC had the dubious distinction of being the most decorated RAF pilot to be killed during the siege of Imphal, and one of the most senior.

Well before this incident, Dereck in frustration decided to do something about the poor quality of his aircraft.

The Wellington Mk IC aircraft with which 215 Squadron was equipped could only be described as 'clapped out'. Most of them had been used operationally in the UK, then in the Middle East and after much servicing had been sent to the India–Burma theatre. They would have been a valuable asset to us had there been sufficient spare parts on hand to keep them serviceable.

The Wellington was of geodetic structured frame covered with a fabric skin. During the monsoon period when it rained daily they absorbed a great amount of water, which added to each aircraft's weight and reduced its 'ceiling' accordingly. As the mountains between Jessore and our targets in Burma rose to 10,000 feet and more, the Wellingtons with their ceiling of about 9,900 feet were not good enough for the job.

Each morning I received a 'scrambled' phone call from Headquarters in Calcutta asking for the aircraft serviceability for the day and was given the target for that day or night. One day when this call came through I replied that our serviceability was 'nil'. When the panic subsided, I invited HQ to send up a group of 'plumbers' (technical officers) to air test the aircraft. They arrived by car and were given a choice of aircraft and crews. The first plane they selected was bombed-up for them but would not give the required number of engine revs so the bomb load was shifted to another plane. This took off with the 'plumbers' aboard, but would not fly above 9,500 feet. The test upset the experts severely and Wellington ICs did not fly on bomber operations again.

At this stage we were offered a replacement for them of B-24 Liberators. I investigated these aircraft and found that they would be no better than the Wellington ICs as regards range and bomb load and a change to them would entail a complete change of ancillary equipment – engines, airframes, armour – and retraining or replacing all of the ground crews. The offer was absurd so I argued that we be re-equipped with the more powerful and up-to-date Wellington Mk X. We eventually got these and they did a good job.[3]

During our stay at Puri, we witnessed an event of ornithological interest. One morning, anxious to make the most of the magnificent food available at the Nagpur Railway Hotel, we had gone down early to indulge in one of their excellent breakfasts. No one else was about in the dining room so we sat quietly at one of the tables waiting for service. Through an open window came a House or Indian crow that landed on a nearby table. It looked at us casually, then removed the glass lid from the sugar bowl, took a beak full of sugar and flew out of the window. Next morning we witnessed a repeat of the same sugar stealing act!

A squadron commander's duty at that time was to periodically recommend personnel for decorations for flying or others duties of an outstanding nature. This was easy as we did little operational work to warrant such recommendations, however, shortly before my departure for Australia I had occasion to recommend a Sgt Pilot for a DFM for outstanding operational work over Burma. The following week I had occasion to submit a case to HQ for him to be court-martialled as he had been caught offering his service pistol for sale in a Calcutta brothel. I still wonder whether he got a DFM or a court martial! Another duty of command was to recommend NCOs for commissions. I once received a letter from an Australian Member of Parliament telling me that one RAAF sergeant with the squadron should be commissioned. Nothing was done.

During the aircraft change over to the Mk X Wellingtons we were hardly operational and my job gave little satisfaction. With this in mind, and the fact that I had heard that my father, who I had not seen for six years was very ill, I decided to apply for a posting to Australia.

Dereck's final mission was a routine affair. On 14 December 1943, he and his crew in Wellington Mk X, HZ401, successfully bombed the Prome railhead some 150 miles from Rangoon. Following this, with every new day Dereck waited with increasing impatience for his posting home to Australia.

22

Home

Melbourne, Easter 1944. On most weekends, Barbara Rigg would travel home to East St Kilda in Melbourne from her work as a bank clerk at the National Bank branch in Romsey, a small town in the Shire of the Macedon Ranges. Romsey station was a significant stop on the Clarkefield-Lancefield railway line located some 38 miles to the north of Melbourne.

Barbara had studied at Central Business College in Collins Street, Melbourne, in 1935. At the age of nineteen, after an introduction to a staff manager at the National Bank she was appointed as a ledger keeper to the Balaclava branch, which had two other staff members, a manager and a teller, and being within walking distance from home was a bonus.

The outbreak of war that year took many of the male staff away so before long she became one of the first of only a few female tellers. 'We were required to handle a pistol which was kept in the drawer near the cash,' she recalled. 'Males had weekly pistol practice but females had none. I loved the job and bank hold-ups were very rare.' Female staff members were paid half the male salary for doing the same work, 'yet the customers preferred us girls.' In fact, one of the customers fell madly in love with her!

Accommodation in Romsey was in short supply but the manager and his wife, Jack and Doris King, came to the rescue by insisting she board with them until she found somewhere else. She never did. She remained with them for four happy years. 'This was a wonderful period of my life. They were like parents and their three daughters were like sisters.' The quality of Barbara's work was such that she progressed to become a full-time bank teller. In fact, she was the first in the National Bank.

Barbara's father, Donald Rigg, had died in 1929 leaving her grief-stricken mother, Margaret (nicknamed Lexie), with two small girls and barely enough money. She provided them with a comfortable

280

home through housekeeping positions. With Barbara grown up, at East St Kilda, Barbara's mother took on another housekeeping position in the home of a Mrs Stachan. As the years passed Mrs Stachan appreciated Lexie's care and she became a good and loving friend. 'Her nice home was ours to treat as our own. We held many good parties there and later my wedding reception.' It was during this time that Barbara's sister, June, met and married Arthur Bentley, a soldier who was much older and still in uniform. The couple married in a little church in the same street, Denman Avenue, East St Kilda.

While Barbara was back from Romsey for the 1944 Easter weekend, Mrs Strachan's next-door neighbours, Henry and Joyce Jacksch, invited her to a welcome home party they were having. It was for a friend from Brighton who was back in Australia from the Burma war zone. His return had been headlined in the Melbourne newspapers as he had been the very first Australian decorated with Britain's Distinguished Flying Cross in the Second World War. He was Wing Commander D. J. French DFC and Bar. Barbara recalled later that at the party: 'We were introduced and spent the evening sizing each other up. In RAAF uniform he was a sight to behold.'

'There was definitely chemistry at work,' Dereck remembered. He also remembered there was other chemistry at work as well. 'Henry, who was of German origin, produced a quantity of his latest home-brew (stout). This was so frothy that it could only be opened safely if over a bath!'

Later that evening when celebration ended, Barbara and Dereck parted company and went their separate ways. Dereck disappeared from East St Kilda and with the Easter holidays over, Barbara went back to Romsey...

After the party, Dereck had reported to the RAAF's Transit Depot at the Melbourne Cricket Ground (MCG). His return to Australia had for the most part deteriorated into a frustrating and discouraging experience – but that was before the party. Back in India, although his application for a posting home had been approved, a long delay followed. He was informed that there was simply nobody else available to replace him as CO of 215 Squadron.

Eventually, I left Jessore for Australia in a not very happy mood as I had learned that during the delay in finding a replacement for me my father had died. I travelled for days by train and ferry to Colombo where I waited weeks more for a ship to continue on to Australia. The only unusual incident during the trip to Ceylon was when, in the middle of nowhere, our train came to a stop and could not proceed further because of a derailed train blocking the line. The problem was overcome by all passengers carting their baggage past the wreck to a train waiting beyond it.

While waiting at Colombo for a boat to Australia I met a few RAAF chaps also on their way home and palled up with F/Lt Forbes-Gordon from Bungendore NSW. Together we explored Ceylon. He had been away from home for some years and wished to return to his wife, who he said had hazel eyes, with a suitable gift. He finally chose an unmounted yellow sapphire about as large as a small almond shell. It was a beautiful stone, being cut with a large rectangular face. Many people saw it and argued as to whether or not such a stone as a yellow sapphire existed. The discussion led to the face of the stone being scraped with a diamond which left a bad scratch. We learned later that the stone was indeed a genuine and very valuable yellow sapphire – softer than a diamond!

On 26 February 1944, we boarded a small steamer, the SS *Randfontein*, and again I was OC Troops, the troops being a handful of Australians. The captain of the ship, Captain Remain OBE, was an old character who claimed to be on his last voyage, having done his first trips under sail. He had tales to tell of being sunk while trying to take supplies into Malta and claimed that although he had been at sea for all of his life he still became seasick in bad weather. Nearly three weeks later we berthed at Fremantle and I went ashore to present my credentials to the AOC of the RAAF at Perth, A/Cdr Brownell. I was told to wait as he was busy. I then saw that he was in his office, feet on table, reading a newspaper.

Raymond James Brownell was a Tasmanian born in New Town on 17 May 1894 and had been educated at Scotch College, Melbourne. He served with the 9th Battery, Australian Field Artillery, on Gallipoli and in France, being awarded a MM before transferring to the RFC late in 1916. In 1917 he was posted to No. 45 Squadron in France. The squadron was equipped with new, deadly Sopwith Camels. During his first patrol on 10 September 1917, he shot down a German twoseater which crashed in flames in Houtboulst Wood. Brownell went to Italy with 45 Squadron in November and was later promoted to captain and awarded an MC. He was credited with at least twelve victories but another nine claims were not confirmed.

After the Great War, Brownell joined the new RAAF as a flying officer and reached the rank of wing commander in 1936. During that year he went to England on an exchange scheme with the RAF. At the start of WW2 he commanded the first permanent RAAF units in Western Australia. He then commanded RAAF units in Malaya and was fortunately recalled in 1941, just before the Japanese invasion. When he retired in 1947, he was an Air Commodore CBE.[1]

Dereck was far from impressed by Brownell's attitude, and was even less so by what followed afterwards.

I was eventually admitted [to his office] where I presented my credentials, said my piece and was offered a train trip to Melbourne. I elected to go by sea and a week later arrived in Melbourne. We steamed across Port Phillip Bay during the night and I was amazed to see the shoreline a mass of lights! Our arrival coincided with a wharfie strike so all the passengers had to carry their own baggage ashore.[2]

I found Melbourne strange after more than six years absence. My family had no home there. My father had recently died, and my mother and brother Neil were staying with old friends. Neil was barely 50 per cent fit, mentally and physically.

Much had happened while Dereck was away.

As a child Neil had been a clever talented type, a good violinist. He was educated at Princes Hill State School where he obtained a scholarship to attend University High School and obtained his Intermediate Certificate. The Depression was at its worst when he left school to work at the Commonwealth Bank. His position with the bank was probably obtained due to my father's influence. Off duty, he took up rowing as a hobby and was always a member of the CMF, in his case the Garrison Artillery.[3]

During 1938, while he was employed in NSW by the bank, he was spending a weekend training with his CMF unit, and while riding as pillion passenger on a motorcycle went at great speed through a metal shed. He suffered severe brain damage, was unconscious for weeks and became mentally and physically disabled. It was thought that his brain damage was the cause of him having epileptic fits from time to time. Despite his disability, the bank continued to employ him in less arduous positions; which job he held for more than forty years. Again, this was probably due to my father's influence, and the fact that Neil had by then become a Freemason. Neil remained single until after our mother died and then married an old flame, Dorothy Judge of Newcastle. They had no children. On the death of our mother, Neil inherited her property and so had few financial worries.

My father, Leo, in 1922 bought, for £90, a bush block of nearly eleven acres at Beaconsfield. We spent most of our spare time, weekends and holidays, there and learned to respect and appreciate our native flora and fauna. Leo was an early conservationist and went to the trouble of obtaining metal signs from the Fisheries and Wild Life Department in Melbourne which proclaimed certain areas to be sanctuaries; these he nailed to trees along the Cardinia Creek. He built a large shed on the property which we used for years until we built a house to replace it.

In 1938 when both Neil and myself had left home and Leo was awaiting notice of transfer to Brisbane he sold it to a chap of German origin for £280.

We later heard that when WW2 broke out the local heroes from the nearby Cardinia Hotel went in force to the block and burned the house down by way of showing their patriotism.

My father was a keen student who realised the value of education. In 1904 he had been accepted to join the Commonwealth Public Service and qualified for membership of the Institute of Accountants Victoria in 1914. He became a licensed member of the Tasmanian Companies Auditors Board in 1926 and gained a Diploma of Commerce from Melbourne University in 1928. He earned these qualifications by personal effort and at his own expense. His progress in the Audit Branch of the Public Service was steady. By 1930 he was Chief Inspector of the Victorian Branch of the Commonwealth Audit Office and rose to be Chief Auditor of the Banking Control Division just before his retirement owing to ill health.

Leo French was appointed to many investigations and Royal Commissions. In 1927, he carried out the investigation of the financial aspects of the Royal Commission on the Moving Picture Industry in Australia. In 1930, he was sent to investigate the administration of Northern and Central Australia and the peanut industry in Australia. In 1934 he was sent to Nauru to investigate the accounts section of the administration of the island. Nauru was then under mandate of the Australian Government from the League of Nations. Later he took part in the financial aspects of the investigation to nationalise banking in Australia. He worked on many investigations into frauds and tax avoidance (Customs) which involved the Commonwealth Government.

From early adulthood Leo had indifferent health, having a bout of pneumonia which left him with weak lungs. He was found to be suffering from tuberculosis in 1930. I did not see him for the last six and a half years of his life, but understand that he had trouble speaking, his vocal cords being damaged. He died in 1943, aged fifty-nine. Too young!

As a father, he was to me, the best. He was a good honest man, never overbearing, never dictatorial, always guiding. I have always thought myself lucky, and the best stroke of luck I had was having him as a father. My one regret is that I did not see him before his death.

The RAAF appeared to have no idea what I was to do, so it sent me on extended leave and gave me accommodation in their transit depot below the stands at the MCG – rather grim!

The general atmosphere was unreal – a state of disturbed peace yet not one of a country at war, although the pubs seemed to be full of chaps in uniform.

At this stage of the war, the balance was definitely swinging in our favour. This was mainly due to the enormous effort of the US, which appeared to have the ability to muster the men and equipment required for the job with little trouble. The Australian attitude among the upper echelons of the services was very defeatist with the various factions fighting among themselves and appearing to be politically geared, so much so that military activity was limited to manoeuvres which could not possibly cause the loss of personnel that might result in the loss of votes at the next election. Talk of the 'Brisbane Line' idea was common, displaying more defeatism. This was an idea which resulted in the formation of large bodies of poorly trained, poorly equipped uniformed personnel spread around the country.

I had returned from Bengal with the idea of handing over what 'know-how' I possessed of the RAF bombing experience in Burma, even to the extent of bringing with me a sample of jungle escape gear which we had evolved for use in Burma. However, when I discovered the apathetic attitude of RAAF HQ, I quickly forgot about it.

During my stay at the MCG, I was ordered to attend two parades. One was to take part in a march of service personnel through the streets of Melbourne to help raise the spirits of the population and inspire them to subscribe to the latest issue of war bonds. The other was to attend church parade. This I thought ridiculous in a time of war. At other places where I had served church parades had been voluntary affairs, usually very poorly attended, so much so that on one occasion in Bengal, to prevent our resident RAF padre from preaching to no congregation at all, I had a number of Indian-enrolled followers (who had little or no English) marched to the service he was holding.

After a few weeks of this strange life of filling in time, socialising and boozing, I decided to leave the service and go on the land. I did this by submitting my resignation. Regulations prohibited the resignation of officers of the permanent RAAF in time of war but on my transfer from the regular RAF I had been transferred to the RAAF Reserve, from which I could resign. I had one interview for this with the Officer in Charge RAAF Personnel, A/G/Capt Winneke who was a member of the legal establishment and later the Governor of Victoria, and my discharge was approved.[4] Almost too readily!

This change of career seemed to follow that of a friend, S/Ldr Greg Graham. Greg had been on my senior term at Point Cook, where he had been awarded the Sword of Honour for his course before transferring to the RAF six months before myself. In 1943 he had suggested that I follow his example and transfer from the RAF back to the RAAF, which I did in Cairo. My resignation also followed his example and strangely enough I again followed his example by getting married rather swiftly. It was there that our careers differed – he became a millionaire – I didn't.

Greg 'Shorty' Graham had transferred to the RAAF in April 1943 and after various appointments he left the service in November 1944. In civilian life he enjoyed business success especially in real estate and property development and eventually retired to Queensland's Gold Coast. Later in life he suffered from Parkinson's disease and passed away in 2001.

Some weeks after Dereck's welcome home party, Barbara Rigg was back in Melbourne walking down Collins St when she saw him standing outside the Hotel Australia. This was a meeting place for servicemen home on leave and regarded as a place for them to 'drown their sorrows'. After greeting each other with surprise, they quickly realised that the chemistry they had shared at the party was rekindling as strong as it had been then.

Dereck sprang more surprises – one of them huge! She learned that after the party he had decided to resign from the RAAF in disgust over the treatment of returning airmen. He was going into farming! Would she marry him? There was just one condition. She must agree to be the wife of a farmer.

As a result of my travels and experiences overseas I thought that we would very soon win the war and have a short peace followed by chaos and turmoil in most countries. Under such conditions, a rural life seemed desirable. I had trained as an engineer before I took to flying, but decided not to return to that profession or a business life in Melbourne as my life out of doors as a pilot caused me to look for a life in the open air – farming.

The idea of going into business in Melbourne was a slight possibility. In the early 1930s, I had worked for a year in the office of Calcutta Company (Jute Merchants) who, after my return to Australia, made contact with me and put on a luncheon at the Mitre Tavern in my honour when they presented me with a cheque for war services and tried to persuade me to go into business in the city. I declined the suggestion. Although I had decided to become a farmer on retirement from flying, I had little idea how I should do this!

Although Barbara was realistic enough to realize that marriage would be 'a huge risk' for both of them, she did not hesitate. To start with she soon discovered that Dereck's mother did not see her as the right person: 'Nell French was distraught [after her husband's death] and looked to Dereck to solve her many problems when he came home. He needed more care than she did, and also he soon told her he planned to marry me. Her hopes had been for a marriage to a pre-war girlfriend, the daughter she never had and longed for, so I was not acceptable.'

Dereck's brother, Neil, cast another shadow over the union. His epileptic fits raised the possibility that they might be a hereditary problem. 'When I... was thinking of getting married,' Dereck wrote later,

'...I contacted his surgeon, Dr Hooper, and asked him whether Neil's complaint was genetically or physically caused. Dr Hooper assured me that in Neil's case the epilepsy was the result of brain damage incurred at the time of the accident.'

Dereck and Barbara married on 13 June 1944 at St Stephen's Presbyterian Church in Balaclava Road, Caulfield. 'Squadron Leader Greg Graham was our best man,' Barbara recalled, 'My sister June was my attendant and Uncle Norman Rigg gave me away. I remained in the bank for another year working at the Collingwood Branch, Western Branch and Head Office in Collins Street.'

Dereck demanded the Dept of Agriculture send him somewhere for farming training. Werribee research farm was suggested, to milk cows from 4 a.m. He gladly accepted this challenge, the first of many...

With the idea of learning something about farming I went to see the Victorian Minister of Agriculture (Mr Brake) and asked for his help. He arranged that I take a job as a labourer at the Werribee Research Farm for about six months, learning what I could. It was an interesting experience. The farm at the time had a large dairy herd, milking Red-polls and Friesians, a large area set aside for growing cereals and a unique research section mainly run by Dr Wishart who was doing pioneering work on artificial insemination. It was a good place to learn.

Although a tractor was available on the farm, horses were used for all purposes. I never saw the tractor used. Apart from the good work being done there, I felt that the farm was a hideout for chaps who wanted to keep out of the services. The manager (Wilson) did not welcome my presence. I did not understand this until I learned that his wife had been lured away by a RAAF flight lieutenant from Point Cook, which caused him to treat all air force types with suspicion. A large group of Land Army girls worked very efficiently on the farm.

At this time I began looking to buy a farm in the Gippsland area. I chose this region because relatives (cousins) the Brysons farmed at Poowong, while Fergusons did so at Loch; both dairying in South Gippsland. I tended to be guided by them. I had £2,000 plus which I had accumulated during my service life. This was sufficient, at that time, to make a down payment on a farm.

My search ended when I bought Belmont, 622 acres of hilly land between Loch and Wonthaggi. It had been magnificent blue-gum country which had been cleared years before, stocked with sheep and neglected so that it had become overgrown with bracken fern with a few Blackwoods along the creeks. The property had originally been a square mile (640 acres), subdivision from which, for the areas of unmade roads, had been deducted, leaving 622 acres of freehold land.

Australia was still at war and everything – tools, cars, machinery, and household goods – was in short supply. I had very few possessions apart from a few clothes and about £2,500 in the bank. We had very few of the essentials required and the effort required to get these was a full-time task. We managed to buy an old Buick car, with a trailer. It was a wonderful old vehicle, very useful. It could run quite well on power kerosene, petrol was rationed. As well, I acquired a fair set of tools, some household goods, furniture, etc. My father's sister, Cecilia (Aunt Sue), was a great help in getting things.

Barbara described Belmont as 'a rambling Victorian style weatherboard 50 years old with few improvements. It had no power or water laid on and the original kitchen and bathroom were very basic with just a trough. Another huge risk for both of us...'

23

Epilogue – Nothing Lasts Forever

The risk was worth it. Barbara and Dereck French celebrated their fiftieth wedding anniversary with family and friends at Mitchelton Winery near Nagambie, Victoria, in 1994. But it was not all easy going, especially at first. They had begun their journey by living and farming in Victoria's South Gippsland.

The district was known as Krowera, which I understand is an Aboriginal word meaning 'Windy Place' – a gross understatement. My first aim was to clear it of bracken fern and graze the area. I had neither the agricultural knowledge nor the financial backing required to achieve this. Following the original clearing of the property, erosion had taken place in the steep gullies and formed an ideal habitat for thousands of rabbits. During the two years of our occupation of the property, from figures I kept, we sold 23,000 rabbits off the property. These were bought by buyers who called every few days and paid us 4/6d a pair for them, and exported them to England. The rabbits were trapped, mainly by professional trappers, who were in residence almost permanently. Some I trapped myself.

The place was visited regularly by workers from the Wonthaggi Coal Mines who caught the rabbits by ferreting. This was done in the extensive eroded gullies where many of the ferrets were lost; some of these I subsequently caught in my traps, nursed back to health and resold to new owners.

Another source of income was from the sale of the skins of foxes and feral cats; cat skins, at that time, sold for 5/-. After a couple of years, I could see that I was making little or no progress in improving the farm so decided to sell out and buy a dairy farm where one might anticipate a regular income.

I continued to look for a suitable dairy farm and found one at Beverford, on the Murray River, about 12 miles north of Swan Hill. The area was roughly 80 acres of irrigation, with a large river frontage. It was part of the pre-emptive right of Tyntyndyer Station and was being run as a dairy farm.

Barbara:

The Mallee is a 'dirty word', dust storms, drought, floods, extreme heat and isolation, inhabited by hard-working farming families not used to 'city slickers' and their way of life, in fact not welcome. Having made the decision to become a farmer, either farming sheep, dairy cattle, beef cattle, fruit or vegetables, one has to find suitable land with irrigation available, ideally beside the Murray River and with suitable housing. A 90-acre irrigated property on Murray River frontage was on the market for £3,153, a wooden cottage, no electricity or water laid on, very basic, a decision was made to purchase, no arguments. I was struck dumb by the state of the house we were to move into. I had hoped to move somewhere better than Belmont but this was much worse. I did not agree to purchasing the farm but Dereck proceeded. I was furious so there was silence for three weeks and he kept to himself in the shed.

The house was small, wooden, no bathroom, no laid on water and no electricity but Dereck wanted it because it was on the Murray River. Soldier settlement granted him a loan to purchase at 3.75 per cent. The chosen farm was capable of supporting seventy milking cows, dairy-farming rather than sheep suited this small property. Farming started in earnest, milking seventy cows on irrigated pastures, twice a day every day, with only family help. Re-irrigating the farm. When it was our turn for water, a water-bailiff called, telling us to turn on the water-wheel and start watering the farm, through channels, nonstop day and night until all paddocks were well-watered. Maybe two or three days. With milking, this was an exhausting job for one person. Milking machines were operated by generator, often needing repairs. Pre-war training in electrical engineering came in handy. Milk or cream was collected by tanker daily for local butter factory. Pigs were a profitable side-line.

The cows were friendly and responded to sympathetic treatment by their loving owner. He wore his RAF uniform at milking time, until it wore out. New calves were fed on skim milk after separation and a new bull introduced every two years for hybrid vigour, several different breeds were used. With little help, milking shed and yards were modernised and by now a guaranteed regular income. After eighteen years without electricity, an insurance policy paid for connection of power; what a luxury to have powered appliances, washing machine and lamps. Holidays were few, always in one of many caravans owned. Twice around Australia and over much of each state.

Dereck:

Soon after we married, we had four beaut daughters. Secretly, I was pleased that they were not sons, as after seeing many hundreds of magnificent chaps killed wastefully during the war I had no wish to see any male offspring of mine die in a similar manner. We tried to bring up the girls to be unselfish and responsible.

They were always treated equally, and I can never remember seeing them quarrel. They started their schooling at the Beverford State School, where they had a very fine headmaster, Eric Dohnt, and later they went to the Swan Hill High School. It was there that their responsible attitude came to the fore, as they all became form captains, house captains, prefects and good students. Pam became a head prefect. We were, and are, proud of them.

Sue Buckingham:

[Dereck] held a Protestant work ethic ideal and considered idleness a sin. We (female) children worked many hours on the farm in activities that were more suited to males. When I complained about yet another chore, he said, 'It's not what you have done; it's what you *haven't* done.'

Often we grumbled about the work-load, and referred to him as 'the Wing Commander' with us taking orders. And yet we wore his old RAAF uniforms with pride (and some warmth) while we fed the pigs and herded cows. To his credit, we children were not disadvantaged by this lifestyle; in fact he encouraged our interest and wonder in the natural sciences, reading non-fiction, boating, camping and fishing on the Murray River, and participating in local sports.

During post-war years he did not seek the company of other servicemen, and was often critical of the need for ex-servicemen to relive and glorify their war experiences. On one rare occasion when he attended an RAAF reunion in Melbourne, he felt uneasy in the crowd of celebrating 'survivors', and then discovered they thought he had died during the war. My father spent the post-war years away from the horrors of war, in a somewhat isolated and reflective life, in the country.

Barbara:

Leaving behind the life as an 'exceptional pilot' with the RAF and RAAF, regarded by his crew as a God and returning to peacetime life needed a lot of courage, for all concerned. Family were the new 'crew' and had to 'toe the line', take orders without complaining and know who was the boss. Life was hard but rewarding. As the years rolled by, the crew became independent and took on other interests. The boss mellowed and showed some appreciation. Compliments were few and far between, but one stayed with the recipient.

As a Commanding Officer RAF, certain methods were used on recruits for suitability to join a crew, take them out for an evening drinking and 'under the influence' take notice of opinions and judgements they expressed, this was a reliable test of character, etc. [for his daughters' prospective husbands]. The peacetime boss, one evening, 'under the influence' said to his senior 'crew member', 'You are the best wife a man could ever have!'

Rooney Fields:

I remember driving the tractor for hours, pastor, harrowing, checking the flood irrigation levels, feeding the pigs, carrying very heavy buckets, feeding the calves and rounding up the cows— I can never remember a word of thanks or sign of appreciation from Dar.

As a child being taken into the bush to bird watch was not classified as enjoyable, however in later years I now can appreciate this time and the great knowledge that I gained, to the degree that I am a member of BOCA and never miss an opportunity to bird watch the world over. He made wonderful records of the habitats and nesting habits of the mallee fowl in the area just north of Swan Hill and we regularly spent hours silently walking, stalking these magnificent birds to find their unusual mound nests.

Dereck:

Sue and Ann (later known as Rooney) decided to become nurses, which ensured future professions and accommodation while training. Pam was an excellent student and gained a Commonwealth Scholarship to study Science at Melbourne University. She successfully completed the course and joined the Victorian Education Department as a teacher.

Christine decided that she, too, would become a teacher and completed a course in Teacher Training and began to teach. After several postings to primary schools... she decided that teaching was not to her liking and trained to be a nurse at the Royal Melbourne Hospital, where both Sue and Rooney had trained earlier.

Pam Mathieson:

His aim was to ensure that his four daughters were well educated for the times (1960s). I was able to take advantage of this by always claiming that I had homework to do, so was able to avoid working in the dairy after school. He was always proud of our academic achievements, but never told us directly.

Dar's farming techniques and the way he 'lived off the land' reflected his resourceful nature. He regularly supplied us with fresh fish from the river, Murray Cod, Yellow Belly or Red fin and we feasted on Murray Cray sandwiches in our school lunches each winter.

Dereck:

A reason I had chosen the farm at Beverford was because it was situated on the Murray River; noted for its fish, which I anticipated catching when free of farm work. This idea eventuated and during our thirty years in residence there we enjoyed many hours fishing and eating the catch...

To further my interest in ornithology and aboriginal pre-history, during most winter rest periods from milking I made many car trips to the Darling River, and beyond, and three long trips along the Murray river in my 12-foot boat, with a motor. These were very interesting journeys which I did alone, camping each night on the river bank, wherever I chanced to be. The bird life, and the people I met along the way made the trips well worthwhile; while the investigation of hundreds of old aboriginal camp sites, both pre-European and recent, gave me an idea as to what had happened there.

Our farms and river frontages had their share of middens, some of which had been excavated and used for filling and making banks during periods of flood. They contained aboriginal skeletons and tools, and on a large one situated between Tyntyndyer Homestead and the Murray River, I discovered a European earth-closet near where the earlier river boats would have tied-up to service the Station. This contained a treasure in antique bottles and other European artefacts.

While searching the midden for more of these treasures, I came across several skeletons which I reported to the Melbourne Museum authorities, who eventually sent a party to research the find. This party was led by Peter Coutts. He excavated two of the skeletons and decided that they were of recent origin (probably 200 years old), and were probably the victims of one of the epidemics of smallpox which occurred along the river at intervals after about 1788. One skeleton was said to have a stone axe near to its hand. The skeletons were named after me, being known as DF1 and DF2. They were taken away. What became of them, I do not know.

My interest in our pre-history was helped greatly by the fact that Barbara, for seven years, managed the tourist attraction side of Tyntyndyer Homestead which we adjoined. Whenever people with an interest in pre-history came along as visitors, she usually guided them in my direction.

In 1978, after thirty years at Beverford, Barbara and I decided that we should move closer towards civilization (Melbourne), where the girls were continuing their education and training. We had been caravanning along the

South Australian coast, near Robe, and were on our way home to Beverford when we stopped overnight at Nagambie.

We were attracted by the small village and the lake, and contacted a local real-estate agent, Pat McNamara, later Deputy Premier of Victoria, asking for a home with a water frontage. He, in a half-hearted manner, showed us 7 Callaghan Court; over which property we obtained a verbal option to buy, and returned to Beverford to put our farm on the market. It sold easily, within a few days, giving us enough money in hand to buy at Nagambie. It was a good move, placing us little more than an hours' drive from Melbourne.

Rooney Fields:

It was only in the last ten to fifteen years of his life that he would talk to us about his war experiences. I remember about ten years ago when visiting Nagambie I spent the whole two days of my visit reading his memoirs, asking questions along the way. It was probably one of the most interesting times I spent with him.

Dereck:

I have had a great interest in books since my pre-teenage years and had gathered many associated with my interests. At Nagambie I enjoyed adding to the collection and eventually had several thousand volumes. During this period I witnessed the disposal of a valuable collection of books about India, when it was under British control, which had been collected by Barbara's stepfather, C.O. Jolly, during his lifetime. They were given to a furniture carrier. I decided that my books would not suffer a similar fate, and to recycle most of them. This was easily done.

Those relevant to Aboriginal prehistory went to the library of the Koori Heritage Trust in Melbourne; some including Australian history and a collection written by Ion Idriess went to Pamela; while hundreds went in bulk to a second-hand book dealer, Delphina Manor at Benalla. This left me a small library which dealt mainly with the RAF, WW2 and natural history reference works.

Since the end of WW2 many writers have published their version of events of the war, which versions, in most cases, consist of half-truths due to the thirty-year time limit on censored material and do not present the whole story. However, an almost endless number of writers from the generation of children of those who took part in the war are delving into the history of the war and are publishing more unrestricted versions of the story.

Of these, a few have contacted me in search of opinions and help. These include Chris Coulthard-Clark, The Third Brother; Bob Kirby, The Avro

Manchester; Dennis Newton, *A Few of the Few, First Impact* and others. Robin Neillands, with about twenty-five military books to his credit, has produced *The Bomber War*, a summary of Bomber Command.

Contact with these authors made me feel how fortunate I have been to have collected so much memorabilia which gives, perhaps, a truer version of the war as I had experienced it. My collection included my diary; letters I had written home to Australia during the war; a few official records; my Flying Log Book; and a journal I had written about the war during my early farm years. From these sources I was able to obtain much information for the writers. This was appreciated by many of them, as most of those who had taken part in those periods of the war had either been killed at the time or had passed on since then.

After twenty-plus good years at Nagambie we began to think about our next move, to a retirement village, either local or handy to Melbourne. We finally decided to move to the Long Island Retirement Village at Frankston, moving in February 2001.

My life has been spent in a period of great changes, in many spheres of technology, aviation, communications, electronics and the different branches of the media; many of which changes evolved as the result of developments during WW2. Living through much of this era of change, I by chance gathered an amount of memorabilia, letters, diaries, my Flying Log Books and a few official records which I felt should be available to future students. With this in mind, I arranged that the collection should go to the archives of the LaTrobe Australian Manuscript Collection at the State Library of Victoria.

The move to the retirement village was a sensible one, although I consider that it should have been made at least five years earlier.

Barbara:

On 18 June 2008, my beloved Dereck passed away peacefully in our unit, aged ninety-two and a half years. He had donated his body to Melbourne University for research so there was no funeral, although we did have a well-attended memorial service at the village. He survived a remarkable six years in Bomber Command and was highly regarded by all who served with him. We have many publications to remind us of his contribution to WW2. 'A distinctive man in peace and war.'

Barbara stayed on at Long Island Retirement Village after Dereck's passing.

In March 2010, I celebrated my ninetieth birthday in the courtyard off my new apartment at Long Island Village with family and friends. The family

– Sue, Pam, Rooney and Chris – include me in their activities and are so caring. The careers of my grandchildren are progressing well and I am proud of their achievements. Their parents' standards in education, discipline and behaviour are plain to see in this fast-moving and demanding world. I now also have six great grandchildren.

I love living by the bay again and memories keep coming back. Melbourne is so exciting in development and culture. I marvel at the changes in the city and the suburbs of my youth. In December 2009 I hired a large house boat on the Murray for a week. The four girls joined me taking turns to helm up and down the river in South Australia. As we lived on the Murray for thirty years it bought back many memories.

In September 2010, Barbara visited Victoria's Grampian Mountains, staying at Halls Gap with daughters Pam, Rooney and Chris, Sue living in Albany, Western Australia. Sadly, less than two and half years later, Pam succumbed to cancer, passing away very peacefully on Friday, 18 February 2013.

Barbara made her final move late in 2015 to Catherine's Hostel, Wangaratta in northern Victoria, where she could be cared for more closely by Chris, who had moved there during that year. Nearly three years later, in August 2018, the time came at long last for Barbara, now ninety-eight, to rejoin her beloved companion of sixty-four years.[1]

APPENDIX 1

Honours and Awards

1/ The citation of the Distinguished Flying Cross awarded to Flying Officer Dereck Jack French of 50 Squadron RAF reads:_

ROYAL AIR FORCE AWARDS.No. 20.
The King has been graciously pleased to approve of the following awards:-

AWARDED THE DISTINGUISHED FLYING CROSS.
Flying Officer French successfully attacked, in the face of intense anti-aircraft fire, a German cruiser in the Bergen roadstead, enabling his navigator and bomb-aimer, Pilot Officer Mulloy, to secure a direct hit on the cruiser. This operation necessitated more than 1,000 miles flying over the sea.

HRH King George VI presented the decoration to Dereck on 7 May 1940. Just three days later the Germans launched their invasion of France and the Low Countries.

2/ For his work with 455 (RAAF) Squadron, Dereck was awarded a Bar to his DFC:

BAR TO THE DISTINGUISHED FLYING CROSS
Squadron Leader Derek Jack FRENCH DFC No. 455 Squadron. This officer was awarded the Distinguished Flying Cross in April 1940. Since joining his present squadron he has made attacks on Frankfurt, Kiel, Huls, Hanover and other important targets. On one occasion he was detailed to attack the aerodrome at Schipol. Despite unfavourable weather, which necessitated a search for the exact target lasting 5 hours, Squadron Leader French eventually completed a successful attack from 1,600 feet. On February 12th, 1942, he participated in the daylight attack on the German warships at sea. In spite of a heavy and accurate defensive barrage, he made his attack from 800 feet. Apart from his operational work, Squadron Leader French played a large part in the organisation of the squadron, of which he was one of the first two officers, and the unit has benefited greatly by his experience, keenness and efficiency.

The Bar to Dereck's DFC was finally presented to him by the Governor of Victoria at Government House, Melbourne, on 7 September 1945, although it had been promulgated in the *London Gazette* on 26 June 1942, over three years earlier.

APPENDIX 2

Main Aircraft Flown on Operations by Dereck French

HANDLEY PAGE HAMPDEN

The Handley Page Hampden and Vickers Wellington medium bombers were built to the same original 1932 specification (B9/32) calling for fast, well-armed day-bombers that could also be used for night operations. They were intended to operate in small formations, relying on their speed and mutually defensive gun armament to evade or fight off enemy fighters. The prototype Hampden, the HP52, flew for the first time on 21 June 1936. Within two months the Air Ministry ordered 180 aircraft to a revised standard with a streamlined moulded Perspex nose replacing the prototype's original square-cut nose.

Hampdens formed the main equipment of No. 5 Group, RAF Bomber Command, when war was declared and along with the Bristol Blenheim bore the brunt of the fighting in the early daylight raids. Serious losses to enemy fighters revealed the inadequacy of their defences, the lack of firepower and the limited traverse of their machine guns. Their long slim fuselages earned them such nicknames as 'frying-pan', 'panhandle', 'tadpole' and 'flying suitcase', and in combat there could have been possible confusion with the German Dornier Do17 'Flying Pencil'. After improvements in firepower and defensive armament such as the introduction of self-sealing fuel tanks, Hampdens joined the Whitley bombers in the night offensive against Germany. From the end of August 1940, these included attacks on Berlin at the extreme limits of their range.

During the grave days of 1940, two Hampden fliers were awarded the Victoria Cross: pilot F/Lt R. A. B. 'Babe' Learoyd of 49 Squadron for leading the famous raid on the Dortmund-Ems Canal on night of 12/13 August 1940; and New Zealander, Sgt John Hannah, a wireless-operator/air-gunner of 83 Squadron who used up two extinguishers and finally his log book to beat out the flames consuming his aircraft.

Although Handley Page stopped building Hampdens after their 500th aircraft in mid-1940, the English Electric Company produced a further 770 of them between early 1940 and early 1942, and factories in Canada built 160 more. While soldiering on as bombers, the Hampdens had two other main roles, laying magnetic mines and as interim torpedo-bombers.

Early in September 1942, two Hampden squadrons, Nos 144 and 455 (RAAF), flew sixteen Hampdens each to Vaenga airfield near Murmansk in North Russia as part of the protective cover for the convoys to Russia. After completing their Russian mission, the British and Australian crews returned home after handing over their aircraft to the Soviet Air Force.

Finally, early in 1944 war-weary surviving Hampdens were transferred across the Atlantic to serve in OTUs in Canada. The RAF declared the Hampden obsolete in August 1944. Despite its changing roles requiring various modifications, there was only the Mk I Hampden. A proposed Mk II version with Wright Cyclone engines did not materialise beyond the prototype stage.

A version of the Hampden that did develop, powered by a pair of Napier Dagger H-type in-line engines in place of the radial Bristol Pegasus engines, was given a new name – Hereford. The type was built by Short & Harland at Belfast but the 150 that were built did not achieve operational status due to engine troubles. For a time they equipped OTUs but were eventually retired to be used as ground instructional airframes, although some of the last fifty were converted back to Hampdens.

Type: twin-engine medium bomber.
Crew: Four.
Powerplant: Two 1,000hp (746kW) Bristol Pegasus XVIII nine-cylinder, air-cooled, radial engines.
Span: 69 feet 2in.
Length: 53 feet 7in.
Height: 14 feet 11 in.
Wing area: 668 sq feet.
Landing gear track: 17 feet 4in.
Maximum speed: 254 mph at 13,800 feet.
Cruising speed: 167 mph at 15,000 feet.
Initial climb: 980/min; time to 15,000 feet 18.9 minutes.
Service ceiling: 19,000 feet.
Range: With 2,000 lb bomb load, 1,885 miles at 155 mph; with 4,000 lb bomb load, 1,100 miles at 206 mph.
Weight Empty: 11,780 lb.
Weight Loaded: (normal): 18,756 lb.
Maximum take-off: 22,500 lb.
Armament: One fixed and one moveable 0.303 in (7.7 mm) Vickers 'K' gun in nose; twin 0.303 in (7.7 mm) Vickers 'K' guns in ventral and dorsal positions.
Maximum bomb load: two 2,000 lb or four 500 lb bombs in bomb bay; two 500 lb bombs on underwing racks.

AVRO MANCHESTER

Manchester L7246, the first of two prototypes developed out of Air Ministry Specification P.13/36, was test-flown in July 1939. Initially planned to have twin fins inboard on the tailplane, it emerged with twin fins outboard, and shortly after initial testing it was given an additional middle fin. Late production Manchesters, modified as Mk IAs, had the span of their tailplane increased from 22 to 33 feet and the middle fin deleted. The second prototype, L7247, first flown in May 1940, was the first fitted with armament.

An order for two hundred Manchesters manufactured to Air Ministry Specification 19/37 was placed within weeks of ordering the two prototypes. Unfortunately, the power unit, the Rolls-Royce Vulture, which was based on mating two Kestrel V engines into a single 24-cylinder 'X' engine, was not fully developed and tested when the first production aircraft arrived. Nevertheless, due to the dire situation existing in 1940, work was pushed forward. No. 207 Squadron received the first production models in October but from then on trouble plagued the Manchester's career. Much of this is covered in Chapters 10 and 11.

Alternative power units were suggested, but the solution eventually adopted was modified wings to accommodate four engines instead of two. The engines selected were the ubiquitous Rolls-Royce Merlins, despite the Merlin being in huge demand for Spitfires, Hurricanes and other types (even Wellington Mk IIs). The Avro Manchester was transformed into the Avro Lancaster. The former was a failure: the latter was destined to become one of the most successful bombers of the war.

The first Lancaster, BT308, which flew on 9 January 1941, was actually a Manchester airframe married to the redesigned wings housing four Merlin engines and it still had three tail fins. In total, 200 Manchesters were built before the production lines changed to make Lancasters. Manchesters flew operationally until mid-1942, when they were assigned to training units. They were permanently grounded in August 1944.

Mk IA
Type: medium/heavy bomber.
Crew: Seven.
Powerplant: Two 1,760 hp Rolls-Royce Vulture 24-cylinder X-type, liquid-cooled engines.
Maximum speed: 265 mph at 17,000 feet.
Cruising speed: 185 mph at 15,000 feet.
Service ceiling: 19,200 feet.
Range: 1,630 miles with 8,100 lb bomb load; 1,200 miles with 10,350 lb bomb load.
Empty Weight: 29,432 lb.
Loaded Weight: (maximum take-off), 56,000 lb.
Span: 90 feet 1 in.
Length: 69 feet 4 in.
Height: 19 feet 6 in.
Wing area: 1,131 sq feet.
Armament: Eight 0.303in (7.7mm) Browning machine-guns mounted two each in nose and dorsal turrets and four in the tail turret.
Maximum bomb load: 10,350 lb.

VICKERS WELLINGTON
Few, if any, bombers of WW2 had a longer or more distinguished operational career than the Vickers Wellington. Like the Hampden, the Wellington was

planned to be a fast, well-armed day-bomber which could be used for night operations as well. It was to rely on speed to evade trouble and the protection of flying in defensive formations bristling with guns to ward off attacking fighters.

Blooded from the beginning of hostilities, it shouldered most of Bomber Command's night bombing offensive until the debut of the four-engined 'heavies'. Its docile flying characteristics and lively performance for the time endeared it to its crews. It had the ability to absorb an extraordinary amount of battle damage due to its revolutionary geodetic 'basket weave', stress-absorbing structure, which was invented by the ingenious engineer Barnes Wallis.

Originally conceived as a high-wing monoplane with a fixed undercarriage, the prototype emerged as a mid-wing monoplane with a retractable undercarriage partly because of its geodetic construction. Its powerplants were to be Rolls-Royce Goshawks or Bristol Mercury engines but the final decision was to use Bristol Pegasus X engines. An order for 180 aircraft was placed on 15 August 1936, exactly two months after the prototype, K4049, first took to the air. It was tentatively given the name, 'Crecy', but this was changed in favour of 'Wellington'. In service it was soon nicknamed 'Wimpey' after the portly cartoon character 'J. Wellington Wimpey' in the popular 'Popeye' comic-strip.

The first production Wellington Mk I (L4212) flew on 23 December 1937 and Mk I Wellingtons were built in three versions. The original Mk I (181 built) had Vickers nose and tail turrets and a Frazer-Nash ventral retractable 'dustbin' turret. The next version, the Mk IA (183 built), had Nash and Thompson two-gun turrets front and rear and retained the ventral retractable 'dustbin' turret. Finally, the Mk IC kept the two-gun turrets front and rear, but dispensed with the ventral 'dustbin' turret in favour of two Vickers 'K' beam guns mounted in the fuselage to eliminate the blind spots on each side.

Facing the early Wellington Mk Is and Mk IAs, German fighter pilots soon realised that relatively safe attacks could be made from the beam and above. The nose and tail guns of the bombers could not traverse around far enough, and the ventral position could not direct fire upward with the fuselage in the way.

One devastating encounter took place on 18 December 1939 when twenty-two Wellingtons on an armed reconnaissance of the Schillig Roads and Wilhelmshaven were caught by *Luftwaffe* fighters. During a running battle, twelve Wellingtons were lost and three others had to force-land after reaching the British coast. Changes were needed. Under attack, the ease with which the Wellingtons leaked fuel or caught fire made it vital to have self-sealing fuel tanks and protective armour fitted for the crews. Bomber Command realised its current heavy bombers were unsuitable for unescorted daylight operations. The early casualties forced the RAF to concentrate on night bombing.

Wellingtons became the mainstay of Bomber Command in the early war years and operating from bases in Britain alone, 63,976 sorties were flown. Meanwhile, shortages of the Pegasus engines led to the use of other engines and other versions to cater for an increasing variety of roles. As well as for bombing, Wellingtons were used as mine layers; sweepers of magnetic mines;

torpedo bombers; anti-submarine bombers with Leigh lights, ASV radar and extra fuel for increased range; troop transports; and transports for dropping paratroops. From 1941 onwards Wellingtons increasingly appeared in other theatres: North Africa and the Middle East in 1941 and the Far East in 1942. They remained operational up to the end of the war.

Altogether, there were 11,461 Wellingtons made, and with 3,804 examples produced the Wellington Mk X was built in far larger numbers than any other version. It was at the controls a Wellington Mk X that Dereck French flew his final operation to bomb a railhead in Burma some 150 miles from Rangoon on 14 December 1943.

B.Mk IC

Type: twin-engine medium bomber.

Crew: Six.

Powerplant: Two 1,050 hp Bristol Pegasus XVIII nine-cylinder, air-cooled, radial engines.

Span: 86 feet 2 in.

Length: 64 feet 7 in.

Height: 17 feet 5 in.

Wing area: 640 sq feet.

Maximum speed: 235 mph at operational height.

Service ceiling: 18,000 feet.

Range: 1,805 miles (normal); 2,550 miles (maximum).

Weight Loaded: 28,500 lb (normal).

Armament: Nash and Thompson two-gun 0.303 in (7.7 mm) turrets in the nose and rear; and two Vickers 'K' guns mounted to fire from positions in each side of the fuselage in lieu of the previous retractable ventral turret.

Bomb load (normal): 4,500 lb.

B.Mk X

Type: twin-engine medium bomber.

Crew: Six.

Powerplant: Two 1,585 hp Bristol Hercules VI or XVI fourteen-cylinder, air-cooled, radial engines.

Span: 86 feet 2 in.

Length: 64 feet 7in.

Height: 17 feet 5 in.

Wing area: 753 sq feet.

Maximum speed: 255 mph at operational height.

Service ceiling: 24,000 feet.

Range: 1,470 miles (normal); 2,085 miles (maximum).

Weight Loaded: 31,500 lb (normal).

Armament: Two 0.303 in (7.7 mm) machine guns in power-operated Frazer Nash front turret; four 0.303 in (7.7 mm) machine guns in power-operated Frazer Nash rear turret.

Bomb load (maximum): 6,000 lb.

Notes

FOREWORD

1. Newton, Dennis and Bungey, Richard, *Spitfire Leader – Robert Bungey DFC, Tragic Battle of Britain Hero* (Gloucestershire, Amberley Publishing, 2019).
2. Ibid
3. Olive, Gordon DFC (Newton, Dennis ed.), *Spitfire Ace* (Gloucestershire, Amberley Publishing, 2015).
4. Newton, Dennis and Bungey, Richard, *Op cit*.

1. DERECK

1. Shakespeare, William, *As You Like It*, Act II, v, 139-141.
2. Lawson, J. H. W., *The Story of 455 (RAAF) Squadron* (Melbourne, Victoria, 1951, Wilke & Co Limited, P.22.)
3. Buckingham, Sue, *A Childhood with Dereck* (Correspondence, March 2011.)
4. Coster, Chris, *Impressions of DJF DFC & Bar as Our Father* (Correspondence, October 2011.)
5. Veitch, Michael, *Flak* (Camberwell, Victoria, Penguin Books, 2006, P.156.)
6. Fields, Rooney, *My Reflections on Dar's Life and Impact on Me* (Correspondence, April, 2011.)
7. French, Barbara Mary), Nothing *Lasts Forever*, Compiled by Pam Mathieson (née French), 2010, P.31.
8. Lawson, J. H. W., *op cit*, P.22.
9. Mathieson, Pam, *Pam's Reflections on DJF* (Correspondence, April, 2011.)
10. Kirby, Robert, *Avro Manchester – The Legend behind the Lancaster* (Leicester, 1995, Midland Publishing Ltd, P.48.)
11. Veitch, Michael, *op cit*, P.156.
12. Lawson, J. H. W., *op cit*, P.22.
13. Cannon, Jack, *My War* (Melbourne, Victoria, 1990, Schwartz & Wilkinson for *The Sun News-Pictorial*, P.104.)
14. Buckingham, Sue, *op cit*.
15. Lawson, J. H. W., *op cit*, P.22.
16. Mathieson, Pam, *op cit*.

17. *Ibid.*
18. Fields, Rooney, *op cit.*
19. Cannon, Jack, *op cit*, P.104.
20. Lawson, J. H. W., *op cit*, P.22.
21. Buckingham, Sue, *op cit.*
22. Mathieson, Pam, *op cit.*
23. *Ibid.*
24. Fields, Rooney, *op cit.*
25. Buckingham, Sue, *op cit.*
26. Mathieson, Pam, *op cit.*
27. Buckingham, Sue, *op cit.*
28. Fields, Rooney, *op cit.*
29. Mathieson, Pam, *op cit.*
30. *Ibid.*
31. Coster, Chris, *op cit.*

3. POINT COOK

1. Eventually Marshal of the Royal Air Force Lord Douglas of Kirtleside GCB MC DFC.
2. Tamara 'Tammie' Beggs married rising political figure John Malcolm Fraser, the Liberal member for Wannon, Victoria, on 9 December 1956. Between 11 November 1975 and 5 March 1983, Malcolm Fraser was Australia's 27th Prime Minister.

4. ENGLAND

1. Ironically, this was a German-designed aircraft. Originally known as British Klemm and formed in 1933, the British Aircraft Manufacturing Company (BA) licence-built the Klemm L.25 and L.32 as the Swallow and Eagle respectively. The Swallow was a two-seat light low-wing monoplane powered by a 56 kW (75 hp) British Salmson or Pobjoy Cataract radial engine. The Eagle was a three-seat cabin monoplane powered by a 97 kW (130hp) de Havilland Gipsy Major or 138kW (185 hp) Gipsy Six engine.

7. GOD HELP 50 SQUADRON

1. It seems that this was likely to have been the light cruiser *Königsberg* which was found the next day moored alongside a wharf in Bergen Harbour by Skua dive bombers of the Fleet Air Arm and sunk.
2. The Allies referred to these Messerschmitt fighters during the war years as 'Me109s' and 'Me110s' but at the time of their design the manufacturing company was *Bayerische Flugzeugwerke* and the prefix 'Bf' was used for these types in official German handbooks and documents. Most modern writers therefore refer to them this way these days, i.e., as 'Bf109' and 'Bf110'. The design team was headed by Professor Willy Messerschmitt who joined the company in 1927 and eventually took over when it was reconstituted as the Messerschmitt A.G. Thus, later types such as the 'Me163' and 'Me262' were written so in official German handbooks and documents. To return to

the mood of the times in this book, it was decided that the 'Me109' and 'Me110' references should be used as employed in Allied documents in WW2.
3. Quoted by Dereck French from *The Royal Air Force and Two World Wars* by Sir Maurice Dean.

8. *TARGET EINDHOVEN*

1. After Dunkirk, Vice Admiral Ramsay faced the threatened German invasion of Britain, and, once that threat receded, was responsible for maintaining British control of the English Channel. In April 1942, he was appointed to work with General Eisenhower, first on the invasion of North Africa as deputy naval C-in-C, then in Sicily as naval commander for General Montgomery's British landings. He was recalled to England for planning the invasion of Normandy in 1944, and with promotion to the rank of admiral was appointed C-in-C Allied Naval Expeditionary Force. Post D-Day, he supervised operations off the invasion beaches. On 2 January 1945, while still conducting the naval side of the Allied drive through north-west Europe, he was killed when the plane that was to fly him to Brussels crashed on take-off from an airfield near Paris.
2. This is the generally accepted figure. The War Office total of men landed in England was 336,427.

9. *OPERATIONS*

1. The loss of 'Slug' Mulloy was a shock to Dereck. See his comments in Chapter 6.
2. Quoted by Dereck in his autobiographical notes.
3. Also quoted by Dereck in his autobiographical notes.
4. Leigh-Mallory's 'Big Wing' ideas won general approval with the Air Staff, and he took command of No. 11 Group in December 1940. He supervised the RAF's return to offensive operations in 1941, and took over Fighter Command itself in November 1942. On 15 November 1943, he was selected to command the Allied Expeditionary Air Force in Operation *Overlord*, the invasion of Normandy. For the invasion he commanded a total of 9,000 RAF and USAAF aircraft which successfully suppressed the *Luftwaffe*, bombed German road and rail communications, and restricted the mobility of German reinforcements within 150 miles (240 km) of the invasion area. In November 1944 he was appointed to command the Allied Air Forces in south-east Asia but, as Dereck noted, his aircraft crashed in bad weather near Grenoble on the 14th. Air Marshal Sir Trafford Leigh-Mallory and his wife were killed.

10. *WITTERING*

1. There is some uncertainty here because one page of Dereck's log book reads 'Hampden X2968' but the next page reads 'Hampden X2986'. There may have been two separate machines but probably the 6 and the 8 have simply been accidentally transposed. Both of these aircraft were brand new at the time having been built by the English Electric company sometime after July 1940. Hampden X2968, was destroyed in a landing accident at Wooten Downs, Upper Heyford, on 20 February 1942. It belonged to 50/16 OTU at the time. Probably the most likely aircraft, Hampden X2986 belonging

to 106 Squadron, the unit Dereck joined in 1940, crashed during a bombing mission to Cologne on the night of 20/21 April 1941.

2. Stanley Charles Widdows was born at Bradfield, Berkshire on 4 October 1909, and joined the RAF in 1926. In 1937 he was a test pilot to A&AEE, Martlesham Heath, where he tested the first production Hurricane, L1547, and the first production Spitfire, K9787. On 16 July 1940, he took command of 29 Squadron at Digby, was awarded the DFC in April 1941 and posted away in June 1941 to command RAF West Mailing. In 1942, he became Group Captain Night Operations at HQ 11 Group and 12 Group. He was SASO 85 Group in 1943-44 and Group Captain Organisation at Supreme HQ Allied Expeditionary Air Forces in 1944. Air Commodore Stanley Widdows retired from the RAF in December 1958, and was made a CB (1.1.59).

11. MANCHESTERS – 207 SQUADRON
1. Ringway later became Manchester Airport.
2. Robert Kirby, *Avro Manchester – The Legend behind the Lancaster* (Leicester, 1995, Midland Publishing Limited, P.34).
3. Figures used by Dereck are from *The Lost Command* by A. Revie.
4. Robert Kirby, *Op cit*, P.48.
5. Parry, Simon W, *Intruders over Britain* (Surrey, 1987, Air Research Publications, P.43).
6. Robert Kirby, *Op cit*, P.51.
7. *Ibid*.

12. MANCHESTERS – 97 SQUADRON
1. Dean, Sir Maurice, *The Royal Air Force and Two World Wars* quoted by Dereck French.
2. Clutton-Brock, Oliver, *RAF Evaders* (London, Grub Street Publishing, 2009, P.408.)

13. 455 (RAAF) SQUADRON – ARRIVAL
1. Dereck is stating the amount in Australian dollars here.
2. Donald Clifford Tyndall Bennett from Toowoomba, Queensland, was one of those rare individuals who had a huge impact on the Second World War. He was the youngest in a family of four brothers. He was the originator of the RAF's Pathfinder Force. During the course of the war, the Pathfinder Force grew from five squadrons of assorted aircraft to eighteen squadrons of Lancasters and Mosquitoes. It flew almost 55,000 sorties and marked over 3,000 targets. The new technology it developed and the proficiency it achieved contributed significantly to RAF Bomber Command's potency in the air war. His autobiography, *Pathfinder*, was published by Frederick Muller Ltd in 1958.
3. Dereck remarked as much to the author on more than one occasion, usually while wearing a big grin because he knew my previous books were about fighter pilots.

14. 455 (RAAF) SQUADRON – OPERATIONS

1. Lawson, J. H. W., *The story of 455 (RAAF) Squadron* (Melbourne, Victoria, 1951, Wilke & Co Limited, P.30.)
2. Ibid, P.38-39.
3. The full story W/Cdr Bob Bungey is told in *Spitfire Leader – Robert Bungey DFC, Tragic Battle of Britain Hero* by Dennis Newton and Richard Bungey, The sudden death of Sybil, Bob Bungey's wife, was also an integral part of the tragedy. (Amberley Publishing, Gloucestershire. 2019).

16. THE END OF ENGLAND – REFLECTIONS

1. Keith Truscott's biography, *Bluey Truscott*, by was written by Ivan Southall and published by Angus and Robertson, Australia, in 1958. He is also featured in many other publications including *Spitfire Leader* by Dennis Newton and Richard Bungey, published by Amberley in 2019.
2. Frank McNamara was the first Australian flier to win the Victoria Cross. In WW1, he was a member of No. 1 Squadron, Australian Flying Corps. On 20 March 1917, although wounded and under fire, he courageously landed in enemy territory and successfully rescued downed pilot Capt D. W. Rutherford.
3. Hugh Birch flew with 10 Squadron in the UK, France, Gibraltar and the Middle East before returning to Australia. After the war he joined Qantas and was one of six pilots who pioneered the flying boat route to Lord Howe Island from Sydney. He retired from Qantas in 1976.
4. Martin Middlebrook and Chris Everitt, *Bomber Command War Diaries* (New York, Viking, 1985, P.711).
5. Seth Manners was the captain of Hampden AE219 of 455 Squadron which failed to return on the night of 10/11 April 1942 during a raid on Essen. All on board were killed and buried in Rheinberg War Cemetery.
6. Charles Harland was navigating Hampden AE219 for Seth Manners when it failed to return on the night of 10/11 April 1942. No. 455 Squadron lost two aircraft that night.
7. Freddy Keck was the navigator of Hampden AT221, one of two aircraft lost on the night of 10/11 April 1942 during a raid on Essen. It crashed at Stürzelberg on the western bank of the Rhine. The entire crew perished and they were buried at Neuss. Their remains were re-interred in Rheinberg War Cemetery after 1945.
8. Geo Weston from Christchurch, New Zealand, had joined the RNZAF in July 1940. He subsequently flew de Havilland Mosquitoes with 105 Squadron RAF and survived the war.
9. The aircraft carrier HMS *Ark Royal* was damaged in the Mediterranean by a U-boat on 13 November 1941 while transporting fighter aircraft to Malta. She was turned back under tow for Gibraltar but was unable to remain afloat and had to be abandoned. She sank just 25 miles (40 km) from the relative safety of her port.
10. Thomas White's book, *Guests of the Unspeakable*, was published by Angus & Robertson in 1928. It was republished in 1990 by Little Hills Press, NSW. The full story of his epic escape is also told in *White's Flight* by Fred and Elizabeth Brenchley (John Wiley & Sons Australia Ltd, 2004).

11. George Jones' autobiography, *From Private to Air Marshal*, was published in 1988 when he was aged ninety-eight. He was an ace in WW1 and joined the new RAAF in 1921. In a long career he rose to become Chief of Air Staff in 1942, a position he held for almost ten years. By 1948 he had attained the rank of Air Marshal and was knighted by the Queen in 1954. Upon retiring from the RAAF, he worked with the Commonwealth Aircraft Corporation for five years and was a director of the board of Ansett Transport Industries for twenty years. He died in 1992.

12. Alan Deere, one of New Zealand's most famous fighter aces, has been credited with as many as 21 and 1 shared enemy aircraft destroyed. His autobiography, *Nine Lives*, published by Hodder & Stoughton, was first published in 1959.

13. In France on 10 May 1940, the first day of the German *Blitzkrieg*, David Mawhood was a member of 85 Squadron in the RAF's No. 80 Wing, Air Component. His Hurricane was damaged by a Ju88 which he counterattacked and claimed to have shot down. He managed to land his damaged plane safely despite his near blindness caused by Perspex splinters entering his eye.

14. P/O Paton of 233 Squadron was a member of the crew of Lockheed Hudson N7224 piloted by P/O J. H. Horan, an Australian, lost at Trondheim on 31 July 1940. It was presumably the victim of AA fire, but there is also the possibility it was shot down by Me109s, two German pilots claiming Blenheims destroyed on this day. Patton's body was recovered from the sea and buried at Kristiansand but the other crewmembers were never found.

15. Brian Carbury, another of New Zealand's high scoring fighter aces, has been credited with as many as 15 and 2 shared enemy aircraft destroyed. He was finally required to resign his commission in 1944. He returned to New Zealand where he died in July 1962 at the age of only forty-four.

16. Allen Mulligan in Alex Gould's *Tales from the Sagan Woods*, published by Alex Gould, Bundanoon, 1994.

17. S/Ldr R. M. Bradley, a member of 150 Squadron, had his aircraft, Fairey Battle L5591, shot up by Me109s on 13 June 1940 but he managed to make a crash-landing. Despite his spine injury, he and his observer got his wounded gunner to a hospital and then by 18 June made their way by road and train to Nantes from where they were evacuated back to England by air just before France collapsed.

17. CONVOY
1. Anzac Day is commemorated in Australia and New Zealand on 25 April.

18. THE DESERT AIR FORCE
1. Terraine, John, *The Right of the Line – The Royal Air Force in the European War1939-1945* (Hodder and Stoughton, London, 1985).
2. Chappell, R. F., *Wellington Wings – An RAF Intelligence Officer in the Western Desert* (William Kimber & Co Ltd, London, 1980).

19. EL ALAMEIN
1. W/O C. T. Ord is commemorated on the Alamein Memorial.
2. Williams, Eric, *The Wooden Horse* (Collins, London, 1949).

20. *INDIA AND FERRY COMMAND*

1. Air Ministry and Central Office of Information, *Wings of the Phoenix – The official story of the Air War in Burma*, His Majesty's Stationary Office, London, 1949.
2. Dereck's daughter Sue stayed overnight in this very same building some twenty years later.
3. A Dhow is a traditional sailing vessel used in the Red Sea and Indian Ocean region. They have one or more masts with lateen sails and are usually used to carry heavy items like fruit, fresh water or goods along the coasts of Eastern Arabia and coastal South Asia. Larger dhows can have crews of around thirty, smaller ones normally around twelve.
4. See Chapter 19.

21. *215 SQUADRON RAF*

1. A/Cdr H. V. Rowley was AOC of 221 Group RAF up to 17 February 1944.
2. Tony Ennis's father was also a distinguished pilot and a squadron leader with RAF Coastal Command.
3. After a year, Wellington Mk Xs were finally withdrawn from operations on 23 June 1944, and No. 215 moved back to Kolar to convert to Liberators which became the standard bomber in the theatre. Day and night bombing operations were resumed on 1 October 1944 but in the following April the squadron's role was changed to transport, its Liberators being replaced by Douglas Dakotas. Supply-dropping missions for the 14th Army continued for the remainder of the war and in October 1945 the squadron moved to Malaya. 215 Squadron was renumbered 48 Squadron on 15 February 1946.

22. *HOME*

1. Ray Brownell later wrote his autobiography titled *From Khaki to Blue*, but he died on 12 April 1974 before it was published by the Military Historical Society of Australia in 1978.
2. Strike by wharf labourers.
3. Citizens' Military Forces.
4. Sir Henry Winneke was the Governor of Victoria 3 June 1974–1 March 1982.

23. *EPILOGUE – NOTHING LASTS FOREVER*

1. The quotes for this chapter are a compilation from the French family papers and correspondence with the author over the years.

Bibliography

The main source for this title are the private papers of Dereck and Barbara French and family.

Buckingham, Sue, 'A Childhood with Dereck' (Correspondence, March 2011.)

Coster, Chris, 'Impressions of DJF DFC & Bar as Our Father' (Correspondence, October 2011.)

Fields, Rooney, 'My Reflections on Dar's Life and Impact on Me' (Correspondence, April, 2011.)

French, Barbara Mary, 'Nothing Lasts Forever' (Compiled by Pam Mathieson (née French), 2010.

French, Dereck, Log Book, Diaries, Family histories, photo album, etc., plus correspondence with the author since 1992.

Mathieson, Pam, 'Reflections on DJF' (Correspondence, April, 2011.)

The French Family has entrusted much of Dereck's memorabilia to the RAAF Museum Point Cook.

Official records via the Imperial War Museum include Operations Record Books and reports of 50, 97, 207 and 215 Squadrons RAF; and via the Australian War Memorial include Operations Record Books and reports of 455 (RAAF) Squadron, and taped interview with Dereck French.

Published works

Air Ministry and Central Office of Information, *Wings of the Phoenix – The official story of the Air War in Burma*, (London, His Majesty's Stationary Office, 1949).

Air Ministry, *The Battle of Britain — an air ministry account of the great days from August 8 to October 31, 1940* (Ministry of Information, London, 1941).

Bingham, Victor, *Blitzed! – The Battle of France May–June 1940* (Surrey, England, Air Research Publications, 1990).

Blair, Clay, *Hitler's U-Boat War – The Hunters 1939-1942* (London, Wellington House, 1996).

Brenchley, Fred and Elizabeth, *White's Flight* (John Wiley & Sons Australia Ltd, 2004).

Cannon, Jack, *My War* (Melbourne, Victoria, Schwartz & Wilkinson for *The Sun News-Pictorial*, 1990).

Chorley, W. R., *Royal Air Force Bomber Command Losses of The Second World War, Volume 1, 1939-1940* (Leicester, Midland Counties Publications, 1992).

_____, *Royal Air Force Bomber Command Losses of The Second World War, Volume 2, 1941* (Leicester, Midland Counties Publications, 1993).

_____, *Royal Air Force Bomber Command Losses of The Second World War, Volume 3, 1942* (Leicester, Midland Counties Publications, 1993).

_____, *Royal Air Force Bomber Command Losses of The Second World War, Volume 9, Roll of Honour 1939-1947* (Leicester, Midland Counties Publications, 2007).

Clutton-Brock, Oliver, *Footprints on the Sands of Time – RAF Bomber Command Prisoners Of War in Germany 1939-45* (London, Grub Street, 2003).

_____, *RAF Evaders* (London, Bounty Books, 2012).

Collier, Richard, *1940 – The World in Flames* (Harmondsworth, Penguin, 1980).

Foreman, John, *Air War 1941: Vol. 1 The Turning Point* (Surrey, Air Research Publications, 1993).

_____, *Air War 1941: Vol. 2 The Turning Point* (Surrey, Air Research Publications, 1994).

Franks, Norman, *Images of War – The RAF Air Sea Rescue Service in the Second World War* (South Yorkshire, Pen and Sword, Aviation, 2016).

_____, *The Air Battle of Imphal* (London, William Kimber & Co, Ltd, 1985).

Gould, Alex, *Tales from the Sagan Woods* (Bundanoon, Alex Gould, 1994).

Green, William, *Famous Bombers of the Second World War* (London. MacDonald, 1959).

_____, *Famous Bombers of the Second World War*, Second Series (London. MacDonald, 1960).

Gunby, David & Pelham, Temple, *Royal Air Force Bomber Losses in the Middle East and Mediterranean, Vol 1: 1939-1942* (Hinkley, Midland Publishing, 2006).

Halley, James J., *The Squadrons of the Royal Air Force & Commonwealth 1918-1988* (Tunbridge, Air-Britain, 1988).

Harper, Helen, *Twenty Two Temporary Gentlemen* (Goulburn NSW, H. Harper, c.1996).

Harris, Sir Arthur, Marshal of the RAF, *Bomber Offensive* (London, Greenhill Books, 1990).

Herington, John, *Australia in the War of 1939-1945, (Air)* Vol. III, 'Air War Against Germany and Italy, 1939-1943' (Canberra, Australian War Memorial, 1962).

His Majesty's Stationary Office, *RAF Middle East – The Official Story of Air Operations in the Middle East, from February 1942 to January 1943* (London, Ministry of Information, 1945).

Johnson, Frank (ed.), *RAAF Over Europe* (London, Eyre & Spottiswoode, 1946).

Long, Gavin, *The War of 1939-1945, (Army) Vol. I, To Benghazi,* (Canberra, Australian War Memorial, 1961).

Kirby, Robert, *Avro Manchester – The Legend behind the Lancaster* (Leicester, 1995, Midland Publishing Ltd.)

Lawson, J. H. W., *The Story of 455 (RAAF) Squadron,* (Melbourne, Victoria, 1951, Wilke & Co Limited.)

Lumsden, Alec, *Wellington Special* (London, Ian Allen Ltd, 1974).

McCarthy, John, *Australia and the Imperial Defence 1918-1939* (St Lucia, University of Queensland Press, 1976).

Middlebrook, Martin and Everitt. Chris, *Bomber Command War Diaries* (New York, Viking, 1985).

Moyle, Harry, *The Hampden File* (Tonbridge, Kent, Air-Britain, 1989).

Newton, Dennis, *A Few of 'The Few' – Australians and the Battle of Britain* (Canberra, ACT, Australian War Memorial, 1990).

Newton, Dennis, *First Impact – Australians in the Air War of World War 2, 1939-40* (Maryborough, Queensland, Banner Books, 1997).

_____, *A Spitfire Pilot's Story – Pat Hughes, Battle of Britain Top Gun* (Gloucestershire, Amberley Publishing, 2016).

Newton, Dennis & Bungey Richard, *Spitfire Leader – Robert Bungey DFC, Tragic Battle of Britain Hero* (Gloucestershire, published by Amberley Publishing, 2019).

Olive, Gordon DFC, (Newton, Dennis (ed.), *Spitfire Ace* (Gloucestershire, Amberley Publishing, 2015).

Otter, Patrick, *Lincolnshire Airfields in the Second World War* (Berkshire, Countryside Books, 2012).

Parry, Simon W, *Intruders over Britain* (Surrey, Air Research Publications, 1987).

Ramsey, Winston G. (ed.), *The Blitz Then And Now*, Vol.1 (London, After the Battle, 1987).

Ramsey, Winston (ed.), *The Blitz Then And Now*, Vol. 2 (London, After The Battle, 1988).

Roberts, Tom, *Wingless – An Alphabetical List of Australian Airmen Detained in Wartime* (Ballarat, Australia, Thomas V. Roberts, 2011).

Shores, Christopher & Williams, Clive, *Aces High* (London, Grub Street, 1994).

Southall, Ivan, Bluey *Truscott* (Sydney, Angus and Robertson, 1958).

Terraine, John, *The Right of the Line – The Royal Air Force in the European War1939-1945* (Hodder and Stoughton, London, 1985).

Thompson, W/Cdr H. L., *New Zealanders with the Royal Air Force*, official history of New Zealand in the Second World War 1939-45, Vol I: 'European Theatre September 1939- December 1942' (Wellington, New Zealand, War History Branch, Department of Internal Affairs, 1953).

Trevor-Roper, H. R., (ed.), *Hitler's War Directives 1939-1945* (London, Pan, 1973).

Veitch, Michael, *Flak* (Camberwell, Victoria, Penguin Books, 2006.)

Williams, Eric, *The Wooden Horse* (Collins, London, 1949).

Wixley, Ken, *Forgotten Bombers of the Royal Air Force* (London, Arms and Armour Press, 1997).

Index